Current Issues in the International Economy: A Reader

edited by

Linda S. Goldberg
New York University

Michael W. Klein
Tufts University

HarperCollins*CollegePublishers*

Current Issues in the International Economy: A Reader edited by Linda S. Goldberg and Michael W. Klein

 For information, address HarperCollins Publishers Inc., 10 E. 53d. Street, New York, NY 10022

ISBN: 0-06-501021-3

92 93 94 95 96 9 8 7 6 5 4 3 2 1

CONTENTS

ACKNOWLEDGMENTS

Reading 1 *"Is Free Trade Passe?,"* Paul R. Krugman, *Journal of Economic Perspectives*, Vol. 1, No. 2, Fall 1987, pp. 131-144.

Reading 2 *"Protection: Is There a Better Way?"* Robert Z. Lawrence, *American Economic Review*, Vol. 79, No. 2, May 1989, pp. 118-122.

Reading 3 *"Jumpstarting Gatt,"* Jagdish Bhagwati. Reprinted with permission from *Foreign Policy* 83 (Summer 1991). Copyright 1991 by the Carnegie Endowment for International Peace. pp.105-118

Reading 4 *"The Political Economy of Trade Policy,"* Robert E. Baldwin, *Journal of Economic Perspectives*, Vol. 3, No. 4, Fall 1989, pp. 119-135.

Reading 5 *"U.S. Trade Protection: Effects on the Industrial* and Regional Composition of Employment," Linda C. Hunter, Federal Reserve Bank of Dallas, Economic Review, January 1990, pp. 1-13.

Reading 6 *"Foreign Direct Investment in the United States and U.S. Interest,"* Edward M. Graham, *Science*, Vol.253, December 20, 1991, Copyright 1991 by the AAAS.

Reading 7 *"Mexican Maquiladora Growth: Does It Cost U.S. Jobs?"* William C. Gruben, *Federal Reserve Bank of Dallas Economic Review*, January 1990, pp. 15-29.

Reading 8 *"Integration with the Global Economy,"* From *World Development Report 1991*. International Bank for Reconstruction and Development, part of Chapter 5 of World Development Report 1991: The Challenge of Development, Oxford University Press, Oxford England, pp. 96-108.

Reading 9 *"Asian Trade and Growth Lessons,"* Anne O. Kreuger, *American Economic Review*, Vol. 80, No. 2, May 1990, pp. 108-112.

Reading 10 *"Implications of the U.C. Current Account Deficit,"* David H. Howard, *Journal of Economic Perspectives*, Vol. 3, No. 3, Fall 1989, pp. 153-165.

Reading 11 *"Economic Consequences of Continued U.S. External Deficits,"* Charles Pigott, *Federal Reserve Bank of New York Quarterly Review*, Winter/Spring 1989, pp. 4-15.

Reading 12 *"Anomalies: Foreign Exchange,"* Kenneth A. Froot and Richard H. Thaler, *Journal of Economic Perspectives*, Vol. 4, No. 3, Summer 1990, pp. 179-192.

Reading 13 *"Do Sterilized Interventions Affect Exchange Rates?"* Warren E. Weber, *Federal Reserve Bank of Minneapolis Quarterly Review*, Summer 1986, pp. 14-23.

Reading 14 *"Economic Interdependence Between Nations: Reason for Policy Coordination?"* Norman S. Fieleke, *New England Economic Review*, May/June 1988, pp. 21-37.

Reading 15 *"Thinking About International Economic Coordination,"* Martin S. Feldstein, *Journal of Economic Perspectives*, Vol. No. 2, Spring 1988, pp. 3-13.

Reading 16 *"Europe Without Borders,"* Richard N. Cooper, *Brookings Papers on Economic Activity*, 1989, No. 2, pp. 325-340.

Reading 17 *"Europe's Emerging Economic and Monetary Union,"* Jacob A. Frenkel and Morris Goldstein, Finance and Development, March 1991, pp. 32-34. Reprinted by permission of the International Bank for Reconstruction and Development and the International Monetary Fund.

Reading 18 *"International Debts: What's Fact and What's Fiction,"* Anna J. Schwartz, *Economic Inquiry*, Vol. 27, January 1989, pp. 1-19.

Reading 19 *"Debt Relief Is Cheap,"* Paul R. Krugman. *Foreign Policy*, No. 80, Fall 1990, copyright 1991 by the Carnegie Endowment for International Peace, pp. 141-152.

Reading 20 *"Macroeconomic Developments and Systematic Reform in Eastern Europe and the U.S.S.R.,"* International Monetary Fund, Chapter 2 in World Economic Outlook, May 1991, International Monetary Fund, Washington, D.C., c. 1991, pp. 26-37. Reprinted with permission.

Reading 21 *"Soviet Economic Reform: The Longest Road,"* William D. Nordhaus, *Brookings Papers on Economic Activity*, 1990: 1, pp. 287-308.

Supplementary Data

# 1	*"Uruguay Round: Structure and Summary of the Status of Negotiations,"* (columns 1 - 3), International Monetary Fund, Supplementary Note 7 in World Economic Outlook, May 1991, International Monetary Fund, Washington, D.C., c. 1991, pp. 116-119. Reprinted with permission.
# 2	*"Summary of U.S. International Transactions,"* U.S. Department of Commerce, Table A in "U.S. International Transactions," in survey of Current Business, June 1991, p. 36.
# 3	Balance of Payments tables for the United States, Japan and Germany (Tables A4, A5, and A6) in the Statistical Appendix of International Capital Markets: Developments and Prospects, International Monetary Fund, Washington, D.C., May 1991, pp. 90-92. Reprinted with permission.
# 4	*"Major Industrial Countries, Monthly Average Nominal and Real Effective Exchange Rates, January 1980 to February 1991,"* International Monetary Fund, World Economic Outlook, May 1991, p. 94. Reprinted with permission.
# 5	*"Developing Countries: External Debt and Debt Service, 1983-1992,"* International Monetary Fund, World Economic Outlook, May 1991, p. 192. Reprinted with permission.

Foreword

This book of readings is primarily intended as a supplement to undergraduate or masters level courses in International Trade and International Finance. This book also serves as a useful overview and reference for current issues in the international economy. For International Economics coursework, this book supplements your textbook in a number of important ways. It enables you to place the lessons in the context of current events and debates in the world economy. As a result, it helps you deepen and reinforce your understanding of international economic theory.

This book is divided into eleven sections, each consisting of two or three articles. Each of the first ten sections focuses on a topic that has important ramifications for the conduct of international economic policy. The final section of the book presents useful reference data.

The first five sections of this reader cover topics in the area of international trade. The subject Section 1, the debate over free or managed trade, is as old as the field of international economics. One source of renewed interest in this question is a new set of theoretical challenges to the optimality of free trade. Paul Krugman has been an important contributor to this "new wave" trade theory. In his article he assesses the policy-relevance of these new advances. In a second article, Robert Lawrence surveys recent trade legislation. In the final article in this section, Jagdish Bhagwati reflects on the recent Uruguay round of multilateral trade negotiations for the General Agreement on Tariffs and Trade (GATT) as well as the recent move towards bilateral trade arrangements.

While the case for free trade is based on society-wide criteria, economists recognize that the benefits from free trade may be very different across groups or regions of a country. Recognizing that trade policy is not formed in a political vacuum, the idea of the political economy of protectionism has attracted considerable attention. The articles in the Section 2 of this book focus on the differential impact of trade policy across industries and across regions and their political implications. In an insightful article, Robert Baldwin considers the political implications of the economic policy of free trade. Linda Hunter makes these points more concrete by showing the differential impact of trade policy across industries and regions in the United States.

International factor movements, specifically foreign direct investment, have captured the attention of the American public. In an informative article, Edward M. Graham reviews the behavior of foreign direct investment into the United States and discusses the economic consequences of the surge in FDI in the 1980s. William Gruben looks at one particular type of direct investment, the so-called maquiladora assembly plants in Mexico. He considers the charged issue of whether this type of international factor mobility costs American workers their jobs.

As discussed in Section 4, lessons from international trade theory are essential for confronting one of the greatest challenges to the world community, the economic development of poorer nations. One of the most important international agencies in this struggle is the World Bank. The reading drawn from its World Development Report 1991 lays out some of the key issues in economic development and presents some of the lessons learned over the past four decades. As further argued by Anne Krueger in the article that follows, the recent economic performance of East Asian countries has demonstrated the possibilities for development.

The next three sections of the book focus on international finance. The 1980s witnessed some striking developments in the international economy, including unprecedented movements in current account balances and exchange rates. There was also an internationally coordinated effort to manage currencies and macroeconomic policies in the latter half of the decade. The implications of large current account deficits are studied in Section 5 in the articles by David Howard and by Charles Pigott. Section 6 reviews what we have learned about the behavior of the exchange rate since the advent of floating rates in 1973. The article by Kenneth Froot and Richard Thaler reviews studies of the properties of the exchange rate while the article by Warren Weber reviews studies of the abilities of governments to influence currencies while leaving domestic policy variables unaffected. In Section 7 international linkages across countries and the scope for policy coordination are reviewed in the article by Norman Fieleke. In the second article of Section 7, Martin Feldstein questions the efficacy of international policy coordination.

The European Community (EC) provides us with an example of a group of countries that have tied their economies closely together through policy coordination. Plans for further strengthening the links among members of the European Community are reviewed in the two articles in Section 8. Richard Cooper considers the impact of the removal of barriers to trade and factor movements, as proposed in the EC 1992 plan. Jacob Frenkel and Morris Goldstein discuss plans for closer monetary and macroeconomic integration, culminating in a proposed European System of Central Banks.

The LDC debt crisis, the topic of Section 9, has been one of the most important economic problems of the 1980s. Anna Schwartz interprets the causes of the debt crisis, asking whether its origin was due to bad luck or bad policy. Paul Krugman discusses the likely cost of providing debt relief The issue of LDC debts surely will continue to be one of the premier problems facing the world economy in the 1990s.

As the world economy enters the 1990s, the remarkable changes that have occurred in Eastern Europe and the Soviet Union pose broad challenges to economists. The initial euphoria that greeted liberalization in these countries has given way to a more somber realization of the difficulties facing governments that attempt to switch from a command economy to a marketbased one. In Section 10, the reading from the International Monetary Fund's World Economic Outlook presents a range of topics that countries in Eastern Europe, as well as the Soviet Union, must face. A more in-depth discussion of the challenges facing the Soviet Union is provided in an article by William Nordhaus.

The reader concludes with a section containing some important international economic data including information on the recent Uruguay round of GATT, United States current account data, balance of payments data for Japan and Germany, exchange rates and external debt. This section is a resource for students and professors who want handy access to figures and data that help supplement the material presented in textbooks.

SECTION I

Free or Managed Trade

Over the years, many economists have cited the Theory of Comparative Advantage to argue the merits of free, unrestricted trade between nations. Recently, this debate has been reshaped by the arguments that trade between nations can be motivated by increasing returns-to-scale in production and the existence of imperfectly competitive markets. Moreover, since trade policy must be negotiated in complicated international arenas, the theoretical possibility of welfare-improving restraints on trade must be weighed against the likelihood that this result actually will be achieved. In the articles presented in this section, Paul Krugman, Robert Lawrence and Jagdish Bhagwati provide theoretical and institutional background to the debate on free versus managed trade.

READING 1

Is Free Trade Passé?

Paul R. Krugman

If there were an Economist's Creed, it would surely contain the affirmations "I understand the Principle of Comparative Advantage" and "I advocate Free Trade." For one hundred seventy years, the appreciation that international trade benefits a country whether it is "fair" or not has been one of the touchstones of professionalism in economics. Comparative advantage is not just an idea both simple and profound; it is an idea that conflicts directly with both stubborn popular prejudices and powerful interests. This combination makes the defense of free trade as close to a sacred tenet as any idea in economics.

Yet the case for free trade is currently more in doubt than at any time since the 1817 publication of Ricardo's *Principles of Political Economy.* This is not because of the political pressures for protection, which have triumphed in the past without shaking the intellectual foundations of comparative advantage theory. Rather, it is because of the changes that have recently taken place in the theory of international trade itself. While new developments in international trade theory may not yet be familiar to the profession at large, they have been substantial and radical. In the last ten years the traditional constant returns, perfect competition models of international trade have been supplemented and to some extent supplanted by a new breed of models that emphasizes increasing returns and imperfect competition. These new models call into doubt the extent to which actual trade can be explained by comparative advantage; they also open the possibility that government intervention in trade via import restrictions, export subsidies, and so on may under some circumstances be in the national interest after all.

To preview this paper's conclusion: free trade is not passé, but it is an idea that has irretrievably lost its innocence. Its status has shifted from optimum to reasonable rule of thumb. There is still a case for free trade as a good policy, and as a useful target in the practical world of politics, but it can never again be asserted as the policy that economic theory tells us is always right.

RETHINKING INTERNATIONAL TRADE THEORY

From the early nineteenth century until the late 1970s international trade theory was dominated almost entirely by the concept of comparative advantage, which we can define loosely as the view that countries trade to take advantage of their differences. In formal models, economies were assumed to be characterized by constant returns to scale and perfect competition. Given these assumptions, trade can arise only to the extent that countries differ in tastes, technology, or factor endowments. The traditional Ricardian model emphasizes technological differences as the cause of trade; the Heckscher-Ohlin-Samuelson model emphasizes differences in factor endowments. Additional models can be generated by varying assumptions about the number of goods and factors, by placing restrictions on the technology, and so on. These alternative models have different implications in important respects; for example, income distribution effects are absent in the Ricardian model, extremely strong in the Heckscher-Ohlin-Samuelson model. Nonetheless, the underlying commonality among conventional trade models is such that until a few years ago international trade theory was one of the most unified fields in economics.

Thoughtful international economists have long known that comparative advantage need not be the whole story, that increasing returns can be an independent case of international specialization and trade.[1] Ohlin himself repeatedly emphasized this point. Furthermore, at least since the late 1950s empirical workers and informal observers have been dissatisfied with formal trade theory, so that there has been a sort of "counter-culture" in international trade research, a set of informal arguments stressing sources of trade other than those represented in the formal models. Authors such as Steffan Burenstam-Linder (1961) and Raymond Vernon (1966) emphasized endogenous technological change, while many authors have discussed the possible role of economics of scale as a cause of trade separate from comparative advantage. A few papers attempted formal models of trade under increasing returns. However, all such efforts were plagued by the problem of modeling market structure. Except under the implausible hypothesis that economies of scale are completely external to firms, increasing returns must lead to imperfect competition. Yet until the late 1970s, there was no generally accepted way to model imperfect competition in general equilibrium. Since mainstream trade theory derived its power and unity from being stated in formal general equilibrium terms, alternative views were relegated to the footnotes. As recently as 1980, many textbooks—and even survey articles on the theory of international trade—failed even to mention the possibility that trade might arise for reasons other than exogenous differences in tastes, technology, and factor endowments.

During the 1970s researchers in industrial organization began to develop models of imperfect competition that, while admittedly lacking generality, were easy to use and apply. In particular, Chamberlinian large-group competition was given a grounding in utility maximization and placed in a general equilibrium framework by such authors as A. Michael Spence (1976) and Avinash Dixit and Joseph Stiglitz (1977). It quickly became clear to trade theorists that these new models supplied the necessary framework for formal modeling of the role of increasing returns as a cause of international trade. Simultaneously and independently, Avinash Dixit and Victor Norman (1980), Kelvin Lancaster (1980), and this author (1979) published papers in which economies of scale led to arbitrary specialization by nations on products within monopolistically competitive industries. These models immediately established the idea that countries specialize and trade, not only because of underlying differences, but also because increasing returns are an independent force leading to geographical concentration of production of each good. Indeed, at a logical level, increasing returns are as fundamental a cause of international trade as comparative advantage.[2]

The role of increasing returns in trade was not, as already noted, a new idea, although the new models gave it more clarity and precision than in the past. The main new insight from these models was that to the extent that trade driven by economies of scale is important in the world economy, imperfect competition is important as well. International trade theory thus becomes inextricably intertwined with industrial organization. In retrospect this conclusion is obvious. After all, most trade is in the products of industries that economists classify without hesitation as oligopolies when viewing them in their domestic aspect. For international economics, however, this was a radical reorientation.

Although the new models of trade challenged the traditional view that all trade represents exploitation of comparative advantage, the new trade theory did not at first challenge the proposition that trade is of mutual benefit to the trading nations. Indeed, if anything, the introduction of increasing returns and imperfect competition into trade theory strengthens the case that there are gains from trade. In addition to benefitting from complementary differences in resources and technology, trading countries can specialize in the production of different goods, achieving increased scale of production while maintaining or increasing the diversity of goods available. Admittedly, a second-best world of imperfect competition offers no guarantee that potential benefits from trade will necessarily be realized. In most formal models, however, it turns out that the presence of increasing returns increases rather than reduces the gains from international trade. Furthermore, by creating larger, more competitive markets, trade may reduce the distortions that would have been associated with imperfect competition in a closed economy. Thus than discourage exports, and possibly raise national income.

The strategic trade policy argument is immensely attractive to noneconomists, since it seems to say that views always condemned by international trade theorists as fallacious make sense after all. In defense of free trade, a number of analysts have quickly acted to point out the weakness of strategic trade as a basis for actual intervention. Before considering these arguments, however, I turn to the other justification for governments intervention in trade suggested by the new theory.

External Economies

There is nothing new about the idea that it may be desirable to deviate from free trade to encourage activities that yield positive external economies. The proposition that protection can be beneficial when an industry generates external economies is part of the conventional theory of trade policy.[3] However, the rethinking of international trade theory has given at least the appearance of greater concreteness to the theoretical case for government intervention to promote external benefits.

It is possible to imagine bees-and-flowers examples in which externalities arise from some physical spillover between firms, but empirically the most plausible source of positive externalities is the inability of innovative firms to appropriate fully the knowledge they create. The presence of problems of appropriability is unmistakable in industries experiencing rapid technological progress, where firms routinely take each others' products apart to see how they work and how they were made. In traditional international trade models with their reliance on perfect competition, however, externalities resulting from incomplete appropriability could not be explicitly recognized,[4] because the knowledge investment by firms that is the source of the spillover could not be fitted in. Investment in knowledge inevitably has a fixed-cost aspect; once a firm has improved its product or technique, the unit cost of that improvement falls as more is produced. The result of these dynamic economies of scale must be a breakdown of perfect competition. As a result, perfectly competitive models could not explicitly recognize the most plausable reason for the existence of external economies. This did not prevent trade theorists from analyzing the trade policy implications of externalities, and in fact this is a well-understood topic. Since investment in knowledge was not explicitly in their models, however, external economies seemed abstract, without an obvious real-world counterpart. In traditional trade models, one industry seems as likely as another to generate important external economies—so that the theory seems remote from operational usefulness.

Once increasing returns and imperfect competition are seen as the norm, this problem of abstractness is reduced. The dynamic scale economies associated with investment in knowledge are just another reason for the imperfection of competition that has already been accepted as the norm. External economies can now be identified with incomplete appropriability of the results of R & D, which immediately suggests that they are most likely to be found in industries where R & D is an especially large part of firms' costs. So by making tractable the modeling of a specific mechanism generating externalities, the new trade theory also seems to offer guidance on where these externalities are likely to be important.

The emphasis on external economies suggested by new trade theory is similar to the strategic trade policy argument in offering a reason for government targeting of particular sectors. However, the external economies argument differs in one important respect; policies to promote sectors yielding external economies need not affect other countries adversely. Whether the effect of one country's targeting of high-externality sectors on other countries is positive or negative depends on whether the scope of the externalities is national or international. There is a conflict of interest if knowledge spills over within a country but not between countries. Suppose that the research of each computer firm generates knowledge that benefits other computer firms. This is only a case for sponsoring production of computers in the United States as opposed to Japan if U.S. firms cannot benefit from Japanese research.[5] In many cases it seems unlikely that spillovers respect national boundaries; a firm can "reverse engineer" a product made abroad as well as one made at home. The best candidates for nationally limited externalities are where knowledge spreads largely by personal contact and word of mouth. This is a much more restricted set of activities than R & D in general, although it is presumably the force behind such spectacular agglomerations of high-technology industry as Silicon Valley and Route 128.

Despite the restriction that only externalities at the national level make industrial policy a source of international conflict of interest, it is clear that the changes in trade theory have strengthened the view that nations are competing over who gets to realize these externalities. This reinforces the new strategic trade policy argument in offering a more respectable rationale for deviating from free trade than has been available until now.

CRITIQUE OF THE NEW INTERVENTIONISM

The positive economics of the new trade theory, with its conclusion that much trade reflects increasing returns and that many international markets are imperfectly competitive, has met with remarkably quick acceptance in the profession. The normative conclusion that this justifies a greater degree of government intervention in trade, however, has met with sharp criticism and opposition—not least from some of the creators of the new theory themselves. The critique of the new interventionism partly reflects judgements about the politics of trade policy, to which we turn below. There are also, however, three economic criticisms. First, critics suggest that it is impossible to formulate useful interventionist policies given the empirical difficulties involved in modeling imperfect markets. Second, they argue that any gains from intervention will be dissipated by entry of rent-seeking firms. Third, it is argued that general equilibrium considerations radically increase the empirical difficulty of formulating interventionist trade policies and make it even more unlikely that these policies will do more good than harm.

Empirical Difficulties

The previous numerical example assumed that the European government knew the payoff matrix and knew how Boeing would respond to its policy. In reality, of course, even the best informed governments will not know this much. Uncertainty is a feature of all economic policy, of course, but it is even greater when the key issue is how a policy will affect oligopolistic competition. The simple fact is that economists do not have reliable models of how oligopolists behave. Yet the effects of trade policy in imperfectly competitive industries can depend crucially on whether firms behave cooperatively or noncooperatively, or whether they compete by setting prices or outputs.[6] Furthermore, in many oligopolistic industries firms play a multistage game whose rules and objectives are complex and obscure even to the players themselves.

The externality argument for intervention runs up against the empirical problem of measuring external economies. By their nature, spillovers of knowledge are elusive and difficult to calculate; because they represent non-market linkages between firms, they do not leave a "paper trail" by which their spread can be traced. A combination of careful case study work and econometrics on the history of an industry may be able to identify significant external economies, but what we need for trade policy is an estimate for the future rather than the past. Will a dollar of R & D in the semiconductor industry convey ten cents worth of external benefits, or ten dollars? Nobody really knows.[7]

By itself, the argument that making policy based on the new trade theory is an uncertain enterprise would only dictate caution and hard study, not inaction. When it is linked with the political economy concerns described below, however, it raises the question of whether the political risks associated with action outweigh any likely gains.

Entry

Suppose that a government is somehow able to overcome the empirical difficulties in formulating an interventionist trade policy. It may still not be able to raise national income if the benefits of its intervention are dissipated by entry of additional firms.

Consider first the case of a strategic trade policy aimed at securing excess returns. Our example was one in which there was room for only one profitable firm. Suppose, however, that the market can actually support four or five firms, a sufficient number so that the integer constraint does not matter too much and free entry will virtually eliminate monopoly profits. In this case, as Ignatius Horstmann and James

Markusen (1986) have emphasized, a subsidy, even if it succeeds in deterring foreign competition, will be passed on to foreign consumers rather than securing excess returns for domestic producers. Or as Avinash Dixit has put it, when there is a possibility of new entry we need to ask, "Where's the rent?"

A similar issue arises with policies aimed at promoting external economies. Suppose that external economies are associated with the manufacture of semiconductor chips, seemingly justifying a subsidy to chips production. If additional resources of labor and capital are applied elastically to the industry, the external benefits of larger production will not be confined to the promoting country. Instead, they will be passed on to consumers around the world in the form of cheaper chips. The *national* advantage can come only to the extent that some factors are supplied inelastically to the industry—Santa Clara valley real estate?—or external benefits conveyed by the semiconductor industry to other industries. The point is that entry of new factors and new firms further reduces, though it does not eliminate, the extent to which competition for external economies represents a valid source of international conflict.

General Equilibrium

Even in a world characterized by increasing returns and imperfect competition, budget constraints still hold. A country cannot protect everything and subsidize everything. Thus interventionist policies to promote particular sectors, whether for strategic or externality reasons, must draw resources away from other sectors. This substantially raises the knowledge that a government must have to formulate interventions that do more harm than good.

Consider first the case of strategic trade policy. When a particular sector receives a subsidy, this gives firms in that sector a strategic advantage against foreign competitors. However, the resulting expansion of that sector will bid up the price of domestic resources to other sectors, putting home firms in these other sectors at a strategic disadvantage. Excess returns gained in the favored sector will thus be offset to at least some extent by returns lost elsewhere. If the government supports the wrong sector, the gain there will conceal a loss in overall national income.

The implication of this general equilibrium point is that to pursue a strategic trade policy successfully, a government must not only understand the effects of its policy on the targeted industry, which is difficult enough, but must also understand all the industries in the economy well enough that it can judge that an advantage gained here is worth advantage lost elsewhere. Therefore, the information burden is increased even further.

A similar point applies to externalities. Promoting one sector believed to yield valuable spillovers means drawing resources out of other sectors. Suppose that glamorous high-technology sectors yield less external benefit than the government thinks, and boring sectors more. Then a policy aimed at encouraging external economies may actually prove counterproductive. Again, the government needs to understand not only the targeted sector but the rest of the economy to know if a policy is justified.

The general equilibrium point should perhaps not be emphasized too much. Sectors of the economy differ radically and visibly in both the extent to which they are imperfectly competitive and in the resources they devote to the generation of knowledge. There may not be a one-to-one correspondence between small numbers of competitors and excess returns, or between high R & D expenditure and technological spillovers, but there is surely a correlation. Governments may not know for sure where intervention is justified, but they are not completely without information. However, the general equilibrium critique reinforces the caution suggested by the other critiques.

To say that it is difficult to formulate the correct interventionist policy is not a defense of free trade, however. Thus the economic critique of the new interventionism is only part of the post-new-trade-theory case for free trade. The other indispensable part rests on considerations of political economy.

THE POLITICAL ECONOMY CASE FOR FREE TRADE

Like most microeconomic interventions, the interventionist policies suggested by new trade theory would affect the distribution of income as well as its level. The well-justified concern of economists is that when policies affect income distribution, the politics of policy formation come to be dominated by distribution rather than efficiency. In the case of trade interventions, this concern is at two levels. First, to the extent that the policies work, they will have a beggar-thy-neighbor component that can lead to retaliation and mutually harmful trade war. Second, at the domestic level an effort to pursue efficiency through intervention could be captured by special interests and turned into an inefficient redistributionist program.

Retaliation and Trade War

Strategic trade policy aimed at securing excess returns for domestic firms and support for industries that are believed to yield national benefits are both beggar-thy-neighbor policies that raise income at the expense of other countries. A country that attempts to use such policies will probably provoke retaliation. In many (though not all) cases, a trade war between two interventionist governments will leave both countries worse off than if a hands-off approach were adopted by both. For example, consider the case of the European telecommunications equipment industry. This industry is a likely candidate for targeting on both oligopoly and external economy grounds. It is also a sector where nationalistic procurement by government-owned firms allows countries to pursue protectionist policies without violating agreements on international trade. The result of such protectionist policies, however, is by most accounts harmful to all concerned. Each country tries to be largely self-sufficient in equipment, and no country is able to realize the scale economies that would come from supplying the European market as a whole. Arguably, the structure of the game between countries in telecommunications equipment, and probably in other sectors as well, is that of a prisoners' dilemma where each country is better off intervening than being the only country not to intervene, but everyone would be better off if nobody intervened.

The way to avoid the trap of such a prisoners' dilemma is to establish rules of the game for policy that keep mutually harmful actions to a minimum. If such rules are to work, however, they must be simple enough to be clearly defined. Free trade is such a simple rule; it is easy enough to determine whether a country imposes tariffs or import quotas. New trade theory suggests that this is unlikely to be the best of all conceivable rules. It is very difficult to come up with any simple set of rules of the game that would be better, however. If the gains from sophisticated interventionism are small, which is the import of the economic critique of the last section, then there is a reasonable case for continuing to use free trade as a focal point for international agreement to prevent trade war.

Domestic Politics

Governments do not necessarily act in the national interest, especially when making detailed microeconomic interventions. Instead they are influenced by interest group pressures. The kinds of interventions that new trade theory suggests can raise national income will typically raise the welfare of small, fortunate groups by large amounts, while imposing costs on larger, more diffuse groups. The result, as with any microeconomic policy, can easily be that excessive or misguided intervention takes place because the beneficiaries have more knowledge and influence than the losers. Nobody who has followed U.S. trade policy in sugar or lumber can be very sanguine about the ability of the government to be objective applying a policy based on the Brander-Spencer model.

How do we resolve the problem of interest group influence on decision-making in the real world? As in the case of the problem of international conflict, one answer is to establish rules of the game that are not too inefficient and are simple enough to be enforceable. To ask the Commerce Department to ignore special-interest politics while formulating detailed policy for many industries is not realistic; to establish a blanket policy of free trade, with exceptions granted only under extreme pressure, may not be the optimal policy according to the theory but may be the best policy that the country is likely to get.

THE STATUS OF FREE TRADE

The economic cautions about the difficulty of formulating useful interventions and the political economy concerns that interventionism may go astray combine into a new case for free trade. This is not the old argument that free trade is optimal because markets are efficient. Instead, it is a sadder but wiser argument for free trade as a rule of thumb in a world whose politics are as imperfect as its markets.

The economic cautions are crucial to this argument. If the potential gains from interventionist trade policies were large, it would be hard to argue against making some effort to realize these gains. The thrust of the critique offered above, however, is that the gains from the interventions are limited by uncertainty about appropriate policies, by entry that dissipates the gains, and by the general equilibrium effects that insure that promoting one sector diverts resources from others. The combination of these factors limits the potential benefits of sophisticated interventionism.

Once the expected gains from intervention have been whittled down sufficiently, political economy can be invoked as a reason to forego intervention altogether. Free trade can serve as a focal point on which countries can agree to avoid trade wars. It can also serve as a simple principle with which to resist pressures of special-interest politics. To abandon the free trade principle in pursuit of the gains from sophisticated intervention could therefore open the door to adverse political consequences that would outweigh the potential gains.

It is possible, then, both to believe that comparative advantage is an incomplete model of trade and to believe that free trade is nevertheless the right policy. In fact, this is the position taken by most of the new trade theorists themselves. So free trade is not passé—but it is not what it once was.

ENDNOTES

1 There have been many surveys of the new developments in international trade theory. For a synthetic presentation of much of the positive side of this work, see Elhanan Helpman and Paul Krugman (1985); for an informal presentation of arguments for and against new forms of trade intervention, see the volume edited by Paul Krugman (1986); for a survey that also covers related topics in the border area between trade and industrial organization, see Paul Krugman (forthcoming).

2 One need not, of course, abandon comparative advantage entirely. From early in the development of new trade theory most models have represented trade as arising from both increasing returns and some form of comparative advantage, such as differences in factor endowments. This behavior of such models depends on the underlying parameters. For example, if scale economies are large and countries are similar in their factor endowments, the model will behave very differently from when scale economies are weak and countries differ greatly; in the latter case traditional trade theory yields the right predictions, in the former it does not.

3 See, for example, W.M. Corden (1974). As the conventional literature points out, however, protection is only a second-best policy; direct correction of the domestic market failure is preferable.

4 The one exception is the case of *zero* appropriability. In this case technological progress will occur only through learning-by-doing, because there will be no incentive for firms to invest deliberately in knowledge creation; since the fixed costs associated with knowledge investment are absent, perfect competition may be preserved.

5 Even if externalities are national in scope, one might argue that no conflict need be involved; simply each country provide the optimal subsidy. There are three answers to this. First, in practice countries often pursue industrial policy objectives with second-best trade policy tools. It is interesting to ask why they do this, but as long as they do the attempt to promote sectors is an attempt to promote them at other countries' expense. Second, much of the practical argument over industrial policy in the U.S. concerns the urgency of action when we are reluctant to intervene: if foreign countries' policies crowd out externality-generating domestic sectors, then the costs of not subsidizing become larger. Finally, if economies of scale (internal or external) are large enough, conflict of interest becomes unavoidable. Suppose there is room for only one Silicon Valley in the world, yet the agglomeration will yield valuable external economies to the country that gets it. Then the conflict cannot be avoided except through side payments.

6 In a widely cited paper, Jonathan Eaton and Gene Grossman (1986) showed that in a duopoly model where the optimal strategic policy was an export subsidy with quantity competition, it was an export tax with price competition.

7 Of course, one response is to try to find out. The central direction of current research in the new trade analysis is the effort to produce quantitative models of competition in imperfectly competitive industries. These efforts are currently primitive, and even the authors are skeptical about the robustness of the results, but it is encouraging to see an effort to make the theory operational. See in particular Avinash Dixit Smith (1986), Dani Rodrik (1987), and Richard Harris and David Cox (1984).

REFERENCES

Baldwin, Richard, and Paul Krugman, "Market Access and Competition: A Simulation Study of 16K Random Access Memories." In Feenstra, Robert, ed., *Empirical Research in International Trade*. Cambridge: MIT Press.

Brander, James A., and Barbara J. Spencer, "Export Subsidies and International Market Share Rivalry," *Journal of International Economics*, 1985, 18, 83-100.

Brander, James A., and Barbara J. Spencer, "International R & D Rivalry and Industrial Strategy", *Review of Economic Studies*, 1983, 50, 707-722.

Burenstam-Linder, Steffan, *An Essay on Trade and Transformation.* New York: Praeger, 1961.

Corden, W. Max, *Trade Policy and Economic Welfare*, Oxford: Claredon, 1974.

Dixit, Avinash K., "Optimal Trade and Industrial Policy for the U.S. Automobile Industry." In Feenstra, Robert, ed., *Empirical Research in International Trade.* Cambridge: MIT Press, forthcoming.

Dixit, Avinash K., and Victor Norman, *Theory of International Trade*, Cambridge: Nisbet, 1980.

Dixit, Avinash K., and Joseph E. Stiglitz, "Monopolistic Competition and Optimum Product Diversity," *American Economic Review*, 1977, 67, 297-308.

Eaton, Jonathan, and Gene M. Grossman, "Optimal Trade and Industrial Policy Under Oligopoly," *Quarterly Journal of Economics*, May 1986, CI:2, 383-406.

Harris, Richard and David Cox., *Trade, Industrial Policy and Canadian Manufacturing.* Toronto: University of Toronto Press, 1984.

Helpman, Elhanan, and Paul Krugman, *Market Structure and Foreign Trade: Increasing Returns, Imperfect Competition, and the International Economy.* Cambridge: MIT Press, 1985.

Horstmann, Ignatius, and James R. Markusen, "Up the Average Cost Curve: Inefficient Entry and the New Protectionism," *Journal of International Economics*, May 1986, *203/4*, 225-248.

Krugman, Paul R., "Increasing Returns, Monopolistic Competition, and International Trade," *Journal of International Economics*, 1979, *9*. 469-479.

Krugman, Paul R., ed., *Strategic Trade Policy and the New International Economics.* Cambridge: MIT Press, 1986.

Krugman, Paul R., "Industrial Organization and International Trade." In Schmalensee, Richard, and Robert Willig, eds., *Handbook of Industrial Organization.* Amsterdam: North-Holland, forthcoming.

Lancaster, Kelvin, "Intra-industry Trade Under Perfect Monopolistic Competition," *Journal of International Economics*, 1980, *10*, 151-175.

Rodrik, Dani, "Imperfect Competition and Trade Policy in Developing Countries," Harvard University mimeo, 1987.

Spence, A. Michael, "Product Selection, Fixed Costs, and Monopolistic Competition," *Review of Economic Studies*, 1976, *43*, 217-235.

Venables, Anthony J., and M. Alasdair Smith, "Trade and Industrial Policy Under Imperfect Competition," *Economic Policy*, 1986, *3*, 621-672.

Vernon, Raymond, "International Investment and International Trade in the Product Cycle," *Quarterly Journal of Economics*, May 1966, *80:2*, 190-207.

READING 2

U.S. TRADE POLICY: SHORT-TERM PRESSURES AND LONG-TERM STRATEGY†

Protection: Is There a Better Way?

Robert Z. Lawrence*

It is tempting for an economist to invoke Nancy Reagan's dictum when dealing with trade protection: "just say no." On analytical grounds, it is hard to see why structural change because of trade should be singled out for special policy treatment. Moreover, protection, particularly with quotas, is an inappropriate policy instrument for achieving the purposes to which it is generally put. It is inefficient, its costs are not transparent and it may even be counterproductive when used to save jobs or improve competitiveness. If, for example, quota protection encourages domestic monopolists to reduce output, it could lower employment. (See Clifford Winston and Associates, 1987, for an example.) Similarly, increasing foreign rents, quotas could reduce the long-run competitiveness of domestic industry.

Nonetheless, the pure free traders must deal with political reality. Trade *is* singled out as a source of change in the U.S. Constitution. While the Constitution prohibits interference with interstate commerce it expressly provides Congress the authority (and thus exposes it to the political pressures) to regulate international commerce. No matter how firm their ideological commitment to open markets, all U.S. administrations have found the political pressures for protection irresistible. According to William Niskanen, who served on President Reagan's Council of Economic Advisers, President Reagan, despite his free trade rhetoric, has been the most protectionist U.S. president since Herbert Hoover. Moreover, when granting protection, the Reagan Administration has generally used quotas rather than tariffs. Even if President-elect Bush can resist pleas for new protection—he has already agreed to extending steel quotas in 1989—he still needs a strategy for unwinding existing quota protection in an era of scarce budgetary resources. In this paper, therefore, I will discuss U.S. programs that provide protection and consider how protection could be improved and removed.

I. EXISTING PROGRAMS

The United States has two major routes to protection. The escape clause provides a legal route that has been associated with considerable adjustment and has proved to be temporary. The provision of quota protection by the president and/or Congress through legislation or negotiation, is a second, more political route that has been associated with hidden barriers which tend to be permanent. Let us consider the experience with each route and explain why the second, less desirable route has been used so frequently.

The Escape Clause. Section 201 of the Trade Act of 1974, the escape clause, provides legislators with a safety valve for diverting protectionist pleas. It allows domestic industries to receive temporary protection from imports when they can 1) prove to the U.S. International Trade Commission (ITC) that imports threaten or cause them serious economic injury, and 2) persuade the president that relief is consistent with the national interest. Paralleled by Article XIX of the General Agreement on Tariffs and Trade (GATT), the provisions of the U.S. escape clause have been used since 1947 to protect more than thirty industries, ranging from the integrated steel industry to manufacturers of nuts and bolts. In principle, the escape clause is the major route to protection. In practice, it has become a secondary road.

The escape clause law has performed reasonably well where it has been applied. Relief provided under the escape clause has been temporary. By statute, the president could grant protection for a period no longer than five years; thereafter, domestic interests had to prove that renewed protection was merited. In fact, only two of the more than thirty industries that have won escape clause relief (specialty steel and roofing materials) remained protected in 1988. Moreover, according to Gary Hufbauer et al. (1986), protection under the escape clause has been associated with considerable adjustment, most of which has occurred through downsizing.

Relief under the provisions of the escape clause has not been easy to obtain. Only about 6 out of 10 domestic petitioners for relief since 1975 have been able to prove their case before the ITC, and only 1 out of 4 of the 201 petitions filed since 1975 has ultimately resulted in the president providing import relief. Econometric studies (such as Robert Baldwin, 1985) indicate ITC decisions have been largely determined on their economic merits, relatively free from political pressures.

Nevertheless, the escape clause has three major flaws. As estimated for example by Hufbauer et al., such protection is costly; escape clause protection has taken the less desirable form of quotas as well as tariffs; and the denial of any aid by the president to more than half the industries that proved their case before the ITC has emerged as a problem. With relief so uncertain, even in cases such as footwear in 1986 where injury is demonstrated, lawmakers have been tempted to legislate costly quantitative import restrictions.

Special Protection

Several, typically large industries with political clout, have obtained special protection from the president or the Congress. When granted, such protection has generally taken the form of legislated quotas or voluntary restraint arrangements (VRAs) with foreign exporters. Recent examples include President Reagan's use of VRAs to limit imports of automobiles, carbon steel, and machine tools. In addition, statutory frameworks have been used to place quantitative restraints on textiles and apparel imports, and quotas on dairy, peanut, cotton, and sugar imports.

Protection obtained in this manner does not require meeting any particular standard or criterion — not even one as vague as "serious injury." Such protection has tended to be permanent and unrelated to the current fortunes of the industry. As noted by Hufbauer and Howard Rosen (1986), import quotas have been applied to sugar, peanuts, and dairy products in the United States for more than thirty years. Domestic shipbuilders have been shielded from foreign competition in coastal traffic since 1920. Most costly of all, in terms of higher prices paid by consumers, have been the limits on textile and apparel imports, set through quotas negotiated bilaterally under the auspices of the Multifiber Arrangement.

If industries are to be protected, most economists and the GATT would prefer tariffs over quotas. But quotas have greater political appeal (Arye Hillman and W. Heinrich Ursprung, 1988, and James Cassing and Hillman, 1985). The costs of quotas are hidden. If foreigners can be made to comply "voluntarily," the home country avoids explicitly violating the letter of the GATT which has bound tariff rates. Trade officials sometimes suggest that discriminatory VRAs do less damage than global quotas or tariffs. Indeed, as Baldwin (1982) has argued, where transshipment through third countries is possible or where close substitutes are available in other countries, VRAs may be circumvented or ineffective. But experience (with textiles and steel, for example) has shown that where import pressures are diverted, the measures are soon extended to (and by) other countries. Quotas appeal to domestic producers, particularly those with some monopoly power, because, unlike tariffs, they may reduce demand elasticities and thus raise optimal prices. Foreign firms also like quotas, since *they* are directly compensated with higher profit margins. Under the GATT, the country, (but not the industry) hurt by new protection is supposed to receive compensation.

II. FUTURE POLICY

The new administration needs creative approaches to provide a plausible alternative to new and embedded cases of quantitative protection. In an era of budgetary stringency, the best advice of trade theory, to use subsidies rather than tariffs, is not always practical. A second-best approach is to use only self-liquidating tariffs where protection is unavoidable and to use the revenues from such tariffs to compensate those hurt by imports and/or the removal of existing quotas.

The escape clause should serve as the center of the relief program for all claimants. Similarly, only countervailing duties, rather than VRAs or cartels, should be used in response to dumping and subsidies. The tilt toward this form of relief can be achieved by making other forms of protection less attractive and by making the escape clause more attractive. Because the political appeal of VRAs is considerable, the government should tie its hands to prevent the use of such measures by amending the antitrust laws. Following the proposals of Jan Tumlir (1985), the Sherman Act should be extended to prohibit the foreign cartels (even those blessed by foreign governments) necessary to make VRAs work. A weaker measure would be to require estimates (by the Office of Management and Budget) of the tariff and revenues foregone by any new quota measures.

The 1988 Trade Act makes the escape clause more attractive by easing eligibility standards and limiting (but not removing) presidential discretion in denying relief. The next president could enhance this attractiveness. In instances where the ITC recommends action but the president does not feel protection is warranted, he should *automatically* extend two alternative forms of relief. First, mergers of firms should be assessed under liberalized standards. These standards would recognize the full extent of discipline exerted by foreign producers on U.S. firms. Second, an improved trade adjustment assistance (TAA) program should be extended to displaced workers from industries found by the ITC to be injured by trade.

In cases where the president believes temporary protection is warranted, he should use *only* declining tariffs. The model would be the successful experience of the Harley-Davidson company. In addition, as part of the current Multilateral Trade Negotiations, the administration should avoid agreeing to a new Safeguards code that condones discriminatory protection. Instead, it should press for a revised code which permits, once injury has been found by an open (or GATT) judicial hearing, the temporary use of non-discriminatory declining tariffs, without requiring compensation to trading partners.

Improving Trade Adjustment Assistance. The TAA program provides the president with a means of showing concern for the adverse impact of imports without providing trade protection. But it has not provided effective compensation or encouraged adjustment. All workers receive similar benefits so that levels of assistance provided to displaced workers have not reflected the degree of injury they may have suffered because of import competition. Moreover, the form in which assistance has been provided (in effect, extensions of unemployment compensation) does not motivate displaced workers to find new jobs. Trade-adjustment payments might include, in addition to extended unemployment benefits, an earnings insurance component that compensates displaced workers once they accept new employment. Indeed, this proposal is part of the 1988 Trade Act in the form of a pilot project.

Payments would equal a fixed percentage of any erosion in earnings for a particular period of time. This approach would compensate workers for some of their loss of specific human capital—as revealed by subsequent earnings. It would not compensate them fully, however, to maintain some form of copayment to limit moral hazard problems. The proportion of income replaced would decline gradually and could reflect the age and experience of individual workers. By providing extra compensation to workers after they find new employment, the proposal would give them an incentive to adjust. Rather than remain idle in the hope of reemployment, workers would be more likely to accept jobs paying lower wages but offering new career opportunities, training programs and chances to build seniority.

Removing Existing Protection

The United States should convert all current VRAs and quotas into nondiscriminatory tariffs that decline over an extended period of time (see C. Fred Bergsten et al., 1987). The revenues raised from conversion could be used to fund a trade-adjustment program (Hufbauer-Rosen) and to provide compensation to foreign exporters currently enjoying quota rents.

In competitive industries, "tariffication" could proceed in two steps. First, existing quotas (and VRAs) would be globalized and auctioned. For some time, therefore, the domestic industry would receive the same amount of protection it obtains currently, but the globalization of current quotas would afford efficiency gains by allowing a redistribution of imports among foreign firms. Later, tariffs would be set at the rates determined by the final auction of quota rights. Thereafter they would be phased down and eliminated over fairly long periods of time. As Kala Krishna (1988) has pointed out, however, in industries where foreign exporters or domestic distributors have monopoly power, monopolists could reduce auction quota revenues to zero. In these cases, current quotas should be immediately converted into tariffs.

In some cases, in particular where the United States is a small purchaser on the world market, foreign exporters need not be compensated. In other cases, however, they could be explicitly compensated by preferential allocation of transferable quotas, tariff-rate quotas (Robert Feenstra and Tracy Lewis, 1988, and Feenstra, 1988) or direct payments.

This proposal is not without problems. There is some danger that Congress could become hooked on the tariff revenues. Foreigners might also not respond to the loss of quota rents with equanimity and, of course, domestic industry would not find the prospect of losing its protection particularly appealing. Nonetheless, in the absence of new initiatives, the continued drift toward greater, less transparent and more discriminatory protection is likely to continue.

Conditionality

An alternative, but less desirable strategy is to use a more elaborate industrial policy to solve the problem of permanent protection. The industry might be forced to agree to an adjustment plan as a quid pro quo for protection. The 1988 Trade act, for example, encourages (but does not require) an industry requesting relief to submit a plan that outlines the steps it will take to adjust to foreign competition and it makes the plan an important factor when the ITC and the president make their decisions on granting relief.

Advocates of conditionality argue that requirements for industrywide reinvestment, modernization, or other adjustment strategies will make it easier for the government to ensure that workers and communities are taken care of by the beneficiaries of the protection; that protection will achieve adjustment; that firms can be prevented from using the profits from protection to diversify (such as the purchase by U.S. Steel of Marathon Oil); and that protection is temporary.

But embroiling the government in detailed adjustment plans has several problems. Setting conditions for aid presumes that the government—either alone or as part of a tripartite body with representatives of labor and management—can better decide what form adjustment should take and how to accomplish it than firms in the relevant industries and the capital markets on which they depend. Such approaches could induce excess capacity, cartelize declining industries, and, by increasing government responsibility for the industry's adjustment, make protection more difficult to remove. Finally, conditionally is impractical in large competitive industries such as textiles or footwear, with thousands of firms and significant numbers of nonunionized workers. How would such conditions be enforced? Who speaks for labor (or management) in such arrangements? Yet these are precisely the industries that have the political clout to obtain special protection.

Thus far, the U.S. experience with conditionality has not been particularly successful. In 1984, for the first time Congress imposed conditions for trade relief for the steel industry. As a condition for continuing any bilateral import restraint arrangements, the president had to certify each year that the eight major American steel companies were reinvesting all their net cash flow in the steel business. The experience with the steel industry demonstrates some of the pitfalls of this approach. Forcing all steel companies to invest in an industry plagued by excess capacity is inefficient. The commitment by President-elect Bush in the election to renew steel VRAs in 1989 suggests conditionality has had little impact in making protection less permanent. The recent finding that simply holding financial instruments meets the investment conditions points to the problems in making conditions precise.

ENDNOTES

† Discussants: Jagdish Bhagwati, Columbia University; Gza Feketekuty, U.S. Trade Representatives Office; Paul R. Krugman, MIT and NBER

* Senior Fellow, The Brookings Institution, Washington, D.C. 20036. This paper draws heavily on my study with Robert Litan (1986). The views set forth here are solely my own and do not necessarily represent the opinions of the trustees, officers or other staff members of the Brookings Institution.

REFERENCES

Baldwin, Robert, "The Inefficacy of Trade Policy," *Princeton University Essays on International Finance*, 1982, 150.

_______, *The Political Economy of U.S. Import Policy*, Cambridge: MIT Press, 1985.

Bergsten, C. Fred et al., *Auction Quotas and United States Trade Policy*, Washington: Institute for International Economics, 1987.

Cassing, James H. and Hillman, Arye L., "Political Influence Motives and the Choice Between Tariffs and Quotas," *Journal of International Economics*, November 1985, *19*, 270-90.

Feenstra, Robert C., "Auctioning U.S. Import Quotas and Foreign Response," Working Paper No. 318, University of California-Davis, July 1988.

_______, "Negotiated Trade Restrictions with Private Political Pressure," Working Paper, University of California-Davis, August, 1988.

Hillman, Arye L and Ursprung, W. Heinrich, "Domestic Politics, Foreign Interests and International Trade Policy," *American Economic Review*, September 1988, *78*, 729-45.

Hufbauer, Gary and Rosen, Howard, *Trade Policy for Troubled Industries*, Washington: Institute for International Economics, 1986.

Hufbauer, Gary et al., *Trade Protection in the United States: 31 Case Studies*, Washington: Institute for International Economics, 1986.

Krishna, Kala, "The Case of Vanishing Revenues: Auction Quotas With Oligopoly," NBER Working Paper No 2723, September 1988.

Lawrence, Robert Z. and Litan, Robert E., *Saving Free Trade*, Washington: Brookings Institution, 1986.

Tumlir, Jan, *Protectionism: Trade Policy in Democratic Societies*, Washington: American Enterprise Institute, 1985.

Winston, Clifford M. and Associates, *Blind Intersection? Policy and the Automobile Industry*, Washington: Brookings Institution, 1987.

READING 3

Jumpstarting GATT

Jagdish Bhagwati

On December 7, 1990, the Uruguay Round talks on the multilateral trading system broke down. These talks are aimed at redesigning and revitalizing the General Agreement on Tariffs and Trade (GATT), which oversees world trade. In essence, the United States walked out as the European Community (EC) dug in its heels over the issue of agricultural export subsidies.

Washington's negotiating strategy had been to use EC concessions on agriculture, partly to benefit the United States directly, but more to win the support of key developing countries for its position on other trade issues. In return for agricultural liberalization, it had hoped developing countries would consent to new disciplines on trade in services, to stricter intellectual property rights, and to limits on their regulation of foreign investment—matters of interest and profit principally to the United States and other developed nations. The EC agriculture offer was simply not substantial enough to strike this grand deal.

Temporarily suspended, the talks have now resumed at the technical level. But their successful conclusion requires that the fast-track authority granted by Congress to the Bush administration, making possible a straight vote on the entire package of GATT reforms in lieu of votes on each item, be extended beyond the end of May. Barring a highly improbable resolution of disapproval by either house of Congress, fast-track authority will be extended two more years, during which a final deal must be struck.

Having brilliantly maneuvered the EC into a difficult position, the Bush administration is nonetheless unlikely to push the Uruguay Round to a successful conclusion unless it now recognizes that its bargaining leverage is not as strong as earlier believed. The EC may be over a barrel, but the barrel can roll right out of the negotiating arena. The United States has three strategy options: inaction, threats, and incentives. Of these, the last may be the most promising and also the least explored. The strategy of inaction presumes that the EC cannot afford to derail GATT because the stakes are too high and the guilt would be too great. This presumption is not compelling.

The stakes are indeed high. The Uruguay Round, launched in Punta del Este, Uruguay, in 1986, is the single most important trade negotiation since GATT's creation in October 1947. Its agenda is complex, its promise considerable. GATT's rewards rest critically on what economists call a "fix-rule" trading regime: Member nations compete according to rules and generally the chips fall where they may. This conception contrasts with "fix-quantity" trading systems, or what is known popularly as "results-oriented" or "managed" trade. There, bureaucrats and politicians negotiate quantities, not rules, and the former determine who will trade what. GATT matters to many who believe that significant efficiency gains come through a world trading system that lets markers work unimpeded by tariffs, quotas, and other interventions.

A prime example of the Uruguay Round's relevance and importance is the exclusion to date of services from the provenance of GATT, and the intention now to redress that omission. If successful, the Uruguay Round will extend the discipline of a fix-rule trading regime to this new set of sectors, including accounting, airlines, banking, construction, insurance, legal services, medical services, and telecommunications. Such services generate nearly a quarter of world trade today.

At the same time, the Uruguay Round will begin to bring discipline to such older economic sectors as agriculture and textiles. Ironically, it was the United States that in 1955 exempted agriculture from GATT controls with a widely followed waiver. Now the sector is riddled worldwide with myriad market-distorting interventions. Textiles, too, have been heavily protected since 1961 when the United States, under pressure from domestic interests, helped negotiate the Short-term Arrangement on International Trade in Cotton Textiles that survived long term as the Multifiber Agreement (MFA).

Yet the failure to extend GATT's mandate to new sectors and to restore discipline to old ones would entail not only the costs of missed opportunities, great as they are. The probable ensuing consequences also carry costs, which could be very large. The breakdown of negotiations critical to strengthening the common institutions of an increasingly interdependent global economy could undermine confidence in the capacity of key nations to provide necessary leadership. One failure may engender many others.

Further, there are more immediate costs, in particular a resurgence of protectionism. Economists distinguish between the demand for protection (from firms, unions, and communities) and the supply of protection (by the administration and Congress). The supply of protection would probably increase because an irate Congress would more readily accept demands for protection from its constituents if it believed that the EC and others had failed to accept American demands for more open markets. Then again, if the United States were to give in to protectionist demands, which are likely to increase thanks to the recent recession, as all previous experience suggests, so would its trading partners. Competitive "beggar-thy-neighbor" trade restraints could accentuate the recession much the way the global proliferation of tariffs is generally believed to have followed the U.S. Smoot-Hawley Tariff Act of 1930.

Trade restraints and tariff wars are not the only likely outcomes. In agriculture, the failure to reach agreement could mean export-subsidy wars, as the United States starts to match subsidies the EC refuses to surrender. Similarly, reductions in agricultural income-support payments in the 1990 U.S. budget that are contingent on EC concessions on agriculture at the Uruguay Round could be lost. The lost chance to reduce income supports coupled with higher export subsidies would doubly strain the U.S. budget at a time when the United States can least afford it.

Congress is also likely to become less committed to GATT's multilateralism and more enamored with quick-fixes like regionalism and unilateralism—the former leading to the formation of free-trade areas south of the Rio Grande, the latter rooting American use of economic power to extract unilateral concessions from weaker trading partners. Congress has recently flirted with both alternatives, as panic and petulance break out over the continuing trade deficit and the rise of Japan. Regionalism threatens to fragment the world economy; unilateralism undermines GATT's central tenet that the strong and the weak should play by similar rules. Exacerbating these destructive trends in the United States would undermine the world trading system when the pressing task of the day is to reinforce it.

THE BLAME GAME

Could the United States successfully blame the EC for all this mayhem? Not really. Much of the disarray would stem from American actions. Protestations by the Bush administration that a frustrated Congress was the culprit may carry conviction among the experts, but foreign governments will only experience déjà vu.

There is an exaggerated but nonetheless real feeling in the EC bureaucracy that the United States unwisely backed the EC into a corner on an issue of utmost political difficulty. The "blame game" can be played equally well by the EC, and thus seriously undercuts the possibility of unilateral accommodation by the EC to break the Uruguay Round logjam.

If guilt will not work, can shame suffice? Unfortunately, politicians in pluralistic democracies typically suffer from cognitive dissonance on trade policy. Some commentators have criticized French President François Mitterand for the incongruity between the high ground of his rhetoric on Third World needs and the low ground of his support for protection of 10 million relatively well-off EC farmers against hundreds of millions of farmers in less-developed countries. In the same vein, the MFA has protected the senescent textile industries of most industrial countries in the Organization for Economic Cooperation and Development (OECD) at the expense of developing countries, even as these same OECD countries spend large sums on aid programs. Altruism has been easier in aid than in trade, because constituency politics makes trade policy treacherous ground for the national interest. It is not likely, therefore, that Mitterrand will feel particularly embarrassed by his unwillingness, which reflects his political inability, to yield more on agriculture.

A strategy of threats to coerce the EC offers no better prospects. The twin components of a threat strategy would be American regionalism and unilateralism. Neither wound the EC into submission. Instead, both promise to wound GATT.

American regionalism is an empty threat to the EC. Arguably, the "regional card" in the shape of the 1988 U.S.-Canada Free Trade Agreement played a small role in prompting a reluctant EC to join multilateral negotiations it had rejected four years earlier. But when the question is not one of joining negotiations but instead of yielding in them, the threat approach is much less compelling.

Besides, the prospective U.S. regional partners are the troubled countries of Latin America. It is not credible that the United States would divert its energies and trade to a region whose slow growth rates, fragile democracies, inflation, and debts offer a far less attractive market than the burgeoning Far East and EC. If the United States foolishly turns away from the world to its own backyard, the likely EC reaction would be: Go ahead.

Nor can the United States expect the EC to bend because the threat of American regionalism would weaken the multilateral trading system and reduce the benefits accruing to the EC. A staunch believer in the simultaneous practice of regionalism and multilateralism, the EC itself is, of course, a regional arrangement. It is unlikely to view the growth of similar regional arrangements elsewhere as necessarily harmful to the multilateral trading system. A warmer American embrace of regionalism is therefore unlikely to alarm the EC into renewed efforts at the Uruguay Round, no matter how much it frightens those who see greater virtue in multilateralism.

It is tempting to believe, however, that aggressive unilateralism may pay off where regional initiatives do not. Since the passage of the 1988 Omnibus Trade and Competitiveness Act, the United States possesses weapons under sections 301-310, popularly known as Section, Super, and Special 301, designed not merely to enforce American trade rights, but also to extract new concessions through tactics such as the threat of GATT-illegal tariff retaliations. The Super 301 sword, under which unacceptable "priority practices" and "priority countries" can be targeted for retaliation, is now sheathed because of the lapse of its two-year legislative mandate but was used on May 25, 1989, by U.S. Trade Representative Carla Hills against Brazil, India and Japan. The "priority practices" objected to in these countries included many that were in fact compatible with these nations' trading rights as defined by GATT or other treaties.

Resorting to the law of the jungle rather than the rule of law works only against the weak, making its successful application to the EC highly dubious. The EC is a sufficiently sizeable economic power to preclude intimidation. Further, unlike the case of Japan, the imbalance of trade between the United States and the EC is not significant, suggesting a broadly equal stake in trade by both sides and the lack of decisive power by either. For example, the EC was left out of the Super 301 hit list despite many American objections to EC policies. By promising tit-for-tat response, and even adding 301-type legislation into its own arsenal, the EC has inured itself to undue pressure, though not to occasional trade battles like the U.S. invocation of 301 against the EC ban on hormone-fed beef in January 1989.

The EC will only sit back and enjoy the action if the United States lashes out with 301 actions against other weaker states to force one-on-one concessions it cannot procure through multilateral negotiations at the Uruguay Round. Nothing has drawn the wrath and condemnation of the world's trading nations more than America's 301 policy.

Japan, too, is a great economic power capable of resisting 301-style intimidation. But Japan feels seriously exposed and thus far is unwilling to indulge in a tit-for-tat strategy toward either the EC or the United States. It is an interesting question whether, and when, Japan will find the American fixation with Japan, and consequent attempts at imposing solutions on Japan for every imagined perfidy, intolerable and deserving of a tougher response.

Still, all is not lost in the Uruguay Round. An incentive strategy might bring the EC around. Such a strategy can be based on two wholly different by complementary ideas: one addressing fairness in balancing political costs in negotiated concessions between the EC and the United States and the other relating to easing the political cost to the EC.

Economists think of mutual gain from trade transactions; negotiators think of mutual pain from trade concessions. It is improbable that a trade negotiation among equals could reach fruition unless each party felt the political cost of market-opening concessions was matched by costs to the other side. Reciprocity of benefits in terms of increased exports must be broadly matched by reciprocity of costs in terms of the political difficulty of accepting increased imports.

In the current GATT standoff, the agreement that the EC rejected in December appears heavily unbalanced in favor of the United States in terms of political costs, relative to those of the EC, and especially France. The proposed deal essentially involves four elements: services, trade-related intellectual property rights (TRIPs), trade-related investment measures (TRIMs), and agriculture. Only a decade ago this agenda would have seemed strange. After all, why are intellectual property and foreign investment issues included in a trade negotiation, even if they are prefixed by the magic words "trade-related?" TR is, in fact, more aptly read as "tangentially related" than as "trade-related."

The agenda reflects the changed politics of trade policy in the United States, and this in turn explains the imbalance of political costs plaguing the current stalemate. Of late, U.S. trade politics has been marked by increased influence of producer interests in the design and execution of trade policy. Changes in the world economy in the 1980s have strengthened producer interests. The most compelling factor has been the "Diminished Giant Syndrome."[1] There is a national fear of being overtaken by East Asian nations, which will then create a new "Pacific century." Safeguarding U.S. producers against other competitors has gained such enormous importance that it now tends to dominate the definition of national interest.

Interestingly, Japan's role as feared rival has contributed to this ideological shift. Popular attribution of Japan's economic success to a benign, symbiotic partnership between its government and producers has led many to advocate following Japan's example. This belief has undermined the traditional American belief that the national interest is not simply an aggregation of producer interests. Older Democrats who once argued that what was good for General Motors was not necessarily good for the United States have been replaced by younger Democrats whose gut instinct is that what is good for Eastman Kodak cannot help but be good for America.

The institutions defining trade policy have increasingly been reshaped to reflect this ideological shift. Traditionally more responsive to producer interests, Congress has progressively recaptured trade policy from the administration, reversing its surrender to the administration following the Smoot-Hawley Tariff disaster. Particularly evident in the 1988 Omnibus Trade and Competitiveness Act were new limits on the scope of the administration's discretion, with mandatory requirements being imposed in some areas.

Producer influence on trade policy has also arisen from necessity imposed by pluralistic politics during the 1980s. Faced by powerful protectionist pressures, the Reagan administration yielded partially by negotiating export restraints in autos, footwear, and steel. It allowed the dollar to fall. But it also encouraged a coalition of interests to counter protectionist lobbies. Service sectors lobbies were a natural candidate as were industries such as pharmaceuticals and communications that had long felt intellectual property protection abroad was inadequate. Other potential allies were multinational companies that were unhappy with developing-country restrictions and requirements on their operations, chiefly in the form of export-performance targets and local-content rules.

Lobbies for TRIPs and TRIMs were thus eagerly embraced by the administration and dispatched to Brussels and Geneva as part of the elite corps attending the multilateral trade talks. In turn, these lobbies saw in these negotiations a chance to gain concessions denied to them in other forums. The tangential relationship of TRIPs and TRIMs to actual trade issues was ignored, though some developing countries did object. Neither the absence of empirical evidence establishing that lack of intellectual property protection in fact adversely affects technical progress, nor the findings of theoretical research that intellectual property protection can harm developing countries even as it augments world efficiency, were allowed to stand in the way of putting TRIPs on the trade agenda. American spokespersons, such as the current and former U.S. trade representatives, Carla Hills and Clayton Yeutter, shifted from the utilitarian, efficiency-based, and mutual-gain reasoning underlying GATT to a "rights"-based assertion that inadequate intellectual property protection amounts to piracy or theft.

From the perspective of political costs, then, an agreement that yields *any* concessions on services, TRIPS, TRIMS and agriculture (where U.S. grain exports are expected to profit from liberalization) represents a nearly all-win situation for the United States. The only political pain would be from the modest promise of market access on dairy products, peanuts, and sugar, and from concessions on textiles. The American agenda would have triumphed, its lobbies duly rewarded, and the pain principally one of inadequate gain.

For the EC, the role of producer interests in the Uruguay Round is very different. EC producers would profit equally from agreements on services, TRIPs, and TRIMs, but they are relatively ineffective lobbies; therefore, the political payoff is negligible. By contrast, liberalization of agriculture poses tremendous political difficulty in both France and Germany. So from the EC perspective, the agreement currently on the table looks alarmingly like an all-lose proposition in terms of political costs.

The result is a massive imbalance of political costs from the proposed agreement that must be corrected if the Uruguay Round is to be successful. The United States must agree to accept more pain, for example by allowing a substantially greater reduction of production for dairy products, sugar, and peanuts—that is, by going the extra mile where it is politically tough. The United States could also undertake a faster and more comprehensive dismantling of its MFA restrictions than the EC. Now that President George Bush has emerged from Persian Gulf war with great political clout, he can afford to shed the embarrassing MFA in a show of burden-sharing solidarity. It would also be a trade concession to developing nations that have suffered over the years from the MFA.

At this point the spurned accord gives the benefit of concessions in the new areas to OECD countries without comparable concessions to developing countries. By extending benefits to developing countries that can increase textile and clothing exports, the overall settlement at the Uruguay Round could reduce the massive unfairness implicit in the accord currently promoted by the Cairns Group (a coalition of 14 countries exporting farm products) and the United States. In addition, because the EC has an export advantage over the United States in textiles, an accord that substantially opens up textiles trade would afford the EC comparatively greater benefits than the United States, and the United States comparatively greater pain. This would further narrow the gap in political costs that divides the EC from the United States.

The acceptance of more pain would also imply a role reversal, enabling the United States to appreciate that political costs make a difference and to consider acceptable only a modest revision upwards in the final EC offer on agriculture. In turn, the administration must persuade the lobbies and the Congress that the modest gains in regard to services, TRIPs and TRIMs are significant when put into perspective. After all, these areas have escaped effective discipline over the last four decades because of their economic and political complexity. To expect more rapid and substantial progress in them within one negotiation when it took seven to reduce tariffs to their current low levels is to be not utopian but self-destructive.

THE PERESTROIKA SOLUTION

While redressing the imbalance in political costs may well suffice, an added inducement on agriculture for the EC would surely help. Such an inducement could be provided by exploiting the necessity of food imports for the success of *perestroika*. The Soviet Union could offer a significant, if temporary, market for excess European farm production, cushioning the shock to EC farmers of a more substantial cut in agricultural expert subsidies.[2]

An agreement could be reached in which the EC would annually sell up to 20 millions tons of grain and meat to the Soviet Union, close to half of the Soviet Unions's 1989 imports, over a period of perhaps five years. The USSR would be granted long-term credits so that repayment in convertible currency would begin only in the sixth year. This arrangement would ensure that the Soviet Union strapped for foreign exchange, would be able to import this quantity above and beyond its normal imports, thus guaranteeing that the sale would represent a genuine new market.

The sales would naturally gravitate to the furnishers of the credits, ensuring the EC (and the United States insofar as it extends its credits) a share of the extra market. While the EC would lose some subsidy-financed markets by accepting further cuts in export subsidies at the Uruguay Round, it would gain the new Soviet market. The EC's political cost from agricultural liberalization would be greatly eased until the expiration of the Soviet pact in five years, whereas the more competitive Cairns Group countries could immediately pick up markets abandoned by the EC as its currents subsidies dwindled. At the end of five years the EC would be forced to adjust, and the world would retain the gains in agricultural liberalization agreed to at the Uruguay Round, thanks to the cushion provided by the Soviet pact.

The Soviet Union could profitably use credit-financed supplements to its grain and meat supplies. Unfortunately, the Soviet problem was not limited to getting through this past winter with "emergency" food aid—a program that united the EC, the United States, and others. Over a longer period, the USSR will require sustained and sizable supplements to food supplies in order to make the transition to a market economy politically appealing. Supplemental imports need to be integrated systematically into a coherent economic reform plan if they are to have the maximum benefit.

The Soviet problem is not one of falling food production. On the contrary, agricultural production is one of *perestroika*'s success stories. Adjusted for weather variations, Soviet grain yields have increased at an accelerated pace during the Gorbachev years. Farms, by and large, have managed to bypass the state's procurement drive at controlled prices, instead selling food at higher prices in the marketplace. Food shortages in major cities reflect the declining procurement powers of the state: In 1989 the procurement of 59 million tons of foodgrains fell well short of the 86 million ton target. Procurement shortfalls mean that the Soviet government has correspondingly less processed bread and meat to distribute at fixed, low prices in the state shops. As the main problem intensifies, further shortfalls are anticipated and people will begin to drain stores of whatever they can find, leading to unseemly scrambling for vanishing sausages and bread that will fuel still further the frenzied emptying of shelves.

Under the pact with the EC proposed here, imports would largely fill the gap left by lagging procurement. *Perestroika* would be helped in several ways. For example, food would be immediately available in state stores in restive cities. This would help contain the revolution of falling expectations about what Soviet leaders can deliver. Expectations about future shortages and price hikes would be dampened by a large influx of food. Further, a deal with the EC would soak up excess Soviet expenditures, reducing the huge budget deficit —now 10 to 11 per cent of gross national product— that is fueling an inflationary spiral. Moscow's need to slash investment expenditures (and not just defense spending) in order to reduce the budget would be mitigated. One of the principal lessons of developmental planning is that cutting investment for short-run, anti-inflationary objectives is unwise since it saps growth and creates serious problems later.

Simultaneously buttressing *perestroika* and concluding the Uruguay Round by exploiting the complementarity of these tasks is attractive. Tragic events in Lithuania and the increasing likelihood that *perestroika* may succumb to disintegrative tendencies that Gorbachev can no longer control require that the proposed grain and meat agreement be contingent on three factors: the continuation of *glastnost*, the grounding of *perestroika* in a coherent economic plan, and a reasonable prospect for the resolution of the political crisis between the center and the republics, without which no economic reform plan is credible.

The recent resumption of EC credits worth $1 billion, which were suspended over the January 1991 Lithuanian repression, and renewed EC confidence in Gorbachev's democratic credentials and good intentions, if not in his ability to manage the increased domestic turbulence, suggest that marrying the Uruguay Round and *perestroika* remains an attractive way of advancing both causes.

But all will be lost at the Uruguay Round unless U.S. officials reassess their fundamental strategy and develop an approach that takes into account the political realities faced by its key negotiating partners.

ENDNOTES

1 See Jagdish Bhagwati and Douglas Irwin, *"The Return of the Reciprocitarians: U.S. Trade Policy Today,"* The World Economy, June 1987, vol. 10.

2 See Jagdish Bhagwati and Padma Desai, *"Making a Virtue of Moscow's Necessity,"* The New York Times, November 12, 1990.

SECTION II

International Trade and Political Process

While the "free versus managed-trade" debate continues, one undisputed fact is that protectionism makes some parts of the population better-off and some parts of the population worse-off. The distribution of winners and losers has important political ramifications. The benefits of protectionism often are concentrated among small groups, while the costs of protectionism are spreadout over the population. In the political process, intensive lobbying efforts by those who will gain from trade measures can lead to the implementation of policies that will hurt aggregate domestic welfare. In this section, Robert Baldwin and Linda Hunter present insights into the role of the political process and distributional effects as important determinants of trade-policy decisions.

READING 4

The Political Economy of Trade Policy

Robert E. Baldwin

International trade seems to be a subject where the advice of economics is routinely disregarded. Economists are nearly unanimous in their general opposition to protectionism, but the increase in U.S. protection in recent years in such sectors as automobiles, steel, textiles, and apparel, machine tools, footwear and semiconductors demonstrates that economists lack political influence on trade policy.

The type of protectionism chosen does not follow economist' advice, either. A frequently asked question on undergraduate trade exams is why a small country's welfare losses are less when it curtails imports with a tariff rather than by negotiating "voluntary" export-restraint agreements (VEAs) with foreign suppliers.[1] Even though generations of students have correctly pointed out that the equivalent of the domestic tax revenues raised by a tariff is transferred as a windfall gain to foreign countries when VEAs are introduced, these agreements are now the preferred means by which countries pursue protectionism. Moreover, if the purpose of protection is to redistribute income to producers, production subsidies (financed by lump-sum taxes) dominate both tariffs and import quotas on efficiency grounds, since the consumption costs of protection are avoided. Yet governments generally prefer to assist industries by providing import protection rather than production subsidies.

Economists have tended to attribute such disregard for their policy conclusions to a lack of economic education. However, while many consumers still do not seem to know where their economic self-interest lies when it comes to trade matters, it seems clear that today's top policy leaders are quite aware of economists' conclusions on most trade issues. Some economists, consequently, have begun trying to understand the policy-making process that leads politicians to disregard the advice of economists on issues of international trade.

Two broad approaches have been developed to analyze the political economics of trade policy and the processes that generate protectionism.[2] One approach emphasizes the economic self-interest of the political participants, while the other stresses the importance of the broad social concerns of voters and public officials. This paper outlines the nature of the two approaches, indicating how they can explain the above anomalies and other trade policy behavior, and concludes with observations about integrating the two frameworks, conducting further research, and making policy based on the analysis.

THE ECONOMIC SELF-INTEREST APPROACH

Under the economic self-interest approach, an individual favors or opposes a particular trade policy depending on whether the policy increases or decreases the person's real income. Hillman (1989) provides a comprehensive survey of this approach.

In the standard two commodity, two factor Heckscher-Ohlin model with identical, homothetic preferences and perfect competition, this perspective implies that if the imported good is produced in a labor-intensive manner, a worker in an economy facing fixed international terms of trade will favor an import duty, while a capitalist will favor free trade.[3] Consequently, under a majority voting rule, protection would seem to be the outcome if there are more workers than capitalists. But if, as is generally assumed in this model, income redistribution is a costless activity, free trade will be chosen, since gainers under free trade (in this case, the capitalists) can always more than compensate those who lose under this policy and still be better off than under protection. The capitalists will tie the redistribution scheme to the voting outcome.

Costs of Redistribution and Voting

When the assumptions of the model are eased to allow for costs of redistribution or voting, the conclusion, that free trade will be chosen no longer holds. In the situation described above, if redistribution costs plus the compensation to workers required to secure a majority vote for free trade amount to more than the capitalists gain from free trade, a compensation scheme tied to voting behavior will no longer be undertaken by capitalists and popular vote will select the protection option.

The existence of voting costs also can lead to protectionism, especially in situations where the benefits from free trade are quite small for many individual voters. Consider a specific-factors model in which both capital and labor are industry-specific (Baldwin, 1984). In these circumstances, the losses in real income to individual workers and capital owners in an industry subject to a significant increase in foreign competition are likely to exceed their individual costs of voting for protection. In contrast, the fraction of income spent on the industry's product by individual workers and capitalists employed in other sectors, who gain from the decline in the import price, may well be so small that the higher costs of the protected good are each less than the per capita costs of voting against protection or acquiring detailed information about its effects. Consequently, the comparatively small number of people employed in the injured industry all vote for protection and the large number of people working in other industries may not vote at all.

Money, Votes, and Coalition Politics

Protectionism may also be selected because of the well-known free-rider problem associated with public goods (Olson, 1965). Trade policy has the characteristic of a public good, since a beneficiary from a policy such as free trade cannot be excluded from its benefits, even though the person does not contribute to the costs of obtaining this policy. The decision to contribute campaign funds to officials favoring free trade has the structure of a prisoners' dilemma game for individual consumers. If each consumer believes his or her contribution is too small to affect the policy outcome, the individual will conclude that it is best not to contribute, regardless of whether all other consumers do or do not contribute. Thus, the dominant strategy for each consumer is not to contribute in support of free trade, and the outcome is that all end up worse off than if they had contributed.

As Olson points out, a common-interest group is more likely to overcome the free rider problem and raise the funds needed for effective lobbying if the number of its members is small or if the benefits from a particular policy are unevenly distributed, since then some members of the group will have a significant economic stake in the policy outcome. For a large firm with (say) 25 percent of the domestic industry's market that is threatened by import competition, it may pay to lobby, no matter what the other firms in the industry do.

However, in making this decision, such firms must also take into account the anti-protection lobbying of large firms in other sectors who use the industry's output as an intermediate production input. For example, as Destler and Odell (1987) document, the Caterpillar Company vigorously opposed the extension of steel quotas in 1984, claiming to be the largest American steel user as well as the biggest exporter of U.S.-made steel. Furthermore, in these author's view, the active opposition of copper users was the main reason for the failure of this industry to obtain import relief in 1984.

In contrast to Olson, Caves (1976), in stressing the importance of the voting strength of an industry in gaining protection, hypothesizes a negative relationship between the level of protection and the degree of industry centralization both in geographical and market share terms. He argues that a geographically dispersed industry can obtain the support of a larger number of elected representatives than a regionally centralized one, while a low level of firm concentration will attract greater political support from customers and suppliers. However, although most countries studied support the importance of the employment size of an industry as a determinant of the level of protection, they also generally bear out Olson's contention that a high level of industry protection is associated either with a small number of firms or a high degree of market concentration (Anderson and Baldwin, 1987).[4]

The importance of an industry's voting strength for gaining protection is nowhere better supported than in the textile and apparel industries. With nearly two million employees in many firms scattered over a wide geographical area, these industries have been highly successful in using their voting strength to gain import protection. The approval of the Textile Bill of 1985, which tightened textile quotas, by both branches of the Congress illustrates the industry's political clout. (However, the bill was vetoed by President Reagan.) Tosini and Tower (1987) found that the proportion of textile and apparel workers in the total work force of a congressional district or state was the most significant variable explaining the pattern of voting.

In contrast to the textile and apparel sectors, which have managed to hold the ratio of imports to consumption to less than 15 percent, the much smaller leather and leather products industry has been unable to prevent the ratio from rising to over 25 percent. The import ratio for women's footwear, for example, rose from 5 percent in 1965 to 33 percent in 1985.

Differences in market structure seem to influence the manner in which industries lobby for protection. As noted above, the textile and apparel sectors, which are composed of a large number of employees and firms, rely mainly on the voting pressure they can exert directly on individual members of Congress and the president to gain their objectives (Bauer, Pool and Dexter, 1972). They do not launch large lobbying campaigns aimed at the general public. In contrast, the steel and auto industries, which have also been very successful in securing import protection but which are not as large in voting terms and are oligopolistically organized (thus presumably having higher profits), spend large sums lobbying the general public as well as public officials on the merits of their case for protection. Lacking the voting power of textiles and apparel, they seem to believe it is necessary to convince the public that granting protection is desirable on such grounds as "fairness," national security, or the need for a temporary adjustment period, before legislators not dependent directly on their votes will go along with protection. Industries like steel and autos also tend to focus their lobbying efforts on the Senate, where the typical member has more influence and faces the voters less often than in the House. Small industries have little chance of receiving industry-specific protection, although they can sometime free-ride on a politically powerful industry. They usually lobby through general business associations and direct their efforts at securing general changes in the trade laws that make it easier to obtain protection.

Whether it is an industry's voting power or financial strength that create pressures for protection, these pressures are powerful enough that many presidents have made protectionist concessions to improve the chances that Congress would approve a general trade-liberalizing bill. President Eisenhower, for example, felt it necessary to promise to impose oil import quotas to minimize the opposition of congressional members from the oil and coal-producing states to the extension of the Trade Agreements Act in 1955, while President Kennedy agreed to seek an international quota system for cotton textiles in order to minimize opposition to the Trade Expansion Act of 1962. President Nixon increased the likelihood of Congressional approval of the Trade Act of 1974 by renewing steel import quotas and agreeing to negotiate an international textile agreement covering man-made materials, wool, and cotton.[5]

Triggers for Self-Interested Action

Olson (1983) has recently argued that, before a group organizes and undertakes lobbying activities, a crisis like a sudden increase in imports or a decline in employment may be necessary to focus attention on a group's common interests. This view is supported by the success in resisting tariff cuts during the Toyko Round of multilateral trade-liberalizing negotiations (1974-1979) of industries in which employment had been declining and import penetration ratios rising in recent years (Baldwin, 1985). The psychologists Kahneman and Tversky (1979, 1984) also find empirical support for the view that individuals place a greater welfare weight on the loss of a given amount of income than on a gain of the same amount.[6] This would seem to be part of the explanation why protection is usually given only to industries in which profits and employment are declining. Both workers and capitalists are prepared to exert greater efforts to recoup income declines than to gain increases above historically normal levels. In addition, firms may lobby more vigorously for protection when faced with losses, because in bad times they are less concerned that greater protection will attract new entrants to the industry.

One also expects vigorous efforts to secure protection (or resist trade liberalization) in the face of significantly increased import competition by those industries where a substantial part of earnings is due to industry-specific physical and human capital or to the success of unions in raising wages. The extensive (and successful) lobbying activities of the auto and steel industries, where fixed costs are substantial and wages are 55 percent and 40 percent higher, respectively, than the average for all manufacturing sectors, seems to be motivated by this consideration. Even union leaders in the apparel industry, in which wages are low compared to manufacturing generally but high relative to many service sector jobs, recognize the importance of maintaining the rent component in their wages. Sol C. Chaikin, President of the Ladies' Garment Workers, has often indicated that he would be glad to accept free trade in the industry if someone could tell him where his members can find other jobs at wages near what they are currently making.

However, when changes in protection as a result of international trade-liberalizing negotiations or levels of protection across industries are analyzed, high levels of human capital per employee in an industry are generally found to be associated with high duty reductions and low levels of protection (Anderson and Baldwin, 1987; Ray, 1981). As is explained more fully later, these relationships support the social concerns approach to trade-policy determination: specifically, the view that public officials seek to protect workers whose skills and wages are relatively low from the market pressures resulting from liberal trade policies.

If uncertainty is introduced into the self-interest model along with incomplete insurance markets (due, for example, to moral hazard and adverse selection), risk averse economic agents may prefer protective policies that reduce the variability of price or income fluctuations to free trade (Cassing, Hillman, and Van Long, 1986; Newbery and Stiglitz, 1984). This may be why the developing countries have long argued for international commodity stabilization schemes for most of the primary products they export.

Greater certainty about the restrictive effects of quotas than tariffs seems to be a major reason why protection-seekers generally lobby for quantitative restriction in preference to tariffs. Also, their chances of obtaining this form of protection are improved if they lobby for country-selective quantitative restrictions, such as VEAs. When quantitative restrictions apply only to those countries that are the main sources of increased imports, injured domestic industries (and government officials) do not have to be concerned about counter-lobbying from other countries whose exports have not been increasing and who would be hurt by overall restrictions.

The countries selected for export restraint are likely to lobby against protection, but the windfall gains accruing to them from allocating the export quotas among their own producers act to soften their opposition.[7] The importing government loses the revenue that could be collected with a tariff but, since special interest groups recognize the difficulty of securing general revenues through lobbying, this is not likely to lead to objections from very many domestic interest groups. Furthermore, because VEAs are made outside of the rules of the General Agreement on Tariffs and Trade (GATT), government officials do not have to face the domestic political problem of reducing protection in some other industry to compensate other countries for the increase in protection in the injured industry or, if this is not done, of having foreign countries retaliate by increasing protection against some other domestic industry.

The self-interest framework also can be used to explain why most governments use tariffs and quotas more often than domestic subsidies for assisting injured import-competing sectors. Subsidies are more transparent than tariffs and quotas, since they appear in the government's budget and must be financed with taxes or by borrowing. Consequently, industries seeking assistance are concerned that subsidies will be more difficult to obtain politically than import protection and be provided for a shorter

Figure 1
A Perceived Prisoner's Dilemma in Trade Policy

		Country *E*	
		Cooperate	Defect
Country *A*	Cooperate	400, 400	50, 500
	Defect	500, 50	100, 100

time duration. Elected officials also seem to believe they will lose fewer votes of those outside the injured industries and face less anti-protection lobbying pressures if they supply assistance in the form of import protection rather than domestic subsidies. The welfare loss to the general public is, of course, greater under import protection, but poorer knowledge about the consequences of tariffs and quotas compared to domestic subsidies means this does not translate into greater political resistance.

A National Prisoner's Dilemma

The discussion to this point has dealt only with the domestic political economy of trade policy, that is, the manner in which public officials and domestic interest groups interact in determining a country's trade policy. But the manner in which public officials interact with their counterparts in other governments also shapes the nature of trade policies. Viewing these interactions in game theoretic terms has proved helpful in understanding certain aspects of international political economy. For example, Brander (1986) employs the structure of the prisoners' dilemma game to illustrate why countries may end up with protection, even though they would all be better off under free trade. Assuming we can use numbers to represent the net trading benefits perceived by mercantilistically-minded political leaders, suppose two large countries, *A* and *B*, each gains 400 (only the relative size of the numbers are important) if they both follow a free trade policy. However, if one country protects and the other adopts free trade, the country imposing protection gains 500, while the other gains only 50, since the protecting country gains employment and improved terms of trade at the expense of the free trade nation. When both protect, each gains only 100. As is evident from Figure 1, the dominant strategy for each country is to protect, since this yields each country the highest gain no matter what strategy the other country follows. The belief that they were involved in this sort of game may account for the protective policies adopted by many industrial countries in the early 1930s, when the possibility of increasing employment through unilateral protection was especially appealing.

THE SOCIAL CONCERNS APPROACH

The basic idea of the social concerns model is that trade policies are explainable mainly by the government's concern for the welfare of certain social and economic groups and by its desire to promote various national and international goals. Among the goals that have been most widely discussed are preserving the status quo distribution of incomes, redistributing income, or building political power through trade alliances. Proponents of the social concerns approach to analyzing trade policy formation have not been very precise as to why governments seek to implement these various goals, or why one goal is sought in one case and not in another. Most seem to hold to the view that the general public endorses these objectives and that the reelection possibilities of government officials are dependent on the extent to which these goals are implemented. Presumably, they envision each person's voting behavior as being guided by his or her social welfare function, possibly involving interpersonal comparisons based on the individual's ethical postulates.

Since economists tend to prefer models that rely on self-interest, models of social concerns are sometimes taken too lightly. But it should be recognized, as authors like Kau and Rubin (1982) and Andreoni (forthcoming) point out, that many individuals do not free ride even though it is in their narrow economic self-interest to do so, either for ethical reasons or because they gain satisfaction from participating in these activities. An illustration of this point is the refusal of many consumers to buy cheaper foreign goods, even when the country of origin cannot be discerned by others, on the grounds that foreign workers are being exploited or are taking jobs away from American workers.

Concern for the Changing Distribution of Income

Corden (1974, p. 107) attempts to interpret trade policy with a conservative social welfare function, namely that "any significant absolute reductions in real incomes of any significant section of the community should be avoided." This means that increases in income are given relatively low welfare weights and decreases very high welfare weights. Corden believes that this particular set of social values is especially useful in explaining the temporary protection often granted industries seriously injured by rapid increases in imports.

The Reagan administration's pressuring of the Japanese into voluntary limiting their exports of autos to the United States so that the industry could have some time to become competitive in the small car market seems to fit this objective of trade policy especially well. Another example was the governments's 1973 action of freezing the price of domestically produced oil up to the output levels existing prior to the oil crisis in that year. As Kalt (1983) finds, the pattern of voting in the Senate during the oil crisis was motivated mainly by the desire to prevent a significant shift in income away from oil consumers and in favor of domestic oil producers.

Other authors stressing the income distribution goals of government, like Cheh (1974) and Lavergne (1983), argue that trade policies of governments are motivated by a desire to minimize (or delay) adjustment costs, especially to workers. In examining the Kennedy round of multilateral trade negotiations, Cheh found a pattern of low tariff cuts in industries with high proportions of elderly workers, declining employment, and rising import penetration ratios. These findings support the adjustment-assistance hypothesis.

In contrast, Constantopoulos (1974) and Fieleke (1976) believe governments use trade policy not just to maintain the status quo but to promote relative increases in the standard of living of the lowest income groups. This view is supported by the finding in most country studies that industries with high proportions of unskilled workers or low wages tend to have high levels of protection and low tariff cuts in multilateral trade negotiations (Anderson and Baldwin, 1987). U.S. industries for which this relationship holds include textiles, apparel, leather and leather products, furniture and fixtures, and miscellaneous industries such as toys and sporting goods, jewelry, and musical instruments.

One incident illustrating the income distribution concerns of elected officials was the threat in 1979 by many members of Congress to vote against approving the government procurement code negotiated in the Toyko Round, when they discovered that preferences were no longer going to be given to small and minority domestic firms in bidding for government contracts. Ambassador Strauss, the U.S. Trade Representative, quickly negotiated an exception to the code's general principle of national treatment and nondiscrimination that allowed set-asides for these firms.

However, the use of trade policy to promote a more equitable distribution of income can run into problems of inconsistency over time, as Staiger and Tabellini (1987) argue. They consider the case of a country where free trade is the Pareto optimal policy. In this case, the government will have an incentive to announce a policy of free trade to achieve the optimal allocation of labor, but then to surprise the workers with a tariff that improves the distribution of income by raising wages in the import-injured industry. The original announcement of a free trade policy is, therefore, not time-consistent. In this model, the import competition must cause price to decline enough in the industry so that it is advantageous for some workers to move even if they must accept a lower wage (because of their lower level of industry-specific skills). But after the tariff is imposed, the workers who had moved to another industry will not return to the industry of their initial employment because they would have lost their sector-specific skills and thus will have to start again as unskilled workers.

However, workers will recognize that because the government cares about income redistribution, the policy commitment to free trade is not credible. Workers will come to expect the tariff and fewer will leave the import-threatened industry after a price decline. Yet the very fact that they do not leave will make the tariff even more necessary on income-distribution grounds, to prevent wages in the industry from falling even below the level that could be earned as unskilled labor in other industries.

The final outcome is a distribution of income where the expectation of a tariff prevents the economy from adjusting, thus lowering social welfare due to the production and consumption distortions associated with protection. Then the enactment of the tariff restores the income distribution only to a level that would have been achieved by a policy of free trade. The loss of economic efficiency buys no gain in equity.

Thus according to Staiger and Tabellini, the inability of a country to precommit to liberal trade policy becomes the reason for protection. One policy implication of this analysis, according to the authors, is that a commitment to a simple set of trading rules, which preclude the idea of the government attempting or the industry expecting a policy surprise, may often be superior to an activist but discretionary trade policy.

This analysis may help to account for the long-standing import protection of such industries as textiles, apparel, and sugar. The preamble of the international Multifiber Arrangement (MFA) for textiles has for many years included as an objective "the reduction of trade barriers and the liberalization of world trade in these products" (General Agreement on Trade and Textiles, 1974). However, producers in the industrial countries know that the MFA also permits quantitative restrictions as a safeguard against injurious import increases. Consequently, they have an incentive not to undertake the difficult process of adjustment needed to bring about trade liberalization, since they know they can expect continued protection if they do not adjust.

Deardorff (1987) argues that income distribution concerns also may explain why governments seemingly prefer to handle import surges with VEA's rather than tariffs. As he points out, an industry can be seriously injured by increased imports (and thus qualify for protective action by the government under the safeguard provisions of the GATT) before the full extent of the price-reducing increase in imports is known. Consequently, if policy in trade matters is guided by Corden's conservative social welfare function, namely, that income reductions for any significant group should be avoided, the government will be reluctant to use a tariff to provide import relief because of the uncertainty about the extent of the price reduction. Too low a tariff will leave productive factors in the import-competing sector worse off than before the import surge, while one that is set too high will reduce the income level of the productive factors employed in other sectors below what they had been receiving (For simplicity, Deardorff assumes all factors to be sector-specific.)

In contrast, an externally allocated quota set at the import level prevailing prior to the increase in imports—or, what is essentially the same, an agreement by foreign suppliers to restrain their exports to these levels—holds welfare levels of both groups of domestic factors at their pre-import surge levels. Furthermore, if the increased imports are from only a few foreign countries, such a VEA can raise the welfare of these exporting countries above pre-import surge levels due to the quota rents they gain and, at the same time, maintain the income levels of other exporting nations. However, as Deardorff recognizes, the motivation for trying to avoid harm to foreign countries may be related more to national self-interest, namely the fear of retaliation or loss of goodwill, than to a social concern not to take policy actions that reduce the income levels of other countries.

Income distribution concerns may also be a reason why governments generally prefer to assist an import-injured industry by protective measures rather than by providing a production subsidy. By restricting imports and thereby raising the price of the industry's product, the government puts the burden of helping the injured industry on those consumers who benefitted from the initial decrease in the price of this good. If the price returns to its level prior to the increase in imports and even if the tariff revenue is not returned to the good's consumers or its equivalent is given to foreign producers, these consumers are no worse off than initially. In contrast, a production subsidy financed by general taxes leaves those taxpayers who do not consume the import good worse off than initially.[8]

Trade Policy as Foreign Policy

The social concerns approach can be extended to cover various international objectives of the government. In fact, foreign policy has been used as a justification both for protectionism and for liberalizing trade.[9]

Gilpin (1987) and others have argued that hegemonic states, such as the United States after World War II and Great Britain during the latter part of the nineteenth century, adopt liberal trade policies as a mean of inducing other countries to accept their political leadership in the world. The major international political objective of the United States in the early postwar period was to limit the spread of Communism by strengthening the free world economically, and these writers maintain that the liberal U.S. trade and aid policies in this period were largely motivated by this purpose. This may explain why the United States (and Great Britain in the nineteenth century) did not take advantage of its economic power to improve its terms of trade nor to prevent small industrial countries and developing nations from free-riding on its trade concessions and those of other larger countries. National security considerations still play an important role in trade policy determination, as the U.S.-Israel free trade agreement indicates.

Income distribution concerns at the international and domestic levels also may influence countries' foreign economic policies. For example, the comparatively large amounts of untied aid and extensive duty-free treatment provided to developing countries by a number of small industrial countries seems difficult to explain entirely on self-interest grounds. Helleiner (1977) suggests that government officials adopt a mercantilistic attitude in trade negotiations and try to obtain the greatest cuts in protection from others in return for the least cuts by their own country. Minimizing the domestic adjustment problems associated with trade liberalization could be one motivation for this attitude.

SOME CONCLUSIONS

As economists will readily recognize, protectionism does not deem to be just a matter of which sectors have the best social welfare reasons for public assistance. Within a range of social values, the particular social justifications for various trade policies that are accepted by the electorate seem to be significantly influenced by lobbying activities on the part of economic interest groups and the government itself.

In fact, economic self-interest almost always dominates a person's concern for the welfare of other groups or the nation as a whole, when a significant part of an individual's income is affected by a trade policy. One does not, for example, observe workers or managers in import-injured industries opposing protection for their sectors on the grounds that this may cause unemployment in other industries and reduce the real income levels of low-income consumers. National and group concerns are likely to dominate personal economic welfare considerations only when the economic self-interest effects of a trade policy on an individual are small or unclear. Furthermore, the larger the decline in individual economic welfare as a person chooses to support various social goals that only benefit others, the less willing the person seems to be to sacrifice additional economic welfare to promote additional desirable social objectives.

However, the economic self-interest approach cannot stand alone, either. In its pure form, it requires an electorate that is ill-informed or unwilling to participate in the decision-making process due to the high costs of political action or to the free-rider problem. But the considerable attention given to trade issues by the modern media, the extensive efforts undertaken by politicians and others to determine the views of voters, the widespread lobbying activities by all sorts of common-interest groups, and the fact that a substantial number of citizens do vote in elections all suggest that the economic self-interest model by itself is inadequate for explaining either general trade policies or particular industry trade policies.

Many individual decisions on trade and other

economic matters have only a small effect on a person's real income, and the individual's various social concerns can play an important role in shaping his or her decisions. To expand their already substantial contributions toward understanding the policymaking process, economists should integrate such social motivations into their microeconomic optimizing framework. In doing so, they should also include in their models the various imperfections that characterize real world economic and political markets.

I believe that the studies presented here establish that an analytical framework including both economic self-interest and concern for the welfare of others as motivating forces for political action is needed for understanding policy formation in the trade field. The economic self-interest and social concerns approaches are not contradictory; both motivations are included in the standard formulation of an individual's social welfare function. Under Corden's conservative social welfare function, for example, the typical voter is willing to accept the small decrease in his or her own economic welfare and the welfare of other consumers that results from a tariff increase on an imported product, if this prevents a significant real income decline for workers in an important domestic industry. Consequently, declining industries are more likely to receive protection than prosperous ones, not only because of the self-interested lobbying from capitalists and workers who face income losses, but because the typical voter is more willing to grant protection to a declining industry.

Directions for Further Research

A multitude of possible reasons for protection have been outlines. The problem now is to weigh the reasons against one another, weed out those that are less relevant, and combine the others into a more unified theory. To make progress along these lines, there is a need to test the various hypothesis in the self-interest and social concern models with variables that better reflect the key ideas behind the two approaches.

Efforts should be made, for example, to obtain better measures of the extent of political pressures from an industry than such indirect measures as the number of firms in the sector, the industry's concentration ratio, or its growth rate. Information on the size of an industry's lobbying expenditures on a particular issue, the volume of testimony and public statements on the issue by its members, the extent to which industry members make their views known to public officials through visits and letters, and so forth would enable investigators to measure the political demands for protection more accurately.

Similarly, as Bale (1977) has shown, better measures than growth rates in employment or the proportion of older workers in an industry can be estimated to measure the labor adjustment costs associated with increased imports. More complete socioeconomic information on workers in an industry than just wages alone should also be used to measure the conditions under which voters and policy-makers are willing to grant protection on equity grounds. While obtaining improved data is costly and time-consuming, the effort seems necessary if we are to make significant progress in understanding the relative importance of the various political and economic determinants of trade policy.

Policy Recommendations

If economists wish their advice to carry weight in the political process, they must be more willing to examine the influences of institutions and procedures on policies. On the international level, for example, the ability of an organization such as the GATT to obtain adherence to an agreed-upon set of trading rules and to settle disputes among nations is crucial for the degree of order in world trading conditions.

Domestic examples of the importance of political institutions for the degree of protectionism are easy to find. Since 1934, the willingness of the Congress to allow the executive branch to handle most modifications of individual tariffs has had a major effect in reducing protection over the years, since the president has traditionally been more liberal on trade policy matters than Congress, probably because of the special foreign policy responsibilities of the president. Congress has recently attempted to push the executive branch in a more protectionist direction. For example, the Omnibus Trade and Competitiveness Act of 1988 shifts responsibility for the enforcement of U.S. rights under trade agreements (so-called Section 301 responsibilities) from the president to the U.S. Trade

Representative, a political appointee subject to Senate confirmation.

The manner in which the International Trade Commission (ITC) and the president announce their import-injury decisions illustrates the importance of procedures in shaping policy decisions. The ITC is charged with determining whether an industry has suffered serious injury (or the threat thereof) as a result of increased imports, and the public report it issues after its investigation deals only with this issue. The possible effects of protection on the welfare of consumers and industries using the product as an intermediate production input, as well as on the national interest generally, are considered by the president only after receiving an affirmative injury decision from the ITC. Furthermore, the report of the interagency committee established in the executive branch to consider these and other implications of granting protection is not published. In addition, Congress has prohibited members of the International Trade Commission who vote negatively in import-injury decisions, when the majority of members vote affirmatively, from participating in the Commission's decision determining how much protection to recommend to the president. The president usually issues only a very brief statement explaining whether protection is granted and, if so, to what degree and in what form. Thus, while the public learns about the economic problems faced by the petitioning industry and the benefits firms will receive from protection, it learns very little about the social costs of the protection.

This government practice of giving the public only one side of the story biases the entire process toward greater protection. A requirement that the interagency report be published or that some federal agency (perhaps the Council of Economist Advisers?) investigate the costs of granting protection and publish the results of its study would bring a much better balance to the procedures. If the decision-making process for U.S. trade policy is made more open and transparent to the general public, it would tend to reduce import protection or change the form of industry assistance.

Economists should also be careful to distinguish between the economic and political feasibility of policies. A number of explanations for protection provided in this paper rely on the inability of government to use theoretically first-best policies to maximize social welfare for economic reasons. For example, in accounting for protection in an environment of price uncertainty, it was assumed to be impossible to establish complete insurance markets to deal with the uncertainty because of moral hazard or adverse selection. Similarly, redistribution by means of lump-sum taxes and subsidies was ruled out as being too costly in Staiger and Tabellini's explanation of why social welfare-maximizing governments adopt protection and in Deardorff's account of why governments use Pareto-inferior means of protection.

In other cases, certain policies may be economically feasible but appear to be politically infeasible. For most of the industries receiving import relief, especially such industries as textiles, apparel, sugar and steel that have been protected for many years, there appear to be economically feasible policies other than protection for meeting the income distribution concerns about those employed in these sectors, policies that would raise social welfare above the level associated with protection. However, as efforts to deal with the income problems of farmers by using income transfers indicate, groups being assisted by the government often use their political power to block the use of these alternative redistribution means to increase the likelihood they will continue to receive assistance in the form they are used to.

If they are to make policy recommendations, economists need better empirical and expirimental studies of the economic and political feasibility of well-known policy measures as well as greater efforts to devise feasible new policies and political means for carrying out generally accepted economic and social goals. An illustration of promising economic research along these lines is the recent work (Woodbury and Spiegelman, 1987; Lawrence and Litan, 1986) aimed at devising adjustment-assistance measures that provide the same income assistance to displaced workers as existing programs, but encourage economic adjustment rather than unemployment and immobilized resources. An example at the theoretical level of this sort of analysis is the work of Dixit and Norman (1980; 1986), which demonstrates that a system of taxes and subsidies on goods and factors can accomplish the same redistributive goals as lump-sum taxes and subsidies, while requiring less information (and thus presumably being less costly) and also avoiding the many practical problems of lump-sum transfers.

Even if further research along these lines confirms that there are some real world situations where protection would be the best available measure for maximizing social welfare, economists should be very cautious about surrendering the efficiency argument for liberal trade policies. A final insight from viewing how trade policy is make is the readiness of protectionist entrepreneurs to twist the policy analyses of economists to promote their own welfare at the cost national welfare. For example, arguments based on the so-called new trade theory emphasizing imperfect competition and increasing returns are beginning to be made for providing government assistance to a wide variety of industries, even though the empirical work done so far in this field suggests that the case for government intervention on strategic grounds in imperfectly competitive markets is quite limited (Richardson, 1989). Presuming that a liberal trade policy promotes national welfare best and permitting exceptions only if based on careful empirical documentation is likely to yield the highest national welfare in the real world of policymaking.[10]

ENDNOTES

1 As trade economists have long pointed out, if a country is large so that the import supply curves it faces are upward sloping, import taxes can improve its terms of trade by decreasing the prices at which foreigners supply their exports. An optimum set of such taxes couples with lump-sum redistribution arrangements can raise everyone's welfare in the country. However, if foreign countries are also large, retaliation on their part can reduce all countries' welfare levels below what they were before the import taxes.

2 The focus in this paper is on explaining the protection process, that is, on positive political economy. However, there is also a body of literature that analyzes the welfare implications of lobbying for or against protection and lobbying for the rents created by protection. Bhagwati (1988) describes the first type of lobbying efforts as "downstream" activities and the second as "upstream" activities.

3 This follows from the Stolper-Samuelson theorem, which states that the real return to the factor used intensively in producing the import good (in this case, labor) will increase when the domestic price of the import good increases. As Mayer (1984) has shown, if an individual supplies both labor and capital services, the person will favor protection or free trade under the assumed factor-intensity conditions depending upon whether his or her capital/labor endowment is less or greater than the economy's capital/labor endowment.

4 Caves (1976) finds industry protection to be negatively related in a significant manner to market concentration. But Saunders (1980), in a later study of Canadian protection utilizing two-stage least squares estimation, finds a positive (and nearly significant at the 10 percent level) relationship between concentration and industry protection. When both the number of firms and the concentration ratio are included in the same regression equation, the concentration variable has a negative (though insignificant) sign in some of the countries studies, while the coefficient on the number of firms is generally significantly negative. One possible reason for this may be a perception by elected officials that voters are skeptical about their motivation in responding to the petitions of the dominant firms in a concentrated industry, but not to firms in an industry where the number of companies is small but the concentration ratio is not high.

5 When the bill first came before the House Ways and Means Committee in 1973, the textile and apparel unions testified against the bill. However, by the time the bill reached the Senate Finance Committee in 1974, the Multifiber Arrangement had been approved, and they did not testify at all.

6 I am grateful to Joseph Stiglitz for calling my attention to the literature on this point.

7 As Krishna (1989) shows, quantitative restrictions such as VEAs also facilitate collusive behavior between competing firms.

8 Since the sum of consumer and producer surplus is greater when a production subsidy rather than a tariff or quota is used to restore income levels in the injured industry (even if the tariff revenue or its equivalent is retained in the domestic economy), this argument assumes that income-redistribution measures by the government are not feasible.

9 Government policies such as national defense can be explained on the basis of the narrow self-interest motivations of citizens, whereas the concerns for the welfare of others discussed up to this point are based on forms of altruism, such as an implicit social insurance contract.

10 In this journal, Krugman (1987) reached a rather similar conclusion.

REFERENCES

Anderson, Kym, and Robert E. Baldwin, "The Political Market for Protection in Industrial Countries." In El-Agraa, Ali, M., *Protection, Cooperation, Intergration and Development*. London: Macmillan Press, 1987, 20-36.

Andreoni, James, "Why the Free Ride? Strategies and Learning in Public Goods Experiments," *Journal of Public Economics*, forthcoming.

Baldwin, Robert E., *The Political Economy of U.S. Import Policy*. Cambridge: The MIT Press, 1985.

Baldwin, Robert E., "Rent Seeking and Trade Policy: An Industry Approach," *Weltwirtschaftliches Archiv*, Heft 4, 1984, *120*, 646-677.

Bale, Malcolm D., "United States Concessions in the Kennedy Round and Short-Run Labor Adjustment Costs," *Journal of International Economics*, May 1977, 7, 145-148.

Bauer, Raymond A., Ithiel De Sola Pool, and Lewis Anthony Dexter, *American Business and Public Policy: The Policy of Foreign Trade*. Chicago: Aldine-Atherton, 1972.

Bhagwati, Jagdish, "Is Free Trade Passe After All?" Department of Economics, Columbia University, 1988

Brander, James A., "Rationales for Strategic Trade and Industrial Policy." In Krugman, Paul R., ed. *Strategic Trade Policy and the New International Economics*. Cambridge: MIT Press, 1986.

Caves, Richard E., "Economic Models of Political Choice: Canada's Tariff Structure," *Canadian Journal of Economics*, May 1976, *9*, 278-300.

Cassing, James H., Arye L. Hillman, and Ngo Van Long, "Political-Influence Motives and Choice between Tariffs and Quotas," *Journal of International Economics*, November 1986, *19*, 279-290.

Corden, W. M., *Trade Policy and Economic Welfare*. Oxford: Clarendon Press, 1974.

Constantopoulos, Maria, "Labor Protection in Western Europe," *European Economic Reviews*, December 1974, *5*, 313-328.

Cheh, John H., "United States Concessions in the Kennedy Round and Short-Run Labor Adjustment Costs," *Journal of International Economics*, November 1974, *4*, 323-340.

Deardorff, Alan V., "Safeguards Policy and the Conservative Welfare Function." In Kierzkowski, Henryl, ed., *Protection and Competition in International Trade*. Oxford: Basil Blackwell Ltd, 1987.

Destler, I.M., and John S. Odell, *Anti-Protection: Changing Forces in United States Trade Politics*, Policy Analyses in International Economics, No. 21, Washington: Institute for International Economics, September 1987.

Dixit, Avinash and Victor Norman, *Theory of International Trade: A Dual Equilibrium Approach*. Cambridge: Cambridge University Press, 1980.

Dixit, Avinash, and Victor Norman, "Gains from Trade without Lump-Sum Compensation," *Journal of International Economics*, August 1986, *21*, 111-122.

Fieleke, Norman, :"The Tariff Structure for Manufacturing Industries in the United States: A Test of Some Traditional Explanations," *Columbia Journal of World Business*, Winter 1976, *11*, 98-104

General Agreement on Tariffs and Trade, *Arrangement Regarding International Trade in Textiles*, Geneva: General Agreement on Tariffs and Trade, 1974.

Gilpin, Robert, *The Political Economy of International Relations*. Princeton: Princeton University Press, 1987.

Helleiner, G.K. "The Political Economy of Canada's Tariff Structure: An Alternative Model," *Canadian Journal of Economics*, May 1977, *4*, 318-326.

Hillman, Arye L., *The Political Economy of Protection*. New York: Harwood Academic Publishers, 1989.

Kahneman, Daniel and Amos Tversky, "Prospect Theory: An Analysis of Decision under Risk," *Econometrica*, March, 1979, *47*, 263-291.

Kahneman, Daniel and Amos Tversky, "Choices, Values and Frames," *American Psychologist*, April 1984, 4, 341-350.

Kalt, Joseph P., *The Economics and Politics of Oil Price Regulation: Federal Policy in the Post-Embargo Era*. Cambridge: MIT Press, 1983.

Kau, James B., and Paul Rubin, *Congressmen, Constituents, and Contributors*. Boston: Martinus Nijhoff Publishing, 1982.

Krishna, Kala, "Trade Restrictions as Facilitating Practices," *Journal of International Economics*, May 1989, *26*, 251-270.

Krugman, Paul R., "Is Free Trade Passe?," *Journal of Economic Perspectives*, Fall 1987, *1*, 131-144.

Lavergne, Real, *The Political Economy of U.S. Tariffs: An Empirical Analysis*. New York: Academic Press, 1983.

Lawrence, Robert Z., and Robert E. Litan, *Saving Free Trade: A Pragmatic Approach*. Washington, D.C.: The Brookings Institution, 1986.

Mayer, Wolfgang, "Endogenous Tariff Formation," *American Economic Review*, December 1984, *74*, 970-985.

Newbery, David M.G., and Joseph E. Stiglitz, "Pareto Inferior Trade," *Review of Economic Studies*, LI, 1-12, 1984.

Olson, Mancur, *The Logic of Collective Action*. Cambridge: Harvard University Press, 1965.

Olson, Mancur, "The Political Economy of Comparative Growth Rates," In Mueller, Dennis, ed., *The Political Economy of Growth*. New Haven: Yale University Press, 1983.

Ray, Edward J., "The Determinants of Tariff and Nontariff Trade Restrictions in the United States," *Journal of Political Economy*, February 1981, *89*, 105-121.

Richardson, J. David, "Empirical Research on Trade Liberalizations with Imperfect Competition: A Survey," *OECD Economic Studies*, Spring, 1989.

Saunders, Ronald S., "The Political Economy of Effective Protection in Canada's Manufacturing Sector," *Canadian Journal of Economics*, May 1980, *13*, 340-348.

Staiger, Robert W., and Guido Tabellini, "Discretionary Trade Policy and Excessive Protection," *American Economic Review*, December 1987, *77*, 823-837.

Tosini, Suzanne, and Edward Tower, "The Textile Bill of 1985: The Determinants of Congressional Voting Patterns," *Public Choice*, 1987, *54*, 19-25.

Woodbury, Stephen A., and Robert G. Spiegelman, "Bonuses to Workers and Employers to Reduce Unemployment: Randomized Trials in Illinois," *American Economic Review*, September 1987, *77*, 513-530.

READING 5

U.S. Trade Protection: Effects on the Industrial and Regional Composition of Employment

Linda C. Hunter

The dramatic increase in the U.S. trade deficit in recent years has fueled protectionist sentiment. Proponents of trade protection claim that Americans are losing manufacturing jobs to foreign countries and that trade restraints are needed to bolster employment. Although trade protection generally increases employment in the protected industry, it tends to reduce employment in other industries. Higher prices for imports and their domestic substitutes adversely affect industries that use these goods as an input in their production. In the long run, wages will rise or fall in response to an increase or decrease in labor demand caused by trade barriers. This change in wages will ensure that labor demand is in line with labor supply. Consequently, the net effect of trade restraints on overall employment is unclear and is likely to be small.

Trade restraints, however, have a significant effect on the industrial *composition* of employment. Furthermore, because individual industries hire more workers in some states than in others, trade barriers also have a significant effect on the regional composition of employment. This article measures the effects of trade protection on the distribution of employment across industries and regions in the United States. I examine three cases of trade protection: textiles and apparel, steel, and automobiles. They are among the largest industries in the United States to receive protection.

The results of this study indicate that U.S. trade protection benefits only a few industries while harming many others. The gains in employment accrue to the protected sector and its primary suppliers. The losses, on the other hand, are spread across many industries. Manufacturing industries are both winners and losers. Thus, trade barriers have not been successful in alleviating the loss of manufacturing jobs in the United States.

The regional distribution of the gains and losses from trade protection has a similar pattern. Few states gain employment, while many states lose employment. Furthermore, the winning states are only in the East. The greatest winners are concentrated in the southeastern portion of the United States. The losses in employment, on the other hand, are widespread. All states west of the Mississippi River, in addition to some eastern states, lose employment.

THE MODEL

Trade restraints increase employment in the protected industry by raising the price or limiting the supply of competing imported goods. Industries that supply to the protected sector also gain employment. Industries that purchase the protected product as an input face higher costs. These higher costs are then passed on to the consumer and reduce sales. Thus, employment declines in these related industries.

Because trade restraints cause both positive and negative employment effects on the economy, the net effect of protection on aggregate labor demand is unclear. Trade protection may lead to either an excess demand for or an excess supply of labor. In an economy with flexible wages and a functioning labor market, wages will adjust to ensure that the economy remains fully employed. In the long run, trade protection simply alters the composition of employment.

I estimate the gains and losses in employment

for different industries by using an input-output model of the United States. A study by Hufbauer, Berliner and Elliott (1986) provides estimates of the initial increase in domestic production and price of the protected commodity caused by trade restraints that were in place in 1984.[1] I apply the increase in domestic production estimates to the input-output model to examine the gains in employment in industries supplying to the protected sector. I also apply the increase in domestic price estimates to the input-output model, in a different manner, to estimate the losses in employment in industries using the protected product. The Appendix describes this procedure in detail.

Most input-output models that are used to examine the employment effects of trade protection assume a perfectly elastic labor supply.[2] In other words, if protective measures cause the quantity of labor demanded to increase or decrease, the quantity of labor supplied will meet the new demand for labor. This is a reasonable assumption for a country that participates in a broad labor market or suffers from a chronic surplus of labor. This is not a reasonable assumption, however, for a country like the United States. Labor is scarce and in limited supply in the United States because the country does not permit a free flow of labor across its borders and wages are sufficiently flexible to achieve virtually full employment. Accordingly, it is more appropriate to view the national labor supply as *fixed.*

Because I assume the national labor supply is fixed, aggregate employment is not affected by trade restraints To ensure that aggregate employment remains constant, any net gains (losses) generated by the input-output model are subtracted from (added to) the individual industries in proportion to their shares of total employment. This procedure is intended to approximate the employment effects of equilibrating wage adjustments, assuming that industries respond in a similar manner to changing wages.[3]

PROTECTION IN TEXTILES AND APPAREL

The history of protection in the textile and apparel industry is long and complicated. Chart 1 lists the trade agreements negotiated over the past 32 years and illustrates how the level of protection has risen. In a 1957 agreement, Japan voluntarily agreed to restrict its exports of fabrics to the United States. Accordingly, imports from other countries—including Hong Kong, Portugal, Egypt, and India—quickly replaced the Japanese goods. In 1961, the United States reached a one-year agreement with other textile exporters, generally called the Short-Term Arrangement on Cotton Textiles. Its successor, the Long-Term Arrangement on Cotton Textiles, broadened product coverage and extended from 1962 through 1973.

Increased production of man-made fibers induced the Untied States to seek even wider product coverage. In 1974, the United States reached an expanded agreement with its trading partners, known as the Multifiber Arrangement, that provided an international framework for negotiating bilateral agreements. The Multifiber Arrangement has since been renewed three times, each time covering a wider scope of products and countries. The current agreement, which will extend through 1991, includes 54 developed and developing countries.

The tariff or tariff equivalent rate for imports of textiles and apparel rose from 20 percent in 1957 to 30 percent by 1982.[4] As the level of protection increased, the costs and the benefits of these trade agreements increased as well. The trade restraints in effect in 1984 led to a 24 percent rise in the domestic price of textiles and apparel above its free-trade level.

Higher import prices for textiles and apparel enabled American producers to increase their domestic market share. U.S. production of textiles increased 24 percent as a result of protection in place in 1984, while apparel production rose 38 percent. Consequently, employment in the textile and apparel industry expanded. Industries that supply to the textile and apparel industry also increased their production and employment. On the other hand, the rise in domestic textile prices raised costs for firms that use textiles as an input. As these higher costs were passed on to the consumer, sales declined and firms reduced production.

Table 1 lists the percentage changes in employment of 30 U.S. industries caused by trade restraints in textiles and apparel. These changes are from the input-output analysis described in the previous section. As expected, the clear winner from

Chart 1

Textiles and Apparel:
History of U.S. Trade Protection

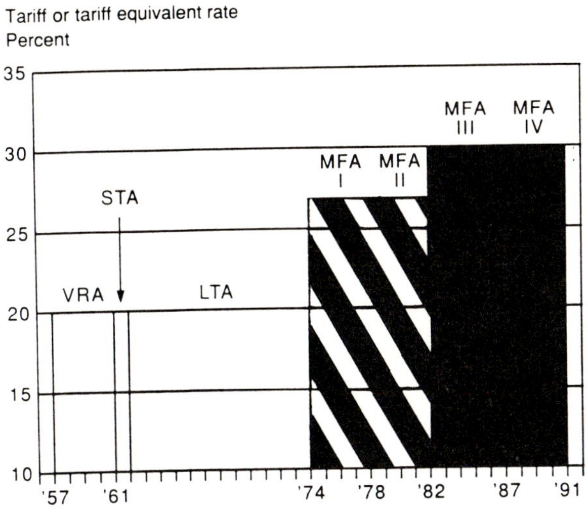

NOTE: If a quota is imposed, the tariff equivalent rate is the tariff rate that would have led to the same level of imports as the quota.
VRA = Voluntary Restraint Agreement.
STA = Short-Term Arrangement.
LTA = Long-Term Arrangement.
MFA = Multifiber Arrangement, Phase I, II, III, or IV.
SOURCE OF PRIMARY DATA: Hufbauer, Berliner, and Elliott (1986).

trade restraints in textiles and apparel is the protected industry itself. Employment in the textile and apparel industry increased 15 percent as a result of the protective measures that were in place in 1984. Because textiles are an input in apparel production, trade barriers in textiles dampen the employment gains from protection in the apparel industry alone.

The next largest winner is the chemical and allied products industry. This industry increased its employment more than 2 percent. Because chemicals are used to produce synthetic fabrics, they are an important input for the textile and apparel industry. Also included in this category are the dyes used to color fabrics. The other four industries gaining employment as a result of trade restraints in textiles and apparel gained a very small percentage of their total employment.

Many industries lost employment as a result of the rise in domestic textile prices. Because fabrics are used in the production of furniture, the furniture and fixtures industry lost almost 2 percent of its employment. Both the motor vehicles and equipment industry and the leather and leather products industry lost about 1 percent of their employment. Included in leather and leather products are luggage and footwear, both of which use fabrics. The loss in jobs in motor vehicles and equipment occurs because textiles are used to carpet and upholster automobiles.

Many of the industries suffering small employment losses did so as a result of wage adjustments. As I mentioned earlier, this analysis assumes that total U.S. employment remains constant. Because textiles and apparel are inputs in relatively few industries, protection in this industry initially causes an excess demand for labor. As wages rise in response to the excess demand for labor, many industries not related to textiles and apparel decrease their employment.

Also listed in Table 1 are the absolute changes in employment caused by trade restraints in textiles and apparel. The textile and apparel industry and the chemicals and allied products industry are again the clear winners. The three industries losing the largest number of jobs are services, government, and wholesale and retail trade. Although these industries lost less than 1 percent of their employment, they are large employers in the United States.

PROTECTION IN STEEL

In 1969, in an effort to forestall a bill limiting U.S. imports of steel, Japan and members of the European Economic Community voluntarily agreed to restrict their exports to the United States. This agreement expired in 1974 and was not renewed. In 1978, the United States imposed the Trigger Price Mechanism, which established import reference prices (for several grades of steel) based on estimates of Japanese costs of production, profit margins, and transportation costs. Countries exporting steel below the reference prices were subjected to expedited antidumping investigations. Countries found dumping steel on the international marketplace—selling steel abroad at a price below their estimated costs of production—faced increased trade barriers.

By January 1982, American steel companies had filed 110 antidumping petitions against 11 countries. In an effort to settle these petitions, the United States negotiated a voluntary restraint agreement with Japan and imposed a quota against the European Economic Community. In 1984 and 1985, other steel exporters also negotiated voluntary restraint

Table 1

Employment Effects of U.S. Trade Protection in Textiles and Apparel in 1984

Industry	Change in employment	
	Percent	Absolute
Textile mill products and apparel	14.95	288,764
Chemicals and allied products	2.07	21,753
Electric, gas, and sanitary services	0.14	1,289
Mining	0.10	997
Rubber and miscellaneous plastics products	0.10	787
Paper and allied products	0.05	333
Agriculture, forestry, and fishing	–0.02	–271
Petroleum and coal products	–0.10	–193
Transportation	–0.13	–3,732
Wholesale and retail trade	–0.22	–37,430
Communication	–0.26	–3,488
Machinery, except electrical	–0.27	–6,722
Finance, insurance, and real estate	–0.28	–16,134
Stone, clay, and glass products	–0.32	–1,899
Government	–0.36	–55,620
Tobacco manufactures	–0.37	–240
Food and kindred products	–0.38	–6,128
Services	–0.39	–95,433
Printing and publishing	–0.43	–5,877
Electric and electronic equipment	–0.48	–8,982
Lumber and wood products	–0.48	–3,369
Primary metal industries	–0.48	–4,123
Fabricated metal products	–0.51	–7,437
Construction	–0.55	–24,015
Instruments and related products	–0.57	–4,011
Transportation equipment, except motor vehicles and equipment	–0.59	–6,093
Miscellaneous manufacturing industries	–0.68	–2,680
Leather and leather products	–0.96	–1,832
Motor vehicles and equipment	–1.05	–9,047
Furniture and fixtures	–1.88	–9,162

SOURCES OF PRIMARY DATA: U.S. Bureau of Economic Analysis.
U.S. Bureau of Labor Statistics.
U.S. Bureau of the Census.

agreements with the United States that were scheduled to expire in September 1989. President Bush recently announced that these agreements will be extended into 1992. Chart 2 shows the various stages of protection of steel and their protective levels.

The level of protection for U.S. steel, like clothing and textiles, increased with every new agreement. In 1974, the tariff or equivalent rate was about 13 percent. It reached 30 percent by 1984. The trade restraints of 1984 led to a 12 percent increase in domestic steel prices.

As a result of the higher import price of steel in 1984, domestic steel production increased 5 percent. Again, industries that supply inputs to steel production increased their output as well. The rise in domestic steel prices, on the other hand, led to reduced production for industries that use steel. These estimates of the rise in production and price of domestic steel have been applied to input-output analysis. Table 2 lists the percentage changes in employment of U.S. industries caused by trade protection in steel in 1984.

Like the case of textiles and apparel, the gains in

Chart 2

Steel: History of U.S. Trade Protection

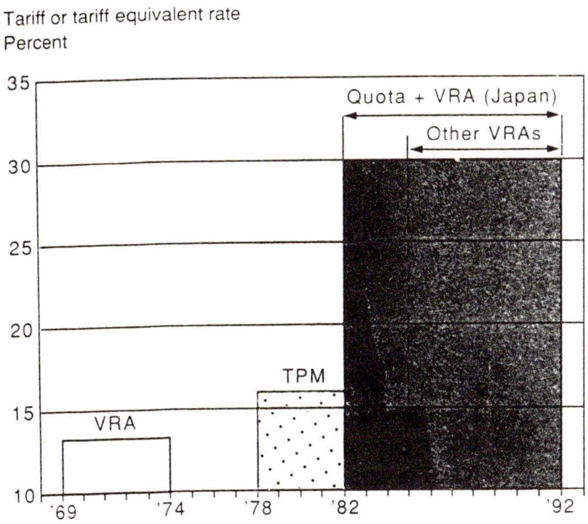

NOTE: If a quota is imposed, the tariff equivalent rate is the tariff rate that would have led to the same level of imports as the quota.
VRA = Voluntary Restraint Agreement.
TPM = Trigger Price Mechanism.
SOURCE OF PRIMARY DATA: Hufbauer, Berliner, and Elliott (1986).

employment are concentrated in the protected industry. The primary metal industries, which include steel, increased their employment by 4 percent. The mining industry is the next largest winner, but the gain there is only one-third of 1 percent. The largest loser is the motor vehicles and equipment industry. It lost more than 1 percent of its employment because of increased steel prices. Four other industries lost more than one-half of 1 percent of their employment—furniture and fixtures; machinery, except electrical; transportation equipment, except motor vehicles and equipment; and fabricated metal products. These industries are all large users of steel.

Unlike textiles and apparel, steel is an input in the production of many goods. Consequently, trade protection in steel initially causes an excess supply of labor. Wages then fall in response to the excess labor supply. As wages decline, some unrelated industries hire more workers. Thus, many industries had very small percentage increases in their employment as a result of the 1984 trade restraints in steel.

Table 2 also lists the absolute changes in employment by industry. Again, the clear winner is the primary metal industries, with a 31,000-job increase. Services and wholesale and retail trade are the only other industries in which employment increased more than 10,000 jobs. The four greatest job declines occurred in nonelectrical machinery, construction, motor vehicles and equipment, and fabricated metal products.

PROTECTION IN AUTOMOBILES

Although steel import restraints in the mid-1980s hurt the auto industry, car production was buoyed by its own protection. In April 1981, the United States negotiated a voluntary restraint agreement with Japan to limit its exports to the United States. The restraints on Japanese car imports greatly increased the production of domestic cars, as well as prices and industry profits. As Chart 3 demonstrates, from 1980 to 1985, the value of U.S. car production increased almost 200 percent, compared with a 43 percent increase in the previous five years. When the voluntary restraint agreement expired in April 1985, the United States did not ask Japan to extend it. Since then, however, Japan voluntarily continues to limit car exports to the United States, although at a less restrictive level.

The agreement between Japan and the United States caused the price of imported cars to increase 11 percent. The higher import price of cars led to a 4.4-percent increase in the price of domestic automobiles in the United States and a 9-percent increase in their production.

Table 3 lists the results of the input-output analysis applied to examine the effects of the trade protection in automobiles that was in place in 1984. The motor vehicles and equipment industry increased its employment almost 7 percent as a result of the voluntary restraint agreement with Japan. Industries that supply the auto industry—such as primary metals, fabricated metals, rubber and miscellaneous plastics, and electric and electronic equipment - also had increases in their employment. In terms of the actual number of jobs gained, the motor vehicles and equipment industry increased its employment by 59,000 jobs. Fabricated metals, primary metals, electrical equipment, and nonelectrical machinery also gained a large number of jobs.

Because cars are rarely inputs in the production

Table 2

Employment Effects of U.S. Trade Protection in Steel in 1984

Industry	Change in employment Percent	Absolute
Primary metal industries	3.61	31,003
Mining	0.34	3,280
Electric, gas, and sanitary services	0.14	1,244
Tobacco manufactures	0.12	78
Finance, insurance, and real estate	0.11	6,108
Printing and publishing	0.09	1,234
Wholesale and retail trade	0.08	12,720
Communication	0.07	965
Transportation	0.07	2,055
Services	0.07	16,177
Leather and leather products	0.06	120
Petroleum and coal products	0.06	117
Government	0.01	2,015
Chemicals and allied products	0.01	125
Textile mill products and apparel	0.01	204
Agriculture, forestry, and fishing	–0.02	–276
Paper and allied products	–0.02	–155
Food and kindred products	–0.03	–480
Instruments and related products	–0.11	–756
Miscellaneous manufacturing industries	–0.19	–746
Stone, clay, and glass products	–0.21	–1,248
Rubber and miscellaneous plastics products	–0.24	–1,882
Lumber and wood products	–0.27	–1,929
Construction	–0.36	–15,763
Electric and electronic equipment	–0.40	–7,464
Fabricated metal products	–0.59	–8,602
Transportation equipment, except motor vehicles and equipment	–0.63	–6,497
Machinery, except electrical	–0.67	–16,914
Furniture and fixtures	–0.70	–3,417
Motor vehicles and equipment	–1.31	–11,311

SOURCES OF PRIMARY DATA: U.S. Bureau of Economic Analysis.
U.S. Bureau of Labor Statistics.
U.S. Bureau of the Census.

of other goods, few jobs were lost as a direct result of the voluntary restraint agreement with Japan. Declines in employment, however, occurred in response to labor market adjustments. Trade restraints in the auto industry lead to an initial excess demand for labor. Wages then rise. With wages rising, industries not related to auto production cut back their employment slightly.

The gains in employment in the auto industry may be temporary. The single protective phase improved the industry's profitability temporarily. Production of cars increased substantially while the voluntary restraint agreement was in place. In 1988, the three largest U.S. auto companies marked their highest profits ever. Recently, however, sales of Japanese cars have been soaring once again, and domestic auto sales have been dropping.[5]

INDUSTRIAL EFFECTS OF PROTECTION

Charts 4 and 5 summarize the industrial effects of protection in textiles and apparel, steel, and

Table 3

Employment Effects of U.S. Trade Protection in Automobiles in 1984

Industry	Change in employment Percent	Absolute
Motor vehicles and equipment	6.83	58,842
Primary metal industries	1.22	10,438
Fabricated metal products	1.03	15,089
Rubber and miscellaneous plastics products	0.58	4,490
Electric and electronic equipment	0.42	7,897
Machinery, except electrical	0.20	5,111
Stone, clay, and glass products	0.18	1,089
Chemicals and allied products	0.11	1,194
Textile mill products and apparel	0.09	1,822
Mining	0.08	774
Electric, gas, and sanitary services	0.03	227
Transportation	–0.04	–1,110
Paper and allied products	–0.04	–278
Lumber and wood products	–0.06	–387
Instruments and related products	–0.08	–558
Petroleum and coal products	–0.09	–165
Wholesale and retail trade	–0.10	–15,989
Furniture and fixtures	–0.11	–522
Finance, insurance, and real estate	–0.13	–7,451
Services	–0.14	–33,657
Communication	–0.14	–1,867
Leather and leather products	–0.15	–287
Agriculture, forestry, and fishing	–0.15	–2,386
Miscellaneous manufacturing industries	–0.15	–600
Printing and publishing	–0.15	–2,095
Tobacco manufactures	–0.17	–106
Food and kindred products	–0.17	–2,750
Government	–0.17	–26,067
Construction	–0.19	–8,297
Transportation equipment, except motor vehicles and equipment	–0.23	–2,400

SOURCES OF PRIMARY DATA. U.S. Bureau of Economic Analysis.
U.S. Bureau of Labor Statistics.
U.S. Bureau of the Census.

automobiles listed in the tables. Chart 4 lists the industries that lose employment as a result of trade protection, while Chart 5 lists the industries that gain employment. These industries are ranked by the percentage changes in their employment. As Chart 5 shows, very few industries actually gain from trade protection. The gains are virtually limited to the protected industries themselves. Individual industries lose very little, on average, relative to the gains of the winning industries.The reason is that the losses in employment are spread across many industries.

In some cases, protection in various industries reinforces the effects on employment. For example, the furniture and fixtures industry is hurt by protection in both steel and textiles and apparel. Consequently, it lost the greatest proportion of jobs. an example on the wining side is chemicals and allied products. The chemicals and allied products industry is a big winner, overall, because it gained employment from protection in both automobiles and textiles and apparel.

On the other hand, the employment effects of trade restraints in one commodity may dampen the effects of protection in another. An example is fabricated metal products, which had a very small loss in net employment. The explanation is that,

Chart 3

Automobiles: U.S. Production and Imports

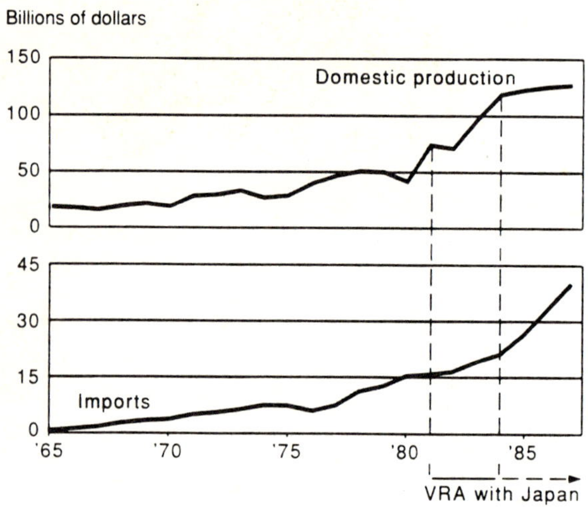

NOTE: VRA = Voluntary Restraint Agreement.
SOURCES: Hufbauer, Berliner, and Elliott (1986).
U.S. Department of Commerce.

Chart 4

Industries Losing Employment from U.S. Trade Protection in 1984 in Textiles and Apparel, Steel, and Automobiles

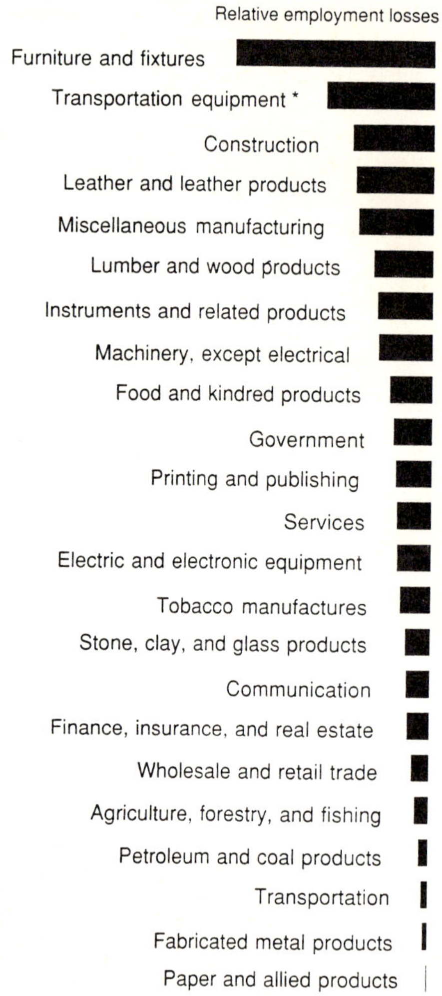

* Except motor vehicles and equipment.
SOURCES OF PRIMARY DATA: U.S. Bureau of Economic Analysis.
U.S. Bureau of Labor Statistics.
U.S. Bureau of the Census.

although the industry is a big loser from steel protection, it is a winner from the voluntary restraint agreement in automobiles.

The largest gains and losses in employment are concentrated in the manufacturing industries. Five of the seven industries that gain employment from trade barriers in textiles and apparel, steel, and automobiles are manufacturing industries. Eight of the top ten greatest employment losses are in manufacturing industries as well. Therefore, unlike the argument set forth by proponents of trade protection, trade barriers in the protected industries have not alleviated the loss of manufacturing jobs in the United States.

The nonmanufacturing industries, in general, are not the big winners or losers from trade protection in textiles and apparel, steel, and automobiles. These industries tend to have small overall changes in their employment, with one exception—construction. Construction suffered large employment losses from trade protection in both steel and automobiles. Thus, it suffered the third greatest percentage loss in employment.

REGIONAL EFFECTS OF PROTECTION

Even if national employment remains constant, trade protection can cause significant regional shifts in employment. Trade protection leads to increases and decreases in the production of goods and, therefore, labor shortages and surpluses in affected industries. Because labor is relatively mobile across states, workers will move from where there is an excess supply of labor to where there is an excess demand for labor.

I estimate the changes in state employment caused by U.S. trade protection by allocating the total net change in an industry's employment (as given in the tables) among the states in accordance with their shares of national production in the industry in 1984.[6] The accompanying map shows which states are the winners and losers from U.S. trade barriers in terms of percentage changes in their employment.

The states that are the greatest winners from trade protection are in the southeastern part of the United States, South Carolina, North Carolina, Georgia, and Alabama rank highest in their percentage increases in employment because they are large textile and apparel producers. Other clear winners from trade protection are Tennessee, Michigan, Rhode Island, and Mississippi. Although Michigan is a big winner from protection in automobiles, its gains are dampened because of protection in steel. Tennessee, Rhode Island, and Mississippi gain most of their employment in the textile and apparel industry. In terms of absolute changes in employment, the five greatest winners are North Carolina (37,000 jobs), Georgia (24,000 jobs), South Carolina (22,000 jobs), Michigan (11,000 jobs), and Alabama (10,000 jobs).

The greatest losers from trade protection, based on percentage changes in state employment, are the District of Columbia, Alaska, Nevada, and Hawaii. The four states lost employment because the protected industries and their suppliers account for a small percentage of their gross state product. Although these states lost the highest percentage of employment, they were clearly not the greatest losers in terms of the number of jobs lost. California lost the greatest number of jobs (30,000 jobs). Florida (13,000 jobs), Illinois (11,000 jobs), and Texas (11,000 jobs) were the next biggest losers in employment.

As the map displays, the gains from trade protection are concentrated among a few states, while the losses are spread across many states. Furthermore, the gains and losses are separated geographically by region. The eastern portion of the United States tends to gain employment, while the western portion of the country tends to lose employment from the trade restraints.

CONCLUSION

In an economy that is virtually at full employment, trade barriers principally affect the

Chart 5

Industries Gaining Employment from U.S. Trade Protection in 1984 in Textiles and Apparel, Steel, and Automobiles

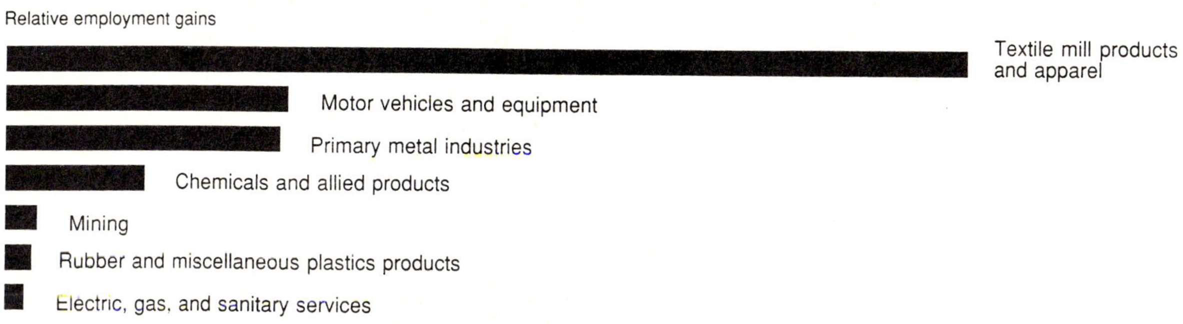

SOURCES OF PRIMARY DATA: U.S. Bureau of Economic Analysis.
U.S. Bureau of Labor Statistics.
U.S. Bureau of the Census.

Textiles and Apparel, Steel, and Automobiles:
Regional Employment Effects of U.S. Trade Protection

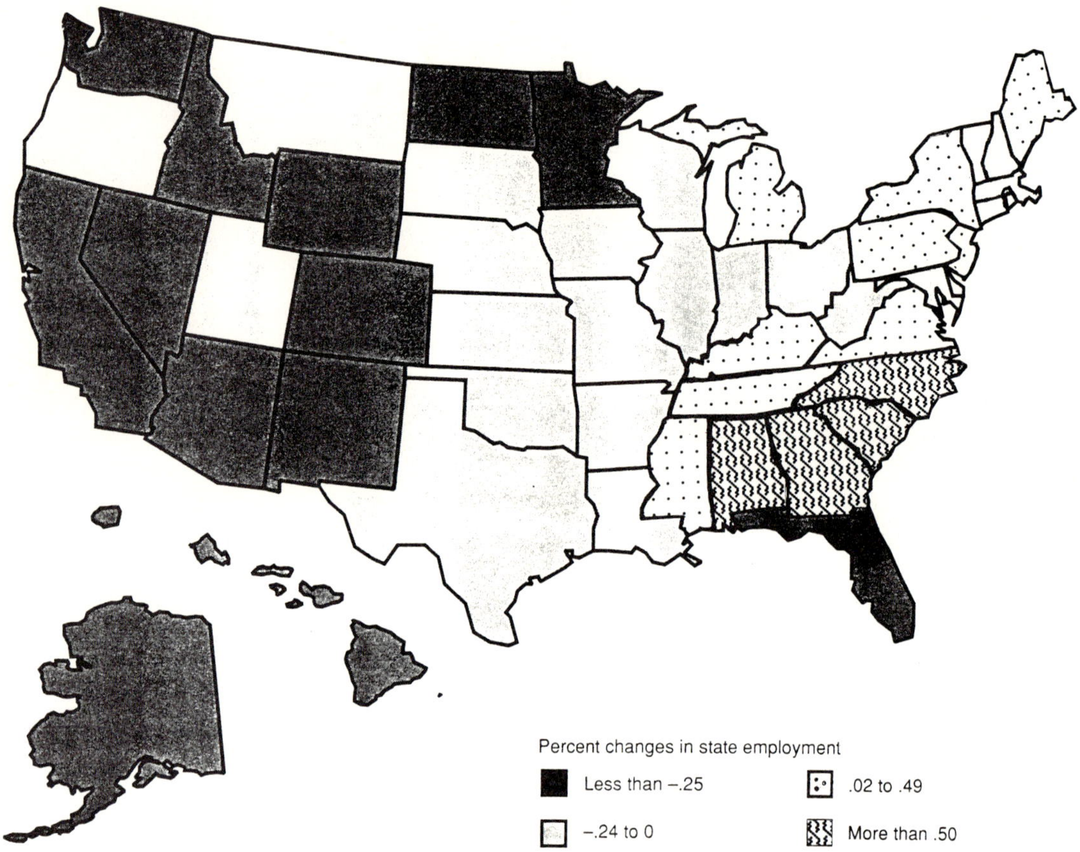

SOURCES OF PRIMARY DATA: U.S. Bureau of Economic Analysis.
U.S. Bureau of Labor Statistics.
U.S. Bureau of the Census.

composition of employment in the long run and not the aggregate level of employment. This article has examined the employment effects of U.S. trade protection in three industries: textiles and apparel, steel, and automobiles. I assume that trade protection does not change the total number of jobs in the economy. Instead, I concentrate on how trade protection affects the *composition* of employment.

The results here indicate that few industries gain employment because of trade protection. The protected industries themselves—textiles and apparel, steel, and automobiles—have experienced substantial increases in employment. The only other industry to gain a significant proportion of employment is chemicals and allied products: chemicals are used extensively in producing synthetic fibers.

Most industries lose employment as a result of trade restraints. The greatest losers are furniture and fixtures; transportation equipment, except motor vehicles and equipment construction; and leather and leather products. These industries use products from protected industries as inputs for their own production. Many industries not related to the protected sectors experience small declines in employment because trade protection raises the cost of labor to all firms in the economy.

For the regional implications of trade protection, a similar pattern exists; few states gain employment, while many states lose employment. The states that gain employment are limited to the eastern portion of the United States.The southeastern states are the greatest winners from trade protection because they are large textile and apparel producers. All states west of the Mississippi River, as well as some others, lose employment as a result of trade protection in textiles and apparel, steel, and automobiles.

APPENDIX

CALCULATION OF EMPLOYMENT CHANGES

This Appendix describes the methods used to estimate the positive and negative employment effects of trade protection. I begin with estimates from Hufbauer, Berliner and Elliott (1986) on the initial production and price effects of trade restraints on the protected industry. The input-output table is provided by the Interindustry Economics Division (1989) of the U.S. Bureau of Economic Analysis. It contains 1983 input-output accounts for the United States, broken down at the two-digit level of the Standard Industrial Classification system (85 industries).

To estimate the positive employment effects of the trade restraints, the increase in production of the protected industry is placed in a vector, with a number of elements equal to the number of industries in the input-output table. Every element in this vector is zero, except the element pertaining to the increase in production of the protected industry. Call this vector ΔO. Using matrix notation, the positive output effects of trade restrains are calculated as follows:

$$\text{(A.1)} \qquad \Delta X = (I - A)^{-1}\Delta O,$$

where I is the identify matrix and A is the input-output matrix. These changes in output, ΔX, are then translated into the positive employment changes.

Calculating the negative employment effects of the price increase caused by trade protection involves several steps. The initial percentage change in price in the protected industry is used to calculated changes in prices in other industries in the following manner:

$$\text{(A.2)} \qquad \Delta P = (I - A')^{-1}\Delta N,$$

where ΔN is the vector containing all zeros, except the percentage price change in the element pertaining to the protected industry. The vector ΔP measures the increase in the prices of goods that use the protected commodity as an input. These price changes are then used to estimate a vector of demand changes, ΔD, where the *i*th element of this vector is defined as

$$\text{(A.3)} \qquad \Delta d_i = -\Delta p_i\left(x_i - \sum_{j=1}^{n} i_{ij}x_j \right),$$

where x, is total output of commodity *i* and a_{ij} is one element of the A matrix pertaining to the *j*th row and *j*th column. The term in parentheses defines final demand for commodity *i*—total output of commodity *i* less intermediate demands for commodity *i*. The ΔD vector is the change in demand for goods as a result of higher prices.

To summarize, equation A.2 defines the effect that an increase in the price of the protected product would have on the price of commodities that use the protected product as an input. Equation A.3 then defines the change in demand for these goods resulting from their increased price. Note that I have assumed unit elasticity of demand with respect to price. The ΔD vector can now be applied to equation A.1 to generate the decline in output in industries that use the protected product as an input.

The positive and negative employment effects are added together to generate net changes in employment caused by trade restraints in a particular commodity. These calculations will lead to a net gain or a net loss in aggregate employment. To ensure that aggregate employment remains constant, the calculated gain (loss) in total employment is subtracted from (added to) each industry's employment in proportion to the industry's share of total employment.

I would like to thank Stephen P. A. Brown, John K. Hill, and Lori L. Taylor for helpful comments without implicating them in my conclusions. I am also grateful to D'Ann M. Ozment and Paul S. Dalberth for their research assistance.

ENDNOTES

1 Although cost and benefit estimates of trade protection vary, the Hulbauer-Berliner-Elliott study provides one set of consistent estimates for all three cases in the study here. for other cost and benefit estimates of trade protection, see Collyns and Dunaway (1987), Crandall (1987), Hickok (1985), and Tarr and Morkre (1984).

2 For examples of such studies, see Denzau (1984) and Mendez (1986).

3 Strictly speaking, wage flexibility ensures full employment, not constant employment. Labor supply, however, tends to be unresponsive to wage changes, especially among adult men (Pencavel 1986). Thus, the constant-employment assumption not only is a clear improvement over the assumption of perfectly elastic labor supply but also is relatively accurate.

4 The tariff or tariff equivalent rate refers to either the actual tariff rate or, if a quota was imposed, the equivalent tariff rate that would have led to the same level of imports as the quota.

5 See White (1989).

6 The shares are based on gross state product data by industry, as published by the U.S. Bureau of Economic Analysis. See Renshaw, Trott and Friedenberg (1988) for a description of the gross state product data.

REFERENCES

Baldwin, Robert E., and Anne O. Krueger, eds. (1984), *The Structure and Evolution of Recent U.S. Trade Policy* (Chicago: University of Chicago Press for National Bureau of Economic Research).

Chiang, Alpha C. (1974), *Fundamental Methods of Mathematical Economics*, 2d ed. (New York: McGraw-Hill Book Company).

Collyns, Charles and Steven Dunaway (1987), "The Cost of Trade Restraints: The Case of Japanese Automobile Exports to the United States," *International Monetary Fund Staff Papers* 34 (March): 150-75.

Crandall, Robert W. (1987), "The Effects of U.S. Trade Protection for Autos and Steel," *Brookings Papers on Economic Activity*, 1987, no. 1: 271-88.

Denzau, Arthur T. (1987), *How Import Restraints Reduce Employment*, CSAB Formal Publication no. 80 (St. Louis: Washington University, Center for the Study of American Business, June).

Hickok, Susan (1985), "The Consumer Cost of U.S. Trade Restraints," Federal Reserve Bank of New York *Quarterly Review*, Summer, 1-12.

Hufbauer, Gary Clyde, Diane T. Berliner, and Kimberly Ann Elliott (1986), *Trade Protection in the United States: 31 Case Studies* (Washington, D.C.: Institute for International Economics).

Interindustry Economics Division (1989), "Annual Input-Output Accounts of the U.S. Economy, 1983." *Survey of Current Business* 69 (February): 21-36.

Méndez, José A. (1986). "The Short-Run Trade and Employment Effects of Steel Import Restraints."*Journal of World Trade Law* 20 (September-October): 554-66.

Pencavel, John (1986), "Labor Supply of Men: A Survey," in *Handbook of Labor Economics*, vol. 1, ed. Orley Ashenfelter and Richard Layard (Amsterdam: North-Holland), 3-102.

Renshaw, Vernon, Edward A. Trott, Jr. and Howard L. Friedenberg (1988), "Gross State Product by Industry, 1963-86," *Survey of Current Business* 68 (May): 30-46.

Standard Industrial Classification Manual 1972, prepared by U.S. Office of Management and Budget, Statistical Policy Division (Washington, D.C.: Government Printing Office).

Tarr, David G., and Morris E. Morkre (1984), *Aggregate Costs to the United States of Tariffs and Quotas on Imports: General Tariff Cuts and Removal of Quotas on Automobiles, Steel, Sugar, and Textiles*, a Bureau of Economics Staff Report to the Federal Trade Commission (Washington, D.C.: Government Printing Office, December).

U.S. Bureau of Labor Statistics (1988), "Time Series Data for Input-Output Industries: Output, Price, and Employment" (Washington, D.C.: Government Printing Office, September).

U.S. Bureau of the Census (1985), *Statistical Abstract of the United States*, 1986, 106th ed. (Washington, D.C.: Government Printing Office).

U.S. Department of Commerce (1986), *1986 U.S. Industrial Outlook: Prospects for Over 350 Manufacturing and Service Industries* (Washington, D.C.: Government Printing Office, January).

U.S. Department of Labor, Bureau of Labor Statistics (1985), *Employment and Wages: Annual Averages 1984*. Bulletin 2249 (Washington, D.C.: Government Printing Office, November).

White, Joseph B. (1989), "Car Wars: After a Brief Pause, Japanese Auto Makers Gain on Detroit Again," *Wall Street Journal*, 23 May, Southwest edition. A1, A12.

SECTION III

International Factor Mobility

International trade is most commonly viewed as the exchange of goods and products between nations. Another form of international exchange is the movement of capital across borders. International capital flows can take the form of portfolio investments, such as purchases of a foreign company's stock, or foreign direct investment. These capital flows will affect the wages of workers and the returns to capital investments in both the source and the host countries. This section begins with an article by Edward Graham that looks at the causes and consequences of foreign direct investment in the United States. The article by William Gruben examines the implications for United States workers of the growth of foreign-owned manufacturing plants in Mexico.

READING 6

Foreign Direct Investment in the United States and U.S. Interests

Edward M. Graham

Foreign direct investment entered the United States at unprecedented rates during the second half of the 1980s. The result has been much higher levels of foreign ownership of U.S. economic activities than those to which the nation has been accustomed. The reasons for this investment include loss of competitiveness of U.S. firms compared to international rivals as well as attractions to foreign investors of the United States itself. The economic effects of greater levels of foreign ownership are generally positive, although some problems with levels of competition could ensure. National security considerations might cause the United States to place some restrictions on this investment, but other restrictions at the present time appear to be unwarranted.

Largely a nonissue until the late 1980s, foreign direct investment (FDI) in the United States, the acquisition of direct managerial control over U.S. real estate or business enterprises by foreign investors, has become the center of much political debate.[1] Critics of FDI in the United States maintain that a large foreign presence in the U.S. economy results in loss of "economic sovereignty" and poses significant threats to national security.[2] Proponents argue that FDI creates new and desirable jobs and brings into the nation new technologies that can improve the global competitiveness of domestic industries.[3] Proponents also maintain that as long as the United States must finance a large balance of payments (BOP) deficit on current account, FDI is a more satisfactory means to finance the deficit than other alternatives

On this last point, the BOP is in deficit whenever the sum of governmental fiscal deficits and domestic private savings is less than domestic private investment. Thus, the BOP deficit falls only if Americans save more, invest less, or local, state, and federal governments reduce their fiscal deficits. Otherwise, to finance the BOP deficit, the United States must sell to foreigners assets such as real estate, short-term instruments such as Treasury bills, or longer term instruments such as bonds or equity. Direct investment falls into this last category: The U.S. government defines direct investment as 10% or more ownership by a single foreign investor (a person or a firm) of a U.S. firm or a real property. The second category (real estate) is of relatively little importance. Most FDI in the United States consists of wholly or majority owned U.S. subsidiaries of foreign firms.

Direct investment is typically held for a much longer duration than other U.S. assets held by foreigners. Although shorter term assets conceivably could be liquidated en mass by foreign investors, likely triggering a precipitous fall of the dollar and an ensuing economic crisis, this is unlikely to happen with FDI. Thus, one case for FDI is that as long as the United States continues to run BOP deficits, FDI is preferable to other forms of foreign investment as a means to finance these deficits.

Apart from this, what is the case for and against foreign direct investment in the United States? In this article I examine the size of FDI relative to the whole U.S. economy, why FDI has occurred, the economic consequences of FDI, national security implications, and finally whether the growing foreign stake in the United States is cause for worry.

HOW MUCH OF AMERICA DO FOREIGNERS OWN?

The book value on balance of payments basis of the annual flow of FDI into the United States for recent years is shown in Fig. 1. As is readily apparent, FDI grew rapidly during the second half of the 1980s, but fell sharply during 1990 and 1991.

The reasons for the recent decline in FDI flows are not wholly clear. Changes in interfirm funds flows account for much of the decline (Fig. 2). The U.S. government counts as FDI the sum of equity held in U.S. affiliates by foreign parent firms, retained earnings of these affiliates, and net intra-firm borrowing between affiliates and parents. In 1990 flows of net lending from parents to affiliates declined sharply. Also, in the first half of 1990, the stock of retained earnings of U.S. affiliates of foreign firms declined sharply because these affiliates paid dividends to their parents in spite of negative net earnings. The decline net lending (and perhaps the accelerated reduction in retained earnings) likely were caused by movements in interest rate differentials favoring borrowing in the United States, expectations of continuing dollar depreciation, or both.

New equity flows were also lower in 1990 than in 1989, but the change was small. Some of this decline was the result of the U.S. recession. But the rate of this decline accelerated in the last quarter of 1990 and the first quarter of 1991, and this acceleration is not easily explained by the recession. It might signal a trend break in new FDI coming into the United States, but it is too early to say this with assurance.

Table 1 details the stock of FDI by major source nation at year end 1986 and 1990. Although the United Kingdom is the largest source nation and Japan is in second place, the growth of FDI from Japan was significantly more rapid between 1986 and 1990 than from other nations. European nations account for almost two-thirds of FDI in the United States.

How large is FDI in the United States when compared to the whole economy? Table 2 presents various measures. By any of these, FDI accounts for a rather small portion of the economy. Alarmist views that foreign interests are buying out America, lock, stock, and barrel, simply are not supported by the facts.

When compared to figures for most other Organization for Economic Cooperation and Development (OECD) countries, the level of FDI in the United States is not high, adjusting for the size of the nation. Table 3 presents comparative figures for the "G-S" nations (the five largest industrialized nations, excluding the U.S.S.R.) compiled by researchers at the Royal Institute for International Affairs in London. Although these figures date from the middle 1980s and suffer from some differences in definition, they do suggest that only in Japan is foreign control of the

Fig. 1. Annual flow of FDI to the United States (balance of payments basis), 1974–1991. The 1991 figure is annualized from preliminary data for the first half of the year. [14]

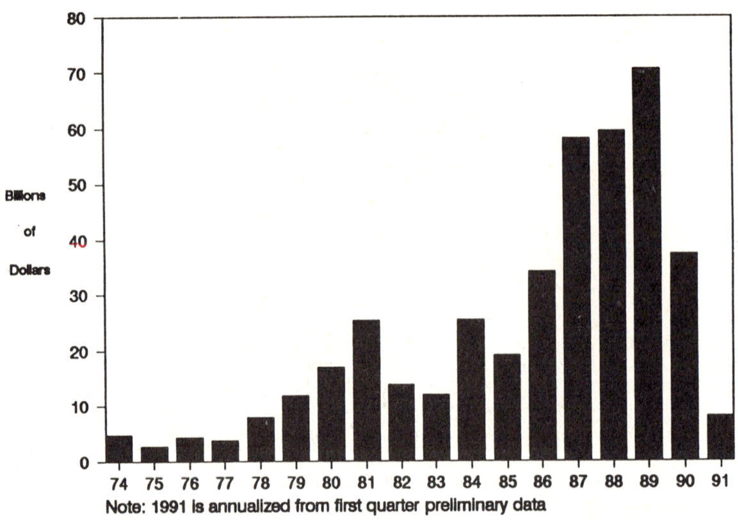

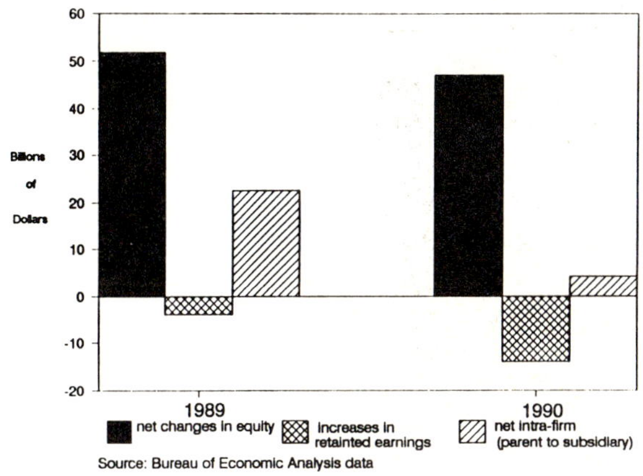

Fig. 2. Composition of FDI entering the United States during 1989 and 1990. [14]

economy lower than in the United States. When compared with western Europe, foreign control of the U.S. economy is relatively low. Since the middle 1980s, the role of FDI has grown significantly in Europe as well as in the United States, but not so in Japan.

Much criticism of FDI in the United States is directed toward investment from Japan in particular. Although Japan is only the second largest source nation to FDI in the United States, Japanese FDI in the United States has surged in recent years. The rate of increase of Japanese FDI fell in 1990, but not by as much as the rates of increase of FDI from the other large investor nations. Until 1985, most Japanese direct investment in the United States was of the "greenfields" variety that is, investment in newly established ventures. In 1986, this investment shifted

Table 1. Foreign direct investment in the United States by source nation. [14]

Nation	Stock of FDI in the United States (dollars × 10^9)	
	1986	1990
United Kingdom	55.9	108.1
Netherlands	40.7	64.3
Other European nations	47.5	84.1
Japan	26.8	83.5
Canada	20.3	27.7
All others	29.0	36.0
TOTAL	220.3	403.7

Source: U.S. Department of Commerce, Bureau of Economic Analysis, Survey of Current Business, June 1987 and 1991 issues

Table 2. Measures of FDI in the United States relative to the whole economy. [14–16]

Measure	Measures (%) by	
	US affiliates of all foreign investors	US affiliates of Japanese firms
FDI stock as percentage of the total net worth of nonfinancial corporations (1990)*	10.5	2.17
Assets of foreign-controlled manufacturing affiliates as percentage of all assets of manufacturing corporations in U.S. (1989)	16.8	1.99
Employment of foreign affiliates as percentage of all U.S. employment (1989)	5.0	0.57
Employment of foreign manufacturing affiliates as percentage of all U.S. manufacturing employment (1989)	9.7	1.26
Value added by foreign affiliates as share of U.S. GNP (1987)	3.4	0.37

*Year in parantheses indicates last year for which base data are available.

Source: from Bureau of Economic Analysis and Federal Reserve Board base data

Nation	Sales*	Manufacturing employment*	Assets*
United States	10	7	9
Japan	1	1	1
France	27	21	
Germany	18	13	17
United Kingdom	20	14	14

Source: D. Julius and S. Thomsen, "Foreign-owned Firms, Trade, and Economic Integration", Tokyo Club Papers 2, London: Royal Institute for International Affairs, 1988

Table 3 Measures of the role of FDI in the economies of five large industrial democracies for the year 1986.[17]

toward takeovers. Even so, takeovers of U.S. firms by Japanese firms during 1987 through 1989 were neither as numerous nor on average as large as takeovers by British firms. But whereas large takeovers of U.S. firms by British firms virtually came to a halt after 1989, large Japanese investments such as the much publicized takeover by Matsushita of MCA have continued.

Indeed throughout the 1980s and into 1990 the vast majority of foreign direct investment in the United States took place through acquisition rather than greenfields investment. Indicative figures are shown in Table 4. These acquisitions occurred concurrently with a mergers and acquisitions boom in the United States involving purely domestically owned firms. Takeovers of major U.S. firms by foreign investors peaked somewhat later than domestic mergers and acquisitions, and while the domestic boom ended somewhere around 1988, foreign acquisitions continued into 1990.

Japanese banks play a larger role in the U.S. economy than do Japanese investors overall. These banks control more than half of all banking assets in the United States under foreign control. Japanese firms also dominate the foreign-controlled portion of the U.S. automotive industry. There are other sectors however where foreign controlled firms account for a substantial portion of domestic activity but where the Japanese presence is slight, such as the chemical and pharmaceutical industries.

There has been much concern about foreign purchases of real estate in recent years. Foreign holdings of U.S. real estate account for only about 1% of U.S. land and no more than 4% of all U.S. commercial properties by value in 1987, and the numbers are unlikely to have grown by much since. Thus, the foreign presence in the real estate sector is much less than the overall foreign presence in the U.S. economy. The attention given real estate doubtlessly has resulted from a rather small number of acquisitions by foreigners (Japanese in particular) of highly visible properties such as New York's Rockefeller Center. In late 1989, the Japanese Ministry of Finance reportedly requested an end to such "showcase" purchases. Most Japanese investors have since sought "low profile" properties away from major city centers, although a few "showcase" purchases by Japanese investors have persisted. In some localities (Honolulu, for example), Japanese purchases of residential properties have bred resentment.

ECONOMICS OF FDI IN THE UNITED STATES

Why did FDI in the United States grow so rapidly? The answer most often given is that FDI in the United States is an inevitable by-product of the U.S. current account deficit, which requires an influx of foreign capital to finance it. But examination of the facts reveals that this is not so. A statistical test of the relation between annual changes in the net flows of FDI and the U.S. current account for the years 1973 to 1989 reveals a weakly negative relation. This is because during the years of rapid rise in the current account deficit, the deficit largely was financed by increased foreign purchases of short term U.S. securities whereas FDI as a percentage of total foreign investment fell sharply. But after 1986, as the BOP

Mode of entry	Total investment ($ billions)								
	1982	1983	1984	1985	1986	1987	1988	1989	1990
Acquisitions	4.8	11.8	20.1	31.5	25.6	33.9	64.9	59.7	56.8
New establishments	3.2	3.4	3.0	7.7	4.9	6.4	7.8	11.5	7.7

Source: U.S. Department of Commerce, Bureau of Economic Analysis, Survey of Current Business, various issues

Table 4. Sources of growth in foreign control of U.S. firms, 1982–1988. [14]

deficit began to shrink, the composition of foreign investment in the United States shifted from short-term securities toward longer term ones and direct investment. In 1989, inward FDI equalled about 52% of the BOP deficit and 56% of the increase in foreign assets in the United States, as opposed to 21% and 28%, respectively, in 1984.

Foreign direct investment is not well correlated with BOP deficits in a number of other countries as well. Japan's outward FDI grew during the late 1980s when her BOP surplus was declining. The United Kingdom has been a large net foreign direct investor in some recent years in spite of BOP deficits.

If the BOP—which measures the net flow of investment funds into or out of a country—is not the determinant of direct investment, what is? It is helpful to remind ourselves that direct investment occurs when foreign persons gain managerial control of a domestic business organization. But those persons" typically are business firms, not individuals. Unlike other forms of foreign investment, then, direct investment is not determined solely or even largely by financial considerations, but rather by considerations of corporate strategy.

FDI specialists thus have observed that direct investor firms (often termed "multinational enterprises", or MNEs) tend to possess firm-specific ownership advantages over their rivals. [4] But the precise nature of the advantage varies from MNE to MNE. In some cases the advantage might be a recognized brand name (Coca-Cola, for example). In other cases, it may be superior technology or management skills. In natural resource industries the advantage can simply be control of low cost sources of supply. For many MNEs, the advantage is some combination of the above.

Firms and industries are not static, and the nature of ownership advantage can change over time. In some instances, MNEs have long since lost the original

Table 5. Measures of economic performance of U.S. affiliates of foreign firms operating in the United States compared with all U.S. firms. [14, 15, 18]

Measure	Manufacturing sector (dollars × 10^3)		All U.S. firms
	U.S. affiliates of foreign firms*	U.S. affiliates of Japanese firms*	
Exports per worker (1989)	14.73	15.6	17.9†
Imports per worker (1989)	18.47	41.2	11.3†
Value added per employee (1987)	48.1	49.8	46.0
Compensation per employee (1989)	35.2	36.4	33.9
R&D per worker (1989)	3.88	2.88‡	3.36

*All data are for industry of affilitate. †Data for "all U.S. firms" for imports and exports per worker are 1988 figures for U.S.–based multinational firms only, otherwise data for "U.S. firms" are for all firms in United States. ‡1987 data available only; 1989 figure is estimated to be about 4.0.

Source: from Bureau of Economic Analysis and National Science Foundation base data advantage that enabled them to become multinational in the first place. Some of these firms may nonetheless be able to continue to operate multinationally because they have established barriers to entry in overseas market (for example, complex distribution networks) that are difficult for rivals to penetrate. Other MNEs that have lost their advantages relative to rivals will, however, over time, experience a shrinking share of global markets.

One interpretation of recent FDI in the United States thus is that non-U.S. firms have improved their status relative to U.S. rivals in terms of ownership advantage. This FDI can thus be seen as symptomatic of overall loss of competitiveness of U.S. firms. But it is unlikely that FDI is a cause of this loss, as some critics maintain. Possession of ownership advantages by foreign firms, implying a loss of competitiveness by U.S. firms, is a precondition for FDI to take place, and thus to the extent that FDI is indicative of loss of U.S. competitiveness, it is the loss that leads to FDI and not the other way around.

Ownership advantages explain why firms become multinational, but they do not explain why they choose to invest in some countries rather than others. To explain this, specialists refer to locational advantages possessed by countries which sought by MNEs possessing ownership advantages. The large amounts of FDI that entered the United States during the 1980s testifies that non U.S.-owned MNEs found considerable locational advantages to be had in the United States. These advantages included large market size, political stability, market growth potential, a generally well-educated labor force, a well-developed infrastructure, and a large R&D base. One can wonder, given the evident deterioration of some of those advantages, if these firms will continue to find the United States an attractive place to locate.

It is commonly accepted by FDI specialists that a firm must also possess economies of internalization as well as specific ownership advantages in order to become multinational. [5] An economy of internalization exists if it is cheaper for a firm to work its ownership advantages internally within its own organization rather than, say, licensing these to overseas rival firms. [6]

There also is evidence that rates of foreign direct investment in the United States have been affected by exchange rate movements and by tax policy changes. These effects however seem to be "at the margin." That is, they have caused short-term deviations in the growth of this investment; but the investment nonetheless is fundamentally driven by considerations of corporate strategies of the investing firms. [7]

Finally, there is a body of literature that holds that at least some FDI is reactive: that firms become multinational because their rivals do. This could be one cause of FDI in the United States. [8] Some implications of this possibility are discussed below.

The economic consequences of FDI in the United States. If FDI indeed is largely a consequence of firm specific advantages held by foreign firms, one would expect the economic performance of U.S. subsidiaries of these firms to be at least as good as or better than that of rival domestically domiciled firms. Table 5 shows five measures of economic performance for the manufacturing sector. By most of these measures, the differences in economic performance of subsidiaries of foreign firms operating in the United States and domestic firms are slight. This certainly hold for value-added and compensation per worker employed, measures which many analysts say best summarize economic performance. Consistent with the hypothesis that the foreign-controlled firms hold advantages over their U.S. rivals, overall the former do slightly better than the latter by these two measures.

The same general result that performance of foreign subsidiaries and their U.S. counterparts arc comparable holds for R&D expenditures per employee in the manufacturing sector as well. All U.S. affiliates of foreign investors in fact do slightly better by this measure than do all U.S. firms, but not U.S. affiliates of Japanese firms. It should be noted, however, that the figure in Table 5 for all U.S. firms is for company-funded R&D only. If governmental funded R&D performed by U.S. manufacturing firms is added, this figure rises to $4.6 thousand per employee. However, given that most R&D performed by U.S. affiliates of foreign firms is company funded, it seems reasonable to use as comparison company-funded R&D by all U.S. firms.

Further bolstering the result that U.S. affiliates of foreign controlled firms perform a share of R&D that is proportional to their size in the economy, one can divide the figure for R&D per worker by value added per worker to get the ratio of R&D to value added. This ratio can be interpreted as share of R&D relative to share of GNP. The figures at 5.6% for all U.S. affiliates of foreign firms, 5.8% for U.S. affiliates of Japanese firms, and 5.0% for all U.S. firms. Thus, by this measure, foreign controlled firms in the United

States more than "pull their oar" in terms of R&D contribution.

In spite of this, two things must be kept in mind. First, the total contribution of foreign-controlled firms to U.S. R&D is rather small, although proportional to the overall role of these firms in the U.S. economy. Secondly, for various reasons multinational firms historically have concentrated their R&D in their home countries. [9] The propensity of multinationals to concentrate R&D in home countries is, however, declining with time. [10] A growing foreign presence in the United States thus probably does translate some increased dependence upon foreign sources of technology. This is not necessarily wholly bad, because inward transfer of technology can benefit the U.S. economy irrespective of where the technology is originally generated. This transfer can even stimulate domestic rivals of foreign-controlled firms to upgrade their own technologies and, in doing so, these rivals might enable recapture by the U.S. economy of some of the externalities associated with the original development that otherwise would fall exclusively on the country where the R&D is performed. To the extent that this occurs, this is one pro-competitive consequence of FDI that acts to the nation's benefit.

Only in foreign trade (exports and imports per worker) do there seem to be significant differences between U.S.-domiciled firms and foreign-controlled U.S. subsidiaries. The figures in Table 5 are for U.S.-based multinational firms with imports and exports of U.S. affiliates of foreign firms in the manufacturing sector. Because the sectoral composition of the two sets of firms are not the same, there are problems of comparability between the two sets of figures. Unfortunately, data limitations prevent a more detailed comparison; figures broken down by industry are not available. The numbers show that the U.S. affiliates imported and exported more per worker than did U.S.-based multinational firms. The gap is especially great for imports per worker: These were about twice as high for U.S. affiliates as for U.S.-based multinationals.

What might have accounted for this difference and of what consequence is it? There are at least two possible explanations. The first is that foreign firms operating in the United States are more "globally integrated" than are their U.S. counterparts and that they therefore ship more so-called "intermediate" goods (for example, parts and subassemblies) between their international subsidiaries than do the latter. If this explanation is correct, one would expect the differences in import propensities to persist over time.

An alternative explanation however is that the differences are largely "life cycle" effects. It is empirically verifiable that newly created subsidiaries tend to rely more on their parent organizations for inputs than do long-established subsidiaries but that as they mature, these subsidiaries substitute locally made inputs for imported ones. Because much FDI in the United States is of recent vintage, many U.S. subsidiaries of foreign firms would be expected to have high import propensities. This is especially true of Japanese-controlled subsidiaries.

To the extent that the "life cycle" explanation is correct, over time the imports per employee of foreign subsidiaries will come down. This indeed does seem to be happening. Whereas in 1982 for U.S. affiliates the ratio of imports per worker to exports per worker was 2.0, this ratio fell to 1.6 in 1988.

These ratios do not, however, clinch the "life cycle" hypothesis. Because much recent FDI in the United States has resulted from acquisition of U.S. firms, the narrowing ratio of imports to exports per worker might reflect nothing more than transfers of ownership of these firms to non-U.S. investors. The issue then is, one under foreign control, do these firms increase their imported inputs? At present, no data exist to address this issue directly.

If U.S. affiliates of foreign firms were to continue to have a higher propensity to import intermediate goods than comparable U.S.controlled firms, what would be the costs to the U.S. economy? One way to measure these is to determine how far the dollar would have to depreciate to reduce net imports of the United States by an amount equal to the difference between levels of imports actually generated by foreign subsidiaries and levels that would be generated if the import propensities were identical to those of U.S.-owned firms. I calculate that the dollar would have to fall by 4% to achieve the required reductions. Such a percentage fall could be swamped in the short term volatility of the dollar; during May 1991 alone, for example, the dollar appreciated on a trade-weighted basis by about 10%.

And so, overall, what are the economic consequences of foreign direct investment in the United States? One cannot help but conclude that this investment is on the whole favorable to the economy. Foreign direct investment creates good jobs at favorable wages. Technologies transferred into the United States help to invigorate the U.S. economy.

If FDI increases competition within the United States, any procompetitive effects must also be counted as benefits. In general FDI does increase competition: As a result of FDI, more firms compete in any given market. This is generally true even if the mode of entry of the foreign firms is acquisition of an existing U.S. firm, because acquisition candidates are usually relatively weak firms whose competitive position stands to be strengthened under foreign ownership. FDI is not, however, always procompetitive. Circumstances where FDI is "reactive" (made in response to previous FDI by rival firms), FDI can have anti-competitive effects. [11] This is likely to happen in industries dominated by a small number of firms. Given the large number of foreign-owned MNEs that established U.S. subsidiaries during the 1980s, if there are industries in the United States where FDI has led to anticompetitive effects, they likely are small in number. But anticompetitive effects in some industries cannot be entirely ruled out.

Empirically it is difficult to determine if and where anticomunictitive effect might be found. Oligopoly industry structure, for instance, is often associated with high R&D intensity. This is especially true for FDI in the United States from Japan, and it is difficult to determine in many industries whether this FDI is the result of firm-specific Japanese advantages or an extension of Japanese oligopoly power. [12]

NATIONAL SECURITY AND FDI IN THE UNITED STATES

If the economic consequences of FDI in the United States are largely favorable, are there any grounds for restricting it? One reason might be national security.

Almost surely there are U.S. firms that should not fall under foreign control—for example, such major defense contracting firms such as General Dynamics, Boeing, or Northrop. The Exon-Florio amendment to the Omnibus Trade and Competitiveness Act of 1988 does allow the president to block foreign takeovers, acquisitions, or mergers of U.S. firms on grounds of national security. This law is not precise with respect to what criteria are to be applied to foreign takeovers of U.S. firms, and the Bush Administration has chosen to implement the authority narrowly. Of upwards of 600 transactions notified to the Committee on Foreign Investment in the United States, the interagency group charged with working level implementation of Exon-Florio, less than a dozen cases have been fully investigated and only one transaction was actually blocked.

The president also has other means to deal with the foreign investor in times of national emergency Under the International Emergency Economics Powers Act, for instance, the President can seize and administer foreign-controlled businesses.

But exactly what are the security threats posed by FDI? As will be argued, these often run counter to conventional wisdom.

We have noted, for example, that the very existence of FDI in the United States implies that foreign firms hold advantages, including technologies ones, over U.S. rivals. Many foreign-held technologies are of military relevance including so-called "dual use" technologies having both military and civilian applications. Does a foreign advantage in such technologies have negative implications for U.S. national security and, if so what should be done about it?

For certain very sensitive technologies the case can be made that the nation should subsidize domestically controlled enterprises to produce products embodying these technologies. Subsidization is costly and presumably the subsidized enterprise would not perform as well as foreign competitors (otherwise, it would not require a subsidy). In the extreme poor performance of the domestic enterprise could actually consign the U.S. military to technological inferiority, the very opposite of the desired result. Thus, subsidized activities should be limited to ones where, in the absence of a domestic supplier, the nation would be so dependent on foreign sources that cutoff of supply would pose a clear, immediate, and credible threat to the national security.

Such instances are likely to be rare. For most activities, a better idea would be to follow the old adage, "If you cannot lick them, join them". That is, steps should be taken to ensure that foreign suppliers of needed technologies contribute positively to national security. This objective is typically better met if the foreign firm operates in the United States (through

FDI) rather than export the relevant products to the United States from the home country. Much the same point is made by the Defense Science Board.

Do U.S. policies currently encourage this? One can argue that current policies are overly restrictive. For example, the Defense Department currently places rather tight strictures on contractor firms under foreign ownership, control, or influence ("FOCI"). Generally, defense contracting operations of any firm subject to FOCI regulations must be structured so that the foreign owners do not have access to information deemed sensitive to national security. Under the most prevalent arrangement, the nonvoting trust, the foreign owners de facto lose managerial control over the defense contracting activities. The effect could be to discourage foreign firms holding proprietary technologies of use to the U.S. defense effort from participating in defense contracting. Intended originally to prevent leakage of militarily sensitive technologies, the regulations might now also encumber access of the U.S. military to desirable foreign-controlled technology. FOCI regulations are, it should be noted, currently being revised.

If the FOCI regulations are too stringent one bill to "strengthen" Exon-Florio could be downright disasterous in terms of its likely effects. This is HR 2624, cosponsored by Representatives Richard Gephardt (D-MO), the House majority leader, and Cardiss Collins (D-IL). Intended to keep under U.S. ownership technology necessary for the defense industrial base, the bill likely would have the opposite effect by discouraging foreigners from investing in the United States in precisely those technologies where their contribution could be most beneficial. [13]

This is not to say that FDI presents no threat whatsoever to national security. One threat, as noted, is excessive reliance on a single (or small number) of suppliers of critical technologies under foreign control. A useful prescription for dealing with this threat is embodied in another proposed bill to amend Exon-Florio, HR 2631, sponsored by Representative Phil Sharp (D-IN). This bill would link Exon-Florio to U.S. antitrust law by spelling out special new provisions for acquisitions of U.S. firms that meet national security criteria. The idea is that dependence on foreigner firms becomes problematic when these firms hold monopoly power. But remedy of monopoly power is precisely what antitrust law is supposed to do. Such remedy is, of course, desirable even if no national security issues are present, and indeed use of antitrust laws can be one remedy to any anticompetitive effects that might be induced by FDI. In some industries, however, problems of competition (or lack therof) are not limited to the U.S. market, and one agenda for the future likely will be international approaches to competition policy. A model might be the new competition policy emerging in the European Community.

FOREIGN DIRECT INVESTMENT: DOES IT THREATEN THE UNITED STATES?

Is the bottom line that there is no reason whatsoever for concern about foreign ownership of U.S. economic activities? The answer is "no." There is a level of foreign ownership above which few Americans would feel comfortable, where indeed "economic sovereignty' would become a real issue. There are specific activities which for defense reasons should be maintained under domestic ownership.

But whatever the level above which overall foreign ownership should not rise, actual levels of such ownership are surely now much below this threshold. Will FDI in the United States grow at a rate such that the threshold will soon be breached? Prediction is a risky business, but the best guess is "no." Flows of FDI into the United States have declined sharply from the high levels of the late 1980s, and earlier experiences of other advanced nations with surges of inward FDI (for example, Canada and the United Kingdom) suggest that those do not last forever.

Although there are some activities that should not be under foreign control for defense reasons, these are likely to be rather small in number. The United States has adequate laws and policies to deal with these cases. In fact, the danger is not so much that the U.S. government will fail to keep activities out of foreign control that should be retained under domestic ownership, but rather that the government's authority could be used over-zealous so as to keep out of the nation activities that should be allowed in. Some FDI might cause problems in the domain of competition (that is, FDI might result in highly oligopolistic global industries) and, although unilateral application of antitrust law might be one remedy, a more international approach to the regulation of competition is likely to be one agenda for future discussion among nations.

REFERENCES AND NOTES

1. E. M. Graham and P. R. Krugman, *Foreign Direct Investment in the United States* (Institute for International Economics, Washington, D.C., 1991), 2nd Ed.
2. S. Tolchin and M. Tolchin, *Buying Into America* (New York Times Books, New York, 1988).
3. R. B. Reich, *The Work of Nations* (Knopf New York, 1991).
4. J. H. Dunning, J. *Int. Bus. Stud.* 19, 1 (1988).
5. P. J. Buckley and M. C. Casson, *The Future of Multinational Enterprise* MacMillan, London 1976)
6. J. Cantwell, *Technological Innovation and Mu[illegible]tional Corporations* (Blackwell,Oxford, 1989).
7. M. W. Klein and E. Rosengren, *J. Int. Econ.*, in press.
8. E. M. Graham, J. PostKeynesian Econ. 1, 82, (1978).
9. R. Vemon, in *Economic Analysis and the Multinational Enterprise*, J. H. Dunning, Ed. (Allen & Unwin, London 1974), pp. 89-114
10. J. Cantwell, in *The Nature of the Transnational Firm*, C. N. Pitelis and R. Sugden, Eds. (Routlege, London, 1990), pp. 16-63.
11. E. M. Graham, *Int. Trade J.* 4, 259, (1990).
12. B. Kogut and S. J. Chang, *Rev. Econ. Stat..* 73, 401 (1991)
13. E. M. Graham and M. E. Ebert, *The World Economy.*
14. Bureau of Economic Analysis, US Department of Commerce, *Surv. Curr. Bus.*, various issues.
15. Bureau of Economic Analysis, US Department of Commerce, *Oper. U.S. Affiliates Foreign Co.*, various issues.
16. Federal Reserve Board of the Unitcd States, *Balance Sheets U.S. Econ.*, various issues.
17. D. A. Julius and S. Thomsen, *Tokyo Club Pap.* 2, 191 (1988)
18. National Science Foundation, *Science and Technology Indicators* (Washington, D.C., 1990)

READING 7

Mexican Maquiladora Growth: Does it Cost U.S. Jobs?

William C. Gruben

The Mexican *maquiladora* sector is a large and growing assemblage of foreign-owned manufacturing plants that produce chiefly for export to the United States. The rise of this sector occurred partly in response to the Mexican government's liberalization of certain tariff laws and of laws pertinent to foreign ownership of manufacturing enterprises.

While changes in Mexican customs law encouraged the emergence of the maquiladoras, certain aspects of U.S. customs law also facilitated this phenomenon, as did several other factors. In fact, the maquiladora sector is just one example of a broader pattern of global reorganization in manufacturing operations.

The rapid growth of the maquiladora sector has generated attention as well as controversy. U.S. labor organizations argue that maquiladoras take jobs from U.S. workers. Defenders of the maquiladora system claim that its growth is simply part of the overall globalization of manufacturing activity. They contend that the competition is not between Mexican and U.S. workers, but between Mexican workers and those in the Pacific newly industrialized countries, or PACNICs.

In this article, I discuss the factors contributing to maquiladora employment growth and offer tentative statistical evidence to suggest that both sides of the controversy are about equally correct. In support of the first argument, maquiladora employment seems to grow faster when differentials between U.S. and Mexican manufacturing wages are widening. Mexican and U.S. workers do compete. In support of the second argument, maquiladora growth accelerates when Mexican wages fall below PACNIC wages. That is, Mexican and PACNIC workers also compete.

THE GLOBALIZATION OF MANUFACTURING

The rise of the maquiladora sector is not an isolated event. Over the last three decades, an international reorganization and integration occurred in the manufacturing sector. Even earlier, firms in developed countries often located manufacturing plants in less developed countries. Those plants, however, generally served local or regional markets. Foreign plants owned by U.S. companies, for example, exported little or none of their products to the United States. If a U.S. firm's foreign affiliate exported an input to the United States, the input was likely to be a raw material, not a manufactured product. The same patterns of production and importization were common for Japanese and European firms.

In the late 1960s, U.S. firms began to integrate their foreign affiliates into global systems of production. As the disparity widened between labor costs in the United States and less developed countries, and as international communication and transport became easier and cheaper, U.S. firms became more likely to use their foreign manufacturing affiliates as parts of a process designed to serve U.S. markets.[1] Accordingly, the share of production that these foreign affiliates sold to U.S. markets rose.[2]

This change was not simply a wholesale shift of U.S.-operated manufacturing activity to foreign locations; it was a geographical reorganization of the stages of production. While manufacturing a given product, some stages of production may involve labor-intensive operations that require less skill or capital than others. As wage differentials widened between the United States and less developed countries, U.S. firms began to locate such labor-intensive stages of production in countries where the cost of unskilled labor was low.[3] Design and capital-intensive production tended to remain in the United States.

The internationalization of production was not unique to U.S. firms. Japanese firms also began to integrate their foreign affiliates into global systems of production, but with a significant difference from the U.S. approach: Japanese firms did not return their affiliates' manufactured products to Japan, but sent them to other markets, such as the United States.

U.S. CUSTOMS LAWS AND MANUFACTURING GLOBALIZATION

Technological changes that facilitated the use of foreign labor were the chief cause of manufacturing's globalization, but U.S. customs law also played a notable role. Particularly relevant are the provisions for reimportation in Items 806.30 and 807.00 of the Tariff Schedules of the United States.[4] These provisions allow manufacturers to export US-made components for processing or assembly, and then to reimport the resulting products under special tariff provisions. That is, the U.S. components imbedded in the reimported products return duty-free to the United States, and only the value added by foreign manufacturing is subject to tariff. Item 806.30 permits the reimport of fabricated metal products into the United States for further processing. Item 807.00 permits only the foreign assembly of finished goods for reexport to the United States, but not other types of manufacturing processes.

While a recent survey suggests that the 806.30 and 807.00 customs law provisions may positively affect the competitiveness of firms that use them, the same survey found that those provisions are not the primary incentives for establishing foreign production facilities.[5] Indeed, the principal reason cited for locating production facilities abroad was labor-cost savings. Importantly, from the standpoint of the maquiladora program, more than half of all survey respondents said that the presence of a free zone or *in-bond* treatment by the foreign government influenced their decision to use foreign assembly facilities.

An additional aspect of U.S. customs law that facilitates the operations of the maquiladoras is the Generalized System of Preferences (GSP). Authorized under the General Agreement on Tariffs and Trade (GATT) and established in Title V of the Trade Act of 1974, the GSP provides for the elimination of import duties on certain designated products made in developing countries. Mexico was designated as a beneficiary developing country in 1975 and has continued as such since then. The largest sectoral group of products imported from Mexico under the GSP traditionally has been chemicals and related products, which are not normally associated with maquiladora activity. The second largest sectoral group of products imported from Mexico under the GSP, however, has been machinery, and most of these products are made in maquiladoras. Several products ineligible for coverage under 806.30 or 807.00 enter the United States from Mexico under the GSP.[6]

THE DEVELOPMENT OF THE MAQUILADORA SECTOR

The maquiladora program developed in response to the cancellation of the U.S. bracero program. During World War II, labor shortages in the railroad industry and in agriculture led the United States to admit Mexican laborers, or *braceros*, to work. Although the provisions for railroad workers expired in 1946, rules allowing the entrance of farm workers remained and were formally sanctioned in the early 1950s. Many farm workers left the interior of Mexico and established permanent homes on the northern border so they could take seasonal agricultural jobs in the United States. These events caused significant population growth in northern Mexico, but they also caused U.S. labor groups to exert political pressure against the program. In 1964, with 185,000 Mexicans working as braceros, the United States terminated the program. As a result, underemployment rates began to exceed 70 percent in some northern Mexican cities.[7]

To find jobs for the thousands of unemployed braceros, the Mexican government designed a program to take advantage of U.S. tariff Items 806.30 and 807.00.[8] Under the Border Industrialization Program, the Mexican government allowed 100 percent foreign control of plant operations in Mexico under specified conditions. it also permitted duty-free imports of materials and equipment, provided that all output would be exported from Mexico. These new rules made it easier for U.S. and other foreign producers to use Mexico's low-cost labor to compete with Asian producers.[9]

At first, Mexican law required maquiladoras to locate on the border, but later allowed plants in the interior. Despite Mexico's relaxation of restrictions on plant location, more than 80 percent of maquiladora employment is still on the border.

Mexico also relaxed its requirement that all maquiladora products be exported. Now only 80 percent of total output must be exported. Most plants still do not sell any of their output in Mexico. Only about one maquiladora in ten has even applied for permit to sell there.[10]

GROWTH IN THE MAQUILADORAS

Maquiladora growth has been rapid but erratic. Chart 1 depicts maquiladora employment for each year from 1966 to 1988. Note that average maquiladora employment for 1988 exceeds that for 1975 by more than five times and more than ninety times that for 1966. Although maquiladora employment grew in all but three years, rates of expansion in maquiladora employment vary considerably (Chart 2).

The greatest variance occurred during the initial stage of maquiladora expansion, 1966-70. While changes in Mexican law brought rapid growth, contradictory rules among Mexican regulatory agencies created uncertainty among investors and dampened investor enthusiasm. After the initial surge of growth, capacity constraints on infrastructure and in some local labor markets impeded expansion. In 1967, for example, maquiladora employment rose by 321 percent, but it fell the next year by more than 5 percent. although maquiladora employment rose in 1969, it remained below the level established in 1967.[11]

During a second stage of expansion, from 1971 to 1976, Mexican policy contradictions began to be

Chart 1

Maquiladora Employment

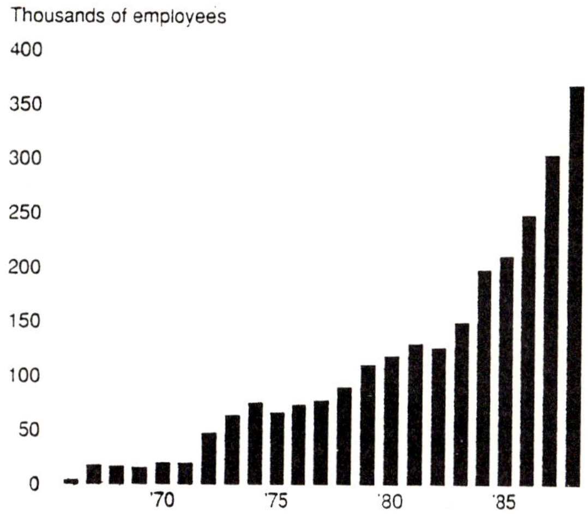

SOURCE OF PRIMARY DATA: Instituto Nacional de Estadística, Geografía e Informática.

Chart 2

Growth in Maquiladora Employment

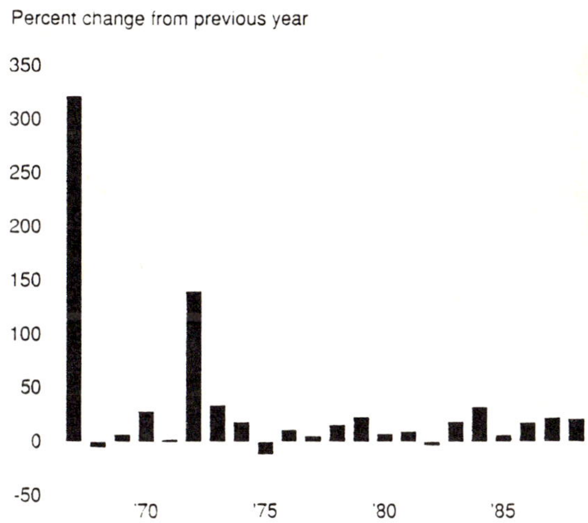

SOURCE OF PRIMARY DATA: Instituto Nacional de Estadística, Geografía e Informática.

resolved and the growth-rate variances diminished. Nevertheless, extreme variance in employment growth remained. For example, maquiladora employment grew 140 percent in 1972, but fell by almost 12 percent in 1975 as a U.S. recession and the overvaluation of the peso discouraged maquiladora activity. A U.S. recovery and a Mexican devaluation prompted a turnaround in 1976.

During the second stage of expansion, it became legal to locate maquiladoras away from the northern border. Sales of as much as 20 percent of a maquiladora's output in Mexican markets also were legalized.

By the third stage of maquiladora expansion, 1977-81, the industry had become much more stable. Employment growth ranged between 5 percent and 23 percent, with no episodes of contraction. As the third period progressed, rapidly rising peso-denominated wages in Mexico, together with intervention in exchange markets, pushed up Mexican wages in dollar terms. These increases, together with episodes of marked weakness in the U.S. economy, dampened enthusiasm for further investment in maquiladoras. Growth was substantially slower in 1980 and 1981 than in 1978 and 1979.

The third stage also became a period of consolidation. Maquiladora employment grew much faster than the number of maquiladoras. In the second stage of maquiladora growth, average employment per maquiladora was 129 workers. In the third stage, this figure rose to 198 and, by 1981, it reached 216. Nevertheless, 1981 brought signs of trouble as the number of plants fell for the first time since 1976. This decline reflected the renewed overvaluation of the peso.

The fourth stage of maquiladora expansion began with instability in both the maquiladora sector and the Mexican and U.S. economies. In 1982, the impact of oil-price declines plunged the Mexican economy into a protracted period of economic weakness. Likewise, in 1982, with the deepening of the U.S. recession, average maquiladora employment fell for the first time since 1975, and the number of plants also declined. These problems were followed by a period of extended growth. A major devaluation of the peso in the third quarter of 1982, a decline in the dollar-denominated level of Mexican manufacturing wages, and a U.S. recovery prompted maquiladora growth in 1983. Since then, maquiladoras have grown every year.

MAQUILADORA EMPLOYMENT GROWTH AND INTERNATIONAL WAGE DIFFERENTIALS

Close ties exist between the growth rate of maquiladora employment and the disparity between Mexican wages and those in other low-wage countries, such as the PACNICs. Chart 3 compares Mexican manufacturing wages, denominated in dollars, with an average of wages in four PACNICs - Hong Kong, Korea, Singapore, and Taiwan. The two lines on Chart 4 depict a ratio of Mexican manufacturing wages to PACNIC manufacturing wages and the rate of growth in maquiladora employment. After the ratio of Mexican wages to PACNIC wages rises, maquiladora employment growth tends to slow because Mexico is not meeting the PACNIC wage competition as effectively. When the ratio of Mexican wages to PACNIC wages is low, the growth rate of maquiladora employment is

Chart 3

Mexican and PACNIC Wages

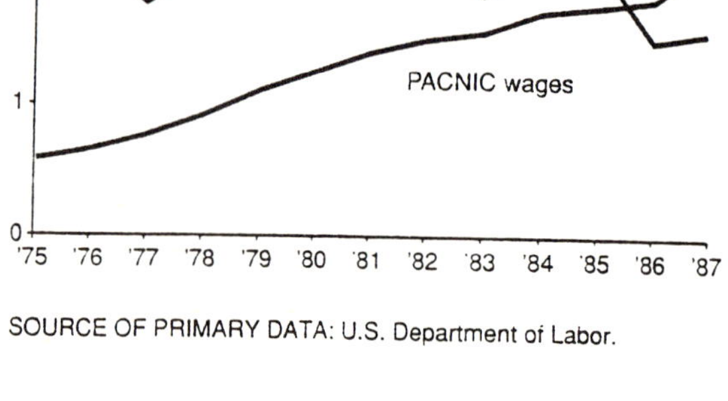

SOURCE OF PRIMARY DATA: U.S. Department of Labor.

Chart 4

Growth in Maquiladora Employment and the Ratio of Mexican Wages to PACNIC Wages

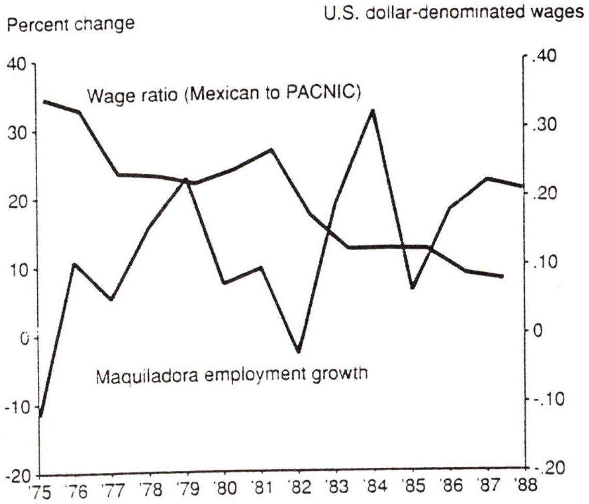

SOURCES OF PRIMARY DATA: Instituto Nacional de Estadística, Geografía e Informática. U.S. Department of Labor.

Chart 5

Growth in Maquiladora Employment and the Ratio of Mexican Wages to U.S. Wages

SOURCES OF PRIMARY DATA: Instituto Nacional de Estadística, Geografía e Informática. U.S. Department of Labor.

high because Mexico is beating the PACNIC wage competition.

Nevertheless, maquiladora employment sometimes grows even when Mexican wages are higher than PACNIC wages. Mexico's proximity to the United States can still make its operations cheaper than those in Asia.[12]

Changes in the ratio between Mexican and PACNIC wages generally lag one year behind changes in maquiladora employment growth rates. Note in Chart 4 that the ratio of Mexican wages to PACNIC wages peaks in 1981, and maquiladora employment falls the following year.

A close relationship also exists between growth in maquiladora employment and the ratio of Mexican manufacturing wages to those in the United States. Chart 5 depicts a ratio of Mexican manufacturing wages to U.S. wages, together with growth rates of maquiladora employment, while Chart 6 compares wages in the two nations. Note the dramatic decline, depicted in Chart 5, in the ratio of Mexican to U.S. wages following the peak in 1981. This reduction prompted the rise in maquiladora employment growth in the middle and late 1980s.

A SIMPLE ECONOMETRIC FORECASTING MODEL OF MAQUILADORA FLUCTUATIONS

The causes of fluctuations in maquiladora output and employment have been the subjects of interest and concern in a number of studies, and there is general agreement on many related issues.[13] There is little dispute that maquiladoras chiefly serve U.S. markets, so that changes in U.S. demand affect rates of change in maquiladora activity. Likewise, there is little dispute that disparaties between wages in Mexico and in other countries hypothesized as competitors explain a substantial portion of the growth of maquiladoras. When Mexican wages fall relative to wages elsewhere, maquiladora employment grows

Nevertheless, a significant controversy over the impact of differentials between Mexican wages and those of other nations remains to be addressed econometrically. This controversy involves the impact of international wage differentials on U.S. manufacturing jobs. U.S. opposition to maquil-

Chart 6

U.S. and Mexican Wages

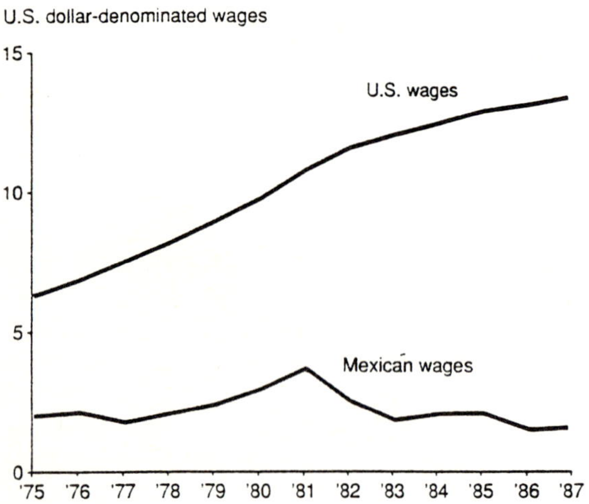

SOURCE OF PRIMARY DATA: U.S. Department of Labor.

adoras, and to U.S. legislation that facilitates their operation, comes principally from organized labor in the United States. Representatives of organized labor contend that maquildora investment by U.S. firms essentially exports jobs. In contrast, advocates of the maquiladoras argue that Mexico competes with the rest of the world for labor-intensive production and that U.S. jobs lost to the maquiladoras would have been lost, in any case, to other low-wage countries.[14]

One approach to addressing this controversy econometrically would be to represent each of the competing arguments by using measures of wage differentials in an equation that explains fluctuations in maquiladora employment.

If the argument from U.S. organized labor were correct, then a measure of the relationship between Mexican and U.S. wages would be significant in explaining fluctuations in maquiladora employment. As Mexican wages fell relative to U.S. wages, maquiladora employment would increase. As Mexican wages rose relative to U.S. wages, maquiladora employment would fall or its growth would slow. Accordingly, this variable would be expected to take on a negative sign in a regression equation that explains variations in maquiladora employment.

If the maquiladora advocates' argument were correct, then a measure of the relationship between Mexican wages and those of other competing low-wage countries would explain fluctuations in maquiladora employment. As Mexican wages fell relative to those of competing low-wage countries, maquiladora employment would rise. As Mexican wages rose relative to those of competing low-wage countries, maquiladora employment would fall or its growth would slow. This variable would also take a negative sign in a regression equation.

If both competing arguments have merit, it may be possible to test the relative strength of each argument by including both wage variables in the same regression equation, and then examining the values of the coefficients. Providing that both coefficient values were significantly different from zero, forming a ratio of the two would suggest something about the relative significance of each argument.

In constructing a model that would allow consideration of these competing arguments, however, labor cost factors are not the only determinants of maquiladora employment fluctuations that deserve consideration. During a 1974-75 crisis in the maquiladora industry, the Mexican Secretary of Industry and Commerce noted that "the degree to which the present problems in the maquila industry have been caused by the United States recession has yet to be analyzed."[15] Both this statement and the econometric conventions of the literature on maquiladoras suggest that a measure of U.S. demand also warrants inclusion in such a model since maquiladoras produce primarily for the U.S.market. As U.S. demand rises, so would maquiladora employment. As a result, I expect the demand variable to take on a positive sign in a regression equation.

Accordingly, three variables appear to be reasonable candidates to explain fluctuations in maquiladora employment. First, to capture the argument of organized labor, I include a ratio of Mexican manufacturing wages to U.S. manufacturing wages. As Mexican manufacturing wages fall relative to U.S. manufacturing wages, maquiladora employment is expected to increase. Second, to capture the argument of maquiladora advocates, I use a ratio of Mexican manufacturing wages to an average of manufacturing wages in Hong Kong, Korea, Singapore, and Taiwan.[16] Third, to capture the effect of fluctuations in U.S. demand, I include U.S. gross national product in 1982 dollars (real GNP).[17]

Table 1 presents the results of three regression equations, each of which incorporates two or more of these variables, using annual data for 1975-87.[18] Regression equations that included, respectively, the Mexico-U.S. wage variable and the U.S. GNP variable and, separately, the Mexico-PACNIC wage variable and the U.S. GNP variable, provide the expected signs.[19] Moreover, the wage variable included in each of the two-variable equations was significant, although the GNP variable was not. A third equation, which contains all three variables,

Table 1

Results of Regression Equations

Equation 1	Intercept	Ratio of Mexican wages to U.S. wages	U.S. GNP
Coefficient	0.079	–0.300	0.739
t statistic	2.089	–2.803	0.812
Summary statistics			
R^2	0.496		
Adjusted R^2	0.369		
Durbin-Watson	2.547		
Autocorrelation check (probability)	0.117		

Equation 2	Intercept	Ratio of Mexican wages to PACNIC wages	U.S. GNP
Coefficient	0.071	–0.314	0.579
t statistic	1.776	–2.743	0.640
Summary statistics			
R^2	0.485		
Adjusted R^2	0.356		
Durbin-Watson	2.743		
Autocorrelation check (probability)	0.070		

Equation 3	Intercept	Ratio of Mexican wages to PACNIC wages	Ratio of Mexican wages to U.S. wages	U.S. GNP
Coefficient	0.078	–0.034	–0.268	0.723
t statistic	1.695	–0.047	–0.390	0.705
Summary statistics				
R^2	0.496			
Adjusted R^2	0.280			
Durbin-Watson	2.572			
Autocorrelation check (probability)	0.155			

SOURCES OF PRIMARY DATA: Instituto Nacional de Estadística. Geografía e Informática.
U.S. Department of Commerce.
U.S. Department of Labor.

provides results whose signs are consistent with expectations but whose levels of significance for the wage variables are not.[20]

Although the coefficients of the Mexico-U.S. wage variable and the Mexico-PACNIC wage variable took on the expected negative signs in an equation that included them and the US GNP variable, neither of the two wage coefficients was significantly different from zero. Although this last result is inconsistent with expectations, these reductions in significance suggest an econometric problem that also appeared in a similar maquiladora-related modeling exercise by Rodolfo Navrete Vargas and José Luis Hernández [*sic*].

The problem is "the existence of multicollinearity between the two variables that express relative costs."[21] That is, movements in the two wage variables are highly correlated with one another.[22] This correlation substantially reduces the ability of regression analysis to separately attribute variations in maquiladora employment to each wage variable. This problem probably explains why, despite years of controversy between pro-and anti-maquiladora groups, no published research ever addressed this question statistically.

We have no direct method for correcting problems of multicollinearity in regression equations beyond increasing the number of observations. Accordingly, the controversy between pro-and anti-maquiladora groups cannot be directly examined by linear regression analysis with the present data.

A procedure does exist, however, that allows for the weighting of the wage variables in a context that avoids multicollinearity. This procedure is *principal components analysis*.

Through principal components analysis, the variation of several variables can be compressed into one or more index variables. The resulting index variable is known as a *principal component*. The principal component is a linear combination of some collection of variables, such as the two wage ratios. A mathematical procedure is used to maximize the amount of variation of each of the two wage variables that can be captured in one index. This variance-maximization procedure suppresses the contaminating effects on one wage variable's correlation with the other. Multicollinearity ceases to be problem.

Through this maximization procedure, a coefficient becomes attached to each original variable. In the context of this study, the wage-ratio variables are the two original variables. More important, the values of the coefficients estimated for the variables used to construct this index "indicate the relative importance of each original variable in the new derived component."[23]

This means that we can compare the weights of the two wage variables when they are used to create the principal components index. Moreover, we can compare these weights with confidence that we have avoided the problems of multicollinearity. Thus, if the weight (or coefficient) for the Mexico-U.S. wage ratio were significantly larger than that of the Mexico-PACNIC wage ratio, this would suggest that the maquiladora opponents were more correct than the maquiladora advocates, and vice versa.

Table 2 provides the results of the maximizing procedure used to create the index number. The index-construction procedure has attached virtually identical weights to the two variables. These weights appear in the rows beneath the heading "eigenvector." Table 3 presents a regression equation using this forecast. The diagnostic statistics of the equation are largely similar to those of the three-variable equation, except that the level of significance on the wage variable easily rejects the null hypothesis at the 0.05 level. Thus, despite the insignificance of the original wage variables in the original three-variable equation, the coefficient of the index wage variable in the new equation is significantly different from zero.

It is interesting to note the ability of alternative models to forecast maquiladora growth out of sample. If the index model forecasted less accurately than the original, multicollinear model, the validity of the weighting scheme would be questionable. Indeed, an important reason for constructing the forecasting equations in this exercise is their usefulness as a means of establishing reliable weights.

Accordingly, I constructed two forecasting equations and used data for 1975-84 to forecast maquiladora employment in 1985, 1986 and 1987. One forecasting equation incorporates the two wage variables and the U.S. real GNP variable. A second equation incorporates the wage index with U.S. real GNP. Each of the two equations rely on data for 1975-84 to forecast maquiladora employment in 1985, 1986, and 1987.

Chart 7 depicts the forecasts of the two

Table 2

Results of Principal Components Analysis

Simple statistics	Ratio of Mexican wages to PACNIC wages	Ratio of Mexican wages to U.S. wages
Mean	−0.129	−0.092
Standard deviation	0.233	0.228
Total variance = 0.1059831		

	Principal component
Eigenvalue	0.104618
Eigenvector	
Mexico/PACNIC	0.714571
Mexico/U.S.	0.699563

SOURCES OF PRIMARY DATA: Instituto Nacional de Estadística. Geografía e Informática.
U.S. Department of Commerce.
U.S. Department of Labor.

Table 3

Results of Principal Components Regression

		Intercept	Principal component index	U.S. GNP
Coefficient		0.074	−0.218	0.665
t statistic		1.927	−2.792	0.735
Summary statistics				
R^2	0.494			
Adjusted R^2	0.367			
Durbin-Watson	2.655			

SOURCES OF PRIMARY DATA: Instituto Nacional de Estadística. Geografía e Informática.
U.S. Department of Commerce.
U.S. Department of Labor.

equations with actual maquiladora employment. Despite the few observations used to construct the equations, the graph suggests that both models forecast maquiladora growth with a high degree of accuracy. The graph also suggests that the index-based model forecasts more accurately than the original model. In this case, statistical measures of the respective forecast results demonstrate that looks are not deceiving.

Tables 4 and 5 provide forecast results and related diagnostic statistics.[24] In these results, root mean square errors (RMSE) appears as a measure of overall out-of-sample forecast accuracy. Note that the index-based model give a lower RMSE than the original three-variable equation, suggesting the usefulness of the index equation as a forecasting instrument. That is, an equation containing an index that weights the two wage variables about evenly forecasts somewhat more accurately than an equation that contains the original wage variables.

This result provides no conclusive proof that the principal components-based weighting scheme can consistently provide a highly accurate picture of the relative effects of fluctuations in each of the two wage variables upon maquiladora growth. There are too few observations to allow inquiry into the stability of the model over time. Nevertheless, the results suggest that the weighting scheme may offer more accurate forecasts than the scheme implicit in the original three-variable equation. This result implies that the principal components-based weighting scheme more accurately characterizes the true relative weights of the two arguments in the maquiladora controversy than do the weights in the original, multicollinear equation.

IMPLICATIONS OF THE ECONOMETRIC RESULTS

Maquiladora job growth is sensitive to differences between Mexican and U.S. wages, but it is about equally sensitive to differences between Mexican and PACNIC wages. Indeed, considering the emphasis that maquiladora opponents place upon maquiladoras as a sink for U.S. jobs, it is striking to see the importance of the Mexico-PACNIC connection.

Chart 7

Comparison of Actual Maquiladora Employment and the Original and Principal Components Forecast

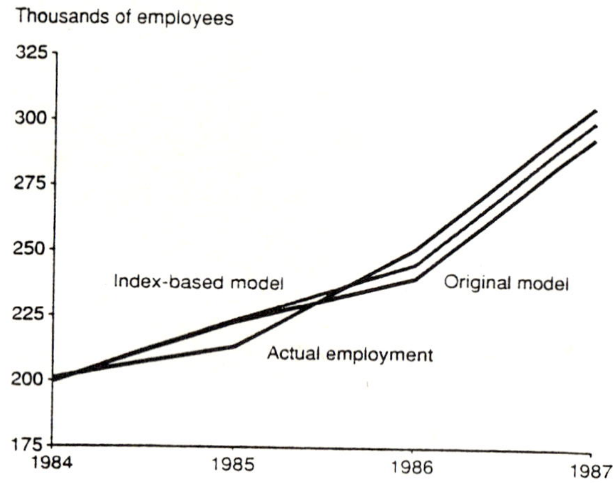

SOURCE OF PRIMARY DATA: Instituto Nacional de Estadística. Geografía e Informática.

The question that remains is, however, how stable are these results over time? The number of observations currently available for the tests are very small. Whether or not the results derived will hold for future observation periods remains to be seen, but the estimation methodology presented here at least permits other researchers to make statistical amendments and reconsiderations as additional data become available. This is an improvement over what was possible before, because the heretofore insoluble problem of multicollinearity appears to have discouraged other researchers from statistically addressing this controversy.

A second useful conclusion from the statistical exercises is that a simple two variable model can provide reasonably accurate out-of-sample forecasts of maquiladora employment. Equally striking is that this degree of forecast accuracy could be achieved despite the use of only a few observations in the estimating equation. The degree of stability of the relationships captured by the forecasting equation, however, remains to be seen. The degree of stability can be examined only through the application of additional observations.

Table 4

Forecast Results Using Original Model

	Actual values			Maquiladora employment		
	Ratio of Mexican wages to PACNIC wages	Ratio of Mexican wages to U.S. wages	U.S. GNP	Predicted	Actual	Residual
1985	0.0112	0.0742	0.0656	0.1099	0.0597	−0.0502
1986	−0.0114	−0.0209	0.0330	0.0851	0.1644	0.0792
1987	−0.3611	−0.3493	0.0281	0.1989	0.2004	0.0014
Root mean square error		0.0542				

SOURCES OF PRIMARY DATA: Instituto Nacional de Estadística, Geografía e Informática.
U.S. Department of Commerce.
U.S. Department of Labor.

Table 5

Forecast Results Using Principal Components Model

	Actual values		Maquiladora employment		
	Principal component index	U.S. GNP	Predicted	Actual	Residual
1985	0.0599	0.0656	0.1133	0.0597	−0.0536
1986	−0.0228	0.0330	0.1011	0.1644	0.0633
1987	−0.5024	0.0281	0.2034	0.2004	0.0030
Root mean square error		0.0479			

SOURCES OF PRIMARY DATA: Instituto Nacional de Estadística, Geografía e Informática.
U.S. Department of Commerce.
U.S. Department of Labor.

SUMMARY AND CONCLUSIONS

The development of the maquiladora sector is not an isolated event, but it is only one artifact of the globalization of the manufacturing industry. Advances in communications and transportation technologies precipitated the use of low-skilled, low-cost labor in Third World countries as part of an increasingly internationalized manufacturing process. A good manufactured by this process cannot really be said to have been made in any particular country. Part of the production procedure occurs in the home country while other portions take place abroad.

Two results of the globalization of manufacturing have been reduced production costs and a shift in demands for manufacturing labor away from the United States and to less-developed countries. This latter result generated controversy among U.S. labor groups, who feel that manufacturing jobs should stay in the United States, even if higher prices to U.S. consumers result.

U.S. labor groups argue that the Mexican maquiladoras take jobs that should go to U.S. workers. They claim that differentials between Mexican and U.S. wages result in a loss of U.S. jobs.

The truth appears to be more complicated than these claims suggest. The econometric results presented here suggest that maquiladora growth is about as sensitive to differentials between Mexican and PACNIC wages as it is to differentials between Mexican and U.S. wages. That is, Mexican workers compete with workers in Asia just as much as they compete with U.S. workers. This result suggests that, if all of the maquiladoras were shut down tomorrow, many maquiladora jobs would not return to the United States. Instead, many of these jobs would go to Taiwan, Hong Kong, Singapore, or Korea.

Considering the trend toward globalization of manufacturing, this result should not be surprising. Indeed, this globalization process originated in Asia, rather than Mexico. Moreover, the original program that facilitated Mexico's first maquiladoras actually came as a response to the stimulus of these Asian phenomena.

In summary, both arguments are partially correct: maquiladoras may take U.S jobs, but the jobs might go to other Third World countries if Mexico's maquiladoras did not exist.

ENDNOTES

1 A related motivation for the globalization of manufacturing activity may be the secular transformation of the nature of industrial production. As the twentieth century progresses, manufacturing output requires fewer raw materials per unit of output. With fewer raw material inputs per unit of output comes a corresponding decline in the quantity of inputs that must be shipped. Accordingly, shipping costs per unit of output fall. For a more extensive discussion of the declining quantity of raw materials per unit of output, see Drucker (1986: 768-91)

2 See Grunwald and Flamm (1985, 2-9) for detailed discussions of this phenomenon.

3 One phenomenon that motivated the international diffusion of production to areas with large supplies of low-skilled, low-cost labor is the process of deskilling. Several technological advances since the mid-1960s allow the use of low-skilled labor in productive processes that formerly used high-skilled, high-wage labor. See Wilson (1989).

4 Items 806.30 and 807.00 were derived from earlier rules. The provisions found in Item 806.30 were originally part of the Customs Simplification Act of 1954 to simplify imports of U.S.-made goods that subsequently were processed in Canada. Item 807.00 arose from an effort to codify a 1954 U.S. Customs Court decision on tariff treatment of U.S. products sent abroad, assembled into other products, and returned to the Untied States. For further discussion of the backgrounds of these items, see Schoepfle and Perez-Lopez (1988).

5 See "Factors that Influence Plant Location Decisions," chapter 5 in U.S. International Trade Commission (1988).

6 For further discussions of the relationship between maquiladora activity and the GSP, see *U.S. International Trade Commission* (1986: 54-67).

7 See U.S. International Trade Commission (1988), 8-1 [sic]

8 Although the intent of this program was to find jobs for the displaced braceros, most of the workers hired by the maquiladoras were not former braceros. Most of the braceros had been men, while the majority of workers hired by maquiladoras are women. The proportion of male workers in the maquiladoras increased over the years, but women still hold most maquiladora jobs.

9 Mexico's Secretary of Industry and Commerce introduced the Border Industrialization Program to facilitate the development of the types of U.S.-owned, labor-intensive assembly operators he had seen in East Asia. See Fernández Kelly (1987, 151).

10 See *Dallas Morning News* (1989, D-1).

11 For additional discussions on these topics and others that are dealt with in this section, see Barajas Escamilla (1988, 27-57).

12 See Grunwald, "The Assembly Industry in Mexico," in Grunwald and Flamm (1985, 137-38) for further discussion. Grunwald notes that the Mexican maquiladora industry has a somewhat different mix of products than its counterparts in Asian countries. Locating in Mexico instead of Asia allows freight-costs savings on such products. Grunwald claims that the location of relatively high transport cost production in Mexico causes Mexican output to be less sensitive to wage changes than Asian output. Whether or not this claim is correct (and Grunwald offers no evidence that it is), Mexican output is highly sensitive to wage differentials both between Mexican and PACNIC wages and between Mexican and U.S. wages.

13 See, for example, Navarette Vargas and Hernández [sic] (1988), Amozzurrutia C. (1988) and Fuentes Flores (1989).
14 For further references to these controversies and their participants, see U.S. International Trade Commission (1986, 24), and Grunwald and Flamm (1985, 14).
15 My translation of a quote that appears in Amozzurrutia C. (1988, 249).
16 The source of all wage data used in the model is U.S. Department of Labor, Bureau of Labor Statistics, Office of Productivity and Technology, Supplementary Table for "International Comparisons of Hourly Compensation Costs for Production Workers in Manufacturing," BLS Report 754 (August 1988) for 1975 and 1977-87 and BLS Report 771 (August 1989) for 1976. These data are annual and are adjusted for differences among countries in worker benefits that are not direct wage payments.
17 In initial tests, we used levels and, separately, logarithms of levels. In these tests, serial correlation was significant. Subsequently, first differences of logarithms were used, and serial correlation was shown not be significant when variables were placed in this form. All regression results displayed in tables depict modeling episodes in which first differences of logarithms were used.
18 This database is obviously very small. Unfortunately, it is the only period for which data exists that corrects for international differences in worker benefits.
19 The wage variables are lagged by one year, while the U.S. GNP variable is contemporaneous. This configuration is based on the following assumptions. First, new plants locate in Mexico in response to changes in wage differentials between that country and other nations. The location or relocation process takes time, in this case, one year. Second, existing plants respond to increases in U.S. demand by hiring more labor. They do not relocate but simply hire more workers. The limited number of observations available for the wage series does not permit much experimentation with alternative lag structures. Lagged wage ratios, however, offer considerably more explanatory power than contemporaneous wage ratios.
20 Durbin-Watson statistics for some of the equations signify degrees of serial correlation in the indeterminate range. In each of these cases, in the case of the index equation below, we constructed ARIMA (autoregressive integrated moving average) equations to characterize the relevant process of serial correlation. In every case, this procedure showed that the null hypothesis of zero intertemporal correlation of error terms could not be rejected at the 0.05 level. That is, these are white-noise processes.
21 Navarrete Vargas and Luis Hernández [*sic*] (1988, 225), my translation. Note that the Navarrete Vargas-Hernández model is quarterly and uses wage data that are not corrected for international differences in worker benefits.
22 Even when the data are transformed into first differences of logarithms, the coefficient of correlation between the two wage variables is 0.985. This is substantive evidence of serious multicollinearity. In contrast, the coefficient of correlation between the transformed versions of the Mexico-PACNIC wage ratio and the GNP variable is only 0.255. The coefficient of correlation between the transformed version of the Mexico-U.S. wage ratio and the GNP variable is 0.311. The latter two coefficients of correlation suggest that the insignificance of the GNP variable in the equations in which it appears is not the result of multicollinearity.
23 Morrison (1967, 226).
24 Note that, in Tables 4 and 5, the forecasts are presented in the form of first differences of logarithms. The forecasts were presented in this form because that is how they were actually constructed, and not as the estimated values of actual maquiladora employment. This presentation facilitates the performance of diagnostic checks. Chart 7 does depict the estimated values of maquiladora employment. In Chart 7, it is possible to see the difference between the employment forecasts and what, in fact, occurred.

REFERENCES

Amozzurrutia, C., Jesús H. (1988), "Generación de empleo por la industria maquiladora: Ciclos economicós en Estados Unidos 1978-1985," in *Maquiladoras (Primera Reunión Nacional Sobre Asuntos Fronterizos)*, ed. Arturo García Espinosa (Monterrey, Nuevo León, Mexico: Press of the Department of Communication Sciences, UANL [Free University of Nuevo León], 249-92).

Barajas Escamilla, Ma. del Rocío (1988), "Estructura y crecimiento de la industrial en México 1965-1986," in *Maquiladoras (Primera Reunión Nacional Sobre Asuntos Fronterizos)*, ed. Arturo García Espinosa (Monterrey, Nuevo León, Mexico: Press of the Department of Comuinication Sciences, UANL [Free Unviersity of Nuevo León], 27-57).

Dallas Morning News (1989), "Mexico Urged to Hike Maquiladora Buying," 7 August, D-1.

Drucker, Peter F. (1986), "The Changed World Economy," *Foreign Affairs* (Spring): 768-91.

Fernández Kelly, M. Patricia (1987), "Technology and Employment Along the U.S.-Mexican Border," in *The United States and Mexico: Face to Face with New Technology*, ed. Cathryn L. Thorup and contributors (New Brunswick, N.J., and Oxford: Transaction Books for Overseas Development Council, 149-66).

Fuentes Flores, Noé Arón (1989), "Ciclos económicos Estadunidenses y actividad maquiladora" (Paper presented at the seminar j"La Industria Maquiladora en México," Mexico City, June).

Grunwald, Joseph, and Kenneth Flamm (1985), *The Global Factory: Foreign Assembly in International Trade* (Washington, D.C., Brookings Institution).

Morrison, Donald F. (1967), *Multivariate Statistical Methods* (New York: McGraw-Hill Book Company).

Navarrete Vargas, Rodolfo, and José Luis Hernández [*sic*] (1988), "Determinantes del crecimiento del empleo en la industria maquiladora de exportación en México," in *Maquiladoras (Primera Reunión Nacional Sobre Asuntos Fronterizos)*, ed. Arturo García Espinosa (Monterrey, Nuevo León, Mexico: Press of the Department of Comuinication Sciences, UANL [Free Unviersity of Nuevo León], 221-47).

Schoepfle, Gregory K. and Jorge F. Perez-Lopez (1988), *U.S. Employment Impact of TSUS 806.30 and 807.00*

Provisions and Mexican Maquiladoras: A Survey of Issues and Estimates, Economic Discussion Paper no. 29, U.S. Department of Labor, Bureau of International Labor Affairs (Washington, D.C., August).

U.S. Department of Labor, Bureau of Labor Statistics, Office of Productivity and Technology (1988), Supplementary Tables for BLS Report 754, "International Comparisons of Hourly Compensation Costs for Production Workers in Manufacturing, 1975-87" (Washington, D.C., August).

________ (1989), Supplmentary Tables for BLS Report 771, "International Comparisons of Hourly Compensation Costs for Production Workers in Manufacturing, 1975-82" (Washington, D.C., August).

U.S. International Trade Commission (1986), *The Impact of Increased United States-Mexico Trade on Southwest Border Development*, Report to the Senate Committee on Finance on Investigation No. 332-223, Under Section 332 of the Tariff Act of 1930, USITC Publication no. 1915 (Washington, D.C. November).

________ (1988), *The Use and Economic Impact of TSUS Items 806.30 and 807.00*, Report to the Subcommittee on Trade, Committee on Ways and Means, U.S. House of Representatives, on Investigation No. 332-244 Under Section 332(b) of the Tariff Act of 1930, USITC Publication no. 2053 (Washington, D.C., January).

Wilson, Patricia A. (1989), "The New Maquiladoras: Flexible Production in Low Wage Regions," Community and Regional Planning Working Paper Series, no. 9, University of Texas, School of Architecture (Austin, April).

SECTION IV

Growth and Development

A fundamental challenge to policy-makers in the United States and the rest of the world is to achieve and sustain per-capita economic growth. In this section, the experiences of developing and industrialized countries are examined for linkages between trade policy and economic growth. Is there evidence that lower tariff and non-tariff barriers to trade stimulate growth? Under what circumstances can interventionist policies prove effective? Both articles in this section address these questions. The first article, from the *World Development Report 1991* of the World Bank, provides a broad spectrum of evidence and linkages between economic growth and trade policies. The second article, by Anne Krueger, explicitly considers the sharply contrasting experiences of a range of Asian countries.

READING 8

Integration with the Global Economy

International Bank for Reconstruction and Development

TRADE POLICY AND ECONOMIC GROWTH

When developing countries establish open trading regimes, they attract DFI for the right reason: foreign investors see opportunities to create internationally competitive businesses. But the gains from liberal trade go far beyond this. Trade restrictions distort the allocation of investment and encourage lobbying by private interests and governments. Consumers pay the costs of restrictive trade policies, while protected sectors gain. In the United States, one study estimated that the cost to consumers of restraints on imports of Japanese automobiles was between $93,000 and $250,000 for each job saved.

Dispersion in the level of protection can lead to significant distortions, even if the average level of protection is low. Buyers of inputs from protected sectors—such as automobile producers who must purchase locally made steel in Brazil, India, or Pakistan—are at a disadvantage in world markets. In the United States, manufacturers of personal computers complain that duties on components reduce their international competitiveness. But if policy makers protect final products instead and allow inputs to be imported duty-free, then the so-called effective protection for these products is often much higher than indicated by official tariff levels..

High tariffs often invite discretionary enforcement: in many countries, official levels of protection are high but actual tariff collections are low. Brazil's import-weighted statutory tariff level for the private sector was 40 percent in 1985, yet total customs revenues as a share of import volumes were only 6 percent. Exemptions (including those for public sector firms) explain a significant part of the discrepancy. In many countries such exemptions are often granted ad hoc, giving politicians a powerful tool for illicit gain.

Freer trade is even more desirable when domestic markets are dominated by only a few firms. In Pakistan, where the domestic market is too small to sustain many bicycle manufacturers, imports could spur competition to improve product quality and lower prices. Evidence on profit margins from countries as diverse as Chile, Colombia, Côte d'Ivoire, Morocco and Venezuela suggests that imports are an important source of competition. In markets that require large production volumes for efficiency, trade leads to consolidation of output and allows specialization in production. Under free trade, Venezuela would not be able to support fifteen auto assembly firms.

By affecting the nature of inputs as well as production processes, trade could generate gains which greatly exceed the short-term benefits from improved resource reallocation (Grossman and Helpman, forthcoming). Access to better-quality inputs is likely to improve productivity and accelerate output growth. Exporters and importers learn about new products and processes arising from international advances in technology. Larger markets, which provide greater returns from research efforts and increase competition, motivate producers to develop or adapt new technology Yet it is sometimes argued that monopoly profits are necessary to reward producers for investing in research and adapting imported technology to local

Box 5.2 Protection in industrial countries: a historical perspective

Centuries before the industrial revolution, countries had learned to protect domestic markets. Beginning in the thirteenth century, England enacted a series of laws that restricted the type and origin of fabrics which could be worn. Although some laws had a social objective—to identify social classes through their costumes—the basis for others was clearly economic. In addition to laws against imports of French products, the British also protected producers against countries such as India. British producers in the seventeenth century succeeded in getting a law passed which prohibited importing or wearing silk and calicoes from China, India, and Persia. Restrictions on imported calicoes provided an impetus to England's calico-printing, silk, and cotton-linen industries.

Yet a comparison of protection levels in industrial countries during the past two hundred years with those prevailing in developing countries today (Box table 5.2) shows that average levels of protection in industrial countries never reached the level of protection presently found in developing countries. In 1820, the average level of tariffs on manufactures for seven countries was 22 percent. Although industrial countries did benefit from higher natural protection before transport costs declined, the average tariff for twelve industrial countries ranged from 11 to 32 percent from 1820 to 1980. For example, in Japan low tariffs were mandated through foreign treaties until 1899. Once these restraints were removed, rates seldom rose above 10-15 percent until 1911. Even after 1911, the overall level of tariffs never exceeded 20 percent. In contrast, the average tariff on manufactures in developing countries is 34 percent (Table 5.3).

Box table 5.2 Tariff rates in industrial countries, 1820–1987
(unweighted average percentages)

Kind of goods and country or region	*1820*	*1875*	*1913*	*1925*	*1930*[a]	*1950*	*1987*
Manufactures							
Austria	. .	15-20	18	16	24	18	9
Belgium	7	9-10	9	15	14	11	7
Denmark	30	15-20	14	10	. .	3	. .
France	. .	12-15	20	21	30	18	7
Germany	10	4-6	13	20	21	26	7
Italy	. .	8-10	18	22	46	25	7
Netherlands	7	3-5	4	6	. .	11	7
Spain	. .	15-20	41	41	63	. .	. .
Sweden	. .	3-5	20	16	21	9	5
Switzerland	10	4-6	9	14	19	. .	3
United Kingdom	50	0	. .	5	. .	23	7
United States	40	40-50	25	37	48	14	7
Average	22	11-14	17	19	32	16	7
All goods							
Australia	. .	. .	16	18	14	17	. .
Canada	. .	14	17	14	13	9	6
Japan •	. .	4	20	13	19	4	8
United States	45[b]	41	40	38	45	13	6
Average	. .	6	23	21	23	11	7

a. For manufactures, the average is for 1931 instead of 1930.
b. Data are for 1821 instead of 1820.
Sources: For 1820 and 1875 (average tariff on duties), Bairoch 1976. For 1987, GATT data reported in Kelly and others 1988. For other years: for the United States (ratio of customs revenues to dutiable imports), U.S. Department of Commerce 1975; for Japan (ratio of customs revenues to dutiable imports), Ohkawa, Shinohara, and Umemura 1979; for Canada and Australia (ratio of customs revenues to dutiable imports), Mitchell 1983; for 1913 and 1925 (average statutory tariffs), League of Nations 1927.

conditions. If domestic investors cannot fully appropriate the gains from innovation or adaptation, they will underinvest in technology. In industry, however, many efforts to apply and diffuse knowledge require in-house technical expertise and may therefore by fully captured by the firm. What does the historical evidence suggest about the relation between protectionist systems and technological change? The answer seems to be that openness has generally promoted faster growth.

The Evidence on Trade

As industrial countries developed, they relied less on protection than do most countries developing today. Since the beginning of the nineteenth century, tariffs in industrial countries have averaged less than 25 percent (Box 5.2). In 1987, the average tariff in developing countries was more than 30 percent, and that was after a decade of extensive reforms (UNCTAD 1987). Tariff protection in South Asia is more than twice as great as the historical average for industrial countries.

Industrial countries rarely used nontariff measures during industrialization, although lately this has been changing—witness the increase in voluntary export agreements for autos and steel and the Multifibre Arrangement (MFA) for textiles. Yet for a sample of eighty-two developing countries, nontariff barriers were applied to 28 percent of all imports in 1987 (Table 5.3). Overall, the evidence suggests that the industrial countries grew with somewhat lower tariffs and substantially fewer nontariff barriers than those employed today by developing countries.

Studies which measure the short-term (static) gains from moving to freer trade find that the gains vary from less than 1 percent to as high as 6 percent of GDP. The gains are larger still if domestic markets are dominated by only a few producers, or if there are economies of scale in production. These studies, however, only measure changes at one point in time; they are not designed to analyze the potential linkages between trade policies and long-term growth.

Most of the studies which have analyzed GDP growth and openness to trade have found a positive relation (Box 5.3). Figure 5.2 also shows that there is a positive association between productivity growth and trade and exchange rate policy, using seven different measures of openness. The accumulated evidence suggests that the long-run gains from increased competition and the spillover of technology are likely to be much greater than the short-term gains.

Yet a degree of skepticism is warranted for two reasons. First, most studies examine the relation between economic growth and trade volumes, not policies; this is partly because measuring "policy" poses difficult questions. Some East Asian economies have achieved high shares of trade in GNP with trade policy intervention. Nevertheless, more recent studies have tried to identify the effect of trade policies in their own right, using information on tariffs, quotas, and relative prices. These still show a positive relation between openness and growth.

Second, interpreting the observed correlation between trade policies and growth is difficult. Policies that are not directly concerned with trade (macroeconomic policy, measures to promote domestic competition, and so on) may be responsible both for superior export performance and for high GDP growth. Moreover, it is difficult to establish the direction of causality between trade policies and growth.

Table 5.3 Tariffs and nontariff barriers in developing countries, 1987

	Manufactures		*All goods*	
Region	*Tariffs*	*NTBs*	*Tariffs*	*NTBs*
East Asia	22	20	21	22
South Asia	81	47	77	48
Europe, Middle East and North Africa	26	31	24	32
Africa	30	30	33	30
Latin America and the Caribbean	34	20	33	21
Average	34	27	32	28

Note: NTBs, nontariff barriers. Data are unweighted tariff averages.
Source: UNCTAD 1987, based on eighty-two individual country sources. For Republic of Korea, World Bank estimates.

Intervention and Growth

The evidence supports two broad conclusions. First, there is a general statistical association between less intervention and lower price distortions on the one hand and higher productivity growth on the other. Second, there is considerable variation in country experience—hence the dispersion of points around the general trends in Figure 5.2. In part, this is because openness is only one factor which explains productivity growth; this Report also documents the importance of establishing macroeconomic stability, providing social services, and fostering a productive climate for enterprises.

Box 5.3 Trade policy and growth: the evidence

In this chapter, openness means access not only to goods, but also to services, technology, foreign investment, and capital flows. Neutrality in trade policy means that incentives are neutral between saving a unit of foreign exchange through import substitution and earning a unit of foreign exchange through exports. Price comparisons between goods sold in domestic and international markets provide one measure of neutrality. If domestic markets are competitive, price comparisons incorporate the effect of the trade and exchange rate policies that affect domestic prices: tariffs, quotas, different exchange rates for imports and exports, and subsidies. But information on relative prices is often unavailable, so many other proxies are used instead (for examples, see Barro, forthcoming).

The simplest measures of trade orientation are based on actual trade flows, such as imports plus exports as a share of GDP. (For an overview of the literature on openness and growth, see the background papers by Dollar, Harrison, and Jen.) Most of these measures show a positive association with GDP growth, even after controlling for other factors. Unfortunately, they are at best an imperfect proxy for *trade policy*. Other factors, such as country size or foreign capital inflows, also affect trade: for example, large countries tend to have smaller trade shares. One improvement over this approach is to use the deviation of actual from predicted trade flows, based on variables such as country size (Balassa 1985; Syrquin and Chenery 1989).

The use of administrative data, which include tariffs and nontariff barriers, are difficult to aggregate into an overall index. Coverage ratios for nontariff barriers cause the greatest difficulty. Because the coverage ratio indicates the percentage of imports covered by trade barriers, an extremely effective barrier that excludes almost all imports in one category would receive little weight. Most studies based on these direct measures of policy find a positive relation between trade and growth (for example, Heitger 1986).

Microeconomic studies also have generally shown a positive association between increased exports and productivity growth. However, the relation between imports and productivity growth is sometimes positive and sometimes negative. (For the work summarized in the last two sentences, see both Nishimizu and Page 1990 and Tybout 1991.) Empirical work has been unable to distinguish between the expected positive effect of imports on productivity growth in the long run and the fact that imports are initially drawn to sectors with low productivity in which a country does not have an international advantage.

Another difficulty in measuring the effect of trade policies on growth is that trade policy itself may be a function of other variables, including growth. Studies that have tried to identify the causal relation between GDP growth and growth in exports or imports have had mixed results (for example, Hsiao 1987; Jung and Marshall 1985).

The majority of the evidence now available shows a positive relation between openness—however measured—and growth. Yet the difficulties in isolating the impact of trade *policies* per se and establishing causality suggest that the debate is not fully resolved. More effort needs to be devoted to gathering detailed data on quotas and tariffs for developing countries.

Yet it is also true that such countries as Korea achieved high rates of export growth in conjunction with selective protection. Why is intervention more risky on average? Why are there exceptions?

From a purely practical point of view, government intervention in trade is risky for several reasons. Countries often underestimate how difficult it can be to offset trade-induced distortions. A duty drawback scheme to reimburse exporters for tariffs paid on inputs is a second-best measure to attack distortions caused by protection. To ensure that incentives to produce for domestic and export markets are truly equal, exporters must also be compensated for any tariffs on their products (which shift incentives toward producing for the domestic market) and the exchange rate overvaluation that arises with protection. One study of Latin American countries found that export subsidies offset only a small fraction of the anti-export bias arising from tariffs and distorted exchange rates. In addition, countries which provide export subsidies become vulnerable to countervailing duties (imposed mainly by the United States) if they have signed the GATT subsidies agreement.

In many countries, the costs of failures in implementation have exceeded gains there might

Figure 5.2 Openness and growth in productivity: partial correlations for developing countries, 1960-88
(percent)

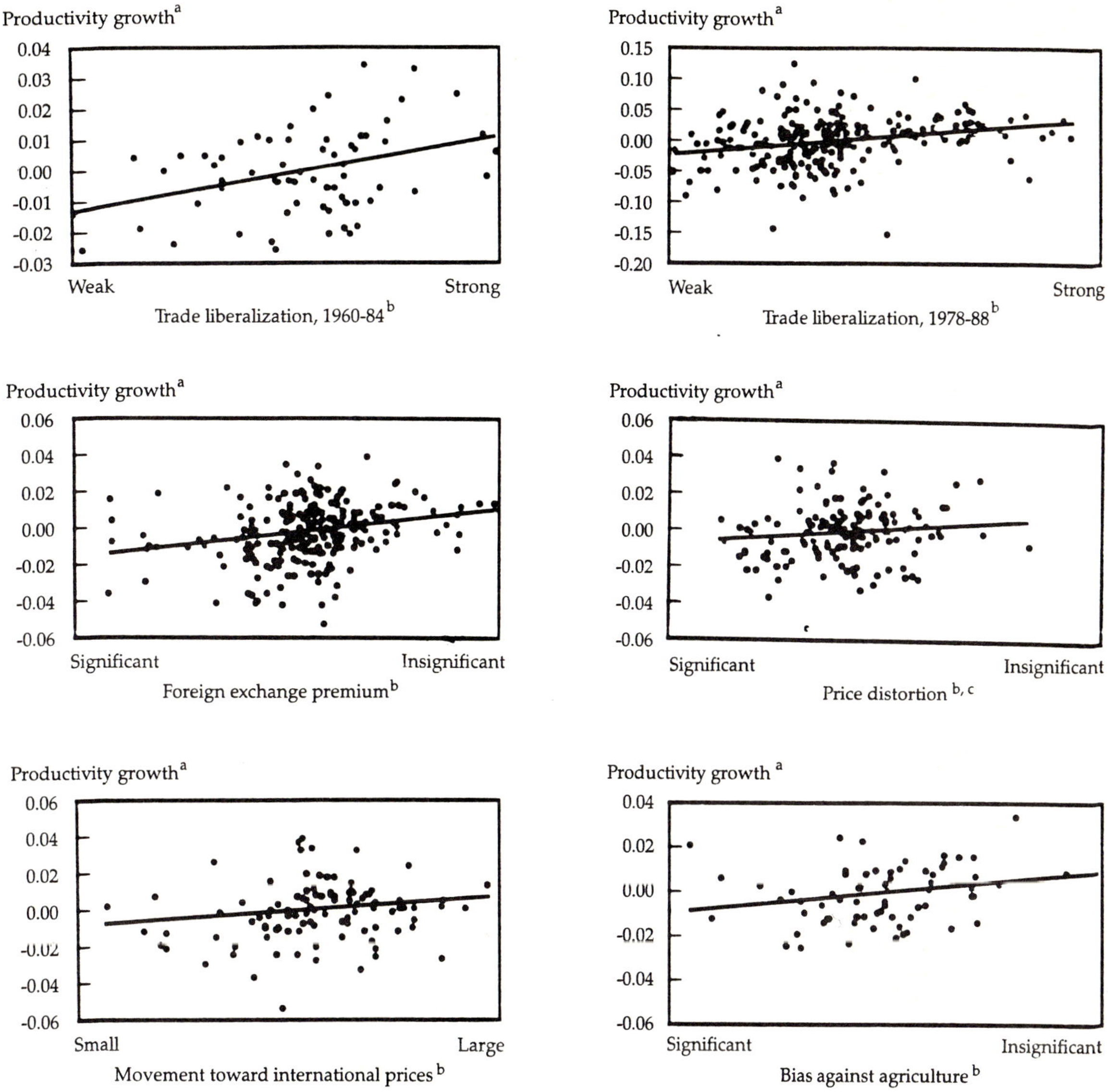

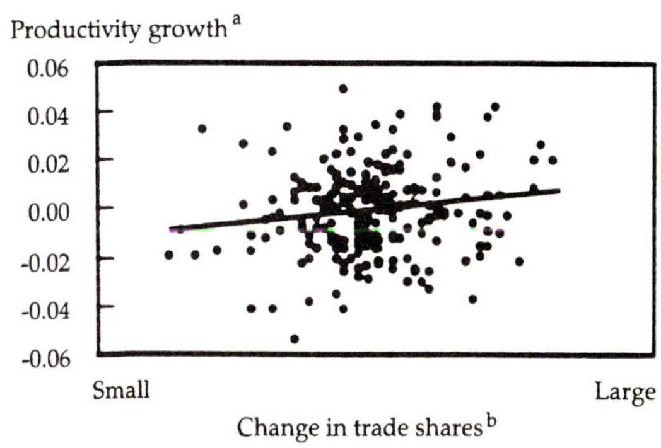

Note: The measures of trade liberalization, foreign exchange premium, price distortion, and change in trade shares are significant at the 5 percent level in a regression of GDP growth on openness, input growth (capital, labor, education, and land), and dummy country variables. The measure of bias against agriculture is significant at the 10 percent level. Data are averages for 1960-66, 1967-73, 1974-81, and 1982-88, except for the trade liberalization index for 1978-88, which uses annual data because of the shortened period. The number of countries sampled ranges from sixty to eighteen.

a. Unexplained residual of GDP growth, after controlling for input growth and country effects.

b. This represents a proxy for trade and exchange rate policy, after controlling for input growth and country effects.

c. The relative price of consumer goods is purged of its nontraded component by taking the residual from a regression of this price index on urbanization, land, and population. See also Dollar, forthcoming.

Source: See the technical note at the end of the main text.

Box 5.4 Should states intervene in trade or shouldn't they?

Arguments for intervention

- Selective state intervention has figured prominently in two of the impressive success stories of development: Japan and the Republic of Korea. Both countries employed taxes and subsidies, directed credit, restrictions on firm entry and exit, and trade protection to encourage domestic industry. In other countries, including resource-rich Canada, Malaysia, and Botswana, moderate intervention supported diversification of the export base and helped new industries get established (Lewis 1988). In Canada, moderate tariffs (10–30 percent) protected industry into the early twentieth century. The government did not use quotas or exchange controls, however, nor attempt to prevent the decline of uneconomic industries. In 1988, manufactures exceeded 50 percent of total exports. Malaysia has also employed modest tariff protection, but it has used exchange controls and import sparingly. Manufactures rose from 6 percent of exports in 1965 to 46 percent in 1988. In Botswana, which has one of the highest GDP growth rates in the world for the postwar period, the value of manufactured exports surpassed that of beef exports in the mid-1980s. At independence beef products had provided almost all of Botswana's export earnings. Although skillful management of the mining sector has been critical to success, modest use of import restrictions promoted both manufactured and horticultural production, with protection conditional on production at import-equivalent prices.
- A long-term decline in the terms of trade for nonfuel commodities, combined with more inelastic demand for some of these products, suggests that countries could well boost export earnings by diversifying into manufactures. In the past, government intervention was sometimes necessary because producers lacked the information or expertise needed to enter industrial production (for example, Brazil, Korea, and Turkey).
- A wide range of market failures, from lack of information to incomplete capital markets, could justify an industrial policy. High rates of return on innovation in agriculture and industry suggest that private agents may be underinvesting in research and development. For industry, less evidence is available, but several studies on industrial development of computers and computerized axial tomography scanners in the United States suggest that consumer benefits from innovations have greatly exceeded research costs. An often-mentioned failure concerns industrywide learning by doing. In principle, governments could use subsidies instead of protection to encourage domestic producers to learn by doing or enter markets with high setup costs. In practice, protection has been a more popular tool because it is more practical administratively and financially.
- A recent argument for trade intervention calls for using trade policy as a strategic tool to give domestic firms an edge in global markets (Helpman and Krugman 1989; Brander and Spencer 1985). When large oligopolies compete in world markets, governments might want to subsidize national firms to shift oligopoly profits to them. Similarly, a government could try to subsidize the entry of national firms into global markets with scale economies that preclude more than a few players.

Arguments against intervention

- The high costs of intervention in trade policy have been documented by a number of studies (Balassa and Associates 1971; Bhagwati 1978). Even in the Republic of Korea, some prominent import-substituting projects were costly failures. The "Big Push" to develop heavy industry in 1973–79 contributed to real appreciation of the exchange rate, loss of competitiveness, and distortions in financial markets (Collins 1990). GNP growth in Korea fell to −4.8 percent in 1980. It turned around again to 6 percent in 1981–82 following devaluation, liberalization of price and import controls, and tax reform. Where interventions have been successful, the evidence suggests that countries do better if the interventions result in neutral incentives. Success also depends on a time limit for the interventions. But most countries do not have the administrative capacity to collect all the information needed to ensure that inter-

have been from correcting market failures. In Argentina and Côte d'Ivoire, efforts to distribute export credits to offset trade and exchange rate distortions were short-lived. Subsidies create financing problems and are often allocated to favored groups or sectors. In Costa Rica, subsidies for nontraditional exports were 5 percent of total central government expenditures in 1990; 80 percent of these subsidies were received by fewer than 20 firms. Korea, which tied credits and subsidies to ventions result in neutral incentives. And protected sectors may continue to lobby for protection of infant industries long after they mature. Europe and Japan provide examples from the industrial countries of the difficulty of trying to dismantle protection of agriculture.

• Efforts to encourage diversification out of commodities and into industry have often resulted in high levels of protection for manufacturing sectors. In the process, many countries undermined their agricultural base and created industrial sectors that depended on indefinite protection for survival (for example, Argentina, Egypt, and India).

• In practice, trade policy is generally not a desirable instrument for encouraging domestic industry. Although protection may encourage learning by doing—by promoting production—and draw more workers to the protected sector, relative prices become distorted in favor of production for domestic markets. To offset the anti-export bias, additional measures are necessary, often resulting in a labyrinth of interventions.

• The case for strategic subsidies to help national firms in developing countries compete on world markets is weak (Bhagwati 1989). Apart from a few isolated cases—such as the Brazilian aircraft industry—producers are more likely to have oligopoly power in home than in global markets. That makes protection even more costly than in the perfectly competitive case. If other countries retaliate by subsidizing their national firms, everyone may be worse off. Studies of the gains from promoting entry by domestic firms into world markets have shown the gains to be small or nonexistent (Grossman 1989). A study of the Brazilian aircraft industry found no welfare gains from subsidizing exports, in part because other countries also subsidized entry (Baldwin and Flam 1989). A study of the global rivalry between a large U.S. airplane manufacturer and a large European one estimated that government subsidies imposed a considerable welfare cost on the United States and brought little (if any) welfare gain to Europe (Baldwin and Krugman 1987).

successful export performance, also made mistakes: the drive to establish heavy industry through widespread subsidies in the 1970s was at best only a partial success. Often, policies designed as short-term measures to give domestic industries a chance to grow or restructure are never dismantled. The main arguments for and against intervention are reviewed in Box 5.4.

What distinguishes the countries which intervened in trade and yet were also able to grow rapidly? First, the successful interventionists preserved incentives for technological change by maintaining international and domestic competition and imposing performance requirements in return for any credit subsidies, import protection, or restriction on domestic entry. In Japan and Korea, subsidies and protection were strictly tied to achieving export success within a defined period. Companies which did not perform well were allowed to fold. In the Japanese synthetic fiber industry, MITI helped firms obtain licenses from several different national sources to ensure new entry - which resulted in excess capacity and ruthless competition.

Successful intervention has also been tempered by a flexible, highly pragmatic approach. The ability to terminate special treatment when intervention fails is critical. In 1980, Korea quickly reversed its 1970s policies of broad support—through protection and subsidies—for the development of heavy industry. In contrast, many industrializing countries have continued to subsidize ailing public sector firms and have restricted exit by poor performers.

Second, their intervention was moderate in the sense that it did not lead to large price distortions. Botswana, Canada, and Malaysia used relatively low tariffs and avoided nonprice measures such as quotas to diversify production. Measures of effective protection for Korea suggest that relative prices never became significantly distorted in favor of production for the domestic market (Westphal 1990). In part, price distortions were minimized in some of the East Asian economies because of their orientation toward global markets. Their commitment to world markets provided an external check on interventionist policies—guiding policy on exchange rates, protection, and subsidies.

In practice, few economies have successfully used infant industry protection to create viable, internationally competitive industries. The cost of government failures has been shouldered most often by the agricultural sector and by the consumers who pay higher prices for low-quality products. If governments do intervene, the guiding principles should be (a) to impose competition by fostering outward orientation and domestic competition, (b) to

Figure 5.3 The share of imports affected by all nontariff measures, 1966 and 1986

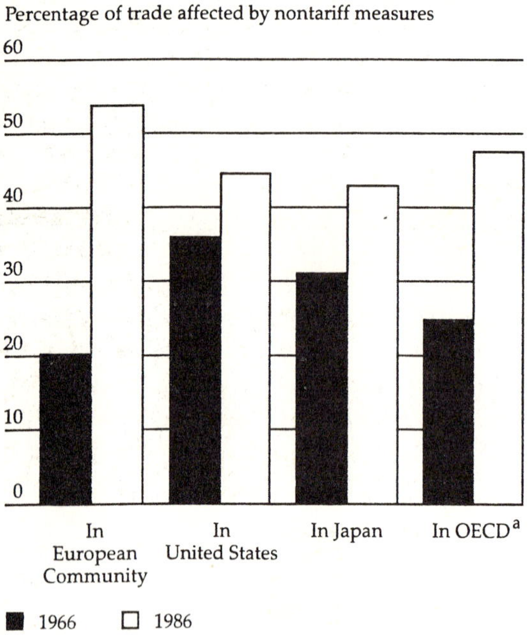

a. Excludes data for Australia, Austria, Canada, Iceland, New Zealand, and Sweden.
Sources: Laird and Yeats 1990b; Walter 1972.

intervene at the source of the distortion (for example, to subsidize education rather than use protection when the problem is lack of human capital), and (c) to intervene only through nondiscretionary, time-bound policies that do not encourage rent-seeking. Economies which do choose to use trade protection should use low tariffs instead of nontariff barriers such as quotas or price controls.

CONDITIONS FOR SUCCESS IN TRADE REFORM

In recent years a growing number of developing countries have embarked on programs of trade policy reform. Where these programs have been maintained, they have generally succeeded—that is, both trade and overall output appear to have expanded as a result. But in many cases programs have been only partly maintained, and often they have collapsed altogether. How far can countries and the international community (which also has a stake in these reforms) improve the chances that trade liberalization will succeed?

One study of thirty-six trade reforms in nineteen countries between 1945 and 1984 found that only fifteen of the reforms were fully sustained, nine were partially sustained, and twelve collapsed (Papageorgiou, Michaely, and Choksi 1990). A study of trade reforms which accompanied World Bank loans in the 1980s found that many countries realigned their exchange rates and offset biases against exporters, and converted quotas to tariffs. Only a few of the countries examined, however, reduced their tariffs substantially. Evidence suggests the merits of phasing out quantitative restrictions rapidly, and reducing tariffs to reasonably low and uniform levels, such as a range of 15-25 percent. Experience supports a substantial and comprehensive reform within, say, five years, with major and decisive actions in the first year.

Despite these difficulties in implementing reform and sustaining it once introduced, liberalizing countries outperformed the others. A study of developing countries in the 1980s found that, holding other factors, countries that implemented trade reforms experienced a higher annual increase in GDP growth (Thomas and Nash, forthcoming). Growth rates for reforming countries were higher even when other effects were taken into account, including external financing, changes in terms of trade, movements in the real exchange rate, and faster growth in the OECD countries.

Microeconomic Aspects

Successful reforms have usually reduced the coverage of quantitative restrictions and the level and dispersion of tariffs. Quantitative restrictions may be phased out in various ways. Where product quotas are used, the quota ceiling can be gradually raised until the quota becomes redundant, a method used by Australia, the EC, and New Zealand. Where import licenses are used, licensing can be phased out by reducing the number of products to which licenses apply, making the licenses transferable, and shifting to "negative lists," which permit unrestricted imports of all products not listed.

Tariffs may be reduced either by making equally proportional cuts in all tariffs or by reducing the top rate to a target level, which is gradually lowered. A nonuniform tariff structure may in principle generate more revenue, with higher tariffs on goods with the most inflexible demand. Designing such a system, however, requires massive amounts of information and could also adversely affect income distribution. Equally important, nonuniform tariffs are subject to lobbying pressures, raise administrative difficulties, and introduce the perception of inequity. Next to a no-tariff system, the best practical policy is to establish a relatively low uniform tariff structure and a duty-drawback program for exporters.

Reforms to promote a more competitive domestic economy (discussed in Chapter 4) are crucial. Restrictions on market entry or exit, price and production controls, or regulations that reduce competition in the nontradables sector may dampen the expected supply response to trade reforms. In Mexico, entry barriers made it difficult for firms to respond to the new incentives. Until recently, regulations in the transport sector steeply increased the cost of shipping products to ports or the U.S. border. Regulations inhibiting exit by insolvent companies (such as bankruptcy laws and institutional or political constraints) also prevent improvements in the structure of production under trade reforms. Restrictions on exit partly explain the failure of earlier trade liberalization attempts in Poland and Yugoslavia. Such cases confirm one of the main themes of this Report: success in one aspect of reform requires complementary efforts in others.

Figure 5.4 Hard-core nontariff measures applied against industrial and developing countries, 1986

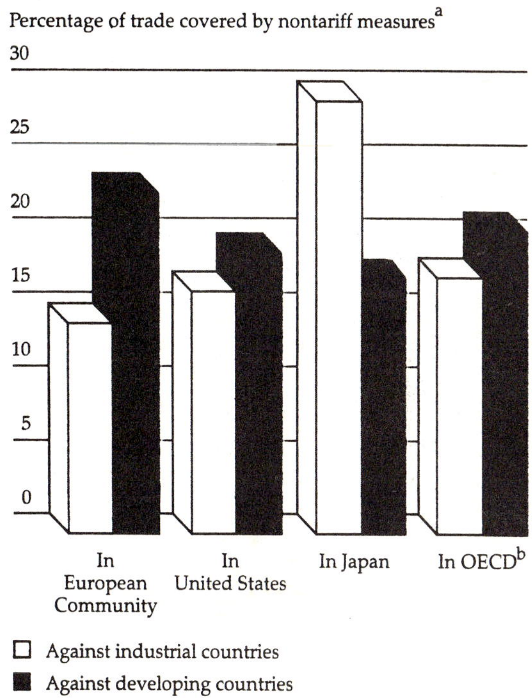

a. Calculated using 1981 trade weights. Hard-core nontariff measures include quotas, voluntary export restraints, the Multifibre Arrangement, and other highly restrictive measures.
b. Excludes data for Australia, Austria, Canada, Iceland, New Zealand, and Sweden.
Source: Laird and Yeats 1990a.

The Macroeconomic Context

This point applies to macroeconomic policy with equal, if not greater, force. Large fiscal deficits and money financing of those deficits worsen the external balance and generate inflation, frequently leading to losses in reserves. If the nominal exchange rate is not allowed to adjust, foreign exchange shortages often oblige the government to return to licensing, higher protection, and trade restrictions.

Although tariffs are a much more distortionary means of raising revenue than sales taxes or value added taxes, administrative weaknesses in many countries lead them to rely heavily on trade taxes as a revenue source.

The effect of liberalization on revenues depends on the mix of policies. Governments need to assess the potential revenue effect of reforms. A switching from quantitative restrictions to tariffs can be undertaken under almost any fiscal situation. Tariff reductions, however, need to be accompanied by measures to convert remaining quotas to tariffs, together with a reduction in tariff exemptions. Declines in tariff revenue—if expenditures cannot be reduced—may need to be compensated for with

Box 5.5 Commodity price movements

Can a country still benefit from trade if a large share of its exports is primary products? In the 1950s, Raoul Prebisch and Hans Singer suggested that the gains from trade for developing countries would decline as the price of commodity exports relative to manufactures imports fell. The Prebisch-Singer hypothesis provided a rationale for import-substituting industrialization. The evidence is not persuasive.

Between 1900 and 1986, nonfuel commodity terms of trade declined by an average of 0.6 percent a year (Box figure 5.5a). If we choose a different period, however, the decline is much smaller. Between 1920 and 1986, the terms of trade fell less than 0.3 percent a year. In addition, these figures are likely to overstate the decline because they ignore improvements in the quality of manufactured goods.

Many developing countries have diversified their exports: the share of manufacturing in the nonfuel exports of developing countries increased from 15 percent in 1963 to 62 percent in 1987 (Balassa, background paper). In addition, small exporters of commodities such as coffee or cocoa have probably benefited from improved terms of trade as grain import prices have declined. Consequently, the terms of trade for developing countries have probably fallen by much less than the nonfuel commodity decline.

Nor do changing prices take into account offsetting increases in trade volumes. Despite significant declines in the relative price of nonfuel commodities since 1973, revenues from commodities have stayed relatively constant in relation to those from manufactures. Export volumes from developing countries over this period nearly doubled, offsetting the declining terms of trade (Box figure 5.5b). Because of differences in domestic policy, some countries did much less well than others: nonfuel commodity export revenues fell 50 percent in South Asia and increased by about the same amount in East Asia.

Box figure 5.5a Nonfuel primary commodities versus manufactures: relative price index, 1900-90

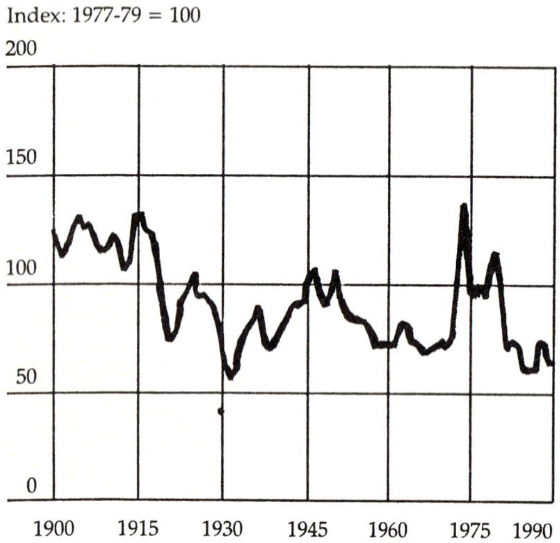

Note: The manufactures price index used is the U.S. wholesale price index.
Sources: World Bank data; Grilli and Yang 1988.

Box figure 5.5b Trends in exports and the terms of trade of developing countries, 1965-88

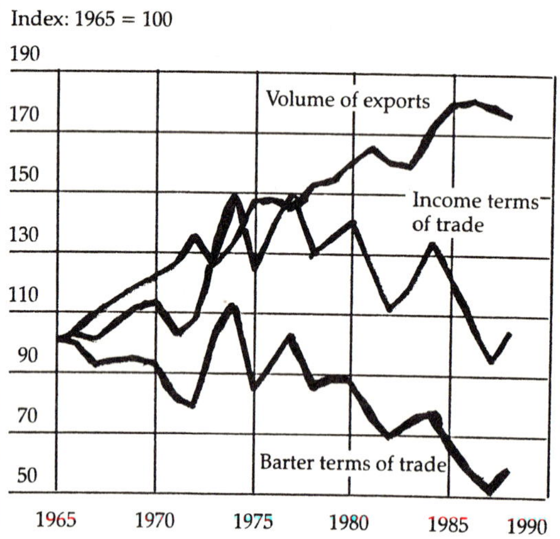

Note: Barter terms of trade are the weighted export unit values of primary commodities deflated by the weighted import unit values of each region. The barter terms of trade multipled by the actual volume of exports yields the income terms of trade. Data are based on a sample of ninety developing countries.
Source: World Bank data.

other measures. Reformers have improved tax administration and collection (in Ghana, Pakistan, and Thailand); increased rates and coverage of sales and excise taxes (in Malawi, Mauritius, Mexico and the Philippines); introduced a value added tax (in Jamaica, Morocco, and Turkey); or increased the price of public sector output and services.

The timing of compensatory revenue measures is of critical importance. Although trade reform in both Mexico and Morocco led to a decline in trade tax revenues, Mexico cushioned the loss through higher revenues from a value added tax instituted before the reform. Morocco, however, rolled back some of its tariff reforms initiated in 1984 when implementation difficulties with its new value added tax and the collapse of world phosphate prices added to its revenue problems.

A World Bank study of nineteen trade-reforming countries found that appreciation of the real exchange rate was often associated with the collapse of a reform episode. Trying to implement trade reforms when the exchange rate is grossly overvalued will make balance of payments problems worse and is likely to sabotage the reform effort. As controls on imports are relaxed, a real depreciation will increase the prices of tradeables, making export production more attractive and temporarily dampening the impact of competition for producers of import-competing goods. (The role of macroeconomic policy in development is discussed in detail in Chapter 6.)

Political-Economy Considerations

Even the best-conceived trade reform may fail because of problems which are not purely economic. Those who stand to lose from a trade reform are generally more organized and politically powerful than those who stand to gain, such as consumers at large or rural agricultural interests. Reform also threatens vested interests within government, from protected state enterprises to trade regulators who derive rents from the status quo to politicians who seek to cultivate support. Getting the pace and sequencing of reform right can help to overcome such difficulties. (Chapter 7 returns to these issues in th e art of reform.)

THE GLOBAL CLIMATE FOR TRADE

Industrial-Country Protection

Trade reform in developing countries is much more likely to go ahead if success in trade is not punished. During the past several decades, average tariffs in industrial countries have been reduced to less than 6 percent. But the use of other protective measures such as quotas, subsidies, voluntary export restraints, and countervailing and anti-dumping measures, has risen alarmingly since the 1960s. Increased protection is largely the result of greater

Table 5.4 Intraunion trade as a percentage of total exports, 1960–87

Economic union	*1960*	*1970*	*1976*	*1980*	*1983*	*1987*
European Community[a]	34.6	48.9	..	52.8	52.4	58.8
Association of South-East Pacific States	21.7	14.7	13.9	17.8	23.1	17.7
Central African Customs and Economic Union	1.6	3.4	3.9	4.1	2.0	0.9
Central American Common Market	7.5	26.8	21.6	22.0	21.8	11.9
Caribbean Community	4.5	7.3	6.7	6.4	9.3	6.3
LAIA-Latin American Free Trade Area	7.7	10.2	12.8	13.5	10.2	11.3
Andean Group	0.7	2.3	4.2	3.5	4.3	3.2
West African Economic Community	2.0	9.1	6.7	6.9	11.6	7.7
Economic Community of West African States	1.2	2.1	3.1	3.9	4.1	5.5
Economic Community of the Great Lake Countries	0.0	0.2	0.2	0.2	0.2	..
Mano River Union	0.0	0.1	0.2	0.1	0.1	..
Regional Cooperation for Development	..	1.0	0.8	5.3	8.5	5.2

a. Includes the original six members up to 1970 and nine after 1980.
Source: Lächler 1989.

competition on world markets, exacerbated by the inability of the GATT to control nontariff barriers. Between 1966 and 1986, the share of imports affected by all nontariff measures increased by more than 20 percent for the United States, almost 40 percent for Japan, and 160 percent for the EC (Figure 5.3). By 1986, 21 percent of imports from developing countries to the OECD were covered by so-called hard-core nontariff barriers: quotas, voluntary export restraints, the MFA, and otherhighly restrictive measures (Figure 5.4). This number does not even include other restrictions such as price restraints or health and safety regulations. If these measures were included, the share of trade covered by nontariff barriers in industrial countries could be equal to the 28 percent of trade covered by all nontariff measures in developing countries in 1987.

Subsidies to agriculture increased by 80 percent in the United States, by 60 percent in Canada, and by 21 percent in Japan between 1980 and 1985, while the number of countervailing and anti-dumping cases filed by Australia, Canada, the EC, and the United States more than doubled. New evidence suggests that anti-dumping and subsidy investigations are being used as a threat against foreign imports, even when the countervailing and anti-dumping duties are not applied. Since the mid-1980s, industrial countries have done almost nothing to roll back the accumulated protection. The increasing use of such measures by industrial countries during the past 30 years provides a disturbing precedent for retaliatory action and for the enactment of similar measures by developing countries.

Laird and Yeats (1987) estimated that the cost (in 1990 dollars) to developing economies in terms of foregone exports was $55 billion in 1980—almost equal to the value of total official development assistance in that year. Action by developing economies to reform their trade policies must be met by equal efforts to reduce protection in the industrial world. But developing economies should not slow their own reform efforts simply because of rising protection in industrial ones. The four East Asian NIEs were able to increase their share in total world trade and manufactured exports more than eightfold between 1965 and 1989, despite rising protection in industrial countries. The scope for increased trade in manufacturers for the rest of the industrializing economies remains significant; they accounted for only 5 percent of manufactured exports in 1988. Can they too continue to benefit from trading opportunities despite declining terms of trade for commodities?

Commodity Price Movements

The evidence in Box 5.5 shows a relatively small decline in primary commodity prices in relation to manufacturers during the course of this century. Nevertheless, falling primary commodity prices since the 1970s and volatility in these markets pose serious problems for low-income primary producers. The solution is not an easy one. If countries produce a large share of world exports (such as coffee or cocoa) or if increasing export volumes from some groups of exporters depress prices, a case could be made for controlling production through export taxes. In practice, however, attempts to stabilize international or domestic producer prices have not met with much success. In many cases, the implicit tax on agriculture is too high because of a combination of export taxes and the protection of manufacturing. Although new financial instruments designed to hedge commodity price risk hold promise, their use has been limited because many poor countries pose an unacceptable credit risk for commercial financing.

Yet both developing and industrial countries have recourse to policies which can make a significant difference (see also Box 54.4). In some low- and middle-income countries during the 1970s, inappropriate policies led to losses in market share and greater dependence on a few primary commodity exports. Industrial countries, which impose greater protection for goods at a higher stage of processing, discourage the development of local processing capacity for industrializing countries.

Regional Trading Blocs

The unification of Europe in 1992, the United States-Canada free trade agreement in 1989, and the proposed inclusion of Mexico in the United States-Canada agreement could herald a new era of regional trading blocs. Although such blocs may constitute a step toward global free trade, it remains to be seen whether they will support or hinder the goal of a more open global trading system.

In principle, the formation of a trading bloc leads to net gains for its members when goods which were domestically produced are not imported from lower-cost partners. Other potential sources of gain include economies of scale and increased competition from larger markets, particularly in countries with emerging infant industries and low domestic demand. Yet a trading bloc may also lead to losses if members replace lower-priced goods from outside the bloc with more expensive goods produced by other members. Even if a regional trading bloc can be designed to generate net gains for its members, these gains are exceeded by the benefits from unilateral trade reform.

What about primary product exporters? The evidence presented in Box 5.5 shows that primary product exporters also stand to gain from rising exports.

The historical evidence (Table 5.4) suggests that regional blocs in all but the EC have not generated a large share of total trade in the post-World War II period. Why? In a number of cases (CARICOM and the Central American Common Market in Central America; UDEAC in Africa) intraregional conflicts have made it difficult to liberate internal trade. In many blocs, such as the Andean Pact, participants sought to rationalize production by allocating specific markets to designated producers instead of allowing the competitive process to determine the allocation of production. These designated producers were not necessarily the most efficient; nor were tariffs low enough in relation to the rest of the world to provide external competition. Consequently, the expected benefits from rationalization of production or increased competition have been limited. Developing-country trading blocs have often imposed high tariffs or quotas against nonmembers, increasing the likelihood that net losses from the bloc will exceed gains. In addition, except in the EC, trading opportunities and pro-competitive effects have been limited by the small size of regional markets in comparison with the rest of the world. Finally, regional trading blocs have frequently produced similar products, limiting the opportunity to exploit differences in skills or endowments.

Do trading agreements between industrial and developing countries show more promise? Larger markets and greater differences in the structure of production could in principle generate greater gains for the participants. But such a strategy could also undermine the GATT and the multilateral trade system, and thus reduce the incentives of partners within such blocs to move toward global free trade. Other countries, reacting to the formation of such blocs, may set up their own network of trading blocs. Such a system is likely to reinforce current protectionist trends, and it could be a blow to developing countries' efforts to reform trade.

Unilateral trade liberalization and multilateral efforts to free up global trade are preferable to the formation of trading blocs; however, steps can be taken to maximize the gains from such unions. First, members should commit themselves to multilateral reform and the GATT. The EC, for example, continued to participate in multilateral trade negotiations in the post-World War II period at a pace similar to other industrial countries (except in agriculture). Second, the external tariffs set by regional blocs should be reduced or limited to those of the most open member; meanwhile, internal efforts should concentrate on freeing up trade and ending efforts to allocate production. Third, participants should continue to move toward freer trade through unilateral reforms. Postponing reforms to win agreement with other members of the trading bloc will greatly increase the costs of such arrangements.

Trade Routes to Growth

Openness to trade has improved resource allocation, increased competition and product specialization, and provided a broad avenue for technology transfer. Ironically, greater competition and a more integrated world have also resulted in a global trading system which is now poised at a critical juncture. The world faces two important trade challenges in the 1990s. First, regional trading arrangements must be carefully managed to ensure that multilateral commitments are strengthened, not forgotten. Second, and even more urgent, the Uruguay Round of trade talks must be revived. However difficult, all participants must reach agreement to open up agriculture, expand the GATT to eliminate quantity restrictions (on autos, steel and textiles), and restrict the use of so-called fair trade legislation (anti-dumping and subsidy measures). In this, the developing countries can play a key role; in their own interests, they should press for free trade and continue to reform their own trading systems. The industrial countries of today grew prosperous through trade. No effort should be spared to ensure that the developing countries can follow that same path to progress.

REFERENCES

Grossman, Gene M. and Elhanan Helpman, Forthcoming. *Innovation and Growth: Technological Competition in the Global Economy.* Cambridge, Mass.: MIT Press.

Laird, Samuel and Alexander Yeats. 1987. "Empirical Evidence Concerning the Magnitude and Effects of Developing Country Tariff Escalation." *Developing Economies* 25, 2: 99-123.

Papageorgiou, Demetrios, Michael Michaely, and Armeane M. Choksi. 1990. *Liberalizing Foreign Trade in Developing Countries. Lessons of Experience.* Washington, D.C.: World Bank.

Thomas, Vinod, and John Nash. Forthcoming. *Best Practices in Trade Policy Reform.* New York: Oxford University Press.

UNCTAD (United Nations Conference on Trade and Development). 1987. *Handbook of Trade Control Measures of Developing Countries.* Geneva.

Westphal, Larry E. 1990. "Industrial Policy in an Export-Propelled Economy: Lessons from South Korea's Experience." *Journal of Economic Perspectives* 4, 3: 41-59.

READING 9

Asian Trade and Growth Lessons

Anne O. Krueger

The Asian experience with trade and growth has been highly varied. There is a strong contrast between the success of the East Asian "superexporters," the still-impressive but less rapid growth of Southeast Asia, and the sluggish growth of much of the South Asian subcontinent, including especially India, Burma, Nepal, and Bangladesh.

No observer of the success of the East Asian exporters can doubt that exports played a key role in accelerating growth. Although the relationship between growth of real per capita GNP and of exports is certainly not perfect, Korea's export growth rate of 22.9 percent accompanied an average annual growth rate of per capita income of 6.4 percent over the 1965-87 period. Hong Kong, Singapore, and Taiwan were also rapidly growing economies whose growth of exports outpaced that of income. By contrast, the Philippines, Sri Lanka, and Pakistan all experienced annual rates of growth of per capita income of less than 3 percent, and had falling shares of exports in GNP. For Bangladesh and Nepal, growth rate and export performance were even worse.

It bears pointing out that the successful East Asian countries had their earlier experience with inner-oriented trade strategies, quantitative controls over imports, and slow growth. In each case, the shift in trade strategy was accompanied by a sizeable increase in the rate of growth of output, in the marginal productivity of capital as judged by the behavior of the incremental capital output ratio, and in total factor productivity.[1]

The interesting questions and lessons therefore arise with respect to how export growth was achieved, and the reasons why export growth was associated with rapid growth of GNP. Consider first the determinants of rapid export growth. Government policies in all the superexporters were clearly set within the context of a commitment to growth through exporting. Several policy instruments were geared to those targets; the real exchange rate received by exporters, the import regime as it affected reexports, and the infrastructure (ports, domestic transport, communications with the outside world by phone and mail) necessary for exporting all were determined by the needs of the export drive. (See Kwang Suk Kim, 1987, and Richard Snape, 1988, for documentation.)

In every country with a successful development-through-exporting strategy, exporters were exempted from whatever restrictions prevailed in the import regime. This was not only necessary for success in exporting, but it restricted the extent to which officials could monitor and regulate imports. Further, the government's commitment to exporting was an implied assurance of the profitability for successful exporting firms. While some of the NICs initially provided export subsidies, subsidized credit, and other special privileges for exporters, all of these became costly as the export drive succeeded, and there was therefore perpetual pressure on government officials to increased reliance on the exchange rates and uniformity of incentives. In Korea, for example, Kim (Table 2.10) estimates that the effective exchange rate for exports was within 6 percent of that for imports for every year after 1965; the variation of incentives between import-competing and exportable commodities was far smaller than in the typical import-substitution regime.

It is certainly not correct to state that the governments in the export-strategy countries provided more incentives for exporting than for import-competing production. What appears to have been the case is that incentives were biased very little away from exporting, and that whatever profits were to be made through import restrictions (in the early stages of the exporting strategy) were channeled to exporters. In the jargon of international trade theory, domestic incentives were reasonably uniform.

It is equally incorrect to state that governments decided which commodities should be encouraged for exporting in the early years of the export-oriented drive. Export subsidies, credit subsidies, and tax exemptions applied to all exporters. Moreover, given the small base on which exports began, any producer who could export was encouraged to do so. (See Jung-ho Yoo, 1989.)

Finally, it must be recognized that in the early years of export-oriented strategies, all relevant participants in the then-poor countries (government officials and producers) perceived themselves to be weak and ineffective in the international market. This perception was significant as a backdrop against which economic policy was framed. Moreover, it permeated the entire structure of governmental decision making, another factor contributing to overall economic growth.

The factors enumerated thus far were all similarities among the successful exporting countries. It may be noted that there were also differences. Chief among these was the contrast in firm size between Korea and Singapore on one hand, and Taiwan and Hong Kong on the other. There were also major differences in the treatment of foreign investors.

It may be concluded that there were a number of factors that contributed to the rapid growth of exports. Certainly, that the initial situation was one in which incentives were highly distorted was one factor. This permitted large efficiency gains. Once rapid growth of exports and real GNP had begun, there was widespread acceptance of the economic strategy which enhanced its credibility, and intensified the mandate of government officials to maintain the momentum of the drive. In all of this, incentives were fairly uniform; decisions were taken regarding prospects for *exporting*; not for particular industries. In addition, labor was relatively abundant, the labor market functioned reasonably well, and hence numerous profitable export opportunities arose.

Interest in the question of why export growth was so rapid has been motivated largely by interest in how other governments' trade policies might be successfully formulated (and in particular the extent to which "picking the winners" is a key element). There has been significantly less effort made to understand how export growth led to such spectacular rates of overall economic growth.

At a superficial level, there are several obvious, and trivially correct, partial explanations for the association between export growth and GNP growth; 1) the East Asian economies had highly protective trade regimes before they embarked on their export-oriented trade and development strategies, and by shifting strategies they achieved gains through realizing their comparative advantage, à la trade theory; 2) associated with that, the incremental capital-output ratio fell sharply, thereby assuring a rapidly rising growth rate even at a constant savings rate; 3) the reliance upon an outer-oriented trade strategy permitted the realization of economies of scale, and the exhaustion of indivisibilities, that would otherwise have arisen; and 4) avoidance of "stop-go" policies associated with balance of payments difficulties that have plagued other developing countries also contributed to more rapid growth.

That these factors were highly significant, especially in the first decade after adopting outer-oriented growth strategies, cannot be doubted. However, questions remain: very rapid growth rates of both exports and real GNP have been sustained for several decades; many of the gains attributed to the four explanations were surely largely exhausted after two decades of rapid growth.

One of the reasons it is difficult to identify the links between export growth and overall growth is that other policies adopted in the superexporting countries have also been conducive to growth. Not only did the trade and payments regime provide reasonably uniform incentives for most tradeables, but the labor market worked fairly efficiently, as already mentioned. In addition, observers have pointed to a host of other factors: educational attainments were quite high; governmental services, including transport and communications, were reasonably efficient; even reactions to changes in the external environment, such as the oil price increases of 1973 and 1979, evoked far swifter and more effective adjustments than in many other developing countries.

Moreover, even in areas of policy (such as financial markets and credit rationing) where initial regulations and controls were not conducive to economic efficiency, there has been a continuing process of liberalization as growth has proceeded. In Korea, real interest rates were negative until 1964, and were positive thereafter; credit rationing thus had less scope for misallocating capital after 1964 than it did earlier. By the early 1980s, financial deregulation was proceeding fairly rapidly, and continues even now. Concurrently, there has been a clear tendency to liberalize international financial transactions, to liberalize the trade regime, and to reduce the domain within which direct controls affect economic activity. Similarly in Taiwan, financial liberalization, tax reform geared to reducing the incentives for misallocation of resources, continuing liberalization of imports and capital account transactions, were hallmarks of the continuing rapid rate of growth. Even the rate of inflation has approached very close to zero in the past several years.

Although there are many questions about these policies and their effects, it is possible to put forward a hypothesis about trade, economic growth, and government policies that is consistent with the trends in the superexporters. It has two parts; first, one of the reasons for the success of the countries adopting outer oriented trade strategies is that an export orientation imposes a discipline and set of constraints on all economic policies that prevent the adoption of very many measures severely antithetical to growth; and second, the extent of liberalization and smooth functioning of markets that is consistent with rapid economic growth increases with the level of output per capita.

Both of these hypotheses are speculative, the second more so than the first. If they are correct, they would suggest a new value of an open economy: not only does openness increase competition, permit the realization of comparative advantage, and provide a means for realizing economies of scale and exhausting indivisibilities, it also constrains government policies in ways that make them conform more closely to those conducive to increases in living standards and rapid economic growth.

Turn first to the ways in which a commitment to an outer-oriented trade strategy imposes a constraint on policies. The fact that anything more than moderate restrictions on imports is inconsistent with such a strategy has already been mentioned. Equally important, however, is the fact that the costs of mistakes become visible fairly rapidly. The mistaken Korean policy of encouraging heavy and chemical industry development in the late 1970s is an example. It was the openness of the economy that made the costs of the policy highly visible (both to policy-makers and to most informed observers of economic activity) quickly. Likewise, when the Singaporean authorities decided to adopt a "high wage" policy in the mid-1980s, growth slackened rapidly, and the policy was reversed. Pressures for realistic exchange rates, budgetary policies, and for restraint in attempting to decide which industries should be developed were strong in all the successful exporting countries because of the fact that they were highly open. Given the huge mistakes in policy that seem to have enormous costs in terms of foregone output and growth in many other developing countries, the fact that an outer-orientation constrains policymakers from making these same mistakes, at least to the same degree, is doubtless one of the reasons for more rapid overall growth.

That heavy-handed direct controls are more inconsistent with an export-oriented trade and growth strategy than with an inner-oriented trade strategy may be tautological. The question really centers on the extent to which it is "better policy," or at least "less bad" policy, that brings about the very high rates of growth, and what the causation is. It could be argued that governments that are able to inaugurate and effect export-oriented trade policies sufficiently to induce any lasting success will also be able to carry out other policies. All that can be said with confidence is that the political penalties for adopting inappropriate policies will be greater in the context of an ongoing outward-oriented strategy. In that sense, success may breed success.

The second hypothesis (that the same policies have different economic costs at different stages of development) is the more tentative of the two. Here, the argument would be that at very low-income levels, most economic activity takes place in agriculture. The costs of direct controls over trade, industry, and factor markets are therefore probably fairly small. Until mechanisms are found that permit satisfactory growth of agricultural output and productivity (or leave the agricultural sector relatively backward and inaugurate industrial growth), there can be very little economic growth. In most countries, this means that a prerequisite for satisfactory economic growth will be the provision of infrastructure (including especially education and health, as well as roads, agricultural research and extension, etc.) and incentives for agriculture.

Once that is accomplished, a given set of restrictions over trade will be consistent with an evermore slowly growing set of industrial activities. For, to the extent that growth occurs, a by-product is the increasing complexity of the industrial production structure, and thus the increasing inefficiency of trade restrictions and other given interventions. A move to an export-oriented trade strategy removes that set of high-cost impediments to growth; at first, the move to an outer-oriented strategy can result in large gains in exports even when credit rationing, duties on imports, and restrictions on capital flows are still in force. Over time, however, as the range of industrial activities (and the service activities supporting them) increases, the costs of these restrictions in turn mount. Sustaining growth therefore entails further liberalizations in the import regime, in financial and capital markets, and in controls in international capital flows as the complexity of the domestic economic increases.

For Hong Kong, there has been virtually complete laissez-faire throughout the thirty-year period of rapid development. For Korea, Singapore, and Taiwan, however, there has been continuing liberalization of economic activity. Certainly this liberalization increased the returns to the trade policies that results in a balance in incentives for production of import-competing and exportable goods. Whether the rapid growth in exports could have been sustained without continuing liberalization in other markets is doubtful, at best.[2]

Seen in this light, a successful export oriented set of trade policies forces the adoption of other efficiency and growth-enhancing liberalization policies. Those policies permit further gains to be realized from the trade strategy, and simultaneously induce further growth and yet greater complexity of the economic structure. The costs of remaining interventions (credit rationing, regulations governing international financial transactions, etc.) then rise further as output increases. The "virtuous" circle then persists. The success of an outer-oriented trade strategy provides the momentum and impetus for further liberalization, which then permits further economic gains from the trade strategy.

Whether the "virtuous policy circle" accounts for the high overall economic growth resulting form the trade strategy adopted by the East Asian countries, or whether other factors are the key explanatory variables is worthy of further research. What seems to be certain is that the South Asian countries that adopted policies of import substitution and industrialization behind high walls of protection failed to adopt policies conducive to rapid economic growth.

ENDNOTES

* Duke University, Durham, NC 27706

1 For a more systematic account of performance than is permitted by space limitations here, see Paul Kuznets (1988).

2 It is an interesting question as to whether costly interventions in agriculture in Korea and Taiwan will come to represent a major bottleneck to growth.

REFERENCES

Kim, Kwang Suk, "The Timing and Sequencing of a Trade Liberalization Policy: The Case of Korea," mimeo., World Bank, February 1987.

Kuznets, Paul, "An East Asian Model of Economic Development: Japan, Taiwan and South Korea," *Economic Development and Cultural Change*, April 1988, Suppl., *36*, S11-S44.

Snape, Richard, "Experiences in East Asia—Korea and Singapore," mimeo., 1988.

Yoo, Jung-ho, "The Korean Experience with an Industrial Targetting Policy," Korea Development Institute, mimeo., May 1989.

SECTION V

Does the Current Account Matter?

In the United States, an important focal point of policy discussions has been the historically large trade and current-account deficits observed since the mid-1980s. Many economists cite the macroeconomic policies of the United States and its trading partners as important contributors to these imbalances. In this section, the causes, as well as the present and future consequences of these deficits are discussed by two economists from the United States Federal Reserve System. As argued by David Howard and Charles Pigott, while there is considerable agreement among economists about the causes of United States deficits, there is much less consensus about their short-term and long-term implications .

READING 10

Implications of the U.S. Current Account Deficit

David H. Howard

In 1988, the United States recorded a deficit of about $135 billion on the current account of its balance of payments with the rest of the world.[1] This sum amounted to roughly 2-3/4 percent of GNP. The evolution of the U.S. current account is presented in Figure 1. Several conclusions can be drawn: $135 billion is a lot of money; 2-3/4 percent is a substantial portion of GNP; the decline in the current account was precipitous; and there are signs of a turnaround. The recent path of the U.S. current account deficit and the consequent accumulation of external debts have raised many interesting economic and policy questions. Some observers have pointed to the deficits and mounting debts and have predicted a large, sharp depreciation of the dollar in the future. Others have worried about the implications of the Untied States as the world's largest "debtor nation," references to the heavily indebted developing countries and the "debt crisis" have been voiced, as have been concerns about the growing foreign control implied by the growth in foreign claims on the United States.

The consensus forecast appears to be for little change in the nominal current account balance in the near term. However, based on current policies, mainstream assumptions about U.S. and foreign growth rates, and limited further currency realignments, many observers expect that within a few years the U.S. current account deficit will resume widening. The consensus forecast seems to be that a U.S. current account balance in the neighborhood of zero is not even a remote possibility in the near or not-so-near future.

As might be expected, the red ink recorded in the U.S. current account during the 1980s has affected markedly the country's net external asset position, since the excess of imports over exports had as a counterpart some type of credit transaction with foreigners. The exact level of net external assets in any particular year is not precisely known for a variety of reasons.[2] However, what is certain is that the cumulated U.S. current account deficit of nearly $700 billion for the 1983-1988 period seriously eroded the U.S. net external asset position, and probably transformed the United States from a substantial net creditor nation into a substantial net debtor. Indeed, the consensus forecast for the U.S. current account indicates that U.S. net external assets will continue to fall steeply for at least the next few years. The official estimate of the net external asset position (the "net international investment position") at the end of 1987—negative $368 billion - was about 8 percent of 1987 GNP.

It is useful to put the recent U.S. experience in perspective. As shown in Figure 1, the size of the 1983-1988 current account deficits as a proportion of GNP is unprecedented (by a wide margin) since 1948. Data reported in Eichengreen (1987) indicate that the deficits have no historical precedent in the United States going back as far as 1890. However, the scale of the present U.S. current account deficit, but not necessarily the circumstances associated with it, does have precedents in other countries' experiences. Leaving aside the history of current accounts in developing countries as irrelevant to an advanced industrial country like the United States, there are many instances in which an industrial country's current account deficit has been on the order of 2 to 4 percent of its GNP or GDP. For example, in the five-year period, 1975-1979, Canada's current account deficit averaged over 2 percent of GDP; in 1974, the British and Italian

Figure 1

U.S. Current Account Relative to GNP

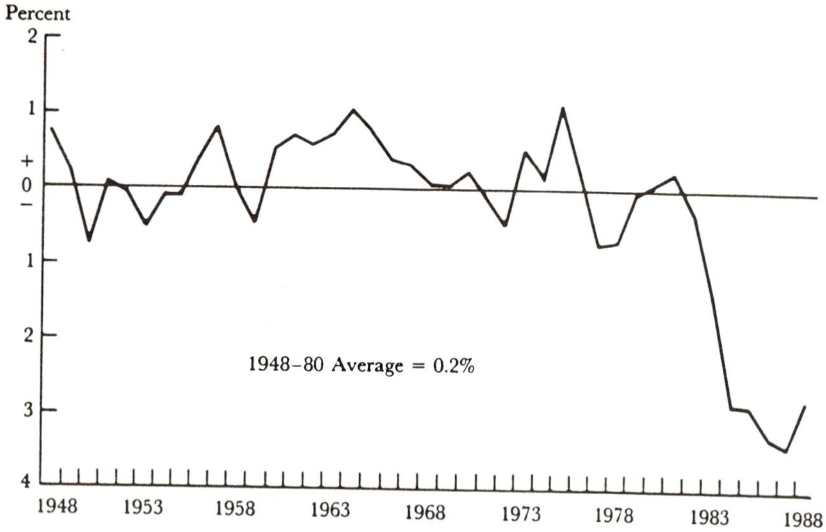

Source: Bureau of Economic Analysis, Department of Commerce.

deficits were 4 percent of GDP, and in some of the smaller industrial countries, annual deficits have been well in excess of 4 percent of GNP or GDP.[3]

THINKING ABOUT THE IMPLICATIONS: ANALYTICAL FRAMEWORK

The implications of a current account deficit depend in part on what caused the deficit in the first place and how the economy adjusts in response—for example, how the deficit is eventually closed. the U.S. current account balance is a general equilibrium phenomenon: it is jointly determined with other endogenous variables in the world economy. The usual proximate determinants of the current account balance—chiefly the terms of trade and relative rates of growth of economic activity—are themselves endogenous variables. Analysis of the current account deficit requires that the fundamental causes as well as the proximate causes be identified. Moreover, spillovers involving other markets and foreign economies must be taken into account. In the present exercise—analyzing the implications of the historically very large U.S. current account deficit—the general equilibrium nature of the problem is not just a theoretical fine point. Anticipating the discussion of the next section of the paper, the conclusion of most economists who have studied the issue is that the U.S. current account deficit is largely the product of the macroeconomic policy mix pursued by the United States and its major trading partners during the 1980s. Reducing the deficit probably, although perhaps not necessarily, would involve a significant reversal of those particular policy choices. Since changes in macroeconomic policies have consequences for the entire world economy—not just the U.S. balance of payments—it is imperative that the entire world economy be incorporated in the analysis.

The economic literature provides several lines of approach for thinking about current account balances. The conventional method—at least in the empirical literature—entails an eclectic model in which trade flows are essentially determined by prices and income flows, supplemented with judiciously and pragmatically chosen additional variables. These explanatory variables are for the most part only the proximate determinants of trade flows, and the trade equations are explicitly or implicitly considered to be a component of a more complete empirical model of the economy. In fact, one approach to modeling the current account involves an econometric model of the entire world economy, consisting of linked individual country models. In these models, trade flows and their proximate determinants are determined endogenously and simultaneously as part of a general equilibrium outcome. Exercises involving such models or components of such models form the basis of what is known—or is believed to be known—quantitatively about the causes of the current U.S. deficit as well as the prospects for its improvement.

Another empirically oriented approach to thinking about current account balances focuses on one aspect of the general equilibrium problem by manipulating the national income accounts to arrive at the identity:

$$X - M \equiv S - I, \quad (1)$$

where X and M represent exports and imports of goods and services, respectively, and S and I denote domestic (including the public sector) saving and investment, respectively. Expressed in this manner, it is natural to view the current account [approximately $(X - M)$ as being reflective of a country's saving-investment behavior and imbalances. For example, in terms of this identify, the U.S. current account deficit can be thought of as being the result of a shortfall in U.S. saving, in which case the level of domestic investment is being supported by flows of foreign saving (equal to the negative of the current account balance). However, viewed in this manner, it is also easy to lose sight of the fact that equation 1 is an identity with no causal significance, and that all four variables are endogenously determined as part of a general equilibrium outcome for the entire international economy. The current account $X - M$ and the saving-investment balance $S - I$ are actually functions of many variables, including importantly income, the exchange rate, and the interest rate. The equilibrium external balance is determined by the intersection of the $X - M$ and $S - I$ functions. Thus, the actual external balance can reflect changes in export and import behavior as well as changes in domestic saving and investment behavior.

Another strand of the economics literature can also be brought to bear on the question of the U.S. current account deficit. The classic Diamond (1965) overlapping generations growth model of public debt provides an analysis of the implications of funding a public sector deficit by borrowing abroad. The open economy aspects of the Diamond model are more fully articulated in Persson (1985). One of Persson's conclusions is particularly interesting (p. 82): "The adjustment towards the higher external debt implied by a higher public debt was shown to involve an extended period of current account deficits following an initial government budget deficit." Persson's explanation of this result essentially involves the use of foreign saving flows (and therefore current account deficits) to supplement domestic saving both during the initial period of the government deficit and during subsequent periods, when domestic saving is depressed by taxes used to service the higher public debt. In fact, Persson's analysis of the interaction between the public sector and current account deficits is similar to that underlying the more-or-less conventional view in official and international financial circles of the relationship between the U.S. budget and current account deficits (the so-called "twin deficits").

CAUSES OF THE CURRENT ACCOUNT DEFICIT

Between 1981 and 1987, the annual U.S. current account balance declined by $160 billion. Quantifying, or even identifying, the main causes of this marked weakening in the current account is difficult for a variety of reasons: it requires an econometrically fitted model with fairly precise and generally accepted estimated coefficients; it requires a view as to what counterfactual baseline should be used for comparison; and such an exercise almost necessarily involves some amount of implicit or explicit causal ordering among simultaneously determined endogenous variables. Nevertheless, some of the leading econometric models of the international economy have been used to address this question.[4]

The explanation of the behavior of the U.S. current account during the 1980s that emerges from the empirical literature is one in which the fundamental cause is the macroeconomic policy mix pursued in the United States and its major trading partners. At the beginning of the decade, the anti-inflation stance of U.S. monetary policy drove real interest rates and the dollar upward. However, the dollar's strength had little effect on the current account since the ensuing U.S. recession dampened the demand for imports. Starting in about 1982, the strongly expansionary course of U.S. fiscal policy began to impart additional upward impetus to U.S. interest rates and the dollar while at the same time fostering a recovery in U.S. economic activity and U.S. demand for imports. The result was a sharp deterioration in the current account in 1983-1984, which was exacerbated by the restrictive posture taken by fiscal authorities in the major foreign industrial countries and the economic problems of the heavily indebted developing countries.[5] The widening of the U.S. current account deficit meant that foreigners in effect were financing more and more of the U.S. government budget deficit, thereby allowing the U.S. private sector to maintain higher levels of consumption and investment expenditures than it otherwise could have.[6]

Steps toward tightening U.S. fiscal policy, starting in 1985, appear to have played a role in reversing the course of the dollar and the current account. Another instrumental factor seems to have been financial market concerns about the longer-run sustainability of the U.S. external position and the recognition that at some point some adjustment would be necessary, a topic that is discussed in the next section of the present paper.

The attempts to *quantify* the various causes of the U.S. current account deficit are, of course, rough, and as one might expect, the results are far from unanimous across models. Nevertheless, the conclusion that one can draw from the empirical literature is that less than half of the deterioration in the current account was associated with the relative strength of U.S. economic activity compared with that abroad, and more than half was associated with the loss of price competitiveness of U.S. goods and services, owing largely to the strong appreciation of the dollar in the first half of the 1980s.

The pace of economic activity at home and abroad as well as the course of the dollar were proximate causes only. Various econometric models indicate that expansionary U.S. fiscal policy coupled with restrictive fiscal policy in the major foreign industrial countries and the anti-inflation stance of U.S. monetary policy can explain a sizable amount of the developments in economic activity and exchange rates. There nevertheless remains a significant portion—perhaps one-third—of the rise in the dollar that remains unexplained, and which perhaps reflects a speculative bubble, and therefore some of the weakening in the U.S. current account is also unexplained.

The models also have been used to investigate the seemingly puzzling persistence of the current account deficit in the face of the dollar's steep decline since early 1985. Several points can be made with regard to the persistence of the deficit. First, in the absence of the dollar's fall, the nominal current account balance probably would have been weaker than the rates actually recorded. Second, the persistence is not too surprising in that the econometric models do not predict a rapid turnaround: trade volumes react with a fairly substantial lag (usually distributed over two years) to changes in prices, and the dollar prices of imports also respond with a lag (again typically distributed over two years) to changes in exchange rates. Moreover, must of the dollar's initial decline represented simply a reversal of its surge at the end of 1984 and early 1985, which probably was not reflected in prices or trade volumes anyway. Finally, the dollar's depreciation between early 1985 and the end of 1987 was more-or-less continuous so that a series of so-called J-curve effects—a weakening of the current account as import prices in dollars rise before import volumes decline in response—would tend to mask the improvement in the underlying current account position for a while. There have been some special (and unpredicted) factors as well, such as the vagaries of the oil market.

SUSTAINABILITY: THE UNITED STATES AS A DEBTOR NATION

There are several statistical indicators or measures of a country's external debt "burden" or debt-servicing requirement. One common measure is the net external debt (D) to GNP (Y) ratio; another scales the debt by the value of a country's exports instead of national output. In either case, the rationale is that the denominator is related to a country's capacity to service its debt. In this paper,

"dollar crash" scenario involving sharp domestic interest rate increases but argues that its deflationary effects can be offset by monetary policy. This seems somewhat optimistic in view of the lags in private economic behavior and policy makers perceptions and actions.

9 Analysts differ more on the relative importance of the various proximate factors, such as the contribution of interest rates to the dollar's rise.

10 A good example is Jeffrey Sachs analysis of the sacrifice ratio of output gains to inflation in the creation of the deficit and its subsequent reversal. See Jeffrey Sachs, "The Dollar and the Policy Mix," *Brookings Papers on Economic Activity*, 1:1985. Similar reasoning underlies John Williamson's calculations of equilibrium dollar exchange rates (*The Exchange Rate System*, Institute for International Economics, Monograph no. 5, September 1983).

11 Of course, a current account deficit cannot absorb more than all available foreign funds (or, more practically, the bulk), nor can the external debt exceed total foreign wealth. Even the most pessimistic projections of the U.S. external deficit and debt are well below such technical limits, however.

12 The measured return on the book value of U.S. investments abroad has typically been significantly greater than that on foreign investments here. Last year, the gap in the two returns was so great that U.S. net service payments were virtually zero despite an officially estimated debt of well over $400 billion. It is possible, although by no means certain, that this country's rate of return on its assets will continue to exceed that paid on foreign liabilities (although not nearly to the degree recorded in 1988). If so, the effective interest rate on U.S. net external debt could remain below the economy's growth rate, making an ongoing trade deficit a technical possibility; this deficit is likely to be fairly small in relation to GNP however. (see Box)

13 Will the present imbalances between national saving and investment and between spending and income stabilize or rise relative to GNP? We can be reasonably assured, based on past experience, that the gap between private saving and investment, which is generally small, will remain stable. Whether the public sector budget deficit will fall (as it has in the past two years) or resume increasing relative to GNP will depend upon policy choices. Stability in the deficit-GNP ratio is not automatic and indeed involves essentially the same technical conditions as apply to the external imbalance (that is, balance or near-balance in the budget excluding interest payments on national debt.)

14 Both U.S. and foreign residents face certain common risks in holding dollar assets, in particular from unanticipated inflation, which reduces the purchasing power of dollar claims. Foreigners, however, face greater losses from fluctuations in the dollar's real value (changes that do not simply offset inflation differentials) than U.S. holders. The reason is that the real depreciation reduces the dollar's value more in terms of foreign goods and services than it does in terms of U.S. goods. Dollar instruments are thus intrinsically more risky to foreign holders than to U.S. holders (the reverse is of course true of foreign currency assets.)

15 See Juann Hung, Charles Pigott, and Anthony Rodrigues, "Financial Implications of the U.S. External Deficit," in this issue of the *Quarterly Review*.

16 In book value terms, the gross stock of foreign direct investment claims on the United States now amounts to about 6 percent of GNP. A doubling in this ratio—probably no more than is likely over the next five years—would place it well above the ratios for Germany and Japan, about equal to the ratio for the United Kingdom, and well below the nearly 25 percent ratio for Canada.

17 As interest payments rise, national income will fall relative to output. Standard consumption functions imply that consumption will vary with income and hence decline as a share of output. To the extent this occurs, the "crowding out" of investment will be reduced. However, this adjustment may well occur slowly, with the higher per capita consumption levels maintained for some time.

18 This is not to claim that lowering the budget deficit will lead to less severe adjustment regardless of the policy used. Reducing the deficit by raising taxes on investment could well have unfavorable consequences, for example.

SECTION VI

Floating Exchange Rates/ Exchange Market Intervention

A variety of approaches are used to explain the movements of short-run and long-run exchange rates. These approaches have met with varied success when used either to confront actual historic data or for predicting future movements in exchange rates. Theory predicts that interest rate differentials should predict future movements in exchange rates. In practice, predictions based on these differentials are usually incorrect. This finding, which has been interpreted as a violation of the premise that foreign-exchange markets are efficient, is the subject of the article by Kenneth Froot and Richard Thaler. Governments have strong incentives to influence the level of the exchange rate. An important question is whether this can be achieved without affecting the money supply. Warren Weber surveys the evidence on this point in his article on sterilized intervention.

READING 12

Anomalies: Foreign Exchange

Kenneth A. Froot and Richard H. Thaler

INTRODUCTION

The one person in your family who ever asks your advice about economics is your uncle, who is in the import-export business. A while back he called you about a foreign exchange issue. "Let's suppose I owe you a million German marks, payable in one month," he said. "We have the money to pay the bill in dollars, so the issue is whether to put the money into marks now or later. I figure we should put the money wherever it would earn the highest rate, but my treasurer, one of those MBA hot shots, tells me that this is irrelevant because if the interest rate is high in Germany that means that the mark is expected to go down. Which I ask her what we should do, she says that it doesn't matter. 'Flip a coin,' she says! Is this what I am paying her so much money for? To flip coins?" You tried to calm your uncle down, and explain the idea of efficient markets to him, but he was unconvinced. "OK," you told him, "if you think you can do better, why don't you run an experiment. You invest some of your money your way, while your treasurer flips coins, and then see who does better." He thought this was a great idea, and promised to let you know what happens.

Much to your surprise, your uncle called back recently. He claims to have a strategy that beats his coin-flipping treasurer. "Here's what I do," he crowed. "When interest rates rise in other countries, I put my money there, and take my chances on the currency falling. On the other hand if rates in the foreign country fall relative to U.S. rates, I keep my money here. It's simple, I admit, but it seems to be working. Of course, my treasurer claimed it was just luck, and said she would do some testing with historical data to prove her point. Well, she just came sheepishly into my office with piles of computer output and has agreed my theory beats her coin flipping. What do you think of this, wise guy?" Baffled, you decide to look into the literature on foreign exchange rates.

The foreign exchange market is among the most active of all financial markets. As of mid-1989, the average volume of trading activity (adjusted for double counting) was about $430 billion per *day*. To get a sense for just how big this number is, consider that daily U.S. GNP is about $22 billion, and daily world trade in goods and services is about $11 billion. Since foreign exchange trading is so much greater in volume than is trade in real goods and services, foreign exchange markets would seem to be highly liquid and efficient.

Partly as a result of the sheer volume of trading, many researchers have focused on the foreign exchange market to examine questions of speculative efficiency. One view—argued initially by Friedman (1955)—is that because speculators buy low and sell high their activity ensures that exchange rates reflect the fundamental or long-run determinants of currency values. A second strand of literature, often attributed to Nurske (1944), holds that speculation in foreign exchange can be destabilizing, and that excess volatility imposes large costs on producers and consumers who as a consequence make less efficient allocative decisions.

Recently this debate has escalated, as both sides try to come to grips with the dramatic, *temporary* 65 percent appreciation in the value of the dollar during the mid-1980s.[1] Some hold that these swings in the dollar's value were attributable to changes in fundamentals, and that given those fundamentals the appreciation was both predictable and optimal. Others, however, point to the experience as evidence of a capricious delinking of the dollar from its usual determinants, and argue that at least some of the dollar's appreciation could have been prevented beneficially. The debate about whether exchange rates are "correctly priced" is particularly important (in comparison to similar debates about the pricing of other assets) since the exchange rate simultaneously affects the prices of all foreign assets, goods, and factors of production. If Nurske's followers are right that speculation drives prices away from fundamentals, then the argument for intervention might be considered strongest in the market for foreign exchange.

In what follows, we discuss the efficiency of foreign exchange markets. Readers interested in more complete treatments should refer to Mussa (1979), Levich (1985), Boothe and Longworth (1986), Hodrick (1987), and Froot (1990). To manage what would otherwise be an enormous task, the question of efficiency is viewed below from the perspective of a single type of test: the test for what is called the forward discount bias. This test is easy to understand, and since it strongly rejects the null hypothesis, statistical power is not an issue. Naturally, in discussing this particular test we mention a variety of other empirical work designed to shed light on alternative explanations of the results.

TEST OF FORWARD DISCOUNT BIAS

If investors are risk neutral and have rational expectations, then the market's forecast of the future exchange rate is implicit in international differences in interest rates. To see this, suppose that the one-year dollar interest rate is 10 percent, and that the comparable German mark interest rate is 7 percent. The dollar interest differential is then said to be 3 percent. Risk neutral, rational investors then must expect the dollar to depreciate against the mark by 3 percent over the next year. This amount of depreciation would be just enough to equalize the expected returns on dollar and mark denominated deposits. If instead these investors expected a different rate of dollar depreciation, say 4 percent, they would all wish to borrow in dollars and lend in marks. Consequently, dollar interest rates would tend to rise and mark interest rates would tend to fall until the interest differential also became 4 percent. This simple relationship between interest differentials and expected currency depreciation is called uncovered interest parity (uncovered because forward markets are not used as a hedge). Thus, uncovered interest parity implies that the interest differential is an estimate of the future exchange rate change. If expectations are rational, then this estimate of future exchange rate changes provided by the interest differential should be unbiased.

Unbiasedness is usually tested by regressing the change in the exchange rate on the interest differential.

$$(1) \qquad \Delta s_{t+k} = a + \beta(i_t - i_t^*) + \pi_{t+k}'$$

where Δs_{t+k} is the percentage depreciation of the currency (the change in the log of the spot dollar price of foreign exchange) over k periods and $(i_t - i_t^*)$ is the current k-period dollar interest rate less the k period foreign interest rate. The null hypothesis is that $\beta = 1$. Some authors include $\alpha = 0$ in the null hypothesis as well. In other words, the realized depreciation of the spot rate is equal to the interest differential plus a purely random error term, π_{t+k}.

A second specification of equation (1) replaces the interest differential by the forward discount; that is, the percentage difference between the current forward and spot exchange rates. (The forward rate is today's dollar price of foreign exchange to be delivered on a specific date in the future.) By arbitrage, the forward discount must equal the interest differential. If it did not, then a strategy of borrowing in the foreign currency, changing the proceeds into dollars, investing those dollars and then selling them forward would yield a riskless profit. Most observers agree that the market respects this arbitrage condition, as banks allow forward rates to be set by interest differentials. Under risk neutrality and rational expectations, the forward discount should also be an unbiased estimate of the subsequent exchange rate change. Indeed, the failure of regressions such as (1) to yield estimates of $\beta = 1$ is often referred to as the forward discount bias.

A very large literature has tested the unbiasedness hypothesis and found that the coefficient β is reliably less than one. In fact, β is frequently estimated it be less than zero. The average coefficient across some 75 published estimates is –0.88 (Froot, 1990). A few are positive, but *not one is equal to or greater than the null hypothesis of* $\beta = 1$.

A coefficient of approximately minus one is difficult to explain. It implies that, for example, when U.S. interest rates exceed foreign rates by one percentage point, the dollar subsequently tends to appreciate at an annual rate of one percent. This is in contrast to the one percent depreciation dictated by the unbiasedness hypothesis.

Two interpretations of these results are common in the literature. Some authors argue that $\beta < 1$ is evidence of a time-varying risk premium on foreign exchange: when the dollar interest rate rises, investments in dollar assets become relatively more risky.[2] Alternatively, others assume that exchange rate risk is purely diversifiable or that investors are risk neutral. They therefore interpret any bias as evidence of expectational errors. The next two sections evaluate the merit of these two types of explanations.

EXCHANGE RISK PREMIA

If investors in foreign exchange markets are risk averse, and if foreign exchange risk is not fully diversifiable, then the interest differential or forward discount can no longer be interpreted as a pure estimate of the expected change in future exchange rates. Rather, the interest differential is the sum of the expected change in the exchange rate plus a risk premium. This, if the dollar is viewed as riskier than the foreign currency, dollar interest rates would have to be higher, even if the exchange rate is not expected to change. If the assumption of rational expectations is maintained, then a finding of $\beta \neq 1$ implies that interest rate movements are related to changes in the risk premium. In particular, a finding of $\beta < 1$ implies that a 1 percent increase in the dollar interest differential is associated with a less than 1 percent expected drop in the value of the dollar. Since the risk premium is just equal to the interest differential less the expected change in exchange rates, this implies that the risk premium on dollar assets must rise with the interest differential or equivalently, the required return on foreign exchange must fall.[3]

Naturally, a finding of $\beta < 0$ is more extreme: an increase is the interest differential is then associated with a *decline* in expected depreciation (since the dollar subsequently appreciates on average) and therefore with an even large rise in the risk premium. As Fama (1984) pointed out, this implies that the variance of the risk premium is greater than the variance of both expected depreciation and the interest differential, and that the covariance of expected depreciation and the risk premium is negative.

By itself, a negative correlation between expected depreciation and the risk premium might be considered plausible: higher expected inflation in the United States might sensibly be associated with both greater expected dollar depreciation and increased riskiness of dollar-denominated assets (Hodrick and Srivastava, 1986). This would be the case if, for example, higher expected inflation reflects greater uncertainty about the future course of monetary policy. The real problem for explanations based on risk premia is whether they can explain why a change in interest rates should produce an even larger change in risk-premia. Three approaches have been advanced to evaluate the merit of the risk-premium interpretation—none of which offer the hypothesis much support.

The first approach specifies and tests what one might call "statistical" models of risk. Rather than exploring whether underlying economic determinants of risk can help explain excess returns on foreign exchange, this approach tests for certain patterns in or across excess currency returns. While this class of tests has provided rich information about the predictable components of exchange rate changes, it has not provided much evidence that these components are actually attributable to risk. Another statistical test asks whether predictable returns can be explained by the expected variance in future returns. This kind of test may, in principle, be more able to distinguish between risk and expectational errors. In practice, however, there is no evidence that measures of expected variance are related to the forward discount bias. Domowitz and Hakkio (1985) present evidence that one such measure of expected future variance, computed using a model of autoregressive conditional heteroskedasticity (ARCH), is uncorrelated with the forward discount's bias.[4]

A second strand of tests for the exchange risk

premium looks beyond relative asset returns themselves and examines various specifications of the fundamental determinants of required returns. One approach, taken initially by Frankel (1982), notes that the capital asset pricing model (CAPM) requires an asset's risk premium to be systematically related to that asset's value share in investors' portfolios. His tests provide no evidence that required returns are positively related to systematic risk in exchange rates. Indeed, using these models it is not possible to reject the hypothesis that the systematic risk is zero; that is, that the exchange risk premium is zero. There is no evidence here that risk premia vary in a way that can explain predictable excess returns in foreign exchange (Frankel and Engel, 1984; Hodrick, 1987). Later work has examined more complex models of time-varying risk, but with similar results (Engel and Rodrigues, 1989, Giovannini and Jorion, 1989, Mark 1985, Obstfeld, 1990).

The third approach for assessing the risk-premium interpretation attempts to measure expected depreciation directly, thereby avoiding reliance on inferences from realized depreciation. If one could actually observe expectations it would be possible to decompose the interest differential's bias into separate components attributable to risk premia and to expectational errors. This would not tell us how the risk premium is formed, but it could tell us the importance of risk and market efficiency in explaining the bias.

The problem, of course, is that market expectations are not observable. However, by gathering independent measures of expectations, one might nevertheless hope to gain insights. Froot and Frankel (1989) use survey data on the expectations of foreign exchange traders as their independent measure of expected depreciation. If the survey expectations are accepted as a measure of expected depreciation, then the bias in the interest differential can be decomposed into a risk premium and a bias in expectations. When this decomposition is performed, the component attributable to risk turns out to be a small and insignificantly different from zero. This is not to say that the surveys don't contain a risk premium, as would be true if the surveys were always equal to the interest rate differential. In fact, the risk premia implied by the surveys are substantially different from zero and move over time. However, these survey risk premia are uncorrelated with the forward discount.

Finally, we might put the alternative hypothesis of a time-varying risk premium to a more informal sensibility check, asking how it would explain the unprecedented behavior of the dollar in the 1980s. From late 1980 until early 1985, dollar interest rates were above foreign rates so the dollar sold at a forward discount, implying that the value of the dollar should fall. However, the dollar appreciated (more or less steadily) at a rate of about 13 percent per year. Under the risk-premium scenario, these facts would suggest that investor's (rational) expectation of dollar appreciation was strongly positive (perhaps even the full 13 percent), but that the risk premium was also positive. Therefore, according to this view, dollar-denominated assets were perceived to be much riskier than assets denominated in other currencies, exactly the opposite of the "safe-haven" hypothesis which was frequently offered at that time as an explanation of the dollar's strength.

The subsequent rapid fall in the value of the dollar would conversely imply a reversal in the risk premium's sign, as investors in 1985 switched to thinking of the dollar as relatively safe. Something very dramatic must have happened to the underlying determinants of currency risk to yield such enormous swings in the dollar's value: during the appreciation investors must have been willing to give up around 16 percent per year (13 percent from dollar appreciation plus 3 percent from an interest differential in favor of the dollar) in order to hold the "safer" foreign currency, whereas during the later depreciation phase they must have been willing to forgo about 6 percent in additional annual returns (8 percent average annual depreciations minus the 2 percent average interest differential) in order to hold dollars. These premia are very large. It is hard to see how one could rely on the risk-premium interpretation alone to explain the dollar of the 1980s.[5]

EXPECTATIONAL ERRORS

The other alternative hypothesis is that expectational errors explain the bias in the forward discount and the interest differential. Under this alternative the risk premium is constant (or at least uncorrelated with the forward discount.) It follows that an increase in the interest differential is associated with an equivalent increase in expected depreciations. Yet the point estimates above suggest that a 1 percent increase in the interest differential tends to be followed by a 1 percent appreciation in the value of the dollar. How could such expectational errors arise, and how could they persist?

Even if such expectational errors appear after the fact to be economically significant for the period studied, they may not imply that market inefficiency or unexploited profit opportunities existed beforehand. Perhaps the period studied was unrepresentative, in which case the usual methods of statistical inference may lead to incorrect conclusions. If investors are in the process of learning about floating exchange rates or other regime changes, then exchange rate changes will be affected by the learning. Lewis (1989) explores whether an explanation of this sort can explain the persistence of the 1980-85 dollar appreciation. She presents evidence that investor's slow learning about an unobservable shift in the U.S. money supply process can explain about half of the error implicit in the forward rate.[6] However, as Lewis notes, the errors do not seem to have died out over time, which is evidence against models of learning about once-and-for-all shifts in regime.

Another example which would generate misleading inferences from regressions is that of "peso problems." This term derives from the 1955-76 Mexican peso, which was fixed by the Mexican government at a constant rate against the U.S. dollar, yet all the while sold at a forward discount. Of course, the large depreciation apparently expected by investors did eventually occur, validating the prediction from interest rates and the forward market—but one could not have guessed this from the 1955-75 sample alone (Rogoff, 1979). In these as well as less extreme circumstances, peso problems will invalidate standard statistical inference procedures.

Michael Mussa has suggested why peso problems might indeed be expected to plague regressions of the type we have been discussing. He argues that the distribution of inflation rates is skewed: most of the time inflation hovers in a restricted range, but occasionally hyperinflation breaks out. For periods in which no hyperinflation actually occurs, increases in expected inflation overpredict the subsequent realized inflation rate. Since such increases in expected inflation are likely to be associated with increases in nominal interest rates and expected depreciation, the ß coefficients will be less than one in more than half of the regression samples.

We can evaluate whether the peso problem is a reasonable explanation for the dollar of the early 1980s by using a skewness argument similar to that proposed by Mussa. During the 1980-85 period the dollar was above its 1980 level by an average of about 33 percent, and appreciated at an average annual rate of 13 percent. Suppose that the market did indeed expect the dollar to appreciate at 13 percent per year if it appreciated at all, but that the alternative was an expected collapse back to its 1980 level.[7] Expected depreciation would then be equal to the probability of collapse, π, times the average size of the expected collapse, 33 percent, minus the probability of appreciation, $1 - \pi$, times the amount of appreciation 13 percent. If we assume that expected depreciation was the 3 percent given by the interest differential, then the probability of collapse in any one year is: $\pi = (13 + 3) / (13 + 33) = 35$ percent. This would imply that the probability that the exchange rate went five years without collapsing was $(1 - \pi)^5 = .12$. If we take this computation seriously, the result suggests that the peso-problem hypothesis is unlikely to be true, although it cannot be rejected at standard levels of statistical significance.[8, 9]

The bias in the interest differential seems less severe for certain types of fluctuations in interest rates. Tests of the bias during the buildup to hyperinflation, in which nominal interest rates move from being small to very large, show ßs that are positive and nearer one. In addition, casual inspection of cross-sectional evidence suggests that interest differentials lead to reasonable predictions: high-inflation countries, such as Italy, typically have had higher nominal interest rates than the U.S., and their currencies indeed did tend to depreciate secularly. Just the reverse has been true for the currencies of low-inflation countries such as West Germany which has had relatively low interest rates. *In other words, the average level of the interest differentials points the right way in forecasting long-run currency changes, even though the short-run correlations usually point the wrong way in forecasting near-term exchange rates changes.*

Nevertheless, the preponderance of evidence

that ß is less than one across different subsamples, currencies, forecast horizons, and asset markets, coupled with the near rejection of the peso explanation of the behavior of the dollar in the early 1980s casts some doubt on the validity of learning and peso problems. To keep these explanations intact, one would need to argue that there is little independence across these many estimates of ß. Perhaps there is the possibility of some important event that has not yet occured—like complete nuclear annihilation—that somehow conditions investors' expectations in such a way as to create the appearance of bias. As the time-series and cross-sectional size of the statistical sample continues to increase, however, such arguments become increasingly strained.

A POSSIBLE EXPLANATION

The primary conclusions reached so far have been negative: a rational efficient markets paradigm provides no satisfactory explanation for the observed results. Perhaps the best we can do is to offer a simple and parsimonious explanation, one that has other testable restrictions but does not require full rationality of all investors. Consider as an example, the hypothesis that at least some investors are slow in responding to changes in the interest differential. It may be that these investors need some time to think about trades before executing them, or that they simply cannot respond quickly to recent information. These investors might also be called "central banks," who seem to "learn against the wind" by trading in such a way as to attenuate the appreciation of a currency as interest rates increase. Other investors in the model are fully rational, albeit risk averse, and even may try to exploit the first group's slower movements. [10]

A simple story along these lines has the potential for reconciling the above facts. First, it yields negative coefficient estimates of ß as long as some changes in nominal interest differentials also reflect changes in real interest differentials. While changes in nominal interest rates have different instantaneous effects on the exchange rate across different exchange-rate models, most of these models predict that an increase in the dollar real interest rate (all else equal) should lead to instantaneous dollar appreciation. If only part of this appreciation occurs immediately, and the rest takes some time, then we might expect the exchange rate to appreciate in the period subsequent to an increase in the interest differential. Hence the possibility of a negative relationship between short-run changes in interest rates and exchange rates. Second, this hypothesis can also explain the cross-sectional and hyperinflation results, in which the interest differential correctly forecasts secular exchange rate changes. A test of this hypothesis could be based on the additional implication that past (not just current) levels of the forward discount should help in predicting exchange rate changes. In fact, this hypothesis suggests that if past levels of the interest differential are added to equation (1), the estimated coefficient should be positive and near one. Froot (1990) presents evidence which is supportive of this latter implication.

Such an explanation (which stresses the lack of "efficiency" in the usual sense) seems to fit the facts well enough, but has an apparently serious flaw: isn't there money to be made by trading on contemporaneous interest rate changes? The empirical case for foreign-exchange market efficiency was made forcefully by Bilson (1981). He argued that the speculative rule suggested by the finding of $ß < 1$—buy the currency whose interest rate is relatively high—could actually provide expected profits without bearing much risk.[11]

Dooley and Shafter (1983) and Sweeney (1986) also examine several types of "filter rules:" trading strategies that are triggered by the past behavior of spot trades. A typical filter rule might specify that an investor should sell the dollar short if the dollar has appreciated by more than 2 percent the last 24 hours. Such rules appear profitable, although the profits are not always statistically significant. Also, Schulmeister (1987) and Cumby and Modest (1987) study a number of trading rules derived from technical analysis and find that these rules generate statistically significant profits.

Whether or not there is really money to be made based on the apparent inefficiency of foreign exchange markets, it is worth emphasizing that the risk-return tradeoff for a single currency is not very attractive. The annualized standard error of the regression estimates of equations (1) is about 36 percent. This implies that a strategy that generates expected profits of \$1 comes with a standard deviation of profits of \$15. To see this note that with ß = – 1, a one percentage point increase in the dollar interest rate is associated with an additional two percent higher annual return on dollar assets than on foreign assets. On a monthly basis, a $500 investment therefore yields about $1 in expected profit, ($500 X .02) / 12 ≈ $1—ignoring compounding. The standard error of profits is then ($500 X .36) / 12 = $15. With transactions costs, the risk-return tradeoff becomes even less favorable. Although much of the risk in these strategies may be diversifiable in principle, more complex diversified strategies may be more costly, unreliable, or difficult to execute.

COMMENTARY

Anomalies in financial markets are often "explained" by economists with the use of some type of risk argument. For example, small firms which earn higher returns than large firms are said to be riskier, though differentials in traditional risk measures such as capital asset pricing model beta's are not high enough to explain the differentials in returns. Similarly, mean reversion in asset prices is often attributed to alleged time-varying risk premia; the amount of risk investors are willing to bear is said to vary over time in a manner that can explain the pattern of returns. Such explanations are often thought to have a decisive debating advantage: untestability. Since risk premia are unobservable directly, how can the explanation ever be disproven? This type of thinking can lead to a false sense of security, because clever researches often think of ways of testing such untestable propositions. An analogy is concept of utility maximization, often considered an untestable tautology. However, as discussed in the previous column (Tversky and Thaler, 1990), subjects can be induced to make conflicting choices when faced with two different version of the same problem, and of course it is impossible for both answers to be consistent with utility maximization.

As we have seen in this column, researchers in foreign exchange markets have been inventive in devising methods of testing whether risk can explain the anomalies. Indeed, the conclusion we draw from the tests completed so far is that there is no positive evidence that the forward discount's bias is due to risk (as opposed to expectational errors). Risk premia which are derived from economists' asset pricing models show no sign of being systematically related to the predictable excess returns derived from econometricians' regressions.

In addition, there is positive evidence which suggests the reverse: that the bias is attributable to expectational errors and not to risk. Attempts to separate the forward discount to expected depreciation and a risk premium using survey data on exchange rate expectations suggest that the bias is entirely due to expectational errors and that none is due to time-varying risk. While such a decomposition cannot itself shed light on whether the expectational errors are generated by learning, peso problems, or by market inefficiency, neither learning nor peso problems seem to offer complete explanations of the facts. Taken as a whole, the evidence suggests that explanations which allow for the possibility for market inefficiency should be seriously investigated.

What are the policy implications of the apparent market inefficiency in foreign exchange markets? Because the evidence for inefficiency is ambiguous, and because there exists no good general equilibrium model of exchange rates, we can say little about whether exchange rate fluctuations are costly enough to merit government intervention. Although the kind of inefficiency discussed above can lead to very large distortions in the level of the exchange rate interventions such as transactions taxes or an exchange rate peg also involve costs to welfare. Future research may help to determine how consumers and producers are affected by the use of such blunt policy instruments.

The authors wish to thank Robert Cumby, Charles Engel, Jeffrey Frankel, Kenneth Kasa, Timothy Luerhman, Robert Hodrick, Karen Lewis, Michael Mussa, Maurice Obstfeld, and Andre Perold for helpful comments and the Division of Research at Harvard Business School (Froot) and Concord Capital Management and the Russell Sage Foundation (Thaler) for generous financial support.

ENDNOTES

1 For a discussion of the performance of exchange rate models over this period, see Meese (1990).

2 Similarly, the results would then also imply that when the

foreign interest rate rises (relative to the dollar interest rate), investments in foreign assets become relatively more risky.

3 Readers may find it difficult to understand how assets denominated in one currency can be riskier than assets denominated in the other currency when there is only a single exchange rate to connect them. The following example may help. Suppose that two equally-sized countries have perfectly integrated trade in gods and assets. Each produces its own good, but consumes both goods in equal amounts. Each country also has an asset which pays off in future consumption of its good. Now suppose that country A's asset represents claims to a greater fraction of country A's good then B's asset represents of country B's good. In other words, the outstanding supply of country A's asset is larger than country B's. Since investors will consume the same amount of each good, all else equal, they will want to invest half of their portfolio in the assets of each country. Investors will agree to hold a greater fraction of their portfolio in the assets of country A—as they must in equilibrium—only if they get paid a premium on the return of A's asset relative to B's. In such a case, we would say that assets denominated in A's goods are "riskier" than those denominated in B's.

4 Another statistical model of exchange rate changes is presented by Engel and Hamilton (1990). They find evidence of "long swings" in the exchange rate and can reject the hypothesis that the exchange rate follows a random walk, but are also unable to find any correlation between their model's predictions and the forward discount's bias.

5 These conclusions can be softened by arguing that investors were repeatedly surprised at the strength (and subsequent weakness) of fundamentals over this period. Rationally expected appreciation (and depreciation) and estimates of the risk premium would then be closer to zero than calculated above. We address such explanations directly in the next section.

6 See also Stulz (1986) for a model of learning about the money supply process.

7 Some support for such skewness in investor's subjective distribution of exchange rate changes can be obtained from the prices of options on the dollar during this period. See Bates (1988) for evidence.

8 This sort of calculation was performed originally by Dornbusch (1982), Frankel (1982) and Krugman (1989). The dollar's collapse could be thought of as coming from a discrete shift in policy, or from the bursting of a speculative bubble.

9 The survey data discussed in Frankel and Froot (1987) report expected depreciation to be about 10 percent on average during this period, much larger than the interest differential which averaged about 3 percent. If we were to use this larger number in the above calculation, the probability of observing no collapse for five consecutive years falls to .03. That is, if investors expected more rapid dollar depreciation, it becomes easier to reject this peso problem argument. Keep in mind, however, a caveat about such casually formed test statistics: their size may overstate their true statistical significance because the 1980-85 subsample is not randomly drawn. See Evans (1986) for more formal methods.

10 For examples of such models see Cutler, Poterba, and Summers (1990) and Kyle (1985).

11 Hodrick and Srivastava (1984) report less favorable risk-return tradeoffs using Bilson's (1981) data.

REFERENCES

Bates, David, "The Crash Premium: Option Pricing under Asymmetric Processes with Applications to Options on Deutsche Mark Futures," Rodney L. White Discussion Paper 36-88, University of Pennsylvania, October, 1988.

Bilson, John, "The Speculative Efficiency Hypothesis," *Journal of Business*, 1981, *54*, 433-451.

Boothe, Paul, and David Longworth, "Foreign Exchange Market Efficiency Tests: Implications of Recent Findings," *Journal of International Money and Finance*, 1986, *5*, 135-52.

Cumby, Robert, and David Modest, "Testing for Market Timing Ability: A Framework for Forecast Evaluation," *Journal of Financial Economics*, 1987, 169-89.

Cutler, David M., James M. Poterba, Lawrence H. Summers, "Speculative Dynamics and the Role of Feedback Traders," *American Economic Review*, May 1990.

Domowitz, Ian, and Craig Hakkio, "Conditional Variance and the Risk Premium in the Foreign Exchange Market," *Journal of International Economics*, 1985, *19*, 47-66.

Dooley, Michael P. and Jeff Shafer, "Analysis of Short-Run Exchange Rate Behavior: March 1983 to November 1981." In Bigman, D., and T. Taya, ed., *Exchange Rate and Trade Instability: Causes, Consequences, and Remedies*. Cambridge: Ballinger, 1983.

Dornbusch, Rudiger, "Equilibrium and Disequilibrium Exchange Rates," *Zeitschrift für Wirtschafts und Sozialwissenschaften*, 1982, *6*, 573-99.

Engel, Charles M., and James Hamilton, "Long Swings in the Foreign Exchange Market: Are They There, and Do Investors Know It?," *American Economic Review*, 1990.

Engel, Charles M., and Anthony P. Rodrigues, "Tests of International CAPM with Time-Varying Covariances," *Journal of Applied Econometrics*, 1989, *4*, 119-38.

Evans, George W., "A Test for Speculative Bubbles in the Sterling-Dollar Exchange Rate: 1981-84," *American Economic Review*, September 1986, *76*, 621-636.

Fama, Eugene, F., "Forward and Spot Exchange Rates," *Journal of Monetary Economics*, 1984, *36*, 697-703.

Frankel, Jeffrey A., "A Test of Perfect Substitutability in the Foreign Exchange Market," *Southern Economic Journal*, 1982, *48*, 406-16.

Frankel, Jeffrey A., and Charles M. Engel, "Do Asset Demand Functions Optimize over the Mean and Variance of Real Returns? A Six Currency Test," *Journal of International Economics*, 1984, *17*, 309-323

Frankel, Jeffrey A., and Kenneth A. Froot, "Using Survey Data to Test Standard Propositions on Exchange Rate Expectations," *American Economic Review*, March 1987, *77*, 133-153.

Friedman, Milton, "The Case for Flexible Exchange Rates," In his *Essays in Positive Economics*. Chicago: University of Chicago Press, 1953, 157-203.

Froot, Kenneth A., "Short Rates and Expected Asset Returns," NBER Working paper no. 3247, January 1990.

Froot, Kenneth A., and Jeffrey A. Frankel, "Forward Discount

Bias: Is it an Exchange Risk Premium?" *Quarterly Journal of Economics*, February 1989, *416*, 139-161.

Giovannini, Alberto and Phillipe Jorion, "The Time-Variation of Risk and Return in the Foreign Exchange and Stock Markets," *Journal of Finance*, 1989.

Hodrick, Robert J., *The Empirical Evidence of the Efficiency of Forward and Futures Foreign Exchange Markets*. Chur, Switzerland: Harwood Academic Publishers, 1987.

Hodrick, Robert J. and Sanjay Srivastava, "An Investigation of Risk and Return in Forward Foreign Exchange," *Journal of International Money and Finance*, April 1984, *3*, 5-30.

Hodrick, Robert J. and Sanjay Srivastava, "The Covariation of Risk Premiums and Expected Future Spot Rates," *Journal of International Money and Finance*, 1986, *V*, S5-S22.

Krugman, Paul R., *Exchange Rate Instability*, Cambridge: MIT Press 1989.

Kyle, Albert F., "Continuous Auctions and Insider Trading," *Econometrica*, November 1985, *53*, 1315-1336.

Levich, Richard, "Empirical Studies of Exchange Rates: Price Behavior, Rate Determination and Market Efficiency." In Jones, R.W., and P. B. Kenen, eds. *Handbook of International Economics*, Volume 2, Amsterdam: North Holland, 1985.

Lewis, Karen K., "Changing Beliefs and Systematic Rational Forecast Errors with Evidence from Foreign Exchange," *American Economic Review*, September 1989, *79*, 621-636.

Mark, Nelson C., "On Time Varying Risk Premia in the Foreign Exchange Market: An Econometric Analysis," *Journal of Monetary Economics*, 1985, *16*, 3-18.

Meese, Richard, "Currency Fluctuations in the Post-Bretton Woods Era," *Journal of Economic Perspectives*, Winter 1990, *4*, 117-134.

Mussa, Michael, "Empirical Regularities in the Behavior of Exchange Rates and Theories of the Foreign Exchange Market." In Brunner, K. and A.H. Meltzer, eds., *Policies for Employment Prices and Exchange Rates*, Vol. 11, Carnegie-Rochester Conference Series on Public Policy, supplement to the *Journal of Monetary Economics*, 1979, 9-57.

Nurkse, Ragnar, *International Currency Experience*, Geneva: League of Nations, 1944.

Obstfeld, Maurice, "The Effectiveness of Foreign-Exchange Intervention: Recent Experience 1985-1988." In Branson, W., J. Frankel, and M. Goldstein, eds., *International Policy Coordination and Exchange Rate Determination*. Chicago: University of Chicago Press, 1990.

Rogoff Kenneth, "Essays on Expectations and Exchange Rate Volatility,": Ph.D. Dissertation Massachusetts Institute of Technology, 1979.

Schulmeister, Stephan, "An Essay on Exchange Rate Dynamics," WZB, Berlin Discussion Paper no. 87-8, July 1987.

Stulz, Rene, "An Equilibrium Model of Exchange Rate Determination and Asset Pricing with Non-Traded Goods and Imperfect Information," mimeo, Ohio State University, 1986.

Sweeney, R.J., "Beating the Foreign Exchange Market," *Journal of Finance*, 1986, *41*, 163-82.

Tversky, Amos, and Richard H. Thaler, "Anomalies: Preference Reversals," *Journal of Economic Perspectives* Spring, 1990, *4*, 201-211.

READING 13

Do Sterilized Interventions Affect Exchange Rates?

Warren E. Weber

On September 22, 1985, at New York's Plaza Hotel, the governments of the Group of Five countries (France, Japan, the United Kingdom, the United States, and West Germany) announced a coordinated program to depreciate the U.S. dollar against other major currencies. A major part of this program was a commitment by these countries to intervene against the dollar in foreign exchange markets. In the next six months or so, the value of the dollar fell about 20 percent (on a trade-weighted basis).

This coincidence of foreign exchange market interventions and a fall in the value of the dollar might seem to indicate that such interventions are a powerful tool with which policymakers can affect exchange rates and, therefore, potentially output and inflation. However, because foreign exchange market intervention involves the exchange of one currency for bonds denominated in another, it can affect an intervening country's monetary base (currency plus commercial bank reserves). As a result, any effects on an intervention on exchange rates may be due to changes in the monetary base—which suggests that the effects may be due to changes in monetary policy rather than intervention.

Nonetheless, a country can intervene in the foreign exchange market without changing its monetary base. Interventions conducted in this way are called sterilized.[1] But do sterilized interventions affect exchange rates? If the answer is yes, policymakers have a third policy tool (besides monetary and fiscal policy) with which to affect the economy. Economic theory suggest that a yes answer is possible. Unfortunately, though, the empirical evidence overwhelmingly says that in fact the answer is no.

STERILIZING FOREIGN EXCHANGE INTERVENTIONS

This section presents the mechanics of a sterilized foreign exchange market intervention. It shows that although a sterilized intervention leaves a country's monetary base unchanged, the intervention does change the quantities of domestic and foreign bonds in the portfolio of its central bank. Thus, the quantities of various bonds available for private agents to hold in their portfolios are also changed—which could affect exchange rates.

To understand the mechanics of a foreign exchange intervention by the United States, compare it to an open market operation conducted by the Federal Reserve. An open market operation involves the exchange of liabilities of the Fed (essentially, commercial bank reserves at the Fed) for U.S.government securities. For example, suppose the Fed sells $50 million of U.S. government securities from its portfolio. The effects of such a transaction are shown at the top of the accompanying table. The Fed's transfer of U.S. government securities to commercial banks is labeled transaction (1). The commercial banks pay for the securities with their reserves at the Fed; that is labeled transaction (2).[2] The overall effect of this open market sale of U.S. government securities is to decrease the reserves of the U.S. banking system—

Accounting for a Foreign Exchange Intervention

Type of Transaction		Federal Reserve: Assets	Federal Reserve: Liabilities	U.S. Commercial Banks: Assets	U.S. Commercial Banks: Liabilities	German Commercial Banks: Assets	German Commercial Banks: Liabilities
U.S. Open Market Operation (Sale of U.S. Securities)	(1)	U.S. Secs. -$50 mil.		U.S. Secs. +$50 mil.			
	(2)		**Reserves -$50 mil.**	Reserves -$50 mil.			
U.S Foreign Exchange Intervention (Sale of German Marks)							
Unsterilized	(1)	German Secs. -$50 mil.				German Secs. +$50 mil.	
	(2)				Deposits of German Banks -$50 mil.	Deposits at U.S. Banks -$50 mil.	
	(3)		**Reserves -$50 mil.**	Reserves -$50 mil.			
Sterilized	(1)	German Secs. -$50 mil.				German Secs. +$50 mil.	
					Deposits of German Banks -$50 mil.	Deposits at U.S. Banks -$50 mil.	
			Reserves -$50 mil.	Reserves -$50 mil.			
	(2)	U.S. Secs. +$50 mil.		U.S. Secs. -$50 mil.			
			Reserves +$50 mil.	Reserves +$50 mil.			

and, therefore, the U.S. monetary base—here, by $50 million.

A foreign exchange intervention also involves the exchange of liabilities of the Fed, but in this case they are exchanged for foreign government securities (denominated in the currency of the issuing country).[3] To continue the above example, suppose that instead of selling $50 million of U.S. government securities from its portfolio, the Fed sells the market equivalent of $50 million of the securities of another government—say, West Germany. This would be considered a foreign exchange intervention by the Fed in favor of the dollar and against the deutsche mark because the intention of such an intervention is to raise the value of the dollar relative to the mark by decreasing the supply of dollars relative to the supply of marks.

The mechanics of this foreign exchange

intervention are shown in the middle of the table. The intervention begins with the Fed selling some of its holdings of German government securities to German commercial banks. This transfer of securities is transaction (1). The German banks pay for the securities out of their accounts with U.S. commercial banks, in transaction (2). On receipt of the payment from the German banks, the Fed debits the reserves of U.S. commercial banks, transaction (3).[4]

This foreign exchange intervention has the same overall effect on U.S. bank reserves as does the open market sale of U.S. government securities. Both actions remove $50 million of U.S. commercial bank reserves. The difference between the two actions is that the open market operation decreases the Fed's holdings of domestic assets whereas the foreign exchange intervention decreases its holdings of foreign assets (more precisely, assets denominated in foreign currency units).[5]

The intervention illustrated in the middle of the table is unsterilized because the U.S. monetary base has been affected. Any such effect can be neutralized—the intervention sterilized—however, by an offsetting open market operation. For example, the Fed's sale of the market equivalent of $50 million of German government securities can be sterilized by a Fed open market purchase of $50 million of U.S. government securities. The bottom of the table shows those transaction. Transaction (1) is the unsterilized foreign exchange intervention; transaction (2) is the open market purchase of U.S. government securities. Clearly, the overall effect of these transactions is a sterilized intervention because they leave the U.S. monetary base unchanged.

Note, however, that something is changed by a sterilized intervention. Though the level of the U.S. monetary base is the same after such an intervention, the composition of the Fed's portfolio of domestic and foreign assets is different.

Since a sterilized intervention does not affect the total available stock of assets, this means that the composition of private agents' portfolios of domestic and foreign assets is also changed. And since, for markets to clear, private agents must adjust their demands for assets to equal the supplies available to them, rates of return and exchange rates might reasonably be expected to adjust as well.

EXCHANGE RATE EFFECTS: A THEORETICAL POSSIBILITY . . .

A simple theoretical model can investigate whether or not exchange rates are affected by a change in the quantities of bonds denominated in domestic and foreign currencies that are available to the private sector. As is appropriate, this model emphasizes private agents' demands for assets denominated in different currencies.[6] In general, the model's results are ambiguous: sterilized interventions may or may not have exchange rate effects, depending on the values of certain parameters. Under certain conditions, however, the model says sterilized interventions do not affect exchange rates.

The model has only two countries—a home country and a foreign country—and four assets—the currencies of the two countries and bonds denominated in each of the two currencies. In such an economy, the liabilities of a central bank must equal its holdings of bonds denominated in either currency, as was illustrated in the last section. Neither country has commercial banks, so each country's money supply equals the liabilities of its central bank.

In more technical terms, then, the home country money supply at time t, $M(t)$, must equal the value of the home central bank's holdings of bonds denominated in units of the home currency, $B_g(t)$, plus the value of its holdings of bonds denominated in the foreign currency, $F_g(t)$ in terms of its own currency. That is

(1) $$M(t) = B_g(t) + e(t)F_g(t)$$

where $e(t)$ is the exchange rate at time t in units of home currency per unit of foreign currency.[7] Similarly, the foreign country money supply, $M^*(t)$, must equal the value of the foreign central bank's holdings of bonds denominated in the foreign currency, $F^*_g(t)$, plus the value of its holdings of bonds denominated in the home currency, $B^*_g(t)$, in foreign currency units. That is,

(2) $$M^*(t) = [B^*_g(t)/e(t)] + F^*_g(t).$$

Throughout the analysis, the levels of the money supplies, $M(t)$ and $M^*(t)$, are assumed to be determined exogenously (outside the model), as are the central bank's holdings of bonds denominated in the foreign currency,.$F_g(t)$ and $F_g{}^*(t)$. Once the levels of these variables have been set, central bank's holdings of bonds denominated in the home currency. $B_g(t)$ and $B_g{}^*(t)$, are determined by (1) and (2), respectively.

The sterilized intervention example of the previous section provides a good illustration of this point. Call the United States the home country and West Germany the foreign country. When the Fed intervenes in the foreign exchange market by selling German government bonds, it decreases its holding of $F_g(t)$. When the Fed sterilizes this intervention by buying U.S. government bonds, it increases its holdings of $B_g(t)$. And since the U.S. money supply must be left unchanged, the Fed's increase in its holdings of U.S. government bonds must be exactly offset by the decrease in its holdings of German bonds; that is, these changes must satisfy $dB_g(t) = -d[e(t)F_g(t)]$. A sterilized intervention by the foreign country must satisfy a similar restriction.

The asset demand functions of private agents in this economy are formulated under two assumptions: private agents can only hold the currency of the country in which they reside, and private agents' asset demands depend only on expected rates of return and aggregate wealth. For now, no restrictions are placed on how interchangeable agents consider bonds denominated in different currencies since there are several reasons agents might consider such bonds less than perfect substitutes. One is the existence of market frictions, such as the risk that currency controls might be imposed. And if agents are risk averse, another is differences in the return distributions of bonds due to uncertain exchange rate changes or differences in default risks, for example.

Specifically, the asset demands of home country residents are assumed to depend on their aggregate wealth, $W(t)$, and the rates of return on the two types of bonds, expressed in terms of the home currency. The rate of return on bonds denominated in the home currency is $r(t)$, and that on bonds denominated in the foreign currency is $r_*-\pi(t)$, where $r_*(t)$ is the rate of return in terms of the foreign currency on bonds denominated in the foreign currency and $\pi(t)$ the expected rate of depreciation of the home currency relative to the foreign currency.[8] Therefore, home residents' demand for bonds denominated in the home currency is

$$(3) \qquad B_p(t) = b_p[r(t), r_*(t) + \pi(t), W(t)].$$

It is assumed to depend positively on $r(t)$ and $W(t)$ and negatively on $.r_*(t) + \pi(t)$. Home demand for foreign bonds is

$$(4) \qquad e(t)F_p(t) = f_p[r(t), r_*(t) + \pi(t), W(t)].$$

It is assumed to depend positively on $r_*(t) + \pi(t)$. and $W(t)$ and negatively on $r(t)$.

Once these two demand functions have been specified, home country residents' demand for money can be determined from their budget constraint

$$(5) \qquad M(t) + B_p(t) + e(t)F_p(t) = W(t)$$

which states that their holdings of money and bonds must equal their wealth.

Similar assumptions are made about the asset demands of foreign country residents. Specifically, the asset demands of foreign residents are assumed to depend on their aggregate wealth, $W^*(t)$, and the rates of return on the two types of bonds, expressed in terms of the foreign currency. The rate of return in terms of the foreign currency on bonds denominated in the home currency is $r(t) - \pi(t)$, and that on bonds denominated in the foreign currency is $r^*(t)$. Therefore, foreign residents' demand for bonds denominated in the home currency is

$$(6) \qquad B^*_p(t) \,/\, e(t) = b_p{}^*[r(t) - \pi(t), r^*(t), W^*(t)].$$

It is assumed to depend positively on $r^*(t)$ and $W^*(t)$ and negatively on $r(t) - \pi(t)$. Foreign demand for bonds denominated in the foreign currency is

$$(7) \qquad F_p{}^*(t) = f_p{}^*[r(t) - \pi(t), r^*(t), W^*(t)].$$

It is assumed to depend positively on $r^*(t)$ and $W^*(t)$ and negatively on $r(t) - \pi(t)$. Given these bond demands, foreign country residents' demand for money can be determined from their budget constraint, which s analogous to (5).

Markets are cleared when supply equals demand. The total stock of bonds denominated in the home currency, $B(t)$, and the total stock of bonds denominated in the foreign currency, $F(t)$, are determined by the past government deficit policies in the respective countries. These policies are assumed to have been set exogenously, so that the total stocks of both type of bonds are given.

Consequently, the market for bonds denominated in the home currency is cleared when

$$(8) \qquad \bar{B}(t) = B_p(t) + B_p{}^*(t) + B_g(t) + B_g{}^*(t).$$

Similarly, the market for bonds denominated in the foreign currency is cleared when

$$(9) \qquad \bar{F}(t) = F_p(t) + F_p{}^*(t) + F_g(t) + F_g{}^*(t).$$

The market for home currency is cleared when the supply of home currency, as given by (1), equals the demand for it, from (5). And when the markets for the two bonds and the home currency are cleared, so will the market for foreign currency, according to Walras' law.

Since the asset demands given by (3), (4), (6), and (7) are specified only in terms of implicit functions, the model cannot be solved explicitly for equilibrium return or exchange rates. However, a very useful linear approximation of the solution for the expected rate of depreciation of the home currency is[9]

$$(10) \qquad \pi(t) = \alpha_0 + \alpha_1 \bar{B}(t) + \alpha_2 e(t)\bar{F}(t)$$
$$+ \alpha_3 M(t) + \alpha_1 e(t) M^*(t)$$
$$+ (\alpha_1 \alpha_2) e(t)[Fg(t) + F_g{}^*(t)]$$
$$+ \alpha_4 W(t) + \alpha_5 e(t) W^*(t).$$

The parameters α_1 through α_5 are complicated functions of the derivatives of the bond demand functions of both home and foreign residents, and unfortunately, the assumptions about the signs of these derivatives do not provide enough information to sign any of the α's. According to (10), the rate of depreciation of the home currency depends in an indeterminate way on the total stock of both types of bonds, home and foreign money supplies, home and foreign wealth, and central banks' holdings of bonds denominated in foreign currency.[10]

Fortunately, the inability to sign the α's does not limit (10)'s usefulness for determining whether or not sterilized interventions can affect exchange rates. Consider the discussion of sterilized interventions in the last section. When the Fed (the home country) intervenes in favor of the dollar by selling German (foreign country) securities and then sterilizes by buying U.S. securities. $e(t)F_g(t)$ decreases with $M(t)$ unchanged. Thus, if $\alpha_1 > \alpha_2$ the sterilized intervention makes the dollar depreciate more rapidly relative to the mark. If $\alpha_1 = \alpha_2$, though, the sterilization leaves exchange rates unchanged.

A natural question, then, is whether theory restricts the value of $\alpha_1 - \alpha_2$. The answer is no: without further restrictions on the derivatives of the bond demand functions, the value of $\alpha_1 - \alpha_2$ is unrestricted, ,and sterilized interventions may or may not affect exchange rates.

A restriction can be placed on bond demands, however, that will make sterilized interventions not affect exchange rates. The restriction is that residents of both countries consider bonds denominated in different currencies *perfect substitutes*: more precisely, while residents of both countries have demand functions for total bond holdings, they are indifferent to the composition of their bond portfolios as long as both types of bonds have the same expected rates of return. Solving the model given by (1)-(9) under this perfect substitutes restriction yields the result that $\alpha_1 = \alpha_2$. Thus, under this restriction, changes in the composition of central bank portfolios, such as those due to a sterilized intervention, leave the rate of depreciation of the exchange rate unchanged. This makes good economic sense because when private agents consider bonds denominated in different currencies perfect substitutes, they do not require any changes in the relative rates of return on those bonds to offset the change in the composition of available bonds which results from the sterilized intervention.

. . . REJECTED BY THE EVIDENCE

Since theory leaves open the question of whether sterilized interventions affect exchange rates, empirical evidence must be consulted. Two basic types of empirical evidence are available. One is evidence on whether bonds denominated in different currencies are perfect substitutes. if they are, then $\alpha_1 = \alpha_2$, and sterilized interventions cannot affect exchange rates. Unfortunately, although most empirical studies show bonds to be perfect substitutes, this evidence is not conclusive. The other type of evidence is direct evidence on the relative magnitude of α_1 and α_2 from empirical studies of the effects of bond holdings on exchange rates, obtained either by estimating equations similar to (10) or by estimating the bond demand equations of the model. These studies provide almost no evidence that sterilized interventions affect exchange rates. And taken together, all the empirical studies make a strong case that sterilized interventions do not affect exchange rates.

Bond Substitutability

When bonds denominated in different currencies are perfect substitutes, their expected rates of return must be equal, so that

$$(11) \qquad r(t) - r^*(t) - \pi(t) = 0$$

If their rates of return were not equal, the demand for the bond with the higher rate would be infinite and markets could not be cleared.

When bonds denominated in different currencies are not perfect substitutes, however, (11) does not have to hold and some or all of the variables on the right side of (10) could help explain $r(t) - r^*(t) - \pi(t)$. Thus, the empirical test of whether bonds denominated in different currencies are perfect substitutes is the test of whether any of the exogenous variables of the model have nonzero coefficients in a regression equation with the term $r(t) - r^*(t) - \pi(t)$ as the dependent variable.[11]

Since the empirical studies of bond substitutability have this term as their dependent variable, they encounter the problem of how to measure the expected future exchange rate to obtain a value for $\pi(t)$. They solve the problem by assuming that expectations are rational, so that $E[e(t+1]$ equals actual $e(t+1)$ plus a white noise error term (an unpredictable element).[12] The studies differ in the currency denomination of the bonds they consider, the period and sampling frequency of their data, and the specification of the right side of their estimating equation.

Frankel (1982a) uses monthly data from January 1974 to October 1978 to examine the substitutability of bonds denominated in West German marks and U.S. dollars. The right side of his regression equation has a constant term and the ratio of mark-denominated bonds to wealth. He finds that neither variable has a regression coefficient significantly different from zero. Though he does not test whether both coefficients are simultaneously equal to zero, he interprets his regression results as indicating that German and U.S. bonds are perfect substitutes. Frankel comes to the same conclusion in a later study (1982b) which uses monthly data for a longer period from (June 1973 to August 1980) to examine bonds denominated in more currencies (six). This study uses a system of regression equations specified so that he can test the null hypothesis that all regression coefficients are simultaneously equal to zero. He is unable to reject that hypothesis, again indicating perfect substitutability of bonds.

Dooley and Isard (1983) obtain very similar results using end of quarter data from 1973 to 1978. They too study the substitutability of bonds denominated in West German marks and U.S. dollars On the right side of their estimating equation, they include only a constant term and dollar-denominated bonds. Like Frankel (1982a), they find no statistically significant coefficients in their regression equations. However, they do not test the hypothesis that both regression coefficients equal zero.

Rogoff (1984) obtains the same type of results for the substitutability of bonds denominated in U.S. and Canadian dollars using weekly data from March 1973 to December 1980. The right side of his regression equation includes only a constant and the ratio of home to foreign bonds. Although he also does not test the joint hypothesis of both regression coefficients equaling zero, he finds significant coefficients only for the subperiod from March 1973 to November 1976, and even then the coefficient on the bond ratio has what he considers an incorrect sign. Thus, overall his evidence argues against imperfect substitutability.

One study which does obtain some evidence of less than perfect substitutability is that by Danker et al. (1985). Using monthly data from February 1975 to December 1981, they study the substitutability of bonds denominated in West German marks, Japanese yen and Canadian dollars with those in U.S. dollars. To study mark- and yen-denominated bonds versus U.S. dollar-denominated bonds, they use two estimating equations. One includes only home country (U.S.) variables (interest rates, income, wealth, and bonds); the other, only foreign country variables (wealth and bonds). To study the substitutability of Canadian versus U.S. dollar-denominated bonds, they combine the home and foreign country variables (interest rates, income, wealth, and bonds) in a single equation. For the mark/U.S. dollar equation with only home variables and for the Canadian/U.S. dollar equation, the hypothesis of perfect substitutability is rejected. But for the mark/U.S.dollar equation with only foreign variables and for both yen/US dollar equations, that hypothesis is not rejected.

Stronger evidence against perfect substitutability is obtained by Loopesko (1983). She studies the substitutability of Eurodollar deposits denominated in West German marks, Japanese yen, French francs, British pounds and Canadian dollars with such deposits denominated in U.S. dollars. She uses daily data starting between 1975 and 1979, depending on the currency denomination, and ending November 6, 1981. Her regression equation includes a constant term, lagged U.S. and German exchange market interventions, lagged exchange rates, and lagged differences between interest rates on the Eurodollars [versions of the term $r(t) - r^*(t) - \pi(t)$ in (11)]. In almost all cases, she is able to reject the null hypothesis of perfect substitutability.

The Danker et al., and Loopesko studies cover more currencies and longer time periods than most of the others, and the Danker et al. study pays the most attention to data construction. Nonetheless, the findings in these two studies do not seem strong enough to completely overturn the others'. For Danker et al., a major reason is that the U.S. interest rate is on both sides of some regression equations. Thus, even if that rate is replaced by an instrument when it appears as a right side variable, its coefficient would not be expected to be zero. This could bias the hypothesis tests in favor of rejecting perfect substitutability. And note that Danker et al. reject perfect substitutability only in those regression equations that have an interest rate as a right side variable. The same problem occurs in Loopesko's study with respect to exchange rates dated period $t - 2$ ($t - 1$ for Canada). If terms involving these exchange rates were modified from the right side of her regression equations, some evidence in her paper suggests that the results would be less unfavorable to the perfect substitutability hypothesis.

In summary, the empiricle studies of bond substitutability provide some evidence that bonds denominated in different currencies are perfect substitutes, so that $\alpha_1 = \alpha_2$, but this evidence is far from conclusive.[13]

Bond Effects

Stronger evidence that $\alpha_1 = \alpha_2$ comes from several empirical studies which include bonds in equations attempting to explain the determination of exchange rates.

Branson, Halttunen, and Masson (1977) estimate a modification of (10) in level form using monthly data from August 1971 to December 1976. They examine the West German mark/U.S. dollar exchange rate in a regression equation which includes both countries' money supplies and private holdings of foreign bonds. Since these asset (bond) variables do not directly correspond to those in (10), their regression coefficients must be interpreted in terms of (10). Since Branson, Halttunen and Masson consider the total stocks of assets (bonds) to be fixed in the short run, I interpret an increase in private holdings of foreign assets as corresponding to a decrease in central bank holdings of foreign assets. Under this interpretation, the regression coefficient on private U.S. holdings of foreign assets in their analysis corresponds to $\alpha_1 - \alpha_2$ in (10), and their regression coefficient on private German holdings of foreign assets corresponds to $\alpha_1 - \alpha_2$. In their regressions, these coefficients have approximately equal but opposite signs as predicted, and neither is significantly different from zero, indicating that $\alpha_1 = \alpha_2$..[14]

Backus (1984) also estimates an equation

similar to (10), but for the U.S. dollar/Canadian dollar exchange rate with quarterly data from 1971 to 1980. He estimates several regression equations, including as right side variables the Canadian money supply, private Canadian holdings of foreign assets, the total supply of assets denominated in Canadian dollars, a U.S. interest rate, and U.S. and Canadian income levels. He obtains negative but statistically insignificant coefficients on the regression coefficient of Canadian holdings of foreign assets which (under the above interpretation of such a variable) suggests that $\alpha_1 = \alpha_2$..

Similar results are obtained by Obstfeld (1983) using a different approach. He constructs a two-asset version of the model in the last section and estimates its demand equations. Specifically, he considers West Germany the home country and the United States the foreign country, and using monthly data from January 1975 to October 1981, he estimates the demand for home country money, the supply of home country money, and home and foreign demand for mark-denominated assets. He then uses these estimated demand functions to simulate the effect of a foreign exchange intervention equivalent to 10 percent of the German monetary base. When the intervention is sterilized, his simulations indicate that the mark would appreciate a mere 0.04 percent.

Altogether, the empirical evidence from the bond effect studies indicates that sterilized interventions do not affect exchange rates. More evidence which supports this conclusion, but is generated in a very different way, comes from two recent studies by Meese and Rogoff (1983a,b). They compare the out-of-sample forecasting performance of several different models of exchange rate determination, one of which is quite similar to (10). They use monthly data from March 1973 to June 1981 of the exchange rates between the U.S. dollar and the West German mark, the Japanese yen, and the British pound as well as for the trade-weighted value of the U.S. dollar. They find that, in general, the best predictor of the log of future exchange rates is the random walk model $\log[e(t)] = \log[e(t-1)] + \varepsilon(t)$, where $\varepsilon(t)$ is a white noise error term.(15) Since bond holdings do not appear in that model, sterilized interventions cannot affect exchange rates.

CONCLUSION

Do sterilized interventions affect exchange rates? Even though theory indicates that the answer may be yes, the empirical evidence shows that the answer is actually no, at least over time intervals of a month or more.

This answer implies that policymakers only have monetary and fiscal policy as tools with which to affect the economy. Thus, if they want to influence the exchange rate, they must use one of those two tools; sterilized interventions will have no effect. But, then, why should central banks intervene in foreign exchange markets at all? If only the size, not the currency composition, of central banks portfolios matters, then it is monetary policy which affects the economy, and any effect achievable by buying or selling foreign bonds is also achievable by buying or selling domestic bonds.

Appendix
Another Type of Foreign Exchange Intervention: The Swap

The Federal Reserve does not have to intervene in the foreign exchange market by selling foreign government bonds from its portfolio. Instead, the Fed can intervene by drawing on its *swap line,* or reciprocal short-term credit agreement, with another country's central bank and using the proceeds to buy that country's commercial bank deposits held in U.S. banks. Such an intervention by the Fed can affect the monetary base in both countries.

As an example, consider how such an intervention works between the United States and West Germany. (Today the Fed has swap agreements with 14 central banks and the Bank for International Settlements.) The Fed's swap agreement with the German central bank, the Bundesbank, lets it borrow marks in return for equivalent dollar deposits at the Fed. A swap of $50 million is shown as transaction (1) in the accompanying table.

Accounting for a Swap Intervention

	Federal Reserve		U.S. Commercial Banks		Bundesbank		German Commercial Banks	
Transaction	Assets	Liabilities	Assets	Liabilities	Assets	Liabilities	Assets	Liabilities
(1)	Deposits at Bundesbank +$50 mil.	Deposits of Bundesbank +$50 mil.			Deposits at Fed +$50 mil.	Deposits of Fed +$50 mil.		
(2)				Deposits of German Banks -$50 mil.			Deposits at U.S Banks -$50 mil.	
(3)	Deposits at Bundesbank -$50 mil.					Deposits of Fed -$50 mil.		
						Reserves +$50 mil.	Reserves +$50 mil.	
(4)		**Reserves -$50 mil.**	Reserves -$50 mll.					
(5)			U.S. Secs. -$50 mil.		U.S. Secs. +$50 mil.			
		Deposits of Bundesbank -$50 mil.			Deposits at Fed -$50 mil.			
		Reserves +$50 mil.	Reserves +$50 mil.					
(6)					German Secs. -$50 mil.		German Secs. +$50 mil.	
						Reserves -$50 mil.	Reserves -$50 mil.	

ENDNOTES

1 Technically, an intervention is said to be sterilized only if the monetary base in all countries is unaffected by the intervention. However, the narrower definition is adequate here and will greatly simplify the discussion. For obvious reasons, an intervention in which the monetary base of one or more countries is affected is called *unsterilized*.

2 Usually, this open market operation would be carried out by the Fed selling the U.S. government securities to a government securities dealer, which would pay for them using a check drawn on its demand deposits with a U.S. commercial bank. Assuming that the securities are sold directly to a commercial bank simply removes the need to carry along an extra account for the securities dealer.

3 For other presentations of the money supply effects of foreign exchange interventions, see Balbach 1978 and Kubarych 1977-78.

4 The mechanics of a foreign exchange intervention are not unique; the German bonds could be sold to agents other than German commercial banks. Thus, the transactions in the table merely illustrate one way the intervention could occur. Nonetheless, no matter how it is accomplished, the final effects on private and central bank portfolios are those shown in the table.

5 Neither the open market operation nor the U.S.foreign exchange intervention affects German commercial bank reserves or the German monetary base. Of course, other countries' central banks can intervene in the foreign exchange market, too. An intervention by West Germany's central bank, the Bundesbank, for example, is the mirror image of this illustration of an intervention by the Federal Reserve. That is, intervention in favor of the dollar by the Bundesbank increases the reserves of the German banking system and the German monetary base without changing U.S. bank reserves or theU.S. monetary base. The reserves of the German central bank could also have been affected if the Fed had used its swap line of credit with the Bundesbank. this type of intervention is described in the Appendix.

6 Because this model of exchange rate determination concentrates on the supplies of and demands for assets, it is very similar to the portfolio balance model of exchange rate determination. For an excellent review of that model, see Branson and Henderson 1985.

7 Because the exchange rate is defined as units of domestic currency per unit of foreign currency, an increase in $e(t)$ indicates that the domestic currency has depreciated.

8 The expected rate of depreciation of home currency, $\pi(t)$, is defined as $\{E[e(t+1)]/e(t)\} - 1$, where E is the expectations operator conditioned on all information available at time t.

9 Equation (10) is a linear approximation of the solution to the model only under the assumption that $e(t)$ is constant when any of the exogenous variables in the model change. This is not the strictly correct solution to the model which would be obtained by solving for $e(t)$ under the assumption that $\{E[e(t+1)]$ is formed rationally. Such a solution is not possible, however, due to the model's implicit functions. Therefore, I opt to solve the model for $\pi(t)$ holding $e(t)$ constant in order to let expected exchange rate changes affect relative rates of return. that is important because the model is one of portfolio choice. Note that solving the model for $e(t)$ holding $\pi(t)$ constant gives a solution similar to (10) except that $\pi(t)$ is on the right side of the equation and all $e(t)$'s are eliminated. More important, the result that the coefficients on the central bank holdings of bonds denominated in the foreign currency have to be nonzero for sterilized interventions to affect exchange rates still holds.

10 Although the assumptions don't sign the α's, they do imply that α_1, α_2 and α_3 all have the same sign.

11 Since $r(t) - r^*(t) - \pi(t)$ is the uncovered interest differential between home and foreign bonds, uncovered interest rate parity is said to exist when (11) holds. Since the uncovered interest differential is assumed to be nonzero when bonds denominated in different currencies are imperfect substitutes, $r(t) - r^*(t) - \pi(t)$ is also referred to as the exchange rate risk premium.

12 Because these studies have this exchange rate expectations assumption, they are actually testing the joint hypothesis that bonds denominated in different currencies are perfect substitutes and exchange rate expectations are rational. Nonetheless, I will consider evidence of nonzero coefficients in regression equations as evidence against perfect substitutability alone.

13 Remember that tests of bond substitutability can only show that sterilized interventions do not have exchange rate effects if they find that bonds denominated in different currencies are perfect substitutes. Finding that such bonds are not perfect substitutes does not indicate that sterilized interventions have exchange rate effects because it does not show that $\alpha_1 \neq \alpha_2$. In other words, lack of perfect substitutability of bonds denominated in different currencies is a necessary but not sufficient condition for sterilized interventions to affect exchange rates.

14 A later study by Branson, Halttunen, and Masson 91979) uses data through March 1978. In it the coefficient on private German holdings of foreign assets remains insignificant, but the coefficient on private U.S. holdings of foreign assets is negative and significantly different from zero. These differences make interpreting this evidence about the relative magnitudes of α_1 and α_2 difficult since the studies don't provide enough information to test whether the coefficients on the asset variables are equal to each other or simultaneously equal to zero.

A drawback of both Branson, Halttunen, and Masson studies (which is explicitly recognized by the authors) is that bond holdings are not measured directly. Instead, the bond series are cumulations of current account balances on some benchmark level of bond holdings. Such a procedure obviously omits any capital gains effects.

15 See Meese and Rogoff 1983a. p. 10, for a description of how the forecasts are generated.

REFERENCES

Backus, David, 1984, Empirical models of the exchange rate: Separating the wheat from the chaff. *Canadian Journal of Economics* 17 (November); 824-46.

Balbach, Anatol B. 1978. The mechanics of intervention in

exchange markets. *Review* 60 (February): 2-7, Federal Reserve Bank of St. Louis.

Branson, William H., Halttunen, Hannu, and Masson, Paul, 1977. Exchange rates in the short run; The dollar-deutschemark rate. *European Economic Review* 10 (December): 303-24.

________, 1979, Exchange rates in the short run; Some further results. *European Economic Review* 12 (October): 395-402.

Branson, William H. and Henderson, Dale W. 1985. The specification and influence of asst markets. In *Handbook of International Economics*, ed. Ronald W. Jones and Peter B. Kennen, vol. 2 pp. 749-805. Amsterdam: North-Holland.

Danker, Deborah J. et al. 1985. Small empirical models of exchange market intervention: Applications to Germany, Japan, and Canada. Staff Study 135. Board of Governors of the Federal Reserve System.

Dooley, Michael P., and Isard, Peter, 1983. The portfolio-balance model of exchange rates and some structural estimates of the risk premium. *International Money Fund Staff Papers* 30 (December): 683-702.

Frankel, Jeffrey A., 1982a. A test of perfect substitutability in the foreign exchange market. *Southern Economic Journal* 49 (October): 406-16.

________, 1982b. In search of the exchange risk premium: A six-currency test assuming mean-variance optimization. *Journal of International Money and Finance* (December): 255-74.

Kubarych, Roger M. 1977-78. Monetary effects of Federal Reserve swaps. *Quarterly Review* 2 (Winter): 19-21. Federal Reserve Bank of New York.

Loopesko, Bonnie E. 1983. Relationships among exchange rates, intervention and interest rates. An empirical investigation. Staff Study 133. Board of Governors of the Federal Reserve System.

Meese, Richard A., and Rogoff, Kenneth, 1983a. Empirical exchange rate models of the seventies: Do they fit out of sample? *Journal of International Economics* 14 (February): 3-24.

________, 1983b. The out-of-sample failure of empirical exchange rate models: Sampling error or misspecification? In *Exchange rates and international macroeconomics*, ed. Jacob A. Frenkel, pp. 67-112. Chicago: University of Chicago Press.

Obstfeld, Maurice, 1983. Exchange rates, inflation and the sterilization problem: Germany, 1975-1981. *European Economic Review* 21 (March: April): 161-89.

Rogoff, Kenneth, 1984. On the effects of sterilized intervention: An analysis of weekly data. *Journal of Monetary Economics* 14 (September): 133-50.

SECTION VII

International Policy Coordination

Large swings in the value of the dollar in the 1980s and the concomitant trade imbalances among industrial countries have prompted economists and politicians to consider the advantages and disadvantages of internationally-coordinated macroeconomic policies. The most recent episode of coordinated interventions began in September 1985 with the Plaza Accord. This agreement led to monetary policy interventions with the objective of influencing exchange rates. The efficacy and desirability of coordinated policy-making are the subject matter of the articles in this section. How are the potential effects of coordination dependent on the extent to which countries are interdependent? Regardless of this interdependence, is international coordination of macroeconomic policies a desirable strategy? Norman Fieleke and Martin Feldstein address these issues in their articles.

READING 14

Economic Interdependence between Nations: Reason for Policy Coordination?

Norman S. Fieleke

When the stock market crashed in October of last year, it crashed around the world. From October 7 through October 28, popular indexes fell between 24 percent and 30 percent in the United States, Germany, France, the United Kingdom, Canada, the Netherlands, and Switzerland, and by 13 percent in Japan. The crash was but the latest in a series of harsh reminders that the world economy is an interdependent system, with each part influencing, and influenced by, the functioning of the whole. Not only the stock market plunge, but oil shocks, Third World debt problems, and record U.S. trade deficits have combined to convey an impression of high interdependence—and vulnerability.

This heightened sense of interdependence has led to more frequent calls for coordination of the economic policies pursued by different nations. Indeed, following the widely reported "Plaza" agreement, "coordination" became one of the economic buzzwords of the 1980s. Meeting at New York's Plaza Hotel on September 22, 1985, the finance ministers and central bank heads in Britain, France, Japan, West Germany, and the United States announced that they were prepared to cooperate to lower the foreign exchange value of the dollar, which had been declining but which they considered still too high in light of underlying economic conditions. Following this announcement, the dollar's foreign exchange value continued to decline, for a while even faster than before, suggesting that coordination efforts might be fruitful.

But is the world economy really more highly integrated or interdependent than it was, say, 30 years ago? Should national governments coordinate their economic policies more closely, and if so, through what institutional means?

MEASURES OF INTEGRATION

Economic integration and economic interdependence have been defined in a number of somewhat different ways. The essence of the concepts is most clearly indicated by likening an economy, as Alfred Marshall did, to a changing biological organism (Marshall 1948, p. 461); the functioning of one part is influenced by that of others, while all contribute to the functioning of the whole. The various national (sub)economies can be tightly or only loosely integrated into this kind of interdependent, organic whole.

While the general concept of economic integration is easily conveyed, a definition that lends itself to quantitative measurement is much more difficult to set forth. One approach is to measure the degree to which prices of similar goods or productive factors are equalized, or at least move in parallel, across national boundaries, with prices of course expressed in a single currency. If prices so measured diverge sharply between countries, the explanation could lie in high transportation or communication costs or in government barriers to commerce (such as tariffs), all of which would serve to prevent the full merger of more or less separate markets into a single market. Another approach is to measure the share of a nation's economic activity that is accounted for by exchanges with other nations. Larger shares are taken to signify closer integration—or at least closer physical ties, or "openness," to the rest of the world.

MOVEMENTS OF GOODS, LABOR, AND CAPITAL

According to the latter measure, economic integration across goods markets has been increasing, at least for the major industrial countries and for the sampling of major less developed countries listed in table 1. For some countries the increase has been remarkable. The average of South Korea's exports and imports as a share of the nation's gross domestic output rose from about 9 percent in 1960-61 to nearly 37 percent in 1984-85; France, Germany, Italy, and Brazil also experienced dramatic increases. For some countries the change has been less impressive, but on average for the countries listed the share of international commerce in domestic output went up from 15.6 percent to 21.7 percent over the 35 years covered by the table.

Such increases in integration have been fostered by improvements in communications and transportation and, at least until the 1980's, by reductions in government barriers to international trade, especially tariff barriers. For example, the cost of a three-minute, off-peak telephone call between Washington, D.C. and Frankfurt, Germany, declined by 95 percent between 1950 and 1985, after adjustment for inflation. the cost of air travel also plummeted. Measured in 1985 dollars, the average fare per passenger mile for international air travel dropped by two-thirds between 1950 and 1983; for air freight, the comparable figure was a decline of nearly four-fifths in the cost per ton mile (Cooper 1985b, pp. 10-11).

Although reductions in communications and transportation costs have favored the movement of capital and labor as well as goods, government barriers to the international movement of labor have proven more unyielding than barriers to merchandise trade; and it is common knowledge that labor services are exchanged among nations much less freely than are the products of labor. Nonetheless, significant transfers of labor do occur. For example, in the United States more than 40 percent of recent yearly growth in the labor force may be attributable to immigrants (Cooper 1985b, p. 8).

With respect to capital, the impression is widespread that its mobility has been greatly enhanced in recent years by the relaxation of government controls and by speedier communications. It would be instructive to examine data on gross capital transactions between nations, but all capital flow data relate to net changes in claims or liability over specified time periods. Fortunately, the net data are helpful. Indeed, it is the net movement of capital, rather than the gross, that represents a transfer of resources between countries. A country that lends, on net, acquiring net claims on other countries, does so essentially by exporting more goods and services than it imports and by accepting IOUs for the excess. The net lending is measured by the country's balance of international payments on current account, similarly, a nation borrows by incurring a deficit in its current account.

One would expect the value of such borrowing and lending to increase over time with economic growth and inflation and with the increase in total saving and investment. An interesting question, then, relating to economic integration, is not simply whether such borrowing and lending have increased but whether they have increased more rapidly than the value of total saving or total investment. In other words, what has happened to the ratio of the current account balance to gross investment or to gross saving? For the sample of 14 industrial countries listed in table 2, the average ratio has risen, but not dramatically. For half of these countries the current account balance declined as a percentage of gross saving (disregarding the algebraic sign) between 1952-53 and 1984-85, but the average of the country percentages increased appreciably. On balance, the data provide some support for the view that national capital markets had become more highly integrated during the 1980s.

However, volatility rather than strong trend seems to characterize this measure of net international capital flows, with sharp fluctuations occurring for many countries. Moreover, as the table shows, the total deficits and surpluses accumulated by most countries over the entire period 1952-85 were small in relation to their gross national saving. (One exception is Ireland, which borrowed relatively

Table 1

International Commerce as a Percentage of Gross Domestic Output, for Selected Countries and Years

Country	1950–51	1960–61	1970–71	1980–81	1984–85
Industrial Countries					
Canada	22.1	18.1	21.5	27.0	26.9
France	15.9	12.4	15.4	22.6	23.7
Germany	13.5	18.3	21.6	29.7	32.7
Italy	12.0[a]	13.1	16.3	22.5	21.9
Japan	n.a.	10.9	10.9	15.7	14.9
United Kingdom	25.5	20.3	21.9	25.8	28.7
United States	4.5	4.6	5.5	10.2	8.8
Average[b]	15.6	14.0	16.2	21.9	22.5
Less Developed Countries					
Argentina	n.a.	n.a.	8.6	9.1	n.a.
Brazil	n.a.	7.2	7.3	9.7	22.1
India	n.a.	6.3	4.5	8.7	8.1[c]
South Korea	n.a.	9.3	19.7	38.5	36.7
Mexico	15.7	11.2	8.4	12.9	14.0[c]
Average[b]	15.7	8.5	9.7	15.8	20.2
Average for All Countries Listed[b]	15.6	12.0	13.5	19.4	21.7

[a] 1951–52
[b] Simple average of percentages
[c] 1983–84
n.a. not available.
Note: A country's international commerce is defined as half the sum of the country's exports and imports, where exports and imports are as defined in the country's national accounts and generally include goods as well as non-factor services (and exclude interest and other income receipts and payments).
Source: International Monetary Fund, *International Financial Statistics*, various issues.

heavily and would require nearly four and one-half years of saving at its 1985 rate in order to pay back its net foreign debt incurred on current account over the years 1952-85.) These data as well as other studies indicate that over the long run very little capital is transferred, net, between nations.[1] To explain this phenomenon various hypotheses have been set forth, including the arguments that net international capital flows are discouraged in the long run, if not in the short, by government controls, by foreign exchange risks and political risks, and by government policies designed to constrain current account deficits and surpluses.[2] Another line of reasoning suggests that the explanation lies not in such constraints over international capital flows but in a low transference of such flows within *domestic* capital markets into less liquid assets such as equities. With higher transferability within domestic markets, net international flows could presumably increase (Frankel, Dooley, and Mathieson 1986). This last hypothesis, however, is somewhat undermined by a recent study that suggests such transferability already is extremely high.[3]

PRICE MOVEMENTS: LABOR AND CAPITAL

A second method, preferred by many, of measuring integration is to compare the levels or movements of prices for similar goods or productive

Table 2

Selected Statistics on Current-Account Balances for 14 Industrial OECD Countries, 1952–85

Country	Current-Account Balance as Percent of Gross National Saving 1952–53 (1)	1960–61 (2)	1970–71 (3)	1980–81 (4)	1984–85 (5)	Cumulative Current-Account Balance (Billions of Dollars) (6)	Col. (6) Divided by 1985 Gross National Saving (7)
Austria	7.2	−3.3	−1.3	−8.9	−1.7	−12.5	−.8
Canada	−4.9	−19.6	4.1	−4.8	1.3	−39.4	−.6
Denmark	3.7	−6.4	−13.1	−25.6	−25.7	−25.0	−2.8
Finland	−2.3	−4.2	−9.7	−6.9	−3.1	−10.4	−.8
Germany	9.8	4.2	1.3	−6.6	8.8	56.9	.4
Ireland	−21.8	−3.8	23.3	−84.9	−24.3	−14.6	−4.4
Italy	−8.3	3.8	5.9	−12.5	−4.5	−11.8	−.2
Japan	.2	−2.4	4.6	−.9	10.5	141.5	.3
Netherlands	30.3	7.3	−3.1	4.2	18.1	31.1	1.0
Norway	−7.8	−1.6	−11.6	9.7	17.3	−5.2	−.3
Sweden	2.9	−.6	.6	−18.2	−2.2	−18.9	−1.1
Switzerland	19.7	−2.1	1.0	−.2	19.7	34.7	1.2
United Kingdom	6.8	−2.8	8.3	10.7	4.1	26.9	.3
United States	−.6	3.4	.2	.8	−17.3	−231.6	−.4
Average of Percentages (Absolute Value)	9.0	4.7	6.3	13.9	11.3		

Note: A negative number signifies a current account deficit, a positive number a surplus.

Source: Organization for Economic Cooperation and Development, *National Accounts, 1960–1985*, Vol. I (Paris: OECD, 1987), and *National Accounts, 1951–1980*, Vol. I (Paris: OECD, 1982); and International Monetary Fund, Balance of Payments Statistics Yearbook, various issues (Washington, D.C.: IMF), *International Financial Statistics* Vol. XL December 1987; and *International Financial Statistics Supplement on Exchange Rates*, Supplement Series No. 1 (Washington, D.C.: IMF, 1981).

factors in different countries. Again, with regard to labor it is well known that the wage rate varies sharply among countries. Some of the variation is attributable to differences in the quality of labor rather than to barriers against labor mobility. In particular, worker efficiency rises with general education and experience with industrial methods. For example, a study of the cotton textile industry has found that a person-hour of labor in a highly literate and industrialized society is about three and one-half times as productive as a person-hour of labor in a much less advanced society (Warke 1986). Even in the absence of such quality differentials, however, obstacles to labor migration would surely prevent the equalization of labor compensation rates across national boundaries.

Barriers to the movement of capital seem less formidable than those to the movement of labor. The price for the services of capital is, of course, the rate of interest. To evaluate the integration of financial markets across countries, then, we must compare the rates of interest paid in different countries. The comparison should be of interest rates paid by borrowers whose likelihood of defaulting is similar, because the interest rate paid varies considerably with the risk status of the borrower, even within the same country.

Chart 1 attempts such a comparison, using the interest rate paid on 90-day certificates of deposit by U.S. banks, on the one hand, and the average of the three-month interest rates paid by foreign borrowers having a similar risk of default in 10 other industrial countries, on the other hand. The chart begins with the first year for which data on the average foreign rate are available. Clearly, these two interest rate series do not move as one. Especially large differences between the two series occur from 1978 to 1981. Nor do the two series move closely in parallel in most years, as is further demonstrated by the correlation coefficients in table 3; for only three of the 12 years represented are the coefficients both positive and greater than 0.8. More detailed analysis discloses similarly low correlations between the U.S. interest rate and rates in other industrial countries

Chart 1

Three-Month Interest Rates in United States and Abroad, and Foreign Currency Value of U.S. Dollar, 1976-87 (Weekly Averages)

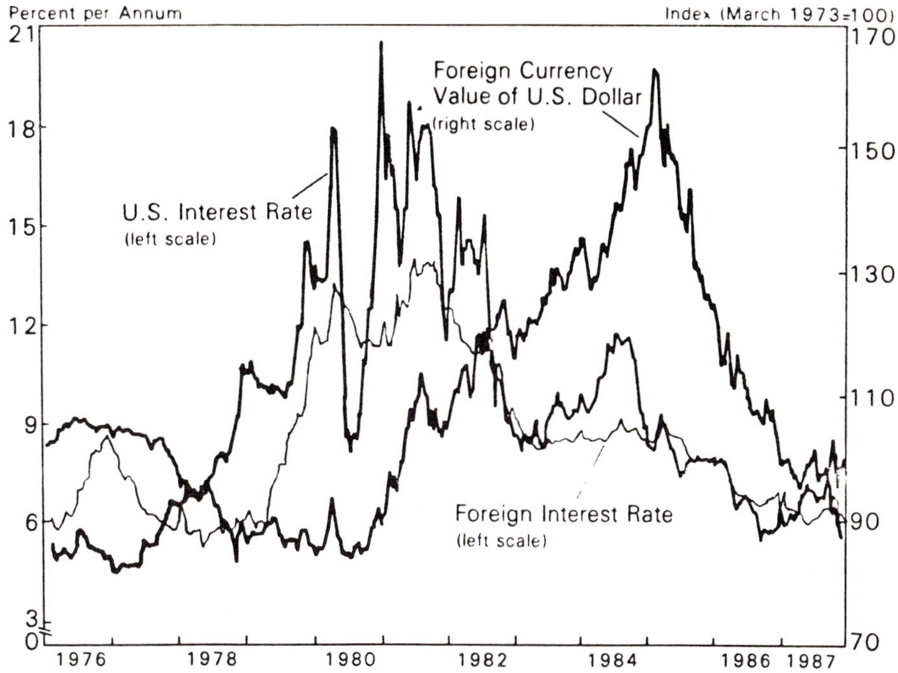

Note: U.S. interest rate is for 90-day certificates of deposit. Foreign interest rate and foreign currency value of U.S. dollar are trade-weighted averages for 10 foreign industrial countries.

Source: Board of Governors of the Federal Reserve System, Macrodata Library.

individually, with the exception of Canada. These data suggest that capital markets are not highly integrated across countries, for nominal interest rates on financial assets with similar default risk can vary substantially between the United States and other industrial countries.

However, the issue is not so simple. The interest returns represented in chart 1 are paid in different currencies, whereas the appropriate test of financial market integration is how nearly equal those rates of return are when measured in a single currency. For example, suppose that a three-month U.S. Treasury bill denominated in U.S. dollars yields 6 percent interest, that a three-month U.K. Treasury bill denominated in U.K. pounds yields 8 percent interest, and that the dollar rises in value against the pound by 3 percent over the three-month period. Taking into account the change in value of the dollar against the pound, an investor could earn 1 percent more (annual rate, ignoring transactions costs) by investing in the U.S. Treasury bill rather than the U.K. Treasury bill, even though the latter offers the higher interest rate. Thus, it is rates of interest adjusted for exchange rate change that should be compared in evaluating financial market integration.

To facilitate this evaluation, chart 1 shows the dollar's average exchange rate as well as U.S. and foreign interest rates. If realized rates of return, taking exchange rate change into account, had in fact been equalized between the United States and abroad, any sustained rise in the dollar's foreign exchange value would have been accompanied by an offsetting interest differential in favor of foreign securities. Instead, the U.S. interest rate exceeded the average foreign rate by a wide margin during much of the period from the second half of 1980 through 1984, even though the dollar's foreign exchange value rose considerably over that period. Moreover, throughout the second half of 1985 and all of 1986 the interest rate differential remained close to zero or in favor of foreign securities, but the foreign exchange value of the dollar generally declined rather than displaying stability or an offsetting appreciation. Thus, the impression remains that capital markets are not highly integrated across countries.

Such incomplete integration can result either

Table 3

Correlation Coefficients Between Weekly Measures of the Three-Month U.S. CD Rate and the Weighted Average Foreign Three-Month Interest Rate, 1976–87

1976	−.205
1977	−.821
1978	.764
1979	.837
1980	.176
1981	.343
1982	.909
1983	.110
1984	.786
1985	.710
1986	.920
1987	.004

Source: Underlying data from Board of Governors of the Federal Reserve System, Macrodata Library.

from inefficiencies in the functioning of private markets or from governmental action. In this case responsibility lies largely with two categories of government activity: issuance of national currencies and intervention in private market transactions. The financial assets compared in chart 1 are denominated in different currencies, and at any time these currencies are usually perceived as likely to change in value against each other by varying degrees. Thus, the assets are subject to differing degrees of exchange rate risk. Moreover, governments impose differing regulations over financial institutions and transactions under their jurisdictions; and on occasion a political risk arises that a government will interfere with payments due to holders of financial assets, especially foreign holders. These exchange rate and political risks and standing government regulations give rise to differences in prices (and interest rates) among financial assets issued in different currencies and countries, even if those assets entail the same commercial default risk. Thus, the interest rates paid will vary, with higher rates required to compensate for higher political risk, for greater suspicion of exchange rate depreciation, and for costs imposed by government regulations.

If the purpose is merely to appraise the basic efficiency with which markets are functioning, rather than their full integration, it seems appropriate to use data that neutralize the effects of government regulation and political and exchange rate risks. Such data as are readily at hand suggest that the freer financial markets in the major industrial countries are linked by very efficient mechanisms, mechanisms that transfer funds quickly to eliminate any discrepancies in rates of return paid after allowing for differential political risk and exchange rate risk. For example, chart 2 shows the interest rate on three-month Eurodollar deposits, which, being located in London, are presumably subject to approximately the same political risk as other assets held there. The chart also shows for pound sterling loans between banks the three-month interest rate after adjustment for the "cost" of insuring against the risk of exchange rate change between the pound and the dollar (the "cost" of forward cover). Thus, neither exchange rate nor political risk influences the

Chart 2

Interest Arbitrage: Three-Month Funds, 1984-87 (Weekly Averages)

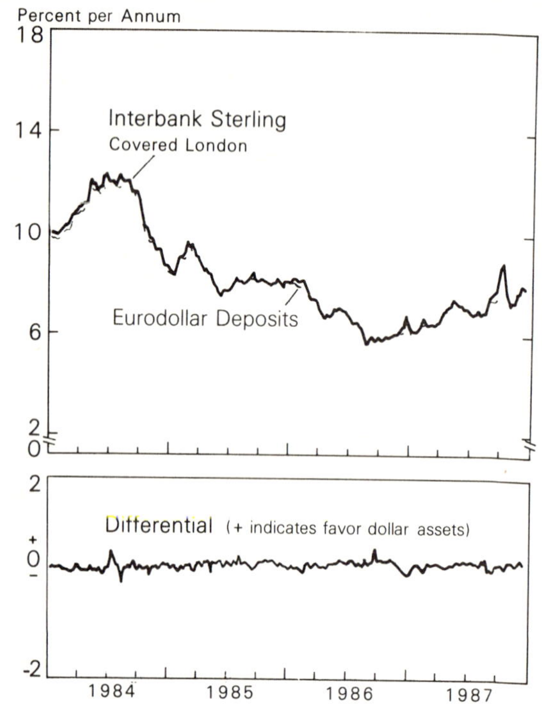

Note: 1 percent on differential scale = 2 percent on rate scale.

Source: Board of Governors of the Federal Reserve System, *Selected Interest and Exchange Rates*, December 28, 1987, Chart 8.

Chart 3

U.S. and Average Foreign Real Long-Term Government Bond Yields Quarterly, 1976-87

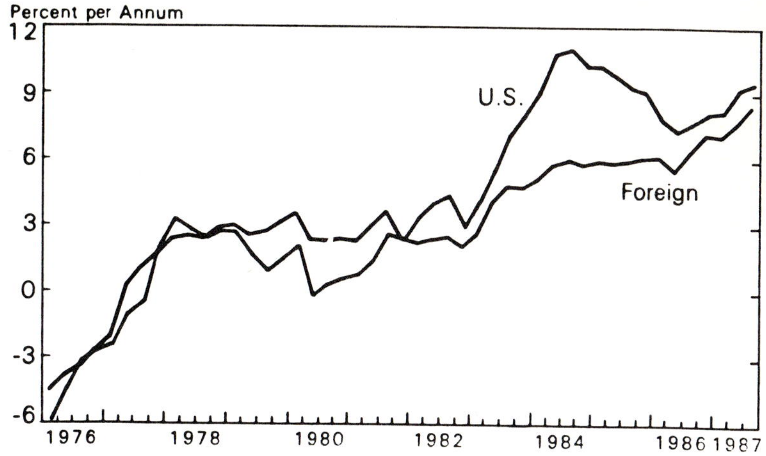

Note: Real yields are nominal yields minus rates of increase in wholesale prices. Foreign countries included are Canada, Japan, Germany, France, the United Kingdom, Belgium, Italy, and the Netherlands. Foreign data are weighted according to relative share of U.S. trade with each country.

Source: Data Resources, Inc.

difference between these two series. The absence of any significant difference is testimony that the financial intermediaries involved are alert and efficient, with very low transaction costs.[4] Such evidence supports our previous claim that factors other than market inefficiency account for the sizable differences between the two series plotted in chart 1.

Another approach to evaluating the international integration of capital markets is to compare the real (adjusted for inflation) rates of interest paid in various national markets. If a country experiences a steady inflation rate of, say, 4 percent per year, the domestic purchasing power of its currency declines accordingly; and annual interest rates must be 4 percent higher in that country than in another country with no inflation if real rates of return in the two countries are to be equal. Judging from chart 3, we conclude that recorded (or ex post) real interest rates have not been equalized by international capital movements. With truly perfect integration, equalization would occur. Only one real interest rate would be observed on bonds of the same default risk, just as only one rate would be observed within a well-functioning national capital market.[5]

PRICE MOVEMENTS: GOODS

The preceding section has shown that the markets for capital and for labor are far from perfectly integrated. Similarly, with respect to the markets for goods, much evidence exists that, from one country to the next, highly similar goods often vary sharply in price (with prices, of course, expressed in a single currency). Most prominent among the goods showing such price differences are the "nontradables," so labelled because the cost of transporting them is prohibitive in relation to their cost of production. The classic example of the nontradable good is the haircut, the dollar price for which is much lower, in say, Mexico than in the United States. In addition to transportation costs, manmade obstacles such as tariffs can prevent the equalization of prices for identical goods.

An item-by-item evaluation of such price differentials and their change over time would be an heroic undertaking. However, a summary evaluation is possible with the aid of aggregate purchasing power parity indexes (PPPs). The PPPs used here are rates that have been calculated to convert overall price levels in different countries to the same level, measured in U.S. dollars.

The rates prevailing for actual transactions in the foreign exchange market commonly differ form these PPPs. In other words, the market does not generally maintain equivalence among the overall price levels of different countries expressed in a common currency, any more than it maintains equivalence among the prices of some individual goods like haircuts. As noted above, transportation costs and trade restrictions help to explain this nonequivalence. The extent of the nonequivalence is

Table 4

Percentage Excess of Market Average Foreign Exchange Rates Over Purchasing Power Parities for Gross Domestic Product, for Six Countries, 1970–84

Country	1970	1972	1974	1976	1978	1980	1982	1984
Canada	14.7	10.0	−.2	−4.3	9.7	8.3	9.2	14.6
France	32.2	18.3	8.2	−.4	−10.3	−19.4	15.9	41.9
Germany	30.7	10.3	−9.5	−7.4	−22.4	−23.3	9.8	32.4
Italy	65.5	48.8	44.2	53.8	31.4	12.8	48.8	64.2
Japan	57.0	31.2	6.6	8.6	−21.2	−5.5	14.8	17.0
United Kingdom	61.2	43.3	43.0	46.5	23.5	−11.7	13.8	47.0

Note: Underlying exchange rates and PPPs are expressed as national currencies per U.S. dollar.

Source: Organization for Economic Cooperation and Development, *National Accounts, 1960–84*, Vol. I (Paris: OECD, 1986), p. 117; and *International Financial Statistics*, 1986 Yearbook and February 1987.

reported in table 4, which presents the percentage excess (positive) or shortfall (negative) of market exchange rates from PPPs for six major industrial countries over a 15-year period. The discrepancies are sometimes enormous. For example, the data imply that Italian prices, measured in U.S. dollars, would have had to rise by 64.2 percent in 1984 to equal the general level of prices in the United States, and that, by contrast, German prices would have had to fall by 23.3 percent in 1980 in order to attain such parity with U.S. prices. Moreover, large discrepancies commonly persist for years.

The generally sizable and uniformly positive discrepancies in 1984 tend to support the view that prices in the United States were then "out of line" with prices in other industrial countries. *Either* prices in these countries had to rise relative to those in the United States *or* the currencies of these countries had to become more expensive in terms of the U.S. dollar. Thus, it is understandable that many currencies rose in value —some vary sharply— against the U.S. dollar during 1985 through 1987.

Since the overall price levels for goods, expressed in a common currency, often differ so much from country to country, the conclusion is inescapable that, in the aggregate, the national markets for goods are not very highly integrated. As in the case of the capital markets, however, this conclusion must be carefully qualified. For goods that have relatively low transportation costs and that are free of government restrictions, evidence is available that prices (again expressed in a single currency) display very similar movement from one country to the next. In other words, after allowing for transportation costs and the like, the goods markets in different countries, like the capital markets, seem to be linked by efficient market intermediaries.

Some illustrations of this seeming efficiency are presented in chart 4, which compares the behavior of prices in Germany and the United States for three basic products over periods of 10 years or more. Multiplying the index of the mark price in Germany by an index of the dollar/mark exchange rate prevailing in the foreign exchange market yielded the "U.S. dollar equivalent of the German mark price." This series should closely correspond to the dollar price in the United States if markets were highly competitive and efficiently linked. In fact, there is little correspondence between these two series during the early 1970s for any of the three commodities, but factors other than market inefficiency seem responsible. The chief explanation surely is the price control program instituted in the Untied States, a program that suppressed the prices of many industrial commodities there during the years 1971 through 1973. After the controls were removed, the U.S. prices for the commodities represented in the chart escalated to the levels previously attained by the U.S. dollar equivalents of German mark prices. This convergence suggests that the German and U.S. markets for each of these commodities were fairly efficiently linked in the absence of such interference as price controls.[6] It

Chart 4

Indexes of Prices for Magnesium in Germany and the United States, 1967-77 (Quarterly Averages of Monthly Data)

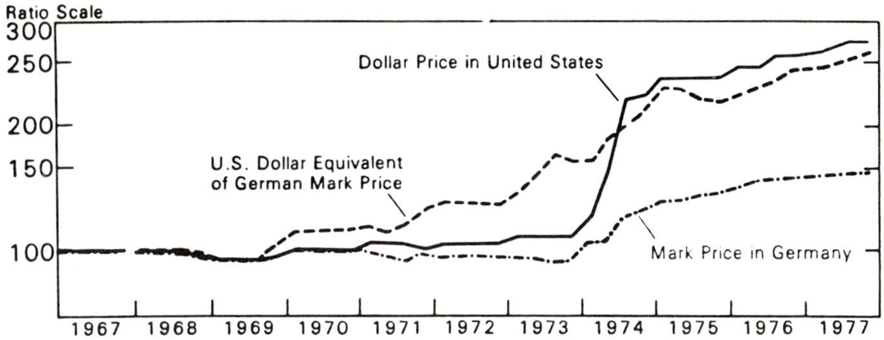

Indexes of Prices for Pig Iron in Germany and the United States, 1966-77 (Quarterly Averages of Monthly Data)

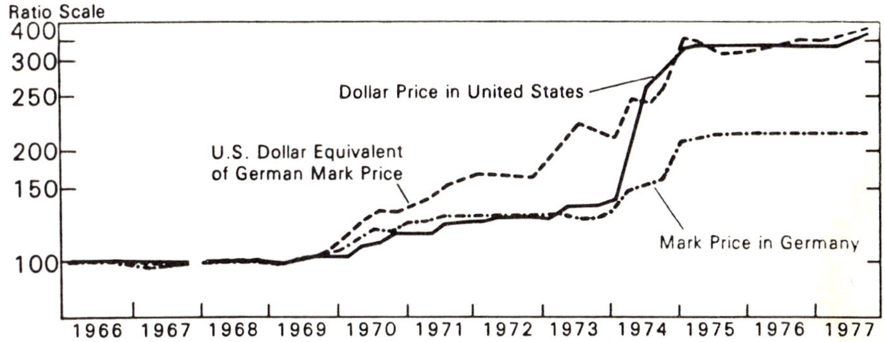

Indexes of Prices for Steel Wire Rods in Germany and the United States, 1965-77 (Quarterly Averages of Monthly Data)

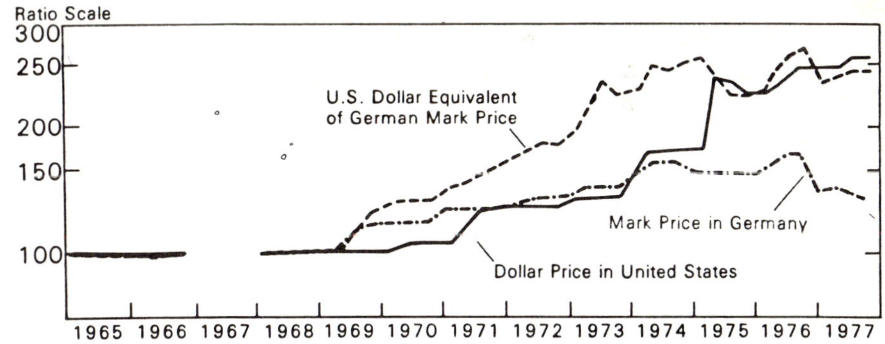

Note: Because of a break in the series for German prices, there are two base periods for each series of indexes. In 1968 and thereafter, Jan.-June 1968 = 100 for all three commodities. Prior to 1968, the base periods are as follows: for magnesium, Jan.-June 1967 = 100; for pig iron, Jan.-June 1966 = 100; and for steel wire rods, Jan.-June 1965 = 100. Data are plotted for every quarter for which observations are available for at least two months.

Source: Norman S. Fieleke, "The International Transmission of Inflation," in *Managed Exchange Rate Flexibility: The Recent Experience*, Conference Series No. 20 (Boston: Federal Reserve Bank of Boston, 1978), p 41.

also suggests, incidentally, that temporary price controls do not succeed in reducing the long-run rate of inflation.

Of course, the less the goods of one country resemble those of another, the less reason to expect correspondence between their prices. Several empirical studies have revealed substantial differences between countries in both price levels and price variations for narrowly defined *groupings* of commodities, after expressing prices in a common currency. However, it is not clear how much of the reported national price differences stems from market imperfections and how much stems from national differences in the commodity categories.[7]

In any event, as table 4 has indicated, *overall* price levels can differ markedly from country to country, so that in the aggregate the goods markets of the world should not be viewed as one single, highly integrated market.

A basic question raised at the beginning of this article is whether the world economy has become more highly integrated or interdependent over the past few decades. The evidence examined here is far from exhaustive, as some of the key data series are available for relatively few years or countries; but neither is the evidence so flimsy that it should be dismissed out-of-hand. Our reading of that evidence is that none of its conclusively contradicts the hypothesis of greater integration, while some supports the hypothesis. The clearest support is offered by table 1, which in our judgement provides the single most meaningful and readily available index of integration of the goods markets.

INTERNATIONAL TRANSMISSION OF ECONOMIC DISTURBANCES

The integration or interconnection of national economies makes possible the transmission of disturbances between them. some of the most dramatic disturbances have been "supply shocks," such as abrupt changes in the supply of oil and in the harvest of major crops such as wheat and coffee. The Organization of Petroleum Exporting Countries raised the average selling price for its crude oil by 230 percent between 1973 and 1974 and by 65 percent between 1979 and 1980. Poor grain harvest in 1972 in the Soviet Union and elsewhere contributed to an 80 percent rise in world food prices between 1972 and 1973. Frosts in Brazil in 1975 destroyed or severely damaged about half of that nation's three billion coffee bushes, and by 1977 coffee prices had risen more than 200 percent.

Although supply shocks have been important, the focus here is on the international impacts of national monetary and fiscal policies, since our purpose is to consider the international coordination of these policies. The chief question raised in this section is whether one country's monetary or fiscal policies can significantly influence the economies of other countries. If not, policy coordination would seem pointless.

To estimate the international effects of national policies, economists have developed econometric models of the linkages between various national economies. What comes out of such a model depends, of course, on what goes into it, not merely the input of raw data but the underlying assumptions about human behavior and the design and number of equations used to estimate the economic relationships that are of interest. It is not surprising, then, that different models yield different results.

These differing results were documented at The Brookings Institution in 1986, when 12 leading econometric models of the international economy were used to estimate the effects of monetary and fiscal policy changes. The policy changes were assumed to occur in the United States or in the rest of the OECD (Organization for Economic Cooperation and Development), whose 24 member countries include all the industrialized market economies. The models employed were the Federal Reserve Board's Multi-Country Model (MCM), the European Economic Community's Compact model (EEC), the Japanese Economic Planning Agency Model (EPA), Project Link (LINK), Patrick Minford's Liverpool model (Liverpool), McKibbon-Sachs's Global model (MSG), the Haas-Masson smaller approximation of the MCM model (MINIMOD), the Sims-Litterman Vector Auto-Regression model (VAR), the OECD Interlink model (OECD), John Taylor's model (Taylor), the Wharton Econometrics model (Wharton), and the Data Resources, Inc., model (DRI). Estimates made with these models are reported in tables 5 and 6.

Table 5 presents the estimated effects of an increase in government spending amounting to 1 percent of GNP. The estimated effects are those that would occur by the second year of such a spending increase. Large differences exist between the estimates yielded by some of the models. For example, suppose that the increased government spending occurred in the United States. The estimated effect on U.S. output is an increase of 1.8 percent according to the MCM, but an increase of only 0.4 percent according to VAR; and the estimated effect on the general price level is a rise of 0.9 percent according to EPA, but a decline of the same magnitude according to VAR. Of course, the effects of an increase in U.S. government spending are not necessarily limited to the United States. In

Table 5

Estimates of Fiscal Policy Multipliers (Simulation Effect in Second Year of Increase in Government Expenditure of 1 Percent of GNP)

	Total Output (Percent)	Consumer Price Index (Percent)	Short-Term Interest Rate (Points)	Currency Value (Percent)	Current Account ($ billion)	Current Account* ($ billion)	Short-Term Interest Rate* (Points)	Consumer Price Index* (Percent)	Total Output* (Percent)
Fiscal Expansion in United States									
	Effect in United States					Effect in Non-U.S. OECD			
MCM	+1.8	+.4	+1.7	+2.8	−16.5	+8.9	+.4	+.4	+.7
EEC[a]	+1.2	+.6	+1.5	+.6	−11.6	+6.6	+.3	+.2	+.3
EPA[b]	+1.7	+.9	+2.2	+1.9	−20.5	+9.3	+.5	+.3	+.9
LINK	+1.2	+.5	+.2	−.1	−6.4	+1.9	n.a.	0	+.1
Liverpool	+.6	+.2	+.4	+1.0	−7.0	+3.4	+.1	+.6	0
MSG	+.9	−.1	+.9	+3.2	−21.6	+22.7	+1.0	+.6	+.3
MINIMOD	+1.0	+.3	+1.1	+1.0	−8.5	+5.5	+.2	+.1	+.3
VAR[c]	+.4	−.9	+.1	+1.2	−.5	−.2	0	0	0
OECD	+1.1	+.6	+1.7	+.4	−14.2	+11.4	+.7	+.3	+.4
Taylor[c]	+.6	+.5	+.3	+4.0	n.a.	n.a.	+.2	+.4	+.4
Wharton	+1.4	+.3	+1.1	−2.1	−15.4	+5.3	+.6	−.1	+.2
DRI	+2.1	+.4	+1.6	+3.2	−22.0	+.8	+.4	+.3	+.7
Fiscal Expansion in Non-US. OECD									
	Effect in Non-U.S. OECD					Effect in United States			
MCM	+1.4	+.3	+.6	+.3	−7.2	+7.9	+.5	+.2	+.5
EEC[a]	+1.3	+.8	+.4	−.6	−9.3	+3.0	0	+.1	+.2
EPA[b]	+2.3	+.7	+.3	−.7	−13.1	+4.7	+.6	+.3	+.3
LINK	+1.2	+.1	n.a.	−.1	−6.1	+6.3	0	0	+.2
Liverpool	+.3	+.8	0	+3.3	−17.2	+11.9	+.8	+3.1	−.5
MSG	+1.1	+.1	+1.4	+2.9	−5.3	+10.5	+1.3	+.6	+.4
MINIMOD	+1.6	+.2	+.9	+.6	−2.2	+3.2	+.3	+.2	+.1
VAR[c]	+.5	−.3	−.2	−2.4	+1.7	−2.6	+.2	−.1	+.3
OECD	+1.5	+.7	+1.9	+.9	−6.9	+3.3	+.3	+.2	+.1
Taylor[c]	+1.6	+1.2	+.6	+2.7	n.a.	n.a.	+.4	+.9	+.6
Wharton	+3.2	−.8	+.8	−2.4	−5.5	+4.7	+.1	0	0
DRI	n.a.	n.a.	n.a.	n.a.	n.a.	n.a.	n.a.	n.a.	n.a.

* Effect in area other than where original stimulus occurred.
n.a. not available.
[a] Non-U.S. short-term interest rate not available; long-term reported instead.
[b] Non-U.S. current account is Japan, Germany, the United Kingdom, and Canada.
[c] CPI not available; GNP deflator reported instead.
Source: Jeffrey A. Frankel. 1987. "Obstacles to International Macroeconomic Policy Coordination." Working Paper /87/29. Washington, D.C.: International Monetary Fund, April 21, p.13.

the rest of the OECD, output would be enlarged by 0.9 percent according to EPA, but would be unaffected according to VAR and Liverpool; and the estimated impact on consumer prices ranges from –0.1 percent to +0.6 percent.

Suppose that the expansion in government spending took place not in the United States but in the rest of the OECD. As the table shows, for the rest of the OECD the estimated effect on output ranges from +0.3 percent to +3.2 percent, the effect on prices from –0.8 percent to +1.2 percent. The United States also could be affected. Depending on the model consulted, the estimated effect on U.S. output ranges from -0.5 percent to +0.6 percent, and on U.S. prices from –00.1 percent to +3.1 percent. Table 6 indicates that the estimated effects of a

Table 6

Estimates of Monetary Policy Multipliers (Simulation Effect in Second Year of Increase in Money Supply of 4 Percent)

	Total Output (Percent)	Consumer Price Index (Percent)	Short-Term Interest Rate (Points)	Currency Value (Percent)	Current Account ($ billion)	Current Account* ($ billion)	Short-Term Interest Rate* (Points)	Consumer Price Index* (Percent)	Total Output* (Percent)
Monetary Expansion in United States									
	Effect in United States					Effect in Non-U.S. OECD			
MCM	+1.5	+.4	−2.2	−6.0	−3.1	−3.5	−.5	−.6	−.7
EEC[a]	+1.0	+.8	−2.4	−4.0	−2.8	+1.2	−.5	−.4	+.2
EPA[b]	+1.2	+1.0	−2.2	−6.4	−1.6	−10.1	−.6	−.5	−.4
LINK	+1.0	−.4	−1.4	−2.3	−5.9	+1.5	n.a.	−.1	−.1
Liverpool	+.1	+3.7	−.3	−3.9	−13.0	+.1	−.1	0	0
MSG	+.3	+1.5	−.8	−2.0	+2.6	−4.4	−1.2	−.7	+.4
MINIMOD	+1.0	+.8	−1.8	−5.7	+2.8	−4.7	−.1	−.2	−.2
VAR[c]	+3.0	+.4	−1.9	−22.9	+4.9	+5.1	+.3	+.1	+.4
OECD	+1.6	+.7	−.8	−2.6	−8.4	+3.1	−.1	−.1	+.3
Taylor[c]	+.6	+1.2	−.4	−4.9	n.a.	n.a.	−.1	−.2	−.2
Wharton	+.7	0	−2.1	−1.0	−5.1	+5.3	−1.3	−.1	+.4
DRI	+1.8	+.4	−2.3	−14.6	−1.4	+14.5	−1.1	−1.3	−.6
Monetary Expansion in Non-US. OECD									
	Effect in Non-U.S. OECD					Effect in United States			
MCM	+1.5	+.6	−2.1	−5.4	+3.5	+.1	−.2	−.2	0
EEC[a]	+.8	+1.0	−1.0	−2.3	−5.2	+1.9	0	+.1	+.1
EPA[b]	0	0	−.1	−.1	−.1	+.1	0	0	0
LINK[d]	+.8	−.6	n.a.	−2.3	−1.4	+3.5	0	0	+.1
Liverpool	+.4	+2.8	−.9	−8.4	+7.1	−8.2	−1.1	−3.4	+1.6
MSG	+.2	+1.5	−.7	−1.4	−15.9	+12.0	−1.2	−.6	+.3
MINIMOD	+.8	+.2	−1.8	−4.8	+3.6	−1.4	−.6	−.5	−.3
VAR[c]	+.7	−.5	−3.0	−5.5	+5.2	−10.0	+.6	−.7	+1.2
OECD	+.8	+.3	−1.3	−2.1	−1.6	+2.3	−.2	−.1	+.1
Taylor[c]	+.8	+.7	−.3	−3.5	n.a.	n.a.	−.2	−.5	−.1
Wharton	+.2	−.1	−.8	+.2	+2.6	+.5	0	0	0
DRI	n.a.	n.a.	n.a.	n.a.	n.a.	n.a.	n.a.	n.a.	n.a.

* Effect in area other than where original stimulus occurred.
n.a. not available.
[a] Non-U.S. short-term interest rate not available; long-term reported instead.
[b] Non-U.S. current account is Japan, Germany, the United Kingdom, and Canada.
[c] CPI not available; GNP deflator reported instead.
[d] Appreciation of non-U.S. currency not available; depreciation of dollar reported instead.
Source: Jeffrey A. Frankel. 1987. "Obstacles to International Macroeconomic Policy Coordination," p. 14.

change in monetary policy also cover a wide range.

Not only do different model yield different estimates, but the same basic model will yield different estimates at different times as underlying data are extended or revised and as the form of the model's estimating equations is revised in accordance with experience and changing theory. No econometric model can remain both static and relevant for very long. Keeping a large model up-to-date is far from effortless. For example, the multicountry model is a system of linked models of the five economies (Canada, West Germany, Japan, the United Kingdom, and the United States) as well as a sector representing the rest of the world. Each of the five national models includes between 150 and

250 behavioral equations and identities, the total number of equations and identities, the total number of equations and identities being in excess of 850.

In spite of the complexities and the differences between various models, the estimates at hand suggest that cross-country effects and international repercussions, whatever their precise magnitudes, may be too large to be ignored for many countries. This conclusion—which fortunately accords with casual observation—leads to the question whether countries should collaborate in designing their economic policies.

THE CASE FOR COORDINATION [8]

If each of two countries can, with its economic policy, significantly affect the economy of the other, it might seem obvious that the two should coordinate their policies. That is to say, they should harmonize their policies to their mutual benefit. The case for coordination is not open and shut, however. We shall first relate some economic arguments on behalf of coordination and then consider some objections.

A common argument on behalf of coordination is that it can reduce the duration for amplitude of economic fluctuations. As transportation and communications have improved, economic disturbances are transmitted more rapidly and fully from country to country than in the past. In these circumstances, might it be possible for countries to destabalize each other's economies by making policy in isolation from each other? Suppose that actions taken by one country to attain its goals (for example, price stability or full employment) shifted the economies of other countries further from their own goals. These other countries might then renew the pursuit of their goals with actions that might incidentally drive the first country even farther from its goals, evoking further destabilizing action by that country, and so on.

No one has demonstrated that such an outcome is impossible. Even if it were, isolated policy making might involve more trial and error than coordination and require more time for countries eventually to attain their goals. Since welfare losses mount with the length of time that countries fall short of their economic goals, coordination would be desirable in such circumstances, provided that the various goals were compatible.

If the goals of different countries are incompatible, coordination again offers a way of coping with the conflict. For example, two countries might have different ideas of what the exchange rate between their currencies should be. Or with respect to the balance of payments countries might aim for balances in their current accounts that, in the aggregate, would sum to a figure substantially different from zero, even though for all countries collectively the balance (correctly measured) must even out to zero.

Such conflicts between goals would provide no ground for concern if the consequences were innocuous. After all, life is replete with such conflicts, and the results are often perceived not as harmful but as desirable. For example, not every firm seeking a high rate of profit can realize it, but the competition for it generally serves society well.

However, under some conditions the world would suffer if the goals pursued by different nations were inconsistent. One illustration of this point uses an example of two nations, each of which sets objectives for its output and rate of inflation that it tries to achieve by manipulating the growth of its money supply, while the exchange rate between the two nations' currencies is allowed to change with market conditions.[9] In this example each country perceives that it can immediately reduce its rate of inflation by reducing its money growth rate so as to raise the value of its currency in the exchange market, thereby lowering the domestic price of imported goods. When both countries actually reduce their money growth rates, the exchange rate remains unchanged—neither currency appreciates—and both countries wind up with unchanged rates of inflation (in the short run) but lower output than if they had jointly adopted more expansionary monetary policies. Given the circumstances, both nations might have benefited from cooperating. At the very least, after exchanging policy plans the two countries would have recognized that neither would achieve the currency appreciation it sought; and that recognition might have induced different policy choices.

Still another argument in support of coordination revolves around the need to provide certain "public goods." A public good is one that one person can partake of without excluding another from partaking; moreover, it is not possible to exclude people from partaking of the good once it is available. National defense is a common illustration.

From the nature of public goods, it is obvious that raising the funds to provide them should not be left to the marketplace but should be the responsibility of government. Where public goods are international in nature, governments generally will have to join forces, or coordinate, to ensure that the supply is adequate. An example would be the preservation of a healthful world environment.

While the matter is debatable, economic stability is also considered by some economists to be an international public good. The management of economic policy in large countries such as Germany, Japan, and the United States has important and unavoidable consequences for other countries. The question arises, then, whether monetary and fiscal policymaking should be subjected to some degree of international negotiation because of public good characteristics.

Finally, coordination is defended as a process through which information important for policy-making is exchanged. To design beneficial policy is difficult even with all extant data, and next to impossible if data are obsolete or otherwise flawed. The pooling of economic information among governments is therefore desirable, and such pooling is more nearly ensured if governments consult frequently on their contemplated policy actions.

SOME ARGUMENTS AGAINST COORDINATION

Reactions to proposals for coordination illustrate the old saw that "One man's meat is another man's poison." In contrast to the favorable views in the preceding section, some penetrating criticisms and caveats have been offered.

One argument against coordination is similar to the argument against centralized government. At the most cynical level, if it is true that all power corrupts, then it is risky to encourage a high degree of collaboration (collusion?) between governments, which might encourage each other in the pursuit of economic policies designed to maintain or promote their own power or wealth rather that to serve their constituencies. Indeed, the very expansion of government paraphernalia required for coordination might be seen as a case in point. (Vaubel 1983, pp. 17-18).

Another, only slightly less cynical, argument is that a formal coordination process would offer the opportunity for evasion of responsibility, if not outright buck-passing. A government might not adopt politically painful but appropriate policies in the hope that foreign action would make such policies unnecessary. Even worse, a government might seek to use its own inaction as a bargaining device to induce desired changes in foreign policies. National officials who mismanaged their economies might then blame the results on foreign governments (Feldstein 1987).

Aside from the possibility of such opportunism, it is the feasibility of coordination that is most often called into question. For example, governments might not be able to resolve conflicts between the goals that they separately pursue, not because they are lacking in either reason or goodwill, but because they are bound by the preferences of their constituencies. If the electorates in all countries coveted surpluses in their international current accounts, co-ordination would not be the answer to the problem. Indeed, governments that agreed to forgo seeking surpluses would have good reason to doubt each other's ability to honor the commitment.

The feasibility of coordination is also undermined by inadequate economic know-how, even if goals could be agreed upon and commitments honored. Thus, the risk arises that the coordination process will embrace a mistaken view of how the world economy works. As illustrated in a preceding section, more than one plausible econometric model of the international economy is available, and different models yield appreciably different results. How are the coordinators to go about choosing among these models? Were they to select the wrong model—and all models might be substantially "wrong"—as a basis for policy coordination, the results for the world economy could be much worse than if no coordination had taken place. Coordinated agreement on disastrous policies would be far inferior to decentralized, independent, even isolated pursuit of a mixture of "good" and "bad" policies.

Coordination could make matters worse even if the coordinators avoided the error of agreeing upon one wrong econometric model. Indeed, it is to be expected that they would not agree on how the world economy should be modeled. Such disagreement need not forestall coordination. Two governments with different models should generally still be able to coordinate their policies in a way that each perceives as beneficial. However, such coordination is about as likely to make matters worse as to improve them as long as the models employed are faulty. In other words, coordination based on several wrong models may be no better that coordination based on a single wrong model.

This point has recently been illustrated by an elaborate experiment with eight different econometric models, any one of which might represent the true functioning of the world economy (Frankel and Rockett 1986). The experiment assumed that the U.S. authorities might select any one of the eight models as the basis for policy formulation and that the authorities in other industrial countries, acting as one, would have the same range of choice. Thus, 64 different combinations of the eight models might be employed for policymaking. The experiment further assumed that for each of these 64 model combinations, any one of the eight models might be the one truly representing the world economy, so that 8 times 64, or 512, possible outcomes were obtained. Coordination of U.S. and other industrial country monetary policies was found to *worsen* welfare for the United States in 206 cases and for other industrial countries in 198 cases. Similarly, coordination of both monetary and fiscal policies reduced welfare for the United States in 228 cases and reduced welfare for other industrial countries in 219 cases, out of the 512 cases examined.[10]

In conclusion, coordination is not an absolute good or bad or even a matter of principle; it is a method to be chosen or rejected depending on the circumstances. In some cases, such as preservation of a healthful environment, coordination seems desirable, if not essential, for successful action. In other areas, such as economic stabilization policy, coordination is more problematical. The issue is not one of decentralized isolation versus full coordination at all times, but of adaptation to the situation. Where governments can agree upon compatible goals and know how to attain them, coordination can offer some gains. At a minimum, governments should share current information on policy measures, and all may profit from frequent discussion and debate in the various international forums.

MECHANISMS FOR COORDINATION

Given the difficult issues involved, efforts to coordinate economic policy are unlikely to succeed without organizations and administrative procedures will adapted to the task. Not suprisingly, then, a number of international organizations with specialized expertise have been formed to facilitate economic cooperation in various areas.

Foremost among these organizations in the international monetary area is the International Monetary Fund (IMF), created toward the end of World War II. In the Articles of Agreement formally establishing the IMF, the first of the listed purposes is "To promote international monetary cooperation through a permanent institution which provides the machinery for consultation and collaboration on international monetary problems" (Articles of Agreement, 1985, p. 2). As the other listed purposes make clear, monetary cooperation is not an end in itself but is intended to promote a free and stable international monetary environment conducive to high employment and economic growth. Toward these ends, the 151 members of the IMF have agreed to a general code of behavior, including abstinence from harmful restriction over foreign exchange transactions and from action that would generate disorder or instability in foreign exchange markets.

A stable international monetary system falls into the category of an international public good, which can be provided only through international cooperation. No government can do it alone. Thus, if the IMF did not exist, governments that sought international monetary stability would no doubt create its analogue.

Much the same could be said about the General Agreement on Tariffs and Trade (GATT) in the realm of international trade. Founded shortly after the IMF, the GATT offers a framework of rules for trade relations, including prohibitions against discrimination and quantitative restrictions, and an international forum for discussion and negotiations on trade among its members (numbering 96 at this writing). the liberal and peaceful trading order that GATT seeks to ensure, free from arbitrary, disguised, and unpredictable government intervention, is another important international public good that governments acting singly would not provide. Insofar as GATT fails, business firms are discouraged from international commerce, and the loss to society is commensurate.

Other international organizations are employed by the community of nations to coordinate the provision of economic assistance to the poorer countries. These organizations, such as the World Bank, the International Development Association, and the International American Development Bank, allocate aid in accordance with internationally agreed criteria that are relatively free from the nationalistic considerations that more strongly influence aid granted directly from one country to another. Also, coordinated assaults on poverty, like coordinated assaults on pollution, probably succeed in marshalling more resources than uncoordinated efforts.

In addition to these organizations, a number of others with smaller memberships play important roles in international economic cooperation. All serve, among other things, as centers for discussion. Among the industrial countries, the Organization for Economic Cooperation and Development (OECD) and the Bank for International Settlements (BIS) have well-established functions. The OECD, with 24 member countries, was established in 1960 to promote policies favoring high economic growth and employment, financial stability, and nondiscriminatory international trade. The BIS acts as a central bankers' bank. In addition, there are the Groups of 5, of 7, and of 10, embracing successively larger subsets of the major industrial countries; in general, the smaller the membership of the organization, the less formal the structure and the larger the economy of the typical member.

Coordination is also an important function of certain regional economic organizations. Preeminent among them is the European Community and its component institutions, which are working toward economic and monetary union of the 12 member nations.

There is, then, no lack of organizations dedicated to economic coordination. What methods of administrative procedures do they employ? A comprehensive survey is not possible here, but one key generalization is that no organization exercises sovereign power over its member countries. Aside from the authority to withhold certain benefits — such as loans—these organizations generally have little power over the policies of individual nations, which can withdraw at any time. All the organizations must rely on the willingness of their members to cooperate.

While it may be next to impossible to compel cooperation, peer pressure and a bad press can have an influence. But before such levers can be employed successfully, there must be generally accepted criteria by which to judge whether, and to what degree, a country is in fact cooperating. The use of such criteria for the purpose of coordinating macroeconomic policies has been formally endorsed by the seven major industrial democracies—he United States, Japan, Germany, the United Kingdom, France, Italy, and Canada. At an economic summit meeting in May 1986, these nations agreed thereafter to forcast their economic performances in terms of quantitative "indicators" and to participate in multilateral reviews of both their forecasts and subsequent deviations therefrom. The presumption was that remedial policy measures would be taken to correct significant deviations. The indicators were to be such variables as gross national product growth rates, inflation rates, interest rates, unemployment rates, fiscal deficit ratios, current account and trade balances, monetary growth rates, reserves, and exchange rates. The IMF staff was to assist in defining the indicators actually employed, and to assist as well in the process of "multilateral surveillance," a process intended both to harmonize the various economic forecasts and to monitor deviations from the forecasts eventually adopted.[11]

While the exchange of information should be enhanced by the use of such indicators, their interpretation is not a simple matter. For example, suppose that Germany agrees to ease its monetary policy in order to stimulate domestic demand. If the money stock then increases more rapidly in Germany, but short-term interest rates go up rather than down, is Germany meeting its commitment? The answer depends on how monetary policy is defined and, more fundamentally, on more detailed information about the workings of the German economy. Or suppose the United States pledges to tighten its fiscal policy with a view to reducing its international current account deficit. If the U.S. economy then enters a recession and the federal budget deficit increases, has the United States met its commitment? Again, an unequivocal answer is not possible without a careful definition of fiscal policy and more knowledge about the U.S. economy.

These complexities have been acknowledged. In September 1986, the IMF's Managing Director, J. de Larosiere, observed that "Indicators should be used with a good element of judgement. They cannot be used in a mechanistic fashion."[12] The dilemma, unfortunately unavoidable, is that ambiguous indicators lack the power of clear standards.

Some governmental economic activities lend themselves to the application of clear standards more readily than macroeconomic policy does. For example, governments have long subscribed to codes of conduct, some fairly detailed, governing their policies in international trade, and significant violations of the more important rules are relatively easily documented. Even where such codes are feasible, however, they are sometimes heavily compromised in practice. Thus, while coordination should be based on the best available information, some of which may take the form of "objective indicators," the process will no doubt continue to be highly political and often subjective in nature.

SUMMARY

A common belief is that the world economy has become more highly interconnected, or integrated, over the past quarter century. Some support for this view is provided by the evidence, admittedly limited, that is examined here. In particular, the rising ratios of international trade to GNP in many countries do suggest that the goods markets, at least, have become more closely interconnected.

In any event, national economies are sufficiently interdependent that economic disturbances get readily transmitted among them. Although econometric models differ on the degree of transmission that takes place, they agree that one country's macroeconomic policies can sometimes have an appreciable impact on other countries. This finding suggests that countries should consider coordinating their policies to their mutual benefit.

Unfortunately, not enough is known about how the world economy functions to ensure that macroeconomic policy coordination would improve the outcome. Even with adequate economic know-how, coordination efforts might founder on the reluctance of countries to compromise with each other when spelling out their economic goals. On the other hand coordination may be essential to secure the provision of international public goods such a healthful environment. At a minimum, the world could benefit from a continuing, close dialogue among national economic policy makers, on the principle that what they don't know could hurt everyone.

Aside from occasional concerted intervention in the foreign exchange markets, little in the way of formally coordinated economic policy has emerged, in spite of the huge current account imbalance between the United States and other nations. In the absence of other major corrective measures, the U.S. dollar depreciated markedly against the Japanese yen, the German mark, and other currencies after the winter of 1985.

The machinery for coordination includes a number of international organizations, none of which is empowered to amend the policies of its member nations. The quest for a mechanism of international discipline over national macroeconomic policies has led to the adoption of a set of quantitative "indicators" in terms of which the major industrial democracies now forcast their economic performances, with multilateral review of both forecasts and the subsequent performances. While the indicators may be helpful, their interpretation is very much a matter of judgement, so that they lack the power of clear standards.

ENDNOTES

1 See Fieleke (1982) and Feldstein and Horioka (1980).

2 Ibid. Also see Summers (1986)

3 Ruffin and Rassekh (1986) conclude that foreign direct investment and foreign portfolio investment by U.S. investors may be perfectly fungible, suggesting a high degree of substitutability of equities for more liquid claims.

4 The absence of a significant covered interest differential is not high proof of high net capital mobility, however. Net capital movements occur only on an uncovered basis. See Fieleke (1985) p. 41.

5 For more detailed evidence on the degree of financial market integration, see Federal Reserve Bank of New York (1987).

6 For an analysis suggesting that this "law of one price" holds in the long run but not the short, see Protopapadakis and Stoll (1986).

7 See Isard (1977), Richardson (1978), and Kravis and Lipsey (1978).

8 This section owes much to Richard N. Cooper (1985a)

9 See Cooper (1985a), pp. 1214-18.
10 For extensions of this analysis, see Frankel (1987)
11 As reported in *The New York Times*, May 7, 1986, p. A10.
12 Quoted in *IMF Survey*, Octover 20, 1986, p.318.

REFERENCES

Articles of Agreement of the International Monetary Fund. 1985. Washington, D.C.: International Monetary Fund.

Cooper, Richard N. 1985a. "Economic Interdependence and Coordination of Economic Policies." in *Handbook of International Economics*, Vol. II, Ronald W. Jones and Peter B. Kensen, eds. New York: North Holland, pp. 1195-1234.

——-1985b. "The United States as an Open Economy." in *How Open Is the U.S. Economy*? R. W. Hafer, ed. Lexington, MA: D.C. Heath and Co., pp. 3-24.

Federal Reserve Bank of New York. 1987. "Research Papers on International Integration of Financial Markets and the U.S. Monetary Policy." December.

Feldstein, Martin. 1987. "Rethinking International Economic Coordination." A Lecture in the Occasion of the Fiftieth Anniversary of Nuffield College, Oxford, 23 October.

Feldstein, Martin and C. Horioka. 1980. "Domestic Saving and International Capital Flows." *The Economic Journal*, vol. 90, June, pp. 314-29.

Fieleke, Norman S. 1982. "National Saving and International Investment." In *Saving and Government Policy*, Conference Series No. 25, Federal Reserve Bank of Boston, pp. 138-57.

———. 1985. "The Rise of the Foreign Currency Futures Market." *New England Economic Review*, March/April, pp. 38-47.

Frankel, Jeffrey A. 1987. "Obstacles to International Macroeconomic Policy Coordination." Working Paper /87/29. Washington, D.C.: International Monetary Fund, April 21.

Frankel, Jeffrey A., Michael Dooley, and Donald Mathieson. 1986. "International Capital Mobility in Developing Countries vs. Industrial Countries: What Do Saving-Investment Correlations Tell Us?" Working Paper No. 2043. Cambridge, MA: National Bureau of Economic Research.

Frankel, Jeffrey A. and Katherine A. Rockett. 1986. "International Macroeconomic Policy Coordination When Policy-Makers Disagree on the Model." Working Paper No. 2059. Cambridge, MA: National Bureau of Economic Research.

Isard, Peter. 1977. "How Far Can We Push the 'Law of One Price'?" *The American Economic Review*, vol. 67, December, pp. 942-48.

Kravis, Irving B. and Robert E. Lipsey. 1978. "Price Behavior in the Light of Balance of Payments Theories." *Journal of International Economics*, vol. 8, May, pp. 193-246.

Marshall, Alfred. 1948. *Principles of Economics*, 8th ed. New York: The Macmillan Co.

Protopapadakis, Aris A. and Hans R. Stoll. 1986. "The Law of One Price in International Commodity Markets: A Reformulation and Some Formal Tests." *Journal of Money and Finance*, vol. .0

READING 15

Thinking About International Economic Coordination

Martin S. Feldstein

I should perhaps begin these remarks by emphasizing that I an not opposed to international cooperation in economic affairs. We as economists recognize that conflict in international trade and the development of protectionist policies would reduce the standard of living around the world. Moreover, the immediate effect of a shift to protectionism could be a major worldwide recession.

The quiet exchange of macroeconomic forecasts and policy plans among government officials that occurs within the framework of the Bank for International Settlement, the OECD, the Group of 7 (the United States, Great Britain, France, Germany, Japan, Italy and Canada) and elsewhere plays an important role in the formulation of domestic economic policies. It is also important for maintaining friendly working relationships among governments that senior officials are not surprised by major policy shifts abroad.

I start with these obvious remarks and with the assertion that I am not opposed to international cooperation in all economic matters because I do not want to be misunderstood when, as in this lecture, I stress the counterproductive consequences of the international coordination of macroeconomic policy.

I do not deny that the economies of the world are linked in a way that makes the monetary and budget policies adopted in one country affect the economic performance of other countries. But I believe that many of the claimed advantages of cooperation and coordination are wrong, that there are substantial risks and disadvantages to the types of coordination that are envisioned, and that an emphasis on international coordination can distract attention from the necessary changes in domestic policy. Moreover, the attempt to pursue coordination in a wide range of macroeconomic policies is likely to result in disagreements and disappointments that reduce the prospects for cooperation in those more limited areas of trade, defence and foreign assistance where international cooperation is actually necessary.[1]

In stressing the limited scope for the international coordination of macroeconomic policy and exchange rates, I do not wish to imply that such action is never appropriate. Far from it. There are some small and very interdependent countries where such coordination should undoubtedly be the general rule. There are also some conditions when the potential gains from coordination are such that all countries could expect to benefit from participation. But the active coordination of the macroeconomic policies and of exchange rates among the United States, Japan, and Germany will generally be inappropriate. Moreover, as I shall explain in these remarks, the United States is particularly unsuited to participate in an ongoing process of economic coordination.

THE MANAGEMENT OF EXCHANGE RATES

After less than a decade of floating exchange rates, the sharp rise in the value of the dollar during the early 1980s caused a renewed interest in the possibility of the international management of exchange rates and even of a return to a system of fixed exchange rates. The rise in the real value of the dollar was the primary reason why the United States shifted from a trade surplus in 1981 to a massive trade deficit by 1986. It is not surprising, therefore, that American businesses and their workers in the wide range of industries hurt by the strong dollar called for government action to stop and reverse the dollar's rise.

Until September 1985, the Reagan Administration argued that the value of the dollar should be left to the market and that it was inappropriate to shift U.S. domestic economic policy or to intervene in currency markets in an attempt to alter the dollar's value. This was a continuing source of conflict with the European and Japanese governments that did not like the dollar's rise because of the inflationary pressures that it imparted in their own economies, the rising real interest rates that resulted from the capital outflow to the United States, and the increased support for protectionist trade policies that was developing in the United States because of the surging U.S. trade deficit.

The Plaza Hotel meeting of the finance ministers of the G-5 countries (United States, Great Britain, France, Germany and Japan) in September 1985 was a political watershed in this process. Faced with the reality that the dollar had been declining for more than six months, Treasury Secretary James Baker abandoned the previous Treasury position that the strong dollar was a measure of foreign investors' approval of the economic policies of the United States. He acknowledged publicly that the high value of the dollar was a serious problem for American Industry. And, most surprisingly and significantly of all, he agreed to participate in coordinated exchange market intervention aimed at lowering the dollar's value.

Immediately after the Plaza meeting, the United States did join with other countries in a major exchange market intervention, selling dollars and buying other currencies. The Japanese central bank also raised short-term interest rates temporarily in order to make yen dominated bonds a more attractive investment and thereby to stimulate the demand for the yen.

Exchange rate targeting and economic policy coordination aimed at achieving desired levels of the exchange rates have been a frequent theme of intergovernmental meetings since that time. The finance ministers of the G-7 countries met at the Louvre in February 1987 to assert their belief in macroeconomic coordination and to call for exchange rate stability. They reaffirmed this call at the June 1987 Venice summit and the September 1987 IMF-World Bank meeting. In more recent days (November and December 1987), European and Japanese government officials have repeated their case for coordinated actions to achieve a stable value of the dollar and a new G-7 communique calling for a stable dollar has been issued.

In contrast to these assertions, I believe that the dollar must continue to decline because the future trade deficit implied by the dollar's correct level would be too large to finance otherwise. Experts estimate that without a further decline of the dollar the U.S. trade deficit will remain at more than $100 billion a year and the current account deficit will grow explosively because of the interest and dividends owed on the U.S. net borrowing from abroad. Only a decline of the dollar can achieve the change in the relative prices of American and foreign goods that can induce American consumers to import less and foreign consumers to buy more American-made goods. The more rapid growth in Japan and Europe that the finance ministers continually stress as an alternative to a dollar decline simply cannot be powerful enough to make a significant dent in the U.S. trade deficit. Similarly, while a decline of the American budget deficit would help to shrink the U.S. trade deficit, it would do so by lowering U.S. interest rates which in turn would reduce the value of the dollar; a decline in the budget deficit, while essential for other reasons, is not an alternative to a decline in the dollar as a means of shrinking the trade deficit. (A longer nontechnical discussion of why the dollar must decline is presented in Feldstein, 1987a.)

I believe that the pursuit of exchange rate goals is likely to be both futile and economically damaging, not just in the current circumstances but more generally as well. In the short term, as the experience of October 1987 painfully demonstrated, the expectation that monetary policy would tighten to defend artificial exchange rate levels can destabilize financial markets. The fear that the Fed would push rates even higher than they were in early October—to offset the downward pressure on the dollar that resulted from the unfavorable trade news of October 14th—was one of the key factors that triggered the stock market crash. Over an extended period of time, the primary risk in the pursuit of exchange rate targets is an increase in the rate of inflation in every country. A policy of targeting exchange rates can also hurt the process of capital formation, weaken the capital goods and construction industries, and delay the recovery of the manufacturing industries that are hurt by an overvalued exchange rate.

NOMINAL AND REAL EXCHANGE RATES

To understand the likely effects of an exchange rate policy, it is crucial to distinguish between changes in nominal exchange rates and changes in real exchange rates. The change in the nominal exchange rate between two countries is the change in the actual exchange rate that prevails in the market. The change in the real exchange rate is equal to the change in nominal exchange rate adjusted for differences in the inflation rates in the two countries. It is, of course, the real value of the currency that influences the competitiveness if the country's products and thus it's exports and imports. This point is worth emphasizing for two reasons.

First, the political discussion about exchange rate targets, target zones and exchange rate management are always in terms of the nominal exchange rates. Therefore even if the politically agreed upon exchange rate targets were achieved and maintained, the relative competitiveness of the countries could change substantially because differences in inflation rates would cause the real exchange rates to change. In short, exchange rate management is likely to be misguided because it focuses on the wrong target.

Second, economic policies that change a country's rate of inflation can easily alter nominal exchange rates without changing the real exchange rates. Therefore, there is a serious danger that an agreement to stabilize exchange rates would lead to increased inflation without any change in the real exchange rates that influence imports and exports.

Consider, for example, the sharp rise in the real value of the dollar that began in 1980 because of the massive increase in current and projected U.S. budget deficits. Reversing the budget deficit could have prevented the dollar's rise or caused it to decline at an earlier time. But on the basis of my experience as a participant in the making of American economic policy at that time, I do not believe that an exchange rate agreement would have produced such a change in budget policy. The Reagan Administration was already trying to reduce the budget deficit by a strategy that combined major domestic spending cuts with a conditional tax increase. There is no reason to think that it would have taken a more conciliatory position with Congress in order to deal with the high dollar. Treasury Secretary Regan apparently believed that the budget deficit had no effect on the dollar. In addition, many experts both inside and outside the government argued that the strong dollar showed only that monetary policy was too tight and therefore argued in favor of depressing the dollar by a monetary expansion.

If the United States had agreed in 1983 to stop the dollar's rise, the easiest way would have been for the Federal Reserve to ease monetary policy. The easier monetary policy would have temporarily lowered real interest rates and that in turn would have caused a temporary decline in the real value of the dollar. More importantly, the easier monetary policy would produce inflation and the inflation would cause the dollar's nominal value to decline. In the end, there would have been no change in the real exchange rate or the trade deficit but a higher price level and a high rate of inflation.

Of course, there are two sides to every exchange rate and the relative value of the dollar could have been depressed by a tightening of monetary policy in Europe and Japan that lowered the inflation rates in those countries. There was in fact some tightening of monetary policy in Europe in response to the rising dollar, but that process was inevitable limited by the increased unemployment that resulted from such a monetary contraction. Political reality would inevitable have required that a change in monetary policy to stabilize the dollar be an inflationary easing by the United States rather than a deflationary tightening in the other countries of the world.

The current attempts to slow the rise of the yen and the German mark provide a further example of the risk that exchange rate coordination is likely to be inflationary. The process of intervention in both Germany and Japan has led to very rapid increases in the money supply and in overall liquidity. This had increased the fear of inflation and raised long-term interest rates in both countries. Although the governments of Germany and Japan have asked the United States to raise interest rates as an alternative way of maintaining the value of the dollar, the U.S. has been reluctant to do so in the context of a recovery that has already lasted five years and with an election this year. Although the German and Japanese intervention has not yet produced any significant rise in inflation, a continuation of the associated increases in money and overall liquidity for an extended period would undoubtedly begin to do so.

GAINS AND LOSSES OF AN OVERSTRONG DOLLAR

There are of course some who believe that the real value of the dollar can be influenced by exchange market intervention alone. Before considering whether such a policy could be expected to work, it is useful to ask whether stabilizing the dollar would in itself have been desirable in today's world economy.

Stopping the rise in the dollar's real value in early 1983 would have reduced the subsequent U.S. trade deficit. Output and employment would have deteriorated less in our export industries and in those firms that compete with imports from abroad. But that is only half of the story. The reduced trade deficit would automatically have meant a reduced capital inflow from abroad. Real interest rates would have been higher in the United States. Investment in plant and equipment and housing construction would have been depressed. The pattern of employment would have been different, but there is no reason to suppose that total employment and output would have been higher. Moreover, the lower rate of capital formation would have reduced the growth of productivity.

In short, stopping the dollar's rise earlier would have had both good and bad effects on the American economy. There is no way to know whether the favorable effects on the export industries and firms that compete with imports would have outweighed the adverse effects on capital investment. I believe that in the absence of clear evidence or analysis to the contrary, it is best to assume that the market produces a better solution than government intervention. That is as true about exchange market intervention as it is about so many other aspects of government interference with the market economy.

The same principle is relevant today. If intervention per se could stop the dollar's fall at the present time, that would contribute to U.S. price stability and would maintain a flow of capital from abroad that dampens real interest rates and provides the funds to finance additional investment in housing and in plant and equipment. But the high dollar would also limit the improvement in the trade deficit, depressing activity in export industries and those that compete with imports from abroad. Ultimately, moreover, the dollar's adjustment would have to occur and would have to be larger because the dollar had contributed to a greater accumulation of net debt from the United States to the rest of the world.

EXCHANGE MARKET INTERVENTION

Although substantial past experience and economic logic both imply that sterilized exchange market intervention (i.e., currency intervention with no change in domestic monetary policy) cannot be expected to have a sustained effect on exchange rates, the fall of the dollar in the year after the G-5 finance ministers meeting at the Plaza Hotel in September 1985 and the relative stability of the dollar in the seven months after the Louvre meeting in February 1987 have led some government officials and others to attribute significant power to coordinated exchange rate intervention. I believe that conclusion is a misreading of the recent experience.

There is in fact no evidence that the G-5 Plaza meeting or the subsequent coordinated intervention had any lasting effect on the dollar's rate of decline. In the days immediately after the G-5 meeting there was a four percent decline in the dollar's value. But the rate of decline of the dollar during the subsequent year was no greater than it had been in the six months before the G-5 meeting.

Immediately after the Louvre meeting the central banks were able to prevent the dollar's continued decline by a combination of massive intervention and the threat of even more intervention in the future. But after a short time, continued stabilizing of the dollar required a significant rise in U.S. interest rates relative to interest rates in Japan and Germany. The resulting tight monetary policy in the United States and the fear of further Fed tightening in response to market pressure for a lower dollar were important causes of the stock market crash. As soon as the United States declared that monetary policy would no longer be directed at stabilizing the dollar, the dollar's value responded to market pressures and began to decline sharply. The experience in 1987 thus again demonstrates the inability of intervention to shift currency values for more than a very short time.

THE COORDINATION OF MACROECONOMIC POLICIES

Coordinated exchange rate intervention is only one aspect of the potential coordination of macroeconomic policies. Indeed there are many who accept that exchange rate intervention per se is powerless and who therefore argue for a more general coordination of monetary and budget policies. The Tokyo summit in May 1986 emphasized such macroeconomic coordination and called for a new "multi-lateral surveillance" procedure managed by the International Monetary Fund.

The first such multilateral surveillance session was held in conjunction with the IMF annual meetings in September 1986. The agenda was predictable. The United States called on Japan and the European countries to expand their economies more rapidly in order to increase their imports from the United States. The Europeans and Japan called on the United States to reduce its budget deficit and to slow the decline of the dollar relative to their currencies, an inherently self-contradictory request. No serious agreements were reached. The Germans explained that their economy was expanding rapidly, that their monetary policy was if anything too loose already, and that a tax cut was scheduled for 1988. The Japanese noted that they were moving gradually toward fundamental changes in their economy and Treasury Secretary Baker said the United States was committed to eliminating the budget deficit over the next five years as promised in the Gramm-Rudman-Hollings legislation. In short, every country said it would go on doing just what it had been doing. And, despite the subsequent pronouncements at the Louvre meeting and the Venice summit, each country continued to pursue what it saw as its own interest, generally unaffected by the "international coordination" process.

Only when the government of Japan became convinced in early 1987 that the sharp rise in the yen-dollar rate during 1986 would create a serious downturn for the Japanese economy did Japan abandon its goal of budget deficit reduction and adopt a package of fiscal and monetary stimulus. In contrast, Germany, despite its high unemployment and zero inflation rate, has not adopted any significant expansionary policies because of a government decision to give primacy to preventing inflation and to reducing domestic labor market rigidities. And the $70 billion decline in the U.S. budget deficit between 1986 and 1987 was not the result of international actions but of domestic policies and peculiarities of budget accounting. This failure of the summit and other international coordination discussions to achieve any changes in domestic economic policies should not be seen as a surprise or as a reflection of the fact that the process of explicit coordination only began in 1986. It should be seen as the most likely outcome of all such meetings. The experience at and immediately after the September 1987 IMF-World Bank meetings again demonstrated the emptiness of the coordination process and the inclination of major governments to pursue their own self interests.

CONSTITUTIONAL LIMITS ON AMERICAN PARTICIPATION.

A primary reason why macroeconomic policy coordination cannot work as envisioned by its advocates is that the United States is constitutionally incapable of participating in such a negotiation. The separation of powers in the American form of government means that the Secretary of the Treasury cannot promise to reduce or expand the budget deficit or to change tax rules. This power does not rest with the president or the administration but depends on a legislative agreement between the president and the Congress. In this sense, the United States' participation in any macroeconomic coordination process is fundamentally different from the participation of a country with a parliamentary system in which the prime minister or the prime minister's representative can commit to a change in the nation's economic policy.

It is sometimes suggested than an American Treasury secretary or president, although incapable of promising the enactment of specific budget legislation, could promise that the American government would support a particular legislative proposal. Such a suggestion ignores the negotiating nature of the relation between the president and the Congress. The president cannot propose the legislative package that he expects Congress to enact and he cannot disclose the extent to which is is willing to compromise on specific issues.

Because it is impossible for the United States to reach an international agreement on specific budget, tax or spending policies, any actual agreement would have to call for a change in U.S. monetary policy. International economic coordination could thus be a recipe for the wrong policy change in the United States. For example, if the United States had entered into an agreement in 1983 or 1984 to shift policy in a way that reduced the value of the dollar, the agreement would have required an inflationary increase in the supply of money. At the present time, the finance ministers of other major industrial countries are urging the United States to defend the dollar by a tight monetary policy that could push the U.S. economy into an unnecessary recession. Moreover, even agreements on monetary policy would be beyond the legal authority of the Treasury secretary or the president since it would require the concurrence of the independent Federal Reserve.

Even if the United States could participate effectively in international macroeconomic coordination, I believe that the incentive for the United States and other major industrial countries to do so is more apparent than real. Uncertainties about the actual state of the international economy and uncertainities about the effects of one country's policies on the economies of other countries make it impossible to be confident that coordinated policy shifts would actually be beneficial. The Germany still remember and regret their agreement to serve as "a locomotive for worldwide expansion after the 1978 Bonn summit meeting. Today the Germans argue that foreign pressure for more expansionary German policy exaggerates the potentially favorable effects of such a change on foreign economies and ignores both the underlying strength of German demand and the need to achieve structural reforms in the German labor market as a precondition for reduced unemployment. A few years ago U.S. Treasury Secretary Regan argued that foreign pressure for the United States to reduce its budget deficit was misplaced because budget deficits do not influence interest rates, exchange rates and capital flows. When there are fundamental disagreements about the way the world economy works, there is little reason to believe that coordinated policy will produce improved performance.

It is important to remember that to a very great extent a nation has the ability to achieve its economic goals by itself. Although the levels of demand, inflation, and interest rates in one country do affect the economies elsewhere, a country can manage its own monetary, budget and tax policies to offset many of the potential influences from abroad. Thus changes in domestic monetary policy can counteract the contractionary or inflationary pressures from abroad and structural tax policies designed to encourage investment can offset the effects of a worldwide rise in real interest rates.

There is also a serious risk that economic summits and ministerial meetings will inhibit appropriate changes in national economic policies. Governments may not take the politically painful steps that they should because they believe that foreign actions will make such policies unnecessary or because they want to use their own lack of action as part of a bargaining strategy to induce desired policies on the part of foreign governments. Thus the assertion at the Louvre ministerial and at the Venice summit that the dollar would stop declining may have contributed to a complacency that reduced pressure on the German government to provide adequate domestic stimulus and that may have contributed to the failure of the American Congress to make greater progress in reducing future budget deficits.

CONCLUDING REMARKS

It is unfortunately easy and often politically convenient to exaggerate the potential gains from international economic coordination and to understate the ability of a nation to guide its own economic future. Our politicians and those of other leading countries should not be allowed to escape their responsibilities by blaming poor domestic economic performance on the policies pursued abroad. Similarly, it would be a serious mistake if the pursuit of international coordination in exchange markets and in macroeconomic policy management became an excuse for not pursing appropriate domestic policies.

Washington's explicit recognition of its responsibility for America's economic future would also reassure a nation that has become unnecessarily frightened by the prospect that international economic coordination will collapse. Unfortunately, ever since the May 1986 summit the U.S. administration and the governments of the other industrial countries have emphatically asserted that international economic cooperation is crucial to a healthy international economy in general and to continued U.S. growth in particular. Since such assertions are not justified by the extent of the actual interdependence of the industrialized nations, Americans have been inappropriately worried about whether policy coordination would continue.

Because foreign governments will inevitably pursue the policies that they believe are in their own best interests, it was inevitable that the process of international coordination would eventually collapse. This began with the actions of the German and Japanese governments in early October and was underscored by the statements of Secretary Baker just before the market crash. But the real problem contributing to the market decline was not the collapse of international macroeconomic coordination per se, but the false impression created by governments that healthy expansion requires such international coordination. Moreover, what appeared as cooperation by the European governments in reducing interest rates since late October was motivated by their desire to offset the contractionary effects of the worldwide stock market declines and the falling dollar, rather than as a gesture of cooperation with the United States.

The United States should now explicitly but amicably abandon the policy of international coordination of macroeconomic policy. We should continue to cooperate with other countries by exchanging information about current and future policy decision, but we should recognize explicitly that Japan and Germany have the right to pursue the monetary and fiscal policies that they believe are in their own best interests.

It is frightening to the American public and upsetting to our financial markets to believe that the fate of our economy depends on the decisions made in Bonn and Tokyo. Portfolio investors, business managers and the public in general need to be reassured that we are not hostages to foreign economic policies, that the United States is the master of its own economic destiny, and that our government can and will do what is needed to maintain healthy economic growth.

Although international coordination of macroeconomic policy-making sounds like a way to improve international relations more generally, there is a serious risk that it will have the opposite effect. An emphasis on international interdependence instead of sound domestic policies makes foreign governments the natural scapegoats for any poor economic performance. Pressing a foreign government to alter its domestic economic policies is itself a source of friction and the making of unkeepable promises can only lead to resentment. It would in general be far better if the major industrial countries concentrated on the pursuit of sound domestic economic policies and reserved the pursuit of international cooperation for those subjects like international trade and national security in which cooperation is truly essential.

This article is a condensed version of the 1987 Distinguished Lecture on Economics in Government, Joint Session of the American Association and the Society of Government Economists, Chicago, December 28, 1987. A copy of the full lecture is available from the author.

ENDNOTES

1 My criticisms of international macroeconomic coordination were sketched first in an article that I wrote for the Economist magazine ("The World Economy Today," June 11, 1983). Earlier versions of the current lecture were presented as one of my two 1986 Horowitz Memorial Lectures of the Bank of Israel and as a lecture on the fiftieth anniversary of Nuffield College, Oxford, (See Feldstein, forthcoming). The general subject of international economic cooperation (in macroeconomic policy, exchange rate policy, international trade and developing country debt management) was unexplored at an April 1987 conference of the National Bureau of Economic Research. The conference volume presents valuable survey papers, personal comments by individuals who have had significant experience in government and business, and an extensive bibliography that makes it unnecessary to provide such references in the current talk; my

own views are summarized in an introductory chapter. The interested reader may also wish to see Feldstein (1987b; forthcoming a ,b).

REFERENCES

Feldstein, Martin, "Correcting the Trade Deficit," *Foreign Affairs*, Spring 1987a, 795-806.

Feldstein, Martin, *International Economic Cooperation: Summary Report*, National Bureau of Economic Research, 1987b.

Feldstein, Martin, "Rethinking International Economic Cooperation," Oxford Economic Papers, forthcoming.

Feldstein, Martin, *International Economic Cooperation*, Chicago: University of Chicago Press.

SECTION VIII

Europe 1992

Since the late 1950s, macroeconomic and trade policies in Europe have evolved toward increased coordination. 1992 marks the target date for the culmination of this process, as the twelve member-countries of the European Community work to resolve the extent of and schedule for economic and monetary integration of their economies. In terms of macroeconomic controls, the union provided by Europe 1992 will emphasize the importance of price and exchange-rate stability, restraints on current-account imbalances, regulation of monetary policy and, to some degree, fiscal policy. The union also provides for the removal of border restrictions on many inter-European movements of goods and factors of production. In this section, the articles by Richard Cooper, and by Jacob Frenkel and Morris Goldstein address some of the key themes associated with this important program of economic integration.

READING 16

Europe without Borders

Richard N. Cooper

As little as five years ago, Europe, its economies stagnating in what numerous observers diagnosed as a serious case of Eurosclerosis, was mired in pessimism. Today, that same Europe is euphoric, if also occasionally anxious, over the prospect of eliminating its internal borders, at least for commercial purposes, by the end of 1992.

In no small measure this dramatic turnabout is the personal achievement of Jacques Delors, President of the European Commission since January 1985. He and his fellow commissioners, especially Lord Cockfield, put forward a program of action that has captured the imagination of Europeans and reinvigorated Europe's economy. Their proposal, outlined in a White Paper, "Completing the Internal Market," published in July 1985, fell on receptive ground, since Europeans were really for new initiatives. The White Paper called for the completion of the internal market—for goods, services, capital, and labor—by the end of 1992. To this end, it suggested the need to adopt more than 300 "directives," which carry the force of law within the European Community, a number that has since been reduced through consolidation to 279.

These proposed directives, which intrude boldly into the midst of governance of economic affairs, cover a wide area: border controls; technical standards, testing, and certifications; professional qualifications; international trade in services such as trucking, aviation, data processing, banking, insurance, and other financial services; government procurement; company law; indirect tax harmonization; and capital market liberalization. More than 70 cover transborder shipment of plant and animal materials, about 30 concern financial services.

It would have been practically impossible to act on these directives as the Community was proceeding at the time: piecemeal, with unanimity required on any issue that any of the 10 member countries (since augmented to 12 with the accession in 1986 of Portugal and Spain) wanted to designate a key issue. So the 1985 program was put forward as a package, not to be selected à la carte, presumably to facilitate compromise across issue areas. And the members passed an amendment to the Rome Treaty, the Single European Act, adopted in July 1987, that removed the requirement for unanimity in the decisionmaking Council and replaced it with a qualified majority requirement for approval of most new directives, such that it would take three (two large and one small) or four (one large and three small) countries to block directives proposed by the Commission, the executive arm of the European Community.[1] That change committed all member countries to the 1992 program and altered substantially the bargaining environment by preventing single countries from holding up the Community for special privileges or compensation.

Americans, slow to take interest in the program for a Europe without borders, did not give it serious attention until late 1988. When queried by Europeans about this lack of curiosity, I suggested only half facetiously that Americans thought Europe had already achieved an economic union back in 1968, when internal tariffs and quantitative restrictions were eliminated. Only those involved in European trade realized how far Europe was from an economic union, as exemplified by the states of the United States. Despite the absence of internal tariffs, commercial traffic in Europe still must endure an average 80-minute delay at European borders, while it takes only 1 second for a truck to roll from Massachusetts to Connecticut. Applying substantially different national excise and value added tax rates requires border tax adjustments. Many technical and most health and safety standards are applied at the national level. Non-European automobiles or textiles cannot be sold freely from one member country to another. Even the so-called Common Agricultural Policy is anything but "common." When agricultural products cross European national borders, exchange rate changes that have taken place since prices for those products were last set require "monentary compensatory adjustments," which, bizarrely, sometimes differ from commodity to commodity, making a total nonsense out of any claim to a common market in agricultural products. Government procurement also remains highly parochial, despite commitments made both within the Community and more widely under the government procurement code of the Tokyo Round multilateral trade negotiations concluded in 1979, with only an estimated 2 percent of government procurement being imported from other members of the Community.[2]

THE ECONOMICS OF 1992

The Community has sponsored much research on the consequences of a Europe without borders, including a major study, by Michael Emerson and his colleagues, of the expected economic effects on the Community.[3] Emerson's group estimated the welfare impact as the summation of various partial equilibrium effects, with a resultant estimated improvement in European welfare of 4.3 percent to 6.4 percent of GDP, depending on the exact assumptions. Then they estimated the expected change in Community GDP, using macroeconomic models to generate dynamic responses to specified changes in costs and prices resulting from the removal of remaining border restrictions. The result was an estimated increase of 4.5 percent after six years, on the assumption of unchanged fiscal policy with constant interest rates and exchange rates. The increased GDP arises from increased real consumption made possible by a decline in consumer prices, and by an improved trade balance brought about by improved international competitiveness.

The two sets of estimates different conceptually, even though the initiating changes are the same. The elimination of border officials and the reduction in inefficient back-haul trucking both represent welfare gains, for instance, because of the resources thus saved; but they lower GDP (other things being equal) because of the resulting decline in employment.

It is interesting to look at the composition of the projected welfare gains shown in the upper panel of table 1. A gain of 2.2 percent is attributed to the removal of border impediments per se, including the direct effects the removal would have on production. Most of this gain arises from elimination of existing national differences in product standards, differences that raise costs as well as causing border delays.

The remaining welfare gains arise from indirect, or market integration, effects, which in turn consist of greater economies of scale, especially significant in government procurement products, such as telecommunications and transportation equipment, and reduction in monopoly profits and "X-inefficiencies" because of greater competition throughout the community, especially in financial services.

These microeconomic effects will result in some layoffs. But they will also lower prices, thus stimulating both consumption and net exports. Tracing the next consequences of those changes over six years (using the Interlink and Hermes multinational macroeconomic models) reveals a 6.1 percent drop in prices, and a 4.5 percent rise in GDP, a reduction in budget deficits of 2.2 percent of GDP, and a net increase in employment of 1.8 million people (lower panel of table 1.) GDP could be further increased if this more benign macroeconomic environment were used for an appropriate combination of fiscal and monetary stimulation, given the relatively high levels of unemployment that persist in the Community.

It sounds almost too good to be true. Significant improvements are recorded under all the major objectives of macroeconomic policy. And, indeed, the estimates, especially those of gains due to potential economies of scale, have been criticized as being exaggerated.[4] But even if gains in scale economies are assumed to be zero, surely an error in the opposite direction, the effects on European economic well-being remain consequential on the Emerson estimate.

It is noteworthy, although Emerson does not

Table 1. Economic Gains from Completing the Internal Market
Percent of Community GDP, except as noted

Item	*Effect*
Welfare gain: partial equilibrium analysis	
Removing barriers	2.2
Economies of scale from restructuring	2.0
Competition effects	1.6
Total	5.8
Macroeconomic gains[a]	
Increase in GDP (percent)	4.5
Decline in consumer prices (percent)	6.1
Increase in employment (millions)	1.8
Reduction in public sector deficit	2.2
Improvement in current account	1.0

Source: Emerson (1988, tables 10.1.1, 10.2.2).
a. After six years.

note it, that these techniques of analysis could be applied as well to the entire OECD, or to the world as a whole. They would no doubt show even greater proportionate gains, since world trade is burdened not only by border controls, differences in national standards, and parochial government procurement, but also by tariffs and quantitative restrictions that do not generally obtain within the Community.

THE BASIC APPROACH TO MARKET OPENING

The original approach of the Commission in building a common market during the 1960's was to "harmonize" the various national regulations and rates of trade-relevant taxation, that is, to set Community-wide standards, regulations, and rates of taxation. The 1986 White Paper abandoned this approach in favor of "mutual recognition," whereby an entity that qualifies to do business in any of the member states can do business in all of them. This principle would apply, for instance, to financial institutions, architectural firms, physicians, and dentists.[5] Similarly, a product that can be sold in one member nation can be sold in all. The principle of mutual recognition, which drew in considerable measure on experience in the United States and other federal countries, might in some cases be qualified by imposing minimum standards for the Community as a whole, for example, on environmental or safety regulations.

Instead of harmonizing fully the rates of trade-related taxes, the Commission proposed a common two-rate value added tax (VAT) system, with tax rates on necessities ranging from 4 percent to 9 percent and rates on other goods and services ranging from 14 percent to 20 percent, with each member able to choose its preferred rate within each range. Taxation, however, remains one of the most difficult problems for achieving the 1992 goals. Britain and others have expressed serious reservations about the Commission's proposal (in Britain's case mainly because of strongly held views that food should not be taxed at all), and taxation is one of those few areas that still requires unanimous consent. More recently, the Commission has suggested that members might agree on minimum indirect tax rates for various categories of goods and services, with members free to set higher rates if they wish and if they are willing to accept the consequences in terms of diversion of purchases to lower-tax jurisdictions.

An analogous issue has arisen for witholding taxes on interest and divided earning. The elimination of capital controls throughout the Community will enable individuals to evade taxes by holding their savings in other member countries.[6] The Commission proposed a uniform witholding tax of 15 percent, but in early 1989 Britain and Luxembourg expressed strong reservations about any witholding at source, thus sending the Commission back to the drawing board. In view of the opposition, Germany, which in 1989 had introduced a witholding tax on interest and experienced a strong outflow of savings, mainly to German banks operating out of Luxembourg, announced that it would rescind its witholding tax.

The approach of mutual recognition will, over time, diminish regulation in most member countries. Footloose firms will gravitate to the countries of least onerous regulation (and taxation) and will operate throughout the Community from those locations. Countries eager to attract economic activity, or to avoid losing it, will ease their regulations, just as the various states of the United States did during 1880-1930, as the U.S. market became increasingly national, not least because of the steady reduction in transportation costs.

The development will be welcomed by some, deplored by others. The pressure of mobile firms and capital will reopen many issues of regulation that were settled years ago at the national level. While there is widespread agreement that regulation in Europe had gone too far by the early 1980's, and therefore that some deregulation was desirable, the extent of deregulation will be highly controversial. Margaret Thatcher's Britain professes a desire for the Community to go very far, but the French tradition leans toward more rather than less regulation. German officials will be caught between their liberal ideology and their frequently highly restrictive practices. There will be considerable debate at the European level over the proper role of government, especially focused on the adoption of minimum standards for the Community.

IMPACT ON OUTSIDE COUNTRIES: CONCERNS ABOUT "FORTRESS EUROPE"

Many outsiders, especially Americans and Japanese, worry that the evolution of policy in Europe will restrict trade, leading to a "fortress Europe."[7] How might outsiders be made worse off? Removing the remaining trade barriers within the Community will of course lead to some trade diversion, as German goods, for example, become on average 2 percent cheaper in France, while U.S. or Japanese goods must still surmount the delays and other costs of entering the market from outside. Some French buyers are likely to switch from outside suppliers to German suppliers. But that possibility worries outsiders much less than the possibility of new barriers being erected where none now exist. This could come about in several ways.

First, as Europeans adjust the national quotas they now maintain on non-European goods, they may increase overall restrictiveness. Britain, France, Italy, and Spain all restrict the importation of Japanese automobiles, while Germany, the Netherlands, and others do not. Brussels says these national quotas must go. On way to do that is to establish an overall Community quota for Japanese autos. That would effectively remove an open market where free entry now exists. (The injury could be compounded in this case by adopting content requirements that lead to Japanese models made in the United States being defined as "Japanese.") Recently, pronouncements from Brussels suggest that any such restriction must be strictly temporary, if it is to exist at all.

Analogous problems exist for a number of products, especially textiles. One that especially concerns Americans is TV broadcasting. The EC Commission has put forward a draft directive, approved by the European Parliament, requiring that the majority of all broadcast programming be European in origin. This directive, which mainly affects TV films as far as international trade is concerned, raises at least three issues. First, it speaks of "European" programming, not merely EC in origin. Thus it seems to discriminate in favor of Swedish or Yugoslav or even Russian programs relative to American or Japanese or Brazilian programs, a violation of the nondiscriminatory provision of GATT insofar as films are considered merchandise trade. Second, it could curtail sales of U.S. (and other non-European) programs to member countries that now permit levels of foreign programming enough higher than 51 percent to compensate for those (for example, Britain, Italy, France, and Spain) that are well below 51 percent. That is a factual question. Conceivably the new directive is actually liberalizing for the non-European films, insofar as the average for Europe is now held to well below 51 percent in practice. But of course even if the directive were liberalizing in its effect, foreign film producers would prefer no restrictions. U.S. producers earn about $1.8 billion a year in sale or lease of films, TV, and home video to the EC, although only TV broadcasting would be directly affected by the directive.

Third, the directive is ostensibly motivated by a

desire to preserve and encourage European "culture." But what exactly is that? Why does it include Russian but exclude American or Brazilian products? Moreover, U.S. studios make many films within Europe, and European studios film outside of Europe. European studios make "westerns" and other films with non-European themes. Why should these be unrestricted but American-made westerns be restricted? Filmmaking, like many other forms of economic activity, has become so internationalized in practice that a restriction in favor of European programming seems motivated less by cultural considerations than by a desire to protect ailing European studios from foreign competition. The "cultural" motivation seems only a cloak designed to achieve wider appeal.

A second source of new barriers is rules for selling services. Here the Commission aroused concern in the U.S. financial community with its first-draft banking directive, which permitted entry of outside banks only on the basis of "reciprocal" treatment, a term that was not defined. But several European countries allow both unlimited branch banking and universal banking (whereby banks can underwrite securities, sell insurance, and provide the whole range of financial services). U.S. banks are restricted in their activities by the Banking Act of 1933, better known as Glass-Steagall, as well as by state boundaries and state regulations and a host of other limitations. Banks in other countries are also restricted. While the regulatory environment is changing rapidly in the United States (and in Japan), few Americans are willing to go as far as universal banking, with the implication that, on this definition of reciprocity, U.S. banks would not be allowed to do business in a unified Community (with those banks already established in Europe possibly subject to a grandfather provision that would permit them to stay).

The ruckus created over this issue led the Commission to redefine its position, making clear it did not mean "mirror-image" reciprocity, and indeed dropping the term reciprocity in favor of the equally ambiguous term "comparable market access." In side comments it was made clear that this qualification was aimed at Japan rather than the United States; but the U.S. financial community correctly took no comfort from such oral assurances, which will have been forgotten by 1995. More recently, Community spokesmen have made clear that genuine national treatment—that is, treating European banks in the same way as domestic banks—will meet the requirement.

It should be acknowledged, however, that just while Europe is eliminating its internal barriers it is also involved with a major multilateral trade negotiation, the Uruguay Round, with the United States, Japan and dozens of other countries. The Europeans quite understandably want to preserve their bargaining position in those negotiations, which are due to conclude in 1990. The Uruguay Round, in fact, can provide a useful forum in which outside countries can make known, and negotiate, their concerns, especially in the various services.

A third source of new barriers is the setting of Community-wide technical, health, safety, and environmental standards. The Emerson study identifies divergent national standards as the most important cost of present arrangements. If borders are to be eliminated for purposes of trade, standards must be effectively harmonized, a process that will often improve trade opportunities for outsiders as well as for Europeans, since a much larger market will be available at common minimum standards. But the standard-setting process could, either by coincidence or by design, work to the disadvantage of outsiders. For instance, a noise limit of 90 decibels has been established, effective in mid-1991, for power lawn mowers. The United States exports to Europe mainly the larger, riding mowers, whose noise typically exceeds this level.[8] The effect will be to reduce U.S. sales of lawn mowers to Europe, or else to force increased costs on U.S. producers for noise reduction, (which in this instance would benefit U.S. consumers as well).

A somewhat analogous situation exists with government procurement. As already noted, only an estimated 2 percent of European government procurement is directly imported. The Commission's proposal to put procurement on a Community-wide basis has been agreed to in principle, with some qualifications. While there may be cases in which Community-wide procurement will damage outside exporters who now supply European governments, those purchases are at present so small that they are likely to be counterbalanced by the greater openness in procurement procedures and practices, even under the existing 1979 Government Procurement Code, especially if it is extended in the Uruguay Round.

Table 2. Indirect Taxes in the European Community, 1987
Percent

Country	*Principal tax rates*	*Indirect taxes as a share of total revenue*	*Indirect taxes as a share of GDP*
Belgium[a]	19	19	8
Denmark	22	35	15
France	19	25[b]	10[b]
West Germany	14'	21	9
Greece[c]	18	33	12
Ireland[a]	25	29	12
Italy	18	20	7
Luxembourg[c]	12	20	8
Netherlands	20	21	11
Portugal	16	28	12
Spain[a]	12	23	7
United Kingdom[a]	15	28	11

Sources: Principal tax rates from Lee and Smith (1988, p. 33). Indirect taxes as a share of total revenue and GDP from International Monetary Fund (1988a and 1988b).
a. 1986.
b. Excludes local government.
c. 1985.

Here the central question is the extent to which government procurement will be formally extended to outside countries as well as members, and that is a matter for negotiation.

Those who have looked closely at the prospects for American business as a result of further integration of European markets find on balance that the results are likely to be beneficial, and that the potentially damaging consequences can be reduced through alert comment on standards or regulations before they get adopted, and in some cases through subsequent negotiation.[9]

PROSPECTS FOR SUCCESS

Will the Community achieve its aim for completing the internal market by the end of 1992? By June 1989 the Commission had put forward proposals under 229 of the 279 headings that make up the total plan. Of these, 121 had been formally adopted, of which over two-thirds concerned plant and animal hygiene, border administration, and technical standards. The most dramatic single directive was perhaps that abolishing controls over capital movements, which commits France and Italy to do so by mid-1990 and the four remaining countries with capital controls, Ireland, Spain, Greece, and Portugal, by later dates.

Since many of the directives, while formally carrying the force of Community law, will nonetheless require national implementing legislation, the directives must largely be adopted by the end of 1990 if border controls are to be totally removed by 1993. Many of the directives are essential for this outcome, but some (for example, those on European company law), while an integral part of the program, are not essential for removal of border controls.

Two essential areas remain exceedingly difficult and will probably not be resolved by 1992. The first concerns trade-related, or indirect tax rates (VAT and excises), and the second concerns the Common Agricultural Policy (CAP).

At present, indirect taxes are levied on the destination principle, which means that taxes of the exporting country are rebated at the border and taxes of the importing country are imposed at the border. If borders are to be eliminated, these border tax adjustments must be eliminated. The "obvious" way to do this is to harmonize tax rates, at least to within a tolerable range, as the Commission has proposed, so that a given product pays roughly the same tax no matter where it is sold in the Community.

The problem is that national tax rates vary greatly, ranging from zero (on food and children's clothing) in Britain to a 25 percent basis rate in Ireland. The national dependence on indirect taxes

Table 3. Private Market Activity in the European Community, 1983–88[a]
Billions of dollars except as noted

Year	*Number of mergers and acquisitions*	*U.S. direct investment*	*Japanese direct investment*
1983	117	−0.7	0.9
1984	155	0.0	1.7
1985	208	11.8	1.9
1986	226	12.8	3.3
1987	303	18.9	6.3
1988	383	4.4	8.3

Sources: U.S. and Japanese direct investment from U.S. Department of Commerce, *Survey of Current Business* (June 1989 and earlier issues), table 10, and MITI news releases, respectively. Mergers and acquisitions from Commission of the European Communities (1989b).

a. Figures for 1983–85 refer to the Community before the entry of Spain and Portugal. Figures for 1986 and later include Spain and Portugal.

as a source of revenue varies too, from 19 percent in Belgium to 35 percent in Denmark (see table 2). Harmonizing tax rates would create windfall revenues for countries such as Spain and Germany, which could respond by reducing income taxes, but it would create significant losses of revenue for countries such as Ireland and Denmark, where it would be much more difficult to restore revenues by raising income tax rates, either because the are already very high or because they are about as high as is enforceable.

An alternative approach would be to shift indirect taxes, at least as far as intra-Community trade is concerned, to an origin basis under which product taxes would be paid in the country of origin. This approach would result in business pressure to reduce tax rates in the high-tax countries, because such taxes put their products at a competitive disadvantage elsewhere in the Community. But as far as the Community is concerned, it would eliminate the need for border tax adjustments on intra-Community trade. Of course, imports from third countries, to which indirect taxes would still apply, would be directed to ports of entry in members with low indirect tax rates, putting further pressure on the high tax rate countries to reduce their rates.

An analogous problem exists with agricultural trade. Under the Common Agricultural Policy, minimum price support levels are set annually, usually in April, in ECU, the European currency unit. But European national currency values fluctuate relative to the ECU. For currencies in the exchange rate arrangements of the European Monetary System these fluctuation are limited, but on occasions, eleven in all between the inception of the EMS in 1979 and early 1987, central rates have been changed. These exchange rate movements imply that minimum farm prices when measured in national currency also should move. But the tolerance of the farmers and their political supporters for reductions in farm prices is distinctly limited. Therefore local currency prices frequently have not been adjusted in response to changes in exchange rates. This result has been accomplished by establishing a set of separate exchange rates, so-called green rates, for agricultural products. To avoid the arbitrage possibilities that would otherwise occur, this system of dual exchange rate requires "monetary compensation adjustments" (MCAs) at internal borders on intra-Community agricultural trade.

With completion of the internal market,the entire system of green rates and MCAs must be dismantled, which can be done only by moving to fixed exchange rates within the Community, with its implications for monetary policy—an important topic not taken up here—or else by persuading farmers to accept a decline in local currency support prices whenever the local currency appreciates against the ECU. The first course represents a significant political as well as technical challenge; the second represents a formidable and possibly insurmountable political challenge. Even if this problem can be solved, the issue of eliminating the current MCAs must be faced. Very likely that will be accomplished be raising agricultural support prices throughout the Community to the highest level, which is where, at market exchange rates, agricultural prices are highest. This European agriculture, already heavily protected, will probably receive a further increase in protection as a result of completing the internal market, with negative effects on agricultural suppliers elsewhere in the world. The Community may hope to finesse the problem of agricultural trade by setting agricultural prices hereafter in German marks rather than in ECU. On the assumption that no other member currency will appreciate against the mark, this approach will assure that local currency support prices will not decline as a result of changes in exchange rates. But that would be a gamble on future exchange rates.

These are the two most formidable obstacles to eliminating Europe's commercial borders (leaving aside Prime Minister Thatcher's insistence that some border controls must be preserved for reasons of public safety). A few other problems have received little attention. First, for purposes of trade West Germany treats East Germany as part of Germany, admitting its goods free of duty. Such goods must now pay duty when they are transshipped to other members of the Community. This practice must cease in a Europe without borders; either East Germany becomes a de facto member of the Community as far as its exports are concerned, or some administrative means must be found to limit transshipment. (It is taken for granted and accepted throughout Europe that West Germany's practice cannot be changed, for political reasons.)

Second, among current members of the Community, Ireland is not a member of the Coordinating Committee for Multilateral Export Controls (COCOM), the officially nonexistent agency that lays down rules limiting sales of militarily significant products and technology to the Soviet Union and its allies. Despite its neutral status, Ireland would have to become a de facto member of COCOM, and enforce its rules, in a Europe without borders unless its members are willing to abandon strategic export controls altogether, which is unlikely.

Third, elimination of borders will eliminate the current sources of statistics on intra-Community trade. A totally new system for estimating trade flows will have to be devised, or else countries will have to learn to live without national trade statistics, just as states within the United States do. Some observers would even see this loss as a positive contribution of the program.

PRIVATE SECTOR RESPONSE

Whether or not European authorities meet their ambitious objective, the prospect of a big reduction in impediments to intra-European trade in goods and especially services is being taken seriously by the private sector, including state-owned enterprises. Both European and non-European firms have addressed the possible changes, and have positioned themselves to take advantage of new opportunities and to fend off stronger competition that, as the Emerson estimates suggest, may have a potent effect on European business in the future. As table 3 shows, mergers and acquisitions within Europe, already rising before the White Paper of 1985, have continued to increase. American direct investment in the Community, which stagnated in the early 1980s, has proceeded strongly since 1985. Japanese direct investment in Europe has also grown sharply, although perhaps not specifically as a result of Europe 1992, since Japanese investment has grown rapidly in the United States as well.

Business managers are not obligated to sort out their motivations for particular actions, as analysts would like, so we do know to what extent this foreign investment is defensive in nature, designed to gain entrance to the Community before new, stiffer rules on entry are promulgated, and to what extent the investment is motivated by new opportunities foreseen for market development within Europe, including a liberalization of government procurement. But in either case the business community is taking seriously the further integration of the European market, both in its own actions and in its support for the Commission's efforts.

CONCLUSIONS

The European program for 1992 is best thought of as a process, with the 1992 deadline being used as a forcing device, a frequent practice in Community affairs. A best guess is that Europe will not be without internal borders in early 1993, mainly because of the intransigence of the tax problem, but that intra-European trade will be substantially freer, and intra-European competition and lot keener, than it is now, especially in the field of financial services. The evolution toward a Europe without borders will open up many issues that were previously settled, and the process of so doing creates uncertainty where heretofore the ground rules, however disagreeable, were understood. The uncertainty is over whether firms will lose or improve their position.

For outsiders, the process on balance is likely to be liberalizing, except in the field of agriculture, for the simple reason that a building a "fortress" is not in Europe's interest. It has a great stake in a liberal trading world, has profited greatly from it, and is likely to contribute further to it.

There are certainly strong protectionist pressures within Europe, partly ideological and traditional, as in France, Italy, and Spain, and partly simply self-interested, as can be found in firms, industries, and labor unions everywhere. Pressures will be strong to confine the benefits to European firms, and even to European-owned European firms. The pressures will be especially strong with respect to government procurement, where they can be avoided only byopening procurement to all, promulgating clear guidelines for tenders, and being willing to punish officials who violate the procedure—something that is difficult to imagine several European governments doing.

Important Brussels officials, however, seem to have a genuine commitment to enhanced competition. The problem for outsiders does not lie so much in the general thrust of Community policy as in the thousands of technical decision that will have to be made to implement the policy. Interested parties will have to be vigilant and to express concerns early about decisions that either by design or by coincidence will put outsiders at a disadvantage. That has been happening, as several extensive reports by American trade associations testify. In that respect expressions of concern about "fortress Europe" are simply part of the process.

ENDNOTES

1 Certain issues still require unanimity, most notably taxation, border controls for law enforcement, working conditions, and environmental protection.

2 Emerson (1988, p. 48).

3 Emerson (1988). For a more popular treatment of the subject see Cecchini (1988).

4 See Davis (1989).

5 Special qualifications might have to be satisfied by lawyers and accountants, because of continuing differences in legal systems and accounting standards.

6 The obvious solution is for income tax authorities to harmonize their reporting requirements and exchange information.

7 This expression seems to have originated with then—Vice-President Willi de Clerq, who was denying what Europe will become.

8 U.S. International Trade Commission (1989, pp. 6-24).

9 U.S. International Trade Commission (1989); U.S. Council for International Business (1989).

READING 17

Europe's Emerging Economic and Monetary Union

Jacob A. Frenkel and Morris Goldstein

After more than a decade of experience with the European Monetary System (EMS), the 12 member countries of the European Community are now engaged in important discussion and negotiation about the path to economic and monetary union (EMU). This article takes a look at key issues relating to the design and implementation of monetary policy in the emerging EMU, without endorsing or dismissing specific institutional proposals for transition to EMU. The emphasis is on the interrelationships among price stability, current account equilibrium, and exchange rate stability, as well as the questions of the degree of coordination and rules versus discretion. Also considered are the critical implications of fiscal policy for the conduct of monetary policy, along with alternative ways of encouraging fiscal discipline.

MONETARY POLICY GOALS

Progress toward EMU necessarily requires a consensus to be reached among participating countries on the goals of monetary policy. During the 1960s and the 1970s, monetary policies in the major industrial nations typically embraced a number of objectives, notably price stability, full employment, and sustainable economic growth (and for some, exchange rate stability and stability of the financial system). But in the last decade or so, governments have concentrated on the objective of controlling inflation, with price stability being regarded—appropriately in our view—as a necessary (albeit not sufficient) condition for achieving other economic goals, including sustainable economic growth.

Consistent with this tendency, there appears to be broad agreement that a European System of Central Banks, or "EuroFed," should have an explicit mandate to pursue price stability (see "Europe: The Quest for Monetary Integration," by Horst Ungerer in *Finance & Development*, December 1990, for a discussion of the institutional aspects of EMU). To give "teeth" to this commitment, some have proposed giving the "EuroFed" substantial independence, while prohibiting it from granting credit to the public sector. What is less clear is how policy-making authorities should respond to developments in current accounts and frame their exchange rate objectives.

Historically, not all potential EMU members have placed the same emphasis on the current account balance relative to other goals. But the further liberalization of European capital markets might increase the importance of any differences among countries in the importance attached to current account objectives, by making it easier to finance intra-European external imbalances. There is also the matter of Europe's aggregate current account position, which could well influence a future ECU/US dollar or ECU/yen exchange rate, (ECU stands for European Currency Unit, a composite basket of the EC currencies.)

What then should the authorities' attitude be on current account imbalances? Several analysts—ourselves included—believe that such imbalances are not inherently good or bad, but must be assessed on a case-by-case basis. For example, imbalances that arise from temporary differences among countries in the age distribution of the population—which in turn yield differences in private saving patterns—are likely to be benign whereas an imbalance that reflects unsustainable borrowing abroad to finance a consumption spree should surely be placed in the malign category.

We see merit in a framework that would consider at least the following factors:

- whether fiscal position is appropriate (in terms of both the level and composition of government spending, as well as the structure of taxes and borrowing used to finance the budget);
- whether increased investment associated with the external imbalance can be expected to provide a rate of return that exceeds the cost of borrowing (including externalities); and
- whether any increased consumption associated with the imbalance is temporary and desirable for purposes of smoothing movements in consumption over time.

One needs to know the origin of an imbalance before one can decide both if the imbalance needs correcting and how that can best be accomplished.

As for the role of exchange rate objectives, several issues arise: the management of the union's exchange rate vis-à-vis non-EMU currencies; the loss of the nominal exchange rate as a policy instrument, and the choice between rapid and gradual approaches to EMU, with "hard" and "soft" exchange rate commitments, respectively.

Exchange Rate Management in a Tri-Polar system

In recent years, we have increasingly felt that a tri-polar exchange rate system, in which exchange rate commitments are "looser" and "quieter" across the poles than within regional currency areas, represents a feasible and desirable evolution of the international monetary system. By tri-polar, we mean a regime where many currencies are linked either to the US dollar, the Japanese yen, or a European currency (e.g., the Deutsche mark or the ECU). "Loose" exchange rate commitments imply that exchange rate targets are altered more frequently and are subject to wider margins than with "tighter" commitments. "Quiet" and "loud" commitments are merely a shorthand for distinguishing between confidential and publicly announced exchange targets.

Several of the arguments for such a system are directly relevant to how an evolving EMU might react to exchange rate movements outside the union. First, an exchange rate system that has as its regional nominal anchors, three relatively independent central banks—each committed to price stability—is not conducive to policy "blueprints" that require monetary policy in the anchor countries to give first priority to keeping exchange rates within loud target zones. Second, real exchange rates across the three poles need some flexibility to be able to reflect changes in real economic conditions over time. Third, better disciplined monetary and fiscal policy within each of the currency areas would go a long way toward establishing more discipline exchange markets across the poles. Fourth, intervention to manage exchange rates across the poles (i.e., \$/ECU, \$/yen, ECU/yen) should be saved for cases where there is strong evidence of bubbles or large misalignments in exchange rates.

This should not be interpreted as a call for return to "benign neglect" in the management of major currency exchange rates. Quite the contrary, as we regard a reasonable degree of exchange rate stability for key currencies as a public good for the system. Our argument instead is that the stabilizing effect of any official exchange rate commitment on expectations depends on its credibility. A looser commitment across the poles—wherein authorities "Keep their powder dry" for large, clear-call misalignments and do not claim that the primary assignment of monetary policy is for external balance—should be more credible than a (nominally) tighter and louder commitment. But the same logic also points to tight, loud exchange rate commitments *within* currency areas, one of which is an emerging EMU. Here, the incentives for stabilizing exchange rates are greater—because these economies are more open, because trade flows among union members account for a large share of members' total trade, because exchange rate stability is closely linked to larger, regional integration objectives, and because there are larger gains in anti-inflationary credibility to be had by "tying ones' hands" on monetary policy via exchange rate fixity.

Nominal Exchange Rates Within the Union

What about the pressing issue of managing exchange rates within, and on the way to monetary union? One key issue relates to the consequences of losing the nominal exchange rate as policy instrument. Economic theory suggests that the types of shocks hitting an economy (monetary or real) should be an important factor in the choice of an exchange rate regime. The potential problem of a monetary union is adjusting to country-specific real shocks. Here, three questions need to be addressed.

- Are the real economic shocks that typically hit European economies industry-specific rather than country-specific? If they are industry-specific and if potential EMU members have well-diversified industrial structures, than it is possible that these shocks largely cancel out at the country level: but if shocks are predominantly country-specific, potential difficulties are obviously greater.
- Will the increased competition in goods and factors markets associated with the 1992 increase the downward flexibility of money wages and prices in Europe? If so — and we do not discount this possibility—it will be less costly to achieve needed changes in real exchange rates via changes in internal wages and prices.
- Is there in operation a federal fiscal authority that could automatically adjust a country's tax and transfer payments in the event of country-specific real shocks—and in a roughly budget-neutral fashion for the union as a whole? As is well known, this kind of tax and transfer system operates as a cushioning device in the United States.

The more confident one can be that the answers to these questions are "yes" the less concerned can monetary authorities afford to be in embracing greater (nominal) exchange rate fixity on the path to EMU.

The Exchange Rate Regime in the Transition to EMU

Assume in keeping with the spirit of EMU, that a judgement has been made to make use of the nominal exchange rate as a policy instrument only in "exceptional" circumstances. This still leaves unanswered whether the transition should be rapid or gradual and whether exchange rate commitments should be absolute or conditional.

One option would be to move rapidly to EMU itself, that is, to a common currency (e.g., the EMU) and to a central monetary authority (e.g., the EuroFed). This would carry a number of attractions. First, it gives maximum credibility to exchange rate stability by eliminating exchange rates within the union. A common currency is harder to "undo" than a commitment to "irrevocably fixed" exchange rates, and market participants presumably know it. Second, a common currency allows EMU participants to obtain more of the efficiency gains associated with moving closer to one money than do fixed exchange rates. Third, a central monetary authority can in principle avoid the negative externalities associated with begger-thy-neighbor policies taken by competing national monetary authorities. Fourth, a central monetary authority may be able to implement monetary control more effectively than individual national central banks—because the demand for money in the wider area may be more stable under open capital markets and full financial liberalization than are individual-country money demands.

On the negative side, two concerns arise about a rapid move to EMU. One is that the participating countries will not be "ready" for a common currency or a common monetary policy, be it because of inadequate convergence of economic performances (particularly of inflation), inadequate consensus on the goals or framework for monetary policy, or inadequate experience with common institutions. To some observers, this lack of readiness calls either for a two-track approach—where the fast track is limited to a subset of potential members who already are ready in terms of convergence of economic performance—or for waiting together until a wider group of members is ready. A second objective is that an administrative, centralized approach to currency and monetary management will result in average—or even worse, collusive, below-average—performance; in contrast, a "competitive" approach—so the argument goes—would allow the market to converge on "the best in the Community."

Another option would be to pursue a slower transition to EMU, characterized by the coexistence of a federal monetary authority and national central banks, and by a looser commitment to fixed exchange rates. This option clearly provides more scope for learning by doing and for making monetary policy more accountable to national governments. But as critics point out, such a strategy cannot escape the constraint that only two of the following three objectives can be obtained simultaneously: open capital markets, fixed exchange rates, and independent monetary policy. With capitol controls all but gone and with increased opportunities for diversification of currency portfolios, a commitment to truly fixed exchange rates will be credible only if monetary policy coordination—ex ante and ex post—is tighter than in the past. In fact, the very liberalization processes that give rise to increased currency substitution, along with any destabilizing speculation, may well call for more frequent recourse to coordinated interest rate adjustments; otherwise, national monetary control is apt to be rendered less effective.

A related challenge thrown up by the coexistence of central and national monetary authorities and by a desire to introduce more symmetry of adjustment into the system, is that the rules of the game may become more difficult to define than at the existing EMS. Not only does the assignment of responsibilities have to be clearly understood, but also that assignment has to respect the primacy of price stability as a goal of EMU.

CARRYING OUT MONETARY POLICY

During the transition to EMU, EC member governments will also have to come to terms with at least two important issues relating to the implementation of monetary policy: the degree of coordination, and rules versus discretion.

We see the current process of financial liberalization, innovation, globalization and securitization as strengthening the case for closer coordination of monetary policy on at least three counts.

• The shift away from credit rationing and qualitative lending restrictions means that the transmission mechanism of monetary policy falls more heavily on interest rates and exchange rates—the "competitive" variables most often the subject of beggar-thy-neighbor complaints. Coordination is a way of discouraging such practices. The degree of conflict that exists at the transition to EMU is not irrelevant for prospects of actually achieving EMU.

• When there is a sudden, large increase in currency substitution, it may become more difficult to implement reliable monetary control at the national level without stronger coordination among monetary authorities.

• The problem of systemic risk does not lend itself easily to an autonomous, competitive approach, and this is of particular relevance to the Europe of 1992 and behond. In an environment where there are increasing competitive pressures in financial services, universal banking throughout the region, equity prices moving more closely across countries, and a desire on the part of monetary authorities to establish or maintain anti-inflationary credibility, it would not be surprising if some financial institutions experienced difficulties. A national monetary authority might act to contain such difficulties by providing emergency liquidity support or by activating official or private deposit insurance schemes. However, official safety nets, as with other types of insurance, raise moral hazard issues: in this case, the encouragement to undertake an unduly high share of risky activities, giving rise to unfavorable consequences for the public sector's liability.

This problem, could be reduced if financial institutions maintained adequate capital requirements, or if access to deposit insurance went hand-in-hand with restrictions on institutions' activities. But in a world of financial liberalization, any single country's attempt to impose stiffer regulatory standards could result merely in firms fleeing to countries with more lax standards (resulting in a form of regulatory arbitrage). A coordinated approach to regulation can accomplish what a competitive approach cannot. The recently concluded Basle Agreement on risk-weighted capital standards for commercial banks in the Group of Ten countries is a case in point.

This brings us to the familiar issue of rules versus discretion, which would need to be addressed whether a coordinated or competitive approach to monetary policy was selected. Those who favor policy rules make essentially three agreements. First, rules are a viable mechanism for imposing discipline on economic policymakers who might otherwise manipulate the instruments of policy for their own objectives and to the detriment of the public. Second, rules can reduce the cost of negotiation and burden-sharing conflicts. Third, rules are regarded as enhancing the predictability of policy actions, thereby improving the private sector's ability to make informed resource allocation decisions.

These arguments in favor of policy rules are powerful, but their immediate operational attractiveness is blunted by two considerations—both of which are relevant to an emerging EMU. One is that rules that do not adapt to major changes in the operating environment run the risk of worsening policy performance. The weakening in many countries of the link between narrow monetary aggregates and the ultimate goals of monetary policy in the face of large-scale financial innovation and institutional change is a leading case in point. In recognition of these changes in the operating environment, several prominent supporters of policy rules have incorporated trend changes in velocity into their money supply or national-income rules (what we might call "evolutionary" rules)—while several monetary authorities have indicated that they now employ a more eclectic approach to monetary policy (where the behavior of monetary aggregates is taken into account along with a set of other variables). A second consideration is that rules that will impart greater discipline to policy only to the extent that penalties for breaking the rules are followed. The sanctions available against sovereign nations for breach of economic policy commitments should not be exaggerated.

SEARCH FOR FISCAL DISCIPLINE

A striking lesson of the 1980s is that when fiscal policy is undisciplined and works in a direction opposite to that of the monetary policy, efforts to promote price stability, effective external adjustment, and exchange market stability will be seriously handicapped. Basically, there are three potential mechanisms for encouraging greater fiscal discipline.

The Exchange Rate Regime

Experience is not kind to the view that the exchange rate regime by itself can enforce discipline on fiscal policy. Thus after more than ten years of operation—and with a clear progression toward fixity of exchange rates—there is little evidence of fiscal policy convergence in the EMS. Monetary policy convergence, yes—but not fiscal policy convergence. In a similar vein, the North American experience with much greater exchange rate flexibility hardly suggests that this exchange rate regime can consistently rein in fiscal policies. It is not difficult to construct theoretical examples where the exchange rate regime sends either a false signal, or no signal at all, about the need for fiscal adjustment. Typically, this comes about because the higher interest rate associated with fiscal expansion induces a capital inflow that either prompts or loosening of monetary policy (to keep the exchange rate within its target), or simply makes the fiscal deficit easier to finance.

The Market

What then about the discipline imposed by "the market?" Such market discipline is usually said to operate via two channels. The first is the higher cost of borrowing associated with constant fiscal imprudence—as the markets exact an increasing risk premium to reflect lower expected repayment. At some point, markets could even impose their ultimate sanction, by refusing to lend altogether to the unrepentant borrower. The second is via pressures for tax harmonization. In short, a government that spends a lot will eventually have to tax a lot, but high taxes will, in turn, induce firms and individuals to move to jurisdictions with lower taxes. Declining tax revenues will then force tax harmonization, and finally, a halt to excessive spending.

For market discipline to work, the following conditions need to be satisfied.

- The market must have accurate and comprehensive information on the size and composition of the debtor's obligations, so that it can make a valid assessment of debt-servicing obligations relative to ability-to-pay. Credit-rating agencies can of course assist in this information processing task, but they need to be cautious since a rating change can become a self-fulfilling prophecy. In addition, debtors may not have incentives to reveal unfavorable information before mandated reporting dates.
- There must not be any implicit or explicit guarantee of a bail-out. For if there is the expectation of a bail-out, then the interest rate charged will reflect the creditworthiness of the guarantor—not that of the debtor. The market's perception of a bail-out is sometimes cited as a reason why in the 1970s interest rate spreads on bank loans to developing countries were so slow to rise. It is of course possible for the overseeing fiscal authority to issue a no bail-out pledge. The problem is that it may be difficult to make this pledge credible if troubled debtors were in the past bailed out.
- The financial system must be strong enough for any given debtor not to be regarded as too large to fail; if other financial institutions are large holders of the troubled debtor's obligations, it will be harder to exercise discipline.
- The borrower's debt must not be monetized by central bank purchases—that is, be allowed to be translated into an expansion of the money supply. This is because the resulting erosion of the real value of the debt will make it difficult for the market to price it accurately.
- There must be neither high costs of mobility nor the provision of public services that compensate for tax differentials (this condition applies specifically to tax harmonization). If mobility costs are high, individuals and firms are less likely to "vote with their feet" when taxes are raised. If better public services are offered in high tax districts, then high taxes do not provide an incentive to leave.

The empirical evidence on market discipline is quite limited. From the viewpoint of an emerging EMU, perhaps the most relevant work is that dealing with common currency areas that have federal fiscal systems (such as the United States and Canada), and where there is no explicit or implicit guarantee of a bail out for fiscal adventurism at the local level. A recent analysis of whether US states with higher debt burdens actually paid higher interest rates on their debt was undertaken by Professor Barry Eichengreen of the University of California at Berkeley. He found only a weak, positive relationship between debt burdens and the cost of borrowing, and no evidence that borrowing costs accelerate at very high debt levels. Moreover, even if stronger empirical evidence linking borrowing costs to fiscal irresponsibility were available, it would give us only half the picture. Still missing is evidence that higher borrowing costs actually induce governments to correct fiscal policy excesses; to our knowledge, no such tests are yet available.

Peer Group Surveillance

This would offer still another mean of encouraging fiscal discipline. One possibility would be a fiscal policy rule that put a ceiling on each participant's fiscal deficit. The main difficulty with rigid fiscal policy rules is that they may not take adequate account of relevant differences between countries—in private savings rates, outstanding debt stocks, the uses to which government expenditures are put, past credit histories, etc. In addition, there may be few sanctions that can be imposed on noncomplying members. For these reasons, peer group surveillance typically takes place in a voluntary, discretionary format. But this mode of operation faces its own obstacles: fiscal policy is inflexible (at least relative to monetary policy); it operates with long and variable lags that depend in good measure on the pace of legislative actions; and the effects of fiscal policy on macro-variables of interest hinge on what kind of fiscal action is taken (taxes versus expenditures, expenditures on tradables versus nontradables, taxes on saving versus investment, etc.). Then, too, surveillance exercises invariably employ multi-indicator methods, where the tendency of different indicators to point in different directions gives considerable scope for discretion in policy diagnosis and prescription.

The likelihood that no single mechanism can be relied upon to yield fiscal discipline means that a broad-based approach that leans both on markets and on surveillance will be called for. The transition to EMU will proceed a lot smoother if fiscal policy can be made to work with monetary policy in achieving EMU's basic economic goals.

SECTION IX

LDC Debt Crisis

The international debt crisis, which began in the early 1980s, slowed the growth of debtor nations and threatened the world economic system. The causes of the debt crisis are disputed. Some economists argue that debtors did not use their resources prudently, while others argue that the creditors were imprudent in supplying funds. Still others argue that the series of shocks that buffeted the debtors were beyond the control and the expectations of both creditors and debtors. Understanding the causes of the debt crisis are important for designing its solutions. Moreover, as creditors resume their large-scale lending activities, the international community must take steps to avoid future debt crises. It remains unresolved whether the initiatives calling for debt-relief and the various menus of debt-reducing instruments provide the solutions sought by debtors and creditors. In this section, the articles by Anna Schwartz and Paul Krugman provide valuable insights into the causes and potential resolution of the LDC debt crisis.

READING 18

International Debts: What's Fact and What's Fiction Presidential Address to the Western Economic Association, July 2, 1988

Anna J. Schwartz*

From the vantage point of 1988, the 1982 judgment that the troubled foreign country debtors had a liquidity problem, not a solvency problem, appears to have been fiction. The fact is that troubled debtors did not use productively the resources they borrowed. Further loans to them only add to the burden of their existing debt. Retaining the loans at face value on the books of the creditor banks is a fiction that financial markets see through. Intervention by regulators and international lending agencies has impeded bilateral bargains between the debtors and the banks.

Next month will mark the sixth anniversary of Mexico's August 13, 1982, announcement that it could not service its $80 billion international debt without an immediate new loan of $3 billion. Up to that time financial markets had taken Mexico's creditworthiness for granted. No one believed that an oil exporter with large known oil reserves would find it difficult to service debt. A possible fall in the price of oil was given no weight. Moreover, national income account measures recorded rapid growth in Mexico from the late 1970s on. Markets had hardly absorbed the shock of Mexico's announcement when Brazil, another country that creditors regarded as a minimal risk, revealed that it could not meet required payments on its $87 billion borrowing. Then Argentina and several dozen other countries of lesser credit standing followed suit.

In retrospect it seems curious that the initial reaction of policymakers and international economists to these developments was that something had gone wrong in the world economy rather than in the management of the debtors' economies. To be sure, conditions in the world economy had changed dramatically between 1979 and 1982 in ways that had an adverse effect on both domestic and international borrowers. No one, however, proposed to solve domestic borrower difficulties by a program comparable to the one recommended for international borrowers who were troubled less-developed countries.

The initial proposed solution had three components: (1) reduce the average rate of interest payable on outstanding loans; (2) foster world economic recovery; and (3) continued lending to less-developed countries by creditor banks, the International Monetary Fund (IMF), the World Bank, and export credit agencies. The first component, lower interest rates, would be achieved by halting the anti-inflationary policy that industrialized countries had pursued beginning around 1980. Lower interest rates would follow, thanks either to temporary liquidity effects of expansionary monetary growth or to a providential decline in the inflationary premium embedded in nominal interest rates. The borrowers' debt burden would thus be eased. The second component, world recovery, would foster growth in demand for developing-country exports. Some of the proceeds of export earnings remitted to international lenders would help to service the debt. Pending world recovery, continued lending to the debtor countries was essential so that they could avoid defaulting and endangering the solvency of the creditor banks.

The proposed solution implicitly assumed that the international debt problem had arisen because the industrialized world was experiencing a sharp recession accompanied by a rise in short-term interest rates in 1980-82. These conditions had aggravated the burden of variable-rate loans that the banks had extended. Evidently the policymakers regarded the solvency of U.S. creditor banks, not that of the troubled debtor countries, as the problem, presumably because Latin American debt to U.S. money-center banks was a multiple of the banks' equity and loan loss reserves.

The money-center banks as well as the regional banks that had participated in loan syndicates assented to the proposed solution of the debt problem. As long as the banks lent the debtors enough to pay contractual interest, they could maintain the fiction that the assets on their balance sheets were performing loans, and that bank income was unimpaired. Asset markets, however, did not play this game. In the U.S. stock market, price-earnings ratios of money-center banks fell after 1982, even though they were already substantially lower than the price-earnings ratios of the Standard & Poor 500.[1] In the limited secondary market for Latin American loans, the average price declined from about 80 cents on the dollar in 1983 to 65 cents in 1986.[2]

From the vantage point of 1988, the judgment made in 1982 that the troubled debtor countries had a liquidity problem, not a solvency problem, appears to have been fiction rather than fact. If external causes were responsible for inability to service debt, all heavily indebted countries should have been similarly affected. Yet East Asian developing countries that had also borrowed heavily until 1982 and that had faced oil shocks and recession in the industrialized world had no debt-service problem.

Despite periodic announcements in 1982 by policymakers and others that resolution of the debt service problem was at hand, it is still in 1988 a festering problem for both creditors and debtors. Perhaps the world would be closer to solving the problem today, had the initial reaction been to investigate the extent to which the borrowings were used productively. Suppose that on a case-by-case basis, an investigation had confirmed that only a fraction of the loans were income producing, even if the debtors' national income accounts reported a rising ratio of investments to Gross National Product (GNP). As Zvi Griliches [1985, 199] has remarked, "It is ... clear that the national income statistics for some of the LDCs are more political than economic documents."[3] Even without such an investigation, capital flight—estimated as a substantial fraction of the change in external debt over the period 1974-1982 (44 percent for Mexico, 62 percent for Argentina, 94 percent for Venezuela, 12 percent for Brazil)—is evidence of policy failure in the countries involved.[4]

If the initial approach had been to determine whether the loans had been used productively, the solution to the problem might have been based less on fiction and more on fact. The predominating theme would not have been that it was feasible in short order to restore the debtors to a growth path simply by arranging for additional loans from private and official lenders. If the debtors' difficulties in fact reflected domestic inefficiency and wasteful use of resources, additional international lending without the elimination of underlying economic distortions would simply create an even larger external transfer problem in the future. Even if effective domestic reform were undertaken by the debtors, greater output and improved allocations of resources would take a long time.

For banks with large third-world exposure, the solution might have been conceived as a workout problem. Regulators might also have asked why it was that, though British, West German, Swiss, and Japanese banks had lent to Latin American countries, only in the United States was anxiety aroused about an impending financial collapse.[5] The U.S. regulators might have applied the lessons that could be learned from the treatment of nonperforming loans in those countries where they did not rank as a serous problem. The U.S. regulators might also have facilitated increased provisioning by the banks by appropriate regulatory changes.[6]

In what follows, I first discuss the economic

issues facing the debtor countries, focusing on their internal policies as the reason the strategies to make them creditworthy have not so far been successful. I then turn to the role of the creditor banks. Initially they did not oppose the official view that the debt problem was a temporary one that would be overcome by continued lending. Eventually they were driven to reject the official view. The banks then embraced reserving against loan losses, adding to capital, and reducing exposure through sales, swaps, and write-offs. In addition to the debtors and creditors, a third set of players has been prominent—the policymakers (in this country, the bank regulators and the Treasury Department) and the international lending agencies. In the third section, I suggest that the intervention of the official players has prolonged and worsened the debt problem. Finally, in summary, I note that optimistic expert forecasts over the period since 1982 have repeatedly been falsified by disappointing performances each year first by one debtor, then by another. The forecasts were based on fiction, not fact.

ECONOMIC ISSUES FACING THE DEBTOR COUNTRIES

Stephen Schuker [1988] has made a telling comparison of troubled Latin American debt today with German reparations after World War I (see also Webb [1988]). He concludes that Latin American debtors of today are following the same course as the Reich, which overborrowed in the 1920s, squandered those resources on public and private consumption, and then for political reasons deliberately failed to adjust its policies to meet its obligations.

What happened to the funds borrowed before 1982 by the troubled Latin American debtor countries? A large part went to finance consumption, including oil and other consumer goods, not to mention extravagant living by corrupt officials. Some funds were invested in inefficient and unprofitable state-owned enterprises producing products at marginal costs in excess of competitive world prices. For some countries, another large part was absorbed by capital flight. Had conditions in the home country changed so as to provide a favorable investment climate, then that capital might have returned.

Given these imprudent uses of the past borrowed funds, it becomes clear why the effort since 1982 to solve the transfer problem for developing countries with troubled debt has had such checkered results. It is questionable whether external capital flows to the troubled debtor economies, both before and since 1982, have contributed to the economic welfare of their citizens. These countries have suffered from overvalued exchange rates (produced in part by the capital inflows), high inflation rates, and low real interest rates. These defects cannot be corrected overnight. Mexico will serve as an illustration.

In 1982 the Untied States shouldered the responsibility for fashioning a financial rescue plan for Mexico. It committed $3 billion in aid, $1 billion as financial guarantees for food exports, $1.85 billion as an emergency bridge loan shared with the Bank for International Settlements (BIS), and $1 billion as a prepayment for Mexican oil (see BIS [1983, 128; 1984, 107-8]).

Other elements of the rescue plan were additional lending by the IMF, the World Bank, industrialized country governments, and creditor banks, and rescheduling of debt. On November 10, 1982, Mexico agreed to reduce its budget deficit and increase its trade surplus, in return for an IMF loan of $3.6 billion, mainly from the Extended Fund Facility drawable over three years, but conditioned on participation by the creditor banks in a $5 billion loan. Agreement with the banks was reached on 2 December although it took until the end of February 1983 for five hundred banks in thirty-seven countries to contribute their shares. In December 1983 the banks extended an additional $3.8 billion, at a lower interest spread and loan fees than earlier.

In 1983, $22.5 billion of sovereign debt maturing up to the end of 1984 was rescheduled. In September 1984, $48.7 billion of sovereign debt, initially maturing in 1982-90, was rescheduled over a fourteen year period, and the margin over London Interbank Offered Rate (LIBOR) reduced and front-end fees or commission were eliminated (see BIS [1984, 107-8; 1985, 136]).

During 1983 Mexico succeeded in meeting its obligations under the IMF loan, and repaid its bridge loan. The improvement in Mexico's trade balance that year was hailed as proof that the three-part strategy to overcome debt repayment difficulties was a success. Skeptics, however, noted that the improvement was unsustainable, because it was mainly attributable to a decline in imports rather than an increase in exports. The decline in imports reduced not only the country's standard of living, but, by limiting inventories of raw materials and spare parts, also the output of firms producing for export. The trade balance in 1985 was only slightly better than in 1982. Even before Mexico's position worsened later in 1985, a new agreement was reached with the IMF in March providing a first $28.6 billion tranche.

Earthquakes in Mexico during the fall of 1985 and (later) the worldwide decline in crude oil prices were cited as reasons for supplementing financial aid to the country and for renegotiating the terms of the multi-year rescheduling agreement. Despite domestic austerity measures in 1985 and falling Gross Domestic Product, the trade surplus shrank from $8.5 to $4.6 billion from 1985 to 1986, even though imports fell sharply and nonoil exports rose. Official reserves rose by the end of 1986, thanks to some return flow of flight capital and financial support provided by the Treasury, the Federal Reserve, the BIS, Latin American central banks, and international commercial banks. Not until March 1987 was an agreement with bank creditors concluded. It provided Mexico with $7.7 billion of new borrowing, rescheduled over half of its external debt, and further reduced the margin of the interest rate over LIBOR. The banks also agreed to increase their loans should the price of oil decline further. official creditors added $6.3 billion in new credit to the commercial bank credits.[7]

The agreement was the first one reached after Secretary Baker proposed a new plan for the resolution of the debt payment difficulties at the October 1985 IMF-World Bank meeting in Seoul. The Baker plan linked continued financial aid to the debtors with their adoption of macroeconomic and microeconomic policies to promote growth, reduce inflation, and adjust their balance of payments.

For Mexico, economic reform is a tall order, Nationalization of Mexican industry gathered momentum over a fifty-year period, culminating in September 1982, when the government took over the entire banking system (after the country's inability to service foreign debt was made known). It has been estimated that the Mexican government operates three-quarters of Mexico's economy. It owns hundreds of enterprises—oil, electrical, communications, railroads, banks, hotels, steel mills, motion picture companies.

Subsidies to state-owned and mismanaged companies are said to be a large fraction of the Mexican government budget deficit Although the government agreed in November 1982 to reduce its deficit (which was then 16 percent of GNP) in return for an IMF loan, five years later that has not yet happened. In 1987 the deficit was 17 percent of GNP. Debt service at domestic interest rates of about 5 percent per month adds substantially to government spending.

The second of two steep devaluations in February and August 1982 was accompanied by the automatic conversion of dollar deposits into pesos on terms highly unfavorable to the depositors. This was hardly a confidence-building action. Foreign exchange was made available at a preferential rate for certain priority imports. The rate was freed for other imports. Export receipts were made subject to surrender at the ordinary exchange rate. Even at the free rates, import licenses were required for about one-third of all items. These import restrictions will have to change because Mexico joined the General Agreement for Tariffs and Trade in 1986, and must comply with the requirement of membership that it lower tariffs and eliminate license conditions.

It is unlikely that Mexico has achieved true progress in subduing inflation. In reaction to an annual inflation rate of about 170 percent, on 15 December 1987, the government signed an "Economic Solidarity Pact" with business, labor, and farmers, stipulating a freeze on wages, some prices, and the exchange rate. The current official inflation figure is 2 percent per month. The partial price freeze was supposed to be replaced by indexation on 1 March, but has since been extended several times to at least 31 August, past the Mexican election on 6 July, and in all likelihood until 1 December, when the new president takes office. Uncontrolled prices continue to rise. Under the frozen exchange rate exports have declined and imports have risen. In the government's view, imports deter local manufacturers of goods not covered by the freeze from raising their prices. It is reluctant to devalue the exchange rate for fear of reigniting inflationary pressure.[8]

What are the prospects for the adoption of policies to promote growth? Divestment initiatives are apparently being seriously pursued in mid-1988.

Seven hundred unprofitable state enterprises are reported to have been sold to the private sector in recent months.[9] This is clearly a positive step that is associated with the program the incoming president introduced as an official of the outgoing administration.

Long-standing Mexican rules have inhibited foreign ventures by barring foreign majority ownership of operations. However, in 1986, IBM was given permission to manufacture personal computers in a plant (retaining 100 percent ownership), on condition that it increase the amount that it originally intended to invest, subject to some marketing restrictions, and to teaching microchip design technology to Mexican companies. The incoming president has announced that he intends to pursue incentives to lure foreign investment to Mexico.

Troubled Latin American country debtors other than Mexico also have unsolved problems with respect to inflation rates, government deficits, and economic growth. The Mexican case is applicable to them even though many details would differ. At the end of 1987 Mexico's foreign debt was $27 billion higher, Brazil's $29 billion higher than in 1982.[10] Additional lending since 1982, like the earlier loans before 1982, has done nothing to eliminate the underlying economic distortions in those economies. Whether that condition will change under the new government in Mexico remains to be seen.

I conclude this section by quoting from a paper that Anne Krueger [1988, 38-39] gave at the Carnegie-Rochester conference in April of this year on the prospects for policy reform in the debtor countries. "Policy reforms have been half-hearted, even to the point of [being] cosmetic in a number of instances. The typical scenario has involved strong resistance to policy reform on the part of key actors within the governments of the debtor countries. Advocacy of reforms has usually been by the international organizations, occasionally supported by some bilateral donors and some economics officials within the government, instigated when the unsustainability of the preexisting policy stance became evident. These advocates have been resisted, and the outcome of negotiations has been a watered-down package. Even then, policies have often retrogressed in the weeks and months following announcement of a program. And, ... in instances where immediate economic difficulties have subsided because of increased export prices or other reasons, politicians have suddenly lost their apparently previously-held convictions as to the desirability of reforms."

Politicians' ambivalence about sustaining an economic reform package is not hard to understand. The short-run consequences of restructuring economics are not in the self-interest of politicians. Austerity (to reduce inflation rates and government deficits) and microeconomic reforms exact social costs in the short run in the shape of increased unemployment, higher prices for subsidized goods, and transitional problems of reallocating resources to more efficient uses. Governments fear riots and political discontent as the short-run price of reform policies.

THE ROLE OF THE BANKS

A common feature of historical and current foreign debt repayment problems is that bargains are struck to stretch out the maturity of debt and modify other conditions to service and repay it. In the past the creditors were generally bondholders. Now the private creditors are commercial banks. In the current case, restructuring agreements require unanimous consent of the hundreds of bank creditors involved. Agreements accordingly are more difficult to achieve than in the past, when representative committees of bondholders were organized.

Scholars have noted that since the beginning of the nineteenth century creditors have paid little attention to the default history of less-developed-country borrowers.[11] If default history raised the probability of rescheduling, creditors should have charged higher premiums, lent at shorter term, or lent less to countries with a default history. While the major banks did indeed lend at shorter term after 1980, they did not discriminate between countries that had or had not defaulted in the past, or those that had or had not required rescheduling by charging the former higher premiums. On the other hand, although they disregarded past performance, the creditors (perhaps fortuitously) did on average in 1976-79 charge higher risk premiums of borrowers that later rescheduled. If the debtor countries did not use the borrowed funds productively, by the same token the Western commercial banks were imprudent lenders.

The current debt problem differs from historical ones in at least two respects. (1) In the present case, international debt settlements involve not only the private creditors and country debtors but also international agencies and creditor-country governments. In the past the two directly concerned parties principally conducted the negotiations. (2) In the present case, the creditors have been urged, if not coerced, to continue lending and, however reluctantly, have continued lending to troubled debtors. That did not happen in the past when the creditors were bondholders.

With respect to the banks' lending "new money," it is informative to compare its distribution between the public and private sectors of thirty-one debtor countries in 1979-82 and 1982-86, as shown by Sachs and Huizinga [1987, 565-66]. In the first period, lending to the public sectors was about two-fifths greater than to the private sectors. In the later period, bank lending to the public sectors was at about the same rate as earlier, but with few exceptions declined substantially to the private sectors. In part, the decline in lending to the private sector reflected the assumption by debtor governments of private sector debt, bank write-offs of claims on private sectors, and sales or swaps of private sector debt. Banks assess the repayment capacity of the private sector as less dependable than that of the public sector. Sovereign debt interest payments have generally been paid when due, although Argentina was in arrears in 1984 and early 1985, and Brazil suspended sovereign debt interest payments in February 1987.[12] Private sector debtors in Latin American countries, however, have defaulted, and in some instances become bankrupt. Given this record, the banks presumably also view investment opportunities in the private sector as less attractive.

"New money," critics of the banks (such as Sachs and Huizinga [1987, 565]) contend, is a misnomer, since the additional bank loans fall short of amortization and interest payments the debtors disburse. For the critics it is scandalous that the shortfall arises. Yet interest payments on a loan should be met out of the income generated by investments financed with foreign capital. New lending to cover debt service should not be required.

One argument for continued lending by banks is that a half-completed project could be salvaged if there were no halt in loan availability, i.e., that lending new money would protect the old money lent. That argument would have force if past lending had indeed been used to finance a project that was worth completing. Peter Lindert [1986], who maintains that creditors in the aggregate can never gain by continued lending in a debt crisis, dismisses the defenses of that idea. One flawed defense is that every individual debt can be repaid if the debt can grow faster than the rate of interest. This is an argument for a kind of Ponzi scheme that would eventually collapse. Another flawed defense is that export growth that exceeds the rate of interest will keep the debt-export ratio from rising. But this defense assumes that the new debt, in excess of interest and amortization, is invested in extremely productive assets. Lindert also challenges the assertion that individual lenders who back off from lending when a default incentive develops can trigger a capital loss for all creditors. That would be true only if the lenders who backed off were in error regarding the ability of the borrower to repay. If the lenders are right about the default incentive, then there need be no extra cost imposed on all the creditors since a default will occur. To argue that continued lending in a debt crisis is in the creditors' collective interest disregards the fact that continued lending does not lessen the capital loss that default would bring.

Until the spring of 1987, U.S. banks passively acquiesced in the strategy policymakers and the international agencies had devised, maintaining the fiction that troubled debt would be repaid at face value. The banks wrote down only $2.2 billion, under 2 percent of their loans to less-developed countries (LDCs), between 1982 and 1985 (see the *Federal Reserve Bulletin* [1986]). They increased loan loss reserves on their total loan portfolio by as little as 1/2 percent of assets per year. Over the same period, however, they increased book capital by sales of new equity and subordinated debt, asset sales, and increased retained earnings.[13] Though exposure to all LDC debtors declined relative to capital between 1982 and 1986, relative exposure of the big banks to troubled LDC debtors rose. Bennett and Zimmerman [1988, 18] find that the percentage of troubled LDC loans in the portfolios of nine money center banks appears to be greater in 1988 than it was in 1981.

The official strategy on the international debt problem was breached in May 1987 when Citicorp, acknowledging the likelihood of credit losses on its Latin American loans, announced that it was increasing its reserves by $3 billion. Nineteen banks between 26 May and 8 July also announced additions to their loan loss reserves, in aggregate amounting to over $12 billion, according to Musumeci and Sinkey [1988]. In May 1988, the General Accounting Office (GAO) estimated that reserves of U.S. banks against their troubled loans to LDCs totaled about $21 billion, whereas adequate provisioning would require reserves of $49 billion (see the *Wall Street Journal*, 19 May 1988).

The GAO used prices on secondary debt markets in determining the adequacy of loan loss reserves. The banks and regulators, however, dispute the GAO's report (see the *Wall Street Journal*, 13 May 1988). The secondary markets, they contend, are thin, and transactions of even moderate size cannot be executed at quoted prices. The price quotations may also misrepresent the prospect of repayment for the following reasons. By holding a foreign country's debt, a creditor bank has been subject to the implied obligation to lend new money pro rata to that country. However, by selling the debt on the secondary market, a creditor bank is released from that obligation, and hence may accept a lower price than would otherwise be the case. On the other hand, as Sachs and Huizinga [1987, 579-87] note, the decline in bank equity prices since 1982 closely matches the secondary market valuation of LDC exposure. The qualifications concerning the significance of the secondary market prices of foreign debt did not apply to prices of foreign bonds that in the past traded at a discount in the market. Those prices reflected solely the probability of repayment of the bond.

The additions to loan loss reserves in 1987 reduced the banks' reported income and their book capital. Equity was reduced by a transfer to reserves, and plans to issue equity were announced by many banks following their additions to reserves. The reserves, however, are not charged against current income for tax purposes. Should write-offs occur in the future or agreements be reached with the debtors to reduce outstanding debt, the losses will be charged to reserves with no effect on reported income. Latin American debt has not been written down because of the additions to reserves, and no forgiveness is involved for LDC debts.

The banks face difficulties in reducing their developing country debt by sales, swaps, and write-offs. Loan agreements may prohibit repurchase of the debt by the borrower, hence limiting the sales option.[14] Swaps for loan currency or equity have had only small effects on debt reduction. J.P. Morgan and Company earlier this year devised a program with Mexico that had the blessing of the U.S. Treasury. Morgan swapped $400 million of its Mexican government debt for $263 million twenty-year Mexican government bonds. The Mexican issue was collateralized by twenty-year U.S. Treasury zero-coupon bonds (at time of sale, priced to pay 8.41 percent annually) that Mexico bought with $2.56 billion of its international reserves. Swaps by other banks participating in this program reduced Mexico's bank debt by about $1 billion, although a $10 billion reduction had been forecast. Morgan regarded the swaps as advantageous because it also served to reduce its obligation to supply future loans to Mexico. For other banks the size of the discount on the swap made the deal unattractive.[15] The third way for the banks to reduce exposure to developing-country debt is write-offs. Write-offs have limited appeal. They risk inciting political pressure to force debt forgiveness.

The regulators, the U.S. government, and international-agency lenders continue to pressure the banks to provide additional loans to the Latin American debtors that are either in arrears on interest payments or pay a large percentage of their trade surplus to cover service charges. Some regional banks demand loan guarantees from the World Bank as a quid pro quo for their contribution to the loan package, since World Bank debt has seniority over commercial-bank debt. Provision of guarantees would offset that advantage.

Over the period that the debt situation has persisted, enormous and clearly wasteful use of bank resources has been required to negotiate new loan agreements that can win the adherence of a sufficient number of bank lenders. One anomaly that characterizes the position of the banks is that every dollar of additional lending that they have advanced has been immediately discounted by the market, whatever the margin of doubt surrounding the quoted price.

Continued lending was originally urged to preserve the financial solvency of U.S. banks. Solvency of the banks may no longer be in question, but they may not be in a position to contest the fiction that continued lending is in their self-interest. The regulators call the tune and the banks are obliged to dance to it.

Lindert [1988] concludes that before World War I, the record of two-party bargaining worked pretty well. Where a revolution occurred, however, as in the decade of the 1910s in Mexico and Russia, the creditors had no effective bargaining position vis-a-vis the post-revolutionary governments. In the 1930s, debt repudiation and the end of lending were the result of the worldwide collapse.

In the post-World War II context, governments initially borrowed from other governments, leaving to the IMF responsibility for loans for balance of payments adjustment and to the World Bank responsibility for development loans. These two agencies subsequently played a role in debt refinancing arrangements between governments. By 1979, however, the creditors were private banks with a high level of exposure. U.S. banks, reluctant to write down nonperforming loans with interest arrears lest it encourage efforts to forgive debts, were eager for third-party help. The IMF grants concessionary loans to a debtor conditional on domestic austerity only when the country has settled on a financing package with the banks. Under this arrangement, the banks have an incentive to demand the maintenance of the original level of interest rates, and the debtors do not hold out for rescheduling agreements that offer debt relief. In Lindert's view, third-party intervention since 1982 has impeded bilateral bargains between the debtor governments and the creditor banks. The two parties directly involved could have resolved the debt repayment problem.

THE ROLE OF THE CREDITOR GOVERNMENTS AND THE MULTILATERAL INSTITUTIONS

In the past, when confronted with foreign debt delinquency, politically dominant creditor governments sometimes actively intervened on behalf of their distressed nationals who had invested abroad. At other times, creditor governments remained aloof. Foreign policy grounds generally determined the decision. In the 1980s international debt crisis, intervention undertaken by the U.S., the dominant creditor country, was a decision of the monetary authorities. They determined that, to preserve financial stability in the domestic banking system, it was essential to create the facade that the foreign borrowers were faced only with a liquidity problem.

The U.S. government took the lead in devising the strategy to cope with the problem. Other creditor governments backed the U.S. approach. The aim of the strategy was to enable the debtor countries to maintain current debt service by providing them with additional loans from official and private bank sources. Income and capital accounts of the U.S. banks would reveal no loss.

In past episodes of foreign default that have recurred from century to century, international agencies did not exist. It was not until 1930 in the inter-war period that the Bank for International Settlements was organized. The post-World War II multilateral agencies were essentially bystanders during the 1970s, when foreign bank borrowing by Third World countries swelled; they had no mandate when originally established to deal with international debt problems. However, they seized the opportunity afforded by the debt crisis in the 1980s to enlarge the scope of their involvement in the economics of the problem countries, becoming active participants in the strategy the U.S. had devised.

The IMF was established to finance temporary international payments imbalances for individual countries under pegged exchange rates. Once the Bretton Woods system collapsed, the initial functions of the IMF evaporated. A deficit in the current account would presumably lead to a decline in a country's floating exchange rate. No temporary IMF adjustment loan would be needed. The commercial banks in the event were prepared to lend to oil importers facing higher bills for energy.

To find a new function, the IMF expanded its activities, principally the Compensatory Financing Facility (introduced in February 1963) that provides financing in the event of export shortfalls. It also established a new upper tranche Extended Fund Facility, covering a three-year period. The rationalization for these innovations was that balance of payments adjustment involved not only aggregate demand conditions but also supply side conditions, such as the need for productivity increases, changes in production structure, and investment. Results on the supply side could not be expected in the short run, hence longer-term financing was needed. The IMF's expanded activities enabled it to extend loans with conditionality provisions to dozens of countries, when previously (under Bretton Woods) it made such loans to only one or two countries a year.

The World Bank followed the same course as the IMF. It introduced Structural Adjustment Loans to support structural changes in industry, agriculture, and energy. The object was to achieve long-term policy reforms that would accelerate development. The bank also introduced sector adjustment loans, as part of the bank's Special Action Program. More countries have been granted loans under the sector than under the structural adjustment program.[16]

The transformation of the IMF's role from a provider of temporary assistance to a source of medium-term financing of heavily indebted countries increased the agency's need for funds. To supplement the resources available to the Fund, Congress approved in 1983 a quota increase and an enlargement of the General Arrangements to Borrow after intense lobbying by the chairman of the Federal Reserve System and the Bankers' Association for Foreign Trade. since then, the IMF has borrowed from Saudi Arabia and Japan, and recently indicated that by April 1989, it would need a 50 percent quota increase.

Similarly, the World Bank, which finances more than 85 percent of its loans by floating debt issues in world capital markets, sought an increase in its capital. Nations with more than 75 percent of the voting shares ratified in April 1988 an increase in its capital from $96.6 billion to $171.4 billion. The U.S. with slightly less than 20 percent of the voting shares has not. The bank has appealed to Congress to grant it $70.1 million as the U.S. share of the first year's increase in its capital (see the *Wall Street Journal*, 21 June and 23 September, 1988).

As I've noted, conditionality, which has always been a feature of an IMF loan, has since 1982 been coupled with a requirement that the debtors reach agreement with their creditor banks before the loan is granted. An IMF agreement is also a prerequisite for debt rescheduling by export credit agencies of the Paris Club creditor governments and for lending by the World Bank and the development banks.[17]

The key feature of lending by the international agencies is that the debtor countries obtain the credits at subsidized rates. Does the subsidy improve the productivity of the use of the borrowings? The loans may be repaid but, as the quotation from Krueger showed, official lenders have not been successful in enforcing the conditionality provisions the debtor countries have accepted to reform their internal economic policies. That is a fact that needs to be acknowledged.

The strategy devised by the U.S. treats not only the debtor countries but also the creditor banks as wards of the U.S. regulators. Neither the accumulation of foreign debt before 1982 nor the strategy to deal with it subsequently was market based. The regulators abetted the accumulation of the debt by U.S. banks, praising them for effectively recycling surplus current account funds of OPEC countries, and abstaining from cautionary injunctions as the portfolio of foreign debt grew.[18] The regulators permitted the banks to evade the provision that limits loans to a borrower to no more than 15 percent of a bank's capital. Loans to various state-operated firms and institutions in a foreign country—all guaranteed by the government—were regarded as individual loans. When the debt problems erupted, the banks were not urged to reduce dividends and build loan loss reserves. Instead public policy was based on the fiction that the Latin American debts on the books of the banks were assets that had full face value, despite their discounted value in secondary markets. No objection was made to the accounting treatment of accrued interest as current income. In conjunction with the IMF, the regulators orchestrated new lending by the creditor banks which far exceeded lending by the international agencies and official government transfers.

It is fair to ask whether the activism of the regulators and the international agencies has contributed to the solution of the debt problem. The three components of the solution proposed in 1982 were all achieved: interest rates on foreign loans were reduced; world economic recovery is still ongoing; and official and private lending has continued. The verdict of the BIS [1988, 132-33] is less than reassuring: "The persistent severe debt service problems, unsatisfactory domestic economic conditions and growing frustration in many developing countries have led to increasing doubts about the adequacy of the strategy used so far to cope with the international debt crisis."

CONCLUSIONS

Why is it that expert opinion on the international debt problem has persistently provided optimistic appraisals of the outcome, despite continued evidence to the contrary? One reason is that some experts have tended to be debt country sympathizers.[19] Further assistance to the debtors in their view is the high-minded way to solve the problem.

Another reason for optimistic appraisals is that projections of the debtor countries' performance in the future extrapolate some variable that would permit them to manage their current debt burden over the long run. Thus Martin Feldstein [1987] conjectured that if Brazil were to obtain additional loans, devote 2-1/2 percent of its GNP to debt service, and grow at 3-1/2 percent a year, the ratio of its external debt to GNP would decline and the economy would grow faster than the interest on its external debt. On this calculation, Brazil would begin repaying its debt by 1997. There is one proviso: "Of course, this prognosis requires sensible economic policies in Brazil." Steven Webb [1987], who analyzes the ability of developing countries to outgrow their debt, projects their growth for forty years as the sum of labor productivity, assumed to grow as fast as it did from 1960 to 1985, and the growth of working-age population. Those countries with rapid productivity growth that paid 2-1/2 percent of GNP toward debt service would greatly reduce their debt burden by the beginning of the next century. Unfortunately, assuming that productivity will grow as fast as it did from 1960 to 1985 begs the key question: will the developing countries adopt "sensible" internal policies?

My conclusions follow.

(1) The troubled debtors did not use their borrowed resources well. They are largely responsible for their own plight. Their own domestic economic policies were and are flawed. Further borrowing by them will only add to the burden of their existing debt. The troubled debtors give little sign that they have improved their domestic economic policies in the six years since their problems surfaced; and even if they now undertake economic reform, improved allocation of resources would yield higher returns only in the long term.

(2) The banks made a mistake when they extended the loans. Retaining the loans at face value on their books has been a fiction, but one that financial markets see through. Inevitably, banks will take losses on Latin American loans; how much loss depends on their leverage in bargaining with the debtor countries.

(3) The interventions of regulators and the international agencies have been a failure. They have coerced the banks to continue lending and have required debtor countries to accept conditionality provisions as the price of an IMF loan. Yet the international agencies have been unable to enforce the conditionality provisions.

At the present juncture, the U.S. Treasury, more than the Federal Reserve System, is in the forefront of debt negotiations. The Treasury serves as a cheerleader for the debtor governments and the international agencies. The Treasury appears to regard the banks as eleemosynary institutions that should be doing more for hard-pressed debtors. since May 1987, when many creditor banks made large additions to their loan loss reserves, the Treasury has repeatedly expressed dissatisfaction with the conduct of the banks. In its view, the banks should have responded more positively to the Mexican debt swap plan, and been more cooperative in raising fresh loans for the countries now in line for new IMF agreements (Brazil and Argentina). The banks have also been charged with failing to reward with timely and adequate loans countries like Columbia, which recently avoided rescheduling, and Ecuador which, according to the Treasury, left it up to the banks to restructure its loans.[20]

The issue is not whether the banks reject the Treasury's complaints. The issue is the ground for the Treasury's intervention in the negotiations between the debtor countries and the banks. It is time for the Treasury and the regulators to discard fiction and base their position on facts. One fact is that bad debts lead to losses. Accounting practices that regulators currently permit the banks to use attempt but fail to hide the fact that these are bad debts. Market value accounting would eliminate the fiction. The debtors will have to help themselves with sound, tough domestic economic actions if they are ever to emerge from their troubles. The losses that must be borne can be distributed in some fashion by voluntary bargains between the debtor countries and the creditor banks without intervention by third parties.

ENDNOTES

* National Bureau of Economic Research, New York, NY.

1 See the chart for 1975-86, based on Salomon Brothers data, in Makin [1987,4].

2 Price quotations by major interbank dealers as market makers in a limited number of country loans became available only in 1986 (see Table 2 in Makin [1987,6]). There were discounts on earlier trades by individual banks, initially rearranging the country composition of their foreign loan portfolios rather than selling off debt; see Sandler [1984,77].

3 Robert Hall [1986, 439] commented on Jeffrey Sachs' proposal to follow a formula in granting debt relief: "One reason not to follow a formula is that the national income accounts kept by many of the debtor countries are simply not believable."

4 These are estimates by Dooley et al. [1983] for 1974-82. Estimates vary according to the period covered and the method of estimation. On three ways of deriving estimates of capital flight and their shortcomings, see Lessard and Williamson [1987, 201-15].

5 See commercial bank exposure in the U.S., U.K., Japan, and West Germany, based on data in the *Economist*, 30 May 1987, in Feldstein et al. [1987,36].

6 See OECD [1987, 241 ff.] for a survey of regulatory and tax provisions for bad and doubtful debts in the U.S. and other industrialized countries.

7 On Mexico's official reserves, see the *Federal Reserve Bulletin* [1986, 702] and BIS [1987,118].

8 See the *New York Times*, 13 June 1988, D8. The freeze on wages, some prices, and the exchange rate was extended on 14 August through 30 November. The government agreed to remove a 6 percent value added tax from all basic foodstuffs and medicines during the next three months. All workers earning $15 a day or less obtained a tax cut of 30 percent. The private sector agreed to reduce by 3 percent prices of about one hundred goods including some not considered in calculating the inflation rate (see the *Wall Street Journal*, 16 August 1988 and the *New York Times*, 16 August 1988, D11).

9 *Wall Street Journal*, 15 July 1988. In April 1988, Mexico announced that it was selling a huge copper mine, state-owned since 1910 (and said to be profitable), to a domestic industrial conglomerate for $910 million. The transaction, opposed by employees of the mine, has not yet been completed (see the *New York Times*, 17 June 1988, A4).

10 Mexico's foreign debt was reported by the country's central bank to have declined in 1988 I. At the end of 1987, government debt was $92.3 billion, private sector debt, $14.7 billion. The government's foreign debt declined in 1988 I by $4.1 billion as a result of a $1.1 billion bond-for-debt swap and of transactions that are still being completed on a debt-for-equity swap suspended in late 1987. After deducting foreign exchange reserves, the central bank study showed net government foreign debt at $88.2 billion at the end of 1988 I. Private sector foreign debt declined $0.2 billion, thanks to purchases in the secondary loan market by the debtors (see the *Wall Street Journal*, 22 June 1988).

11 See the papers in the forthcoming conference volume, edited by Barry Eichengreen and Peter Lindert.

12 Several times in 1988 Argentina also fell behind on interest payments on its medium- and long-term bank debt, but payments at midyear made it current up to April. In August, however, failure to maintain its interest payments made its loans more than ninety days past due, hence subject to classification by banks as nonperforming. Argentina was reported to be seeking a $500 million bridge loan from the U.S. Treasury until it would obtain an IMF and bank loans (see the *Wall Street Journal*, 4 August 1988).

Brazil made payments to its commercial bank creditors to cover interest arrears for March-May 1988. On 22 September it terminated formally the suspension of interest payments that began on 20 February 1987 (see the *Wall Street Journal*, 1 July 1988 and 22 September 1988).

13 The average ratio of equity capital to total assets of all commercial banks rose, 1982-86. In 1987, the ratio declined for the twenty-five largest commercial banks and for banks in the Southwest but rose for the remainder of the industry. The decline for the large banks resulted from the increase of loan loss reserves.

The ratio of primary capital (which includes loan loss reserves) to total assets for all insured commercial banks increased in 1987 (see Heller [1988]).

14 The agreement that Brazil appears to have concluded with its creditor banks in June 1988 for $5.2 billion fresh loans with a twelve-year maturity including a five-year grace period at the start during which no principal payments would have to be made, permits Brazil to buy back a portion of its debt on the secondary loan market (see the *Wall Street Journal*, 22 June 1988).

15 See the *Wall Street Journal*, 25 May 1988. According to the BIS [1988, 137], U.S. regulators ruled that banks that participated in the Mexican scheme would not have to show other claims on Mexico at a lower value.

16 The World Bank has also increased the share of "policy-based loans (loans extended for general budgetary support as compared with the project-based lending that the World Bank has traditionally pursued)" from 8 percent in 1980 to 23 percent in 1987, according to Rep. Walter E. Fauntroy (chairman of the House International Development Institutions and Finance Subcommittee), who interprets the purpose of the loans to be the provision of debt service payments to private

banks. He is an advocate of third world debt relief. See his letters to the editor of the *Wall Street Journal*, 11 July 1988, and to the *New York Times*, 14 July 1988.

17 After three years of resistance, Brazil accepted as a precondition for an IMF loan that it reach an agreement with its creditor banks (see note 14). It formally requested a $1.44 billion loan on 1 July 1988, presenting its economic reform program to the fund (see the *New York Times*, 5 July 1988).

The prerequisite in one African case (countries not otherwise considered in this paper) has not been enforced. It has been reported that Nigeria rejected an IMF loan for $540 million that required reforms including privatization of ninety-six government-controlled enterprises and official devaluation of the naira. The country was nevertheless granted and accepted in place of the IMF loan a $450 million World Bank loan; Nigeria's foreign debt was rescheduled, some export credit was restored, and it obtained $4.3 billion from the World Bank for structural adjustment projects over three years (see the *Wall Street Journal*, 22 June 1988, 24).

18 See the statements by Chairman Burns, 10 March 1977; also the speech by Chairman Volcher, March 1980, quotation from p. 13.

19 Rudiger Dornbusch, for example, exhorts the banks to "Build, Don't Bleed, Economies," *New York Times*, 13 May 1988. Presumably the banks before 1982 believed that they were building the economies of the debtors. Dornbusch does not explain why that belief was mistaken. He now advocates a temporary suspension of interest payments in dollars. Debtors instead would pay interest in local currency, which the creditors would invest in the debtor country, the investments to be managed by the outsiders. The debtor domestic budgets would have to provide for the interest payments, which could not be created by printing money.

20 Ecuador suspended talks with its foreign bank creditors on 8 July 1988, on its unsigned $5.1 billion rescheduling accord with the banks that was reached in October 1987. The country, which has a shortage of foreign exchange because of falling oil prices and an earthquake in March 1987 that halted oil exports for five months, has not paid interest to its creditor banks since January 1988 (see the *New York Times*, 9 July 1988).

REFERENCES

Bank for International Settlements, *Annual Reports*, Basle, 1983-85, 1987-88.

Bennett, Barbara A. and Gary C. Zimmerman. "U.S. Banks' Exposure to Developing Countries: An Examination of Recent Trends." *Economic Review*, Federal Reserve Bank of San Francisco, Spring 1988, 14-29.

Burns, Arthur F. "Statement on the Condition of the Banking System before the Senate Committee on Banking, Housing, and Urban Affairs." *Federal Reserve Bulletin*, Malrch 1977, 238-46.

Dooley, Michael, William Helkie, Ralph Tryon, and John Underwood. "An Analysis of the External Debt Position of Eight Developing Countries through 1990." *Journal of Development Economics*, May 1986, 283-319.

Dornbusch, Rudiger, "Build, Don't Bleed, Economies." *New York Times*, 13 May 1988, A31.

Eichengreen, Barry and Peter Lindert, eds. *A Long Run Perspective on the International Debt Crisis*. 27 May 1988 Conference (volume forthcoming).

Federal Reserve Bulletin, "Foreign Lending by Banks: A Guide to International and U.S. Statistics." October 1986, 694; "Near-Term Contingency Support for Mexico's Reserves." *Ibid.*, 702.

Feldstein, Martin. "Latin America's Debt." *Economist*, 27 June 1987, 21-25.

Feldstein, Martin, Hervé de Carmoy, Koei Narusawa, and Paul R. Krugman. *Restoring Growth in the Debt-Laden Third World*. A report to the Trilateral Commission, 33. Triangle Papers, 1987.

Griliches, Zvi. "The Use and Abuse of Econometrics." *American Economic Association Papers and Proceedings*, May 1985, 196-200.

Hall, Robert. "Comment on Jeffrey Sachs." *Brookings Papers on Economic Activity* 2, 1986, 439.

Heller, H. Robert. "Statement before the Senate Committee on Banking, Housing, and Urban Affairs." 25 May 1988.

Krueger, Anne O. "Resolving the Debt Crisis and Restoring Developing Countries' Creditworthiness." Carnegie-Rochester Public Policy Conference, University of Rochester, 23 April 1988.

Lessard, Donald R. and John Williamson. *Capital Flight and Third World Debt*. Washington, D.C.: Institute for International Economics, 1987.

Lindert, Peter. "Relending to Sovereign Debtors." Working paper, University of California, Davis, Institute for Governmental Affairs, September, 1986.

_________. "Response to Debt Crisis: What is Different about the 1980s?" Conference on a Long-Run Perspective on the Debt Crisis. San Francisco, 27 May, 1988.

Makin, John H. "The Third World Debt Crisis and the American Banking System." *The American Enterprise Institute Economist*, May 1987.

Mesumeci, James J. and Joseph F. Sinkey, Jr. "The International Debt Crisis and Bank Security Returns Surrounding Citicorp's Loan-Loss Reserve Decision on May 19, 1987." Paper presented at the Chicago Federal Reserve Bank Twenty-Fourth Annual Conference on Bank Structure and Competition, 13 May 1988.

New York Times, 13, 17 June, 5, 6, 14 July; 16 August, 1988.

Organization for Economic Cooperation and Development. *Prudential Supervision in Banking*, Paris, 1987.

Sachs, Jeffrey. "Managing the LDC Debt Crisis." *Brookings Paper on Economic Activity* 2, 1986, 397-431.

Sachs, Jeffrey and Harry Huizinga. "US Commercial Banks and the Developing-Country Debt Crisis." *Brookings Paper on Economic Activity* 2, 1987, 555-601.

Sandler, Linda. "The Great Debate Over LDC Loan Swapping." *Institutional Investor*, May 1984, 77-80.

Schuker, Stephen A. *American "Reparations" to Germany, 1919-33: Implications for the Third-World Debt Crisis*. Princeton Studies in International Finance, No. 61, July 1988.

Volcker, Paul A. "The Recycling Problem Revisited." *Challenge*, July-August 1980, 3-14. Originally a March 1980 address at New York University Graduate School of Business Administration.

Wall Street Journal, 13, 19 May; 21, 22 June; 1, 11, 15 July, 4, 16 August, 22, 23 September, 1988.

Webb, Steven B. "Can Developing Countries Outgrow Their Debt?" U.S. Department of State, Bureau of Economic and Business Affairs. Planning and Economic Analysis Staff Working Paper 2, 1987.

________. "Comparing Latin American Debt Today with German Reparations after World War I." U.S. Department of State, Bureau of Economic and Business Affairs. Planning and Economic Analysis Staff Working Paper 5, 1988.

READING 19

Debt Relief is Cheap

Paul R. Krugman

The time has come for the governments of the industrial nations, and for the multilateral institutions that represent their interests, to engineer large-scale debt relief for the Third World. Since Treasury Secretary Nicholas Brady announced support for the debt reduction in March 1989, debt relief of some kind has been official U.S. policy. However, the United States should consider a far more aggressive and comprehensive plan than that which it has championed so far.

Pleas for debt relief have, of course, come frequently since the beginning of the debt crisis. For the most part, those urging a program of debt reduction have assumed that it would represent a major effort justified by large economic benefits to the advanced countries. The real reason to pursue debt reduction now, however, is not that it will be especially beneficial (at least in purely economic terms) but that it will be cheap. The economic health of the Third World is not, sad to say, crucial to the economic health of the advanced world. The North does, however, have a political and humanitarian interest in what happens in the South. If a group of developing countries can be assisted massively at very modest cost to advanced-country taxpayers, such a project is surely worth pursuing. That is now the case with Third World debt.

The origins of the Third World debt problem are familiar and need not be reviewed at length. During the 1970s private bankers in the United States and elsewhere decided that lending to Third World countries was a good idea. Loans to governments, or loans guaranteed by governments, looked safe enough to the bankers to make the higher yields on Third World lending attractive. As Citicorp Chairman Walter Wriston asserted, in remarks he was later to regret, a sovereign nation "does not go bankrupt."

As long as the flow of money continued, everything looked fine. The debtor countries could pay interest and principal easily out of the new loans. In 1982, however, for a variety of reasons confidence evaporated and the flow of money dried up with it. It soon became clear that the countries could not generate enough cash to service their debt. The result was a rolling crisis that continues to this day.

While this is a familiar story, many observers hold onto some important misconceptions about the debt problem. Two of these need to be singled out for attention, because correcting them is crucial to the argument made here for large-scale debt reduction.

The first misconception is the widespread view that the major debtors always have been and will remain economic basket cases—that the willingness of bankers to lend to these countries was never anything but folly. This carries cynicism too far. Bankers surely lent too much money with too little thought, but the economies to which they were lending in the 1970s do not much resemble the disastrous debtors of today. During the decade before the onset of the debt crisis in 1982, the 15 countries that the International Monetary Fund (IMF) now designates as "highly indebted" increased their gross domestic product (GDP) per capita by an average of 2.2 per cent annually in real terms. Such growth does not compare with that of the East Asian countries, but is significant all the same. The same group of countries had an average inflation rate of 39.8 per cent—not a good performance, but nowhere close to hyperinflation. By contrast, the IMF estimated that per capita GDP in these countries fell by .7 percent in 1989, confirming the 1980s as a decade of economic retrogression instead of development. Meanwhile, the advent of hyper-inflation in several debtor nations pushed the average inflation rate to a whopping 481 percent.

The point is that the debt crisis was associated with an unprecedented deterioration in economic performance in the debtor nations. It is virtually certain that the burden of debt was an important cause of that deterioration. The obvious corollary is that reducing the debt burden can help reverse the process.

The second major misconception is that Third World debt is an enormous problem for the world economy. One is often subjected to numbers intended to convey a sense of huge scale, for example, that the developing countries' debt exceeds $1.1 trillion. This emphasis on the magnitude of the problem is clearly appropriate in some respects. Most of Latin America and most of sub-Saharan Africa, as well as a few countries elsewhere, like the Philippines, have been hit hard by the debt crisis. And economic data of course fail to convey the sheer awfulness of the story in human terms; for some of those at the bottom in Latin America and even more in Africa the debt crisis has been quite literally lethal.

As a *financial matter*, however, the debt crisis is not a first-class issue. Most of the widely cited trillion-plus dollars in debt is owed by countries that are not having trouble servicing their debt. The actual amount owed by problem debtors—around $400 billion—still sounds huge, but he world economy is also huge, so huge that $400 billion is really not a very big number from the point of view of the creditor nations.

The sad fact about poor countries is that they do not have much money, and so in purely economic terms they do not count for much. The combined gross national products of all troubled debtors amount to less than 5 percent of world output. The total face value of all loans to troubled debtors comes to less than 1 percent of the wealth of the creditor nations (and its market value to much less). Moreover, the debt service on those loans is less than one-third of 1 percent of the creditors' national incomes. Terrible as it is to say, advanced nations in general and the United States in particular do not have a strong financial interest in what happens to Third World debtors.

Many discussions of debt also overemphasize the indirect economic benefits to the advanced countries that would result from debt relief, such as increased exports to developing countries. The IMF estimates the interest payments of its group of "highly indebted" countries at $47 billion in 1989. Even a massive debt relief program that cut these payments in half would only allow the countries to increase their imports by $23 billion, and the United States would be unlikely to get more than about $8 billion of that. This amount is a drop in the bucket compared with the triple-digit U.S. trade deficit.

That the United States and other industrial countries do not have a large economic interest in the fate of Third World debtors can cut two ways. On one side, the advanced nations can, if they choose, neglect or mishandle the debt situation with little visible economic impact on themselves. On the other hand, if they feel that they have a political or a humanitarian interest in seeing the burden of debt reduced, it would not cost much to achieve that reduction.

In fact, debt reduction can be a remarkably inexpensive policy. Yet before explaining why, it is necessary to review other options and show why debt reduction is appropriate.

THE ROOTS OF CRISIS

The United States and other creditor countries have never tried one option for dealing with Third World debt that, in retrospect, might not have been such a bad idea. This was to do nothing: to treat the whole affair as a private matter between banks and their clients, just as if an ordinary business were having trouble servicing its debts. Instead, the debt crisis from the beginning has received continual high-level government intervention.

At the beginning of the crisis, official involvement was mainly justified by the fear that the debt crisis, if left unattended, could provoke a worldwide banking collapse on the 1931 model. Although the debt of developing countries has never been a large part of the advanced world's wealth, in the early 1980s ownership of that debt appeared to be concentrated precisely where a crisis would do the most damage; in the hands of key money-center banks. When the crisis broke, it appeared that widespread defaults might leave many of the world's major banks insolvent. With today's elaborate bank regulation and supervision, these defaults probably would not have closed the banks but rather put them in government hands. But inadvertent nationalization of the banking industry was not a prospect the Reagan administration welcomed. Today the risk of such an event has diminished greatly because banks have built up their capital as insurance against possible losses. Massive defaults on Third World debt still might put some banks under—among major banks, analysts frequently cite Manufacturers Hanover as a problem case. Still, the kind of wholesale collapse of private banking feared in 1982 now seems a remote prospect.

While the risk of financial crisis resulting from Third World debt has basically passed, the two other reasons for an active government role in managing that debt remain as strong as ever. First, the creditor countries believe they have an interest in the political stability of debtor states and that a confrontation between debtors and bankers could lead to radicalization. The prospect of a leftist-populist movement rising to power in Mexico by denouncing foreign banks and demanding debt repudiation did not seem far-fetched in 1982. Indeed, it is still a reasonable scenario—not for this year or next, but it cannot be dismissed as a possibility in this century. Second, officials at the Federal Reserve Bank, the U.S. Treasury Department, and the IMF believe that government leadership can lead to a better outcome than that which private actors can achieve on their own. But what should this leadership try to accomplish? Here is where experience has forced a change in direction.

Suppose someone who owes you money tells you that he cannot pay in full; after checking out the story, you find that he is telling you the truth and that no purpose would be served by trying to force him to come up with the money. You have two basic options. You can give him time by postponing the payment—in effect lending him the money he cannot pay and hoping that later he will be able to pay. Alternatively, you can tell him to pay what he can, and consider the account settled (mindful that you probably will not lend him money again for a long time).

The same basic options confront the creditors of the Third World. Either they can *finance* the debt by postponing the countries' obligations in the hope that things will look better in the future, or they can *forgive* it, reducing the debtor's obligations to a level that they may be able to pay.

U.S. policy toward Third World debt from 1982 until March 1989 was based on the premise that financing was enough. If debtor nations were given time, they would eventually be able to meet their obligations. In March 1989, treasury Secretary Brady announced that the United States would advocate a strategy of debt reduction. Exactly how this is to be accomplished remains unclear, but it appears that the emphasis on financing has now shifted to forgiving.

During the years of the financing strategy, obligations of countries were postponed in three ways: Repayment of principal was rescheduled, official agencies such as the IMF and the World Bank made new loans that could pay part of the interest coming due; and the banks that had lent money to the countries in the first place were rounded up for "concerted" lending, which mounted to indirect relending of part of the remaining interest. In effect, repayment of debt was very nearly halted, and limited new lending was arranged from both private and public sources.

This strategy could be, and was, described as a plan to put highly indebted countries still deeper into debt. In the early years of the debt problem, this did not seem like a bad idea. Given the past growth rates achieved by debtor nations and the economic reforms that creditors imposed as part of the package, it seemed probable that most major debtors could grow their way out of their debt problems. Even though the debt might grow, the incomes of the debtors would grow faster—and thus the creditworthiness of the debtors would improve, not worsen, over time.

Unfortunately, things did not work out that way. the financing strategy's objective was to buy time until the crisis passed; the definition of that passing would be a restoration of "normal market access"—the ability of the major debtors to attract funding without special arrangements. Yet normal market access has never looked more distant.

Two key indicators of the debtor countries' position reveal the extent of the financing strategy's failure. First, countries have not grown their way out of their debt problems. Concerted lending never materialized on the scale intended; indeed, net lending by banks to heavily indebted countries has been negative since 1985. Also, many debtors have desperately tried to earn more foreign exchange. Yet the ratio of debt to exports of the IMF's heavily indebted group was virtually the same at the end of 1989 as it was at the end of 1982. Second, as the financing strategy's failure has grown apparent, the secondary prices of the Third World debt—the prices at which creditors are willing to sell their claims to others and thus a useful indicator of confidence—have plummeted. With claims on most troubled debtors selling for less than 40 percent of par, a return to normal borrowing on the capital markets looks like a fantasy.

Of course, the slow growth of debtors is no accident. It has a lot to do with the debt itself—with the direct burden of debt service and with the indirect effects on confidence and incentives of a debt overhang larger than the countries are able to pay. Thus there is a vicious circle: Countries are failing to work their way out of their debt problems because of slow growth; they are growing slowly at least in part because of their debt burden.

Even two years ago, U.S. officials vigorously denied the existence of such a vicious circle and officials at the IMF and World Bank alluded to it only guardedly. Their reasons were clear. If a vicious circle exists, then the debt must be reduced. Only since the Brady speech has it become respectable to call for partial debt forgiveness.

But how is debt reduction to be organized and who is to pay for it? These are actually easy questions, but ones that US policymakers have not yet faced squarely.

THE MATHEMATICS OF FORGIVENESS

What should please (and surprise) policymakers when they finally do face up to debt reduction is how cheap it can be. An example from Mexico illustrates the point. How much would it cost *creditors* to forgive, say, $10 billion of Mexico's $80 billion total external debt? It certainly would not cost $10 billion. Nobody has confidence that Mexico will pay all its debt; Mexican debt sells on the secondary market for only about 40 cents on the dollar. So the market value of the debt to be forgiven here is only $4 billion.

But even $4 billion is much too high an estimate. The secondary price reflects the fraction of the debt that creditors expect to be paid on average. The probability that Mexico will pay the last $10 billion is much less. Further, reducing Mexico's debt would improve its growth prospects at least a little, and this would enhance the value of the money still owed after a debt reduction package had been put in place. So the value to creditors of the last $10 billion in overall Mexican debt should be quite small.

It may even be negative. If the vicious circle of high debt and low growth is strong enough, reducing debt may enhance a country's prospects enough to actually increase the total expected debt repayment. Many economists working in this area have accepted the idea of a "debt Laffer curve," a curve that relates the market value of a country's debt to its nominal value. At sufficiently high levels of debt the curve turns down, so that reducing the obligations of a country actually increases its total expected payments. Some recent estimates by Stijn Claessens at the World Bank and other economists suggest that for a number of smaller debtors, such as Peru and Bolivia, debt reduction would actually benefit the creditors as well as the debtors. Larger debtors such as Brazil or Mexico may not be in this paradoxical position, but it is still true that the cost of debt reduction to creditors is very small indeed.

All this leads to a startling conclusion for policy: Large-scale debt relief would not cost very much. The arithmetic works this way. The most heavily indebted countries owe about $400 billion to creditors. A hypothetical scheme of massive debt relief might seek to cut the debt in half, canceling $200 billion. It might also require taxpayers in creditor countries to compensate banks for any losses that result from the plan. At first sight this bailout looks so large that it would be politically unthinkable. But it is not that large.

At current secondary market prices, the $400 billion face value of the debt is worth only about $140 billion. So the market value of the debt to be canceled in this plan is only $70 billion. Yet even this figure heavily overstates the amount by which private creditors would have to be compensated. The likelihood that creditors will be repaid the full $400 billion is far less than 35 percent, the approximate secondary price on the average dollar of debt. Further, debt reduction would enhance the value of the remaining debt. Ultimately, cancelling $200 billion in claims would probably impose a cost on creditors of no more than $25 billion.[1]

Finally, it must be remembered that the United States is not the only major creditor nation. In fact, U.S. banks account for an estimated one-quarter of bank lending to Third World problem debtors. In any internationally coordinated debt-relief plan, the U.S. share would be similar to its share of the original lending. Thus the total cost to U.S. taxpayers of a debt relief plan such as that described here could be as low as $6 billion and would surely be less than $10 billion.

Since this plan would impose only a one-time cost, not a continuing expense, $10 billion is a remarkably small number. For the sake of comparison, the savings and loan bailout has already been given $166 billion in authorized funding, and most experts expect that sum to rise substantially. Massive debt relief for the Third World could cost U.S. taxpayers less than one-twentieth of the cost of the savings and loan bailout.

THE WRONG PATH TO REFORM

If large-scale debt reduction is in fact not an expensive proposition, why is so little debt reduction taking place under the Brady Plan? One reason is that, as in many other affairs of state, advanced countries in general and the United States in particular have been pennywise and pound-foolish on a grand scale. Constrained by Bush administration pledges of "no new taxes" and the spending limits imposed by the Gramm-Rudman-Hollings balanced budget act, a billion dollars in today's budget can seem like a lot of money, even though for an economy the size of America's it is not.

There is, however, a deeper reason. Debt reduction is being seriously impeded by the widespread belief that it can be carried out most effectively through some market mechanism, for example by buying back debt on the secondary market. The phrase "market-based debt reduction" sounds appealing in an era in which the prestige of market economics is high. Yet while market mechanisms are very effective in dealing with many problems, debt reduction is not one of them.

The hypothetical case of reducing the debt of the problem debtors by $200 billion, or about half, can demonstrate this point. As seen earlier, the net loss to creditors from such a reduction would be only about $25 billion, which ideally would be all of the taxpayers' compensation to private creditors. But the public's cost would be much more if, instead of requiring creditors to reduce their claims and then compensating them, debt reduction were made voluntary. In this scenario, creditors would be offered the opportunity to sell off their claims at a discount, but not be required to do so.

Why would this method be far more expensive? The current market value of that $200 billion in loans is about $70 billion, which represents a minimum estimate of the cost of buying the debt on a voluntary basis. Yet the actual price would be much higher, since those creditors who did not sell out would gain much better prospects for payment as a result of the lower debt burden. In practice, the secondary market prices would rise sharply as soon as a policy of buybacks was announced. (Secondary market prices did, in fact, soar in the weeks following the Brady speech.) A debt buyback of $200 billion would probably take place at a price of 55 percent or more of par, so the debt reduction would cost taxpayers not $25 billion but at least $110 billion. The difference represents a windfall gain for creditors—both those who sell at a higher price and those who hold out and face improved payment prospects. Such a huge expense, incurred largely for the benefit of banks rather than debtor countries, would surely be viewed as politically unacceptable.

Many bankers have claimed that this unhappy market arithmetic can be avoided if simple buybacks are replaced with more complex schemes, such as swaps of debt for equity. When one cuts to the essence of such financial engineering, however, it usually turns out to be a disguised buyback, often at less favorable terms for the country than those that could have been achieved through a simple exchange of cash for debt. For example, investments by multinational companies that are financed through debt-equity swaps would typically be made in any case. The result is that foreign exchange that would have come to a debtor country's central bank is diverted to the secondary market to acquire debt for the exchange—usually at an unnecessarily high price.

Debt reduction is a classic example of a situation in which voluntarism and reliance on the market are exactly the wrong approach. For the most heavily indebted countries, it is in the interest of both debtors and creditors to reduce the debt, but it is also in the interest of each individual creditor to hold out while others reduce their claims. The result of this free riding is that too little debt reduction takes place at too high a cost to taxpayers. The right policy answer is concerted debt reduction through which creditors are compensated for their losses but are not given the option of staying out of the program.

That approach was followed in the Mexican debt reduction package, the only major debt reduction under the Brady Plan to date. Although a thin façade of voluntarism was maintained by offering banks a choice of options, they were essentially forced to reduce their claims in return for guarantees on interest and principal that left the market value of their claims unchanged. Unfortunately, the Mexican package covered too little of that country's debt (only $48.9 billion, or less than two-thirds) and was excessively cautious. And while the misplaced emphasis on market mechanisms was dropped in practice, the rhetoric of voluntarism remained, getting in the way of clear thinking. Massive Third World debt reduction is therefore a viable option—but only if policymakers avoid knee-jerk conservatism that assumes the market mechanism is always best.

Most appeals for debt relief assert that a large expenditure of resources is justified either by the need to safeguard world financial stability or by the importance of developing-country markets to the advanced world. Both arguments are essentially wrong: The highly indebted nations are simply too poor to matter much either to global financial markets or to exports.

But 600 million people do matter. If the United States and other creditor countries can do debtors' economies a great service at a modest cost to themselves, they should. The face value of Third World obligations is being maintained at highly unrealistic levels given the actual prospects for repayment. Reducing those obligations will help the indebted economies at little real financial cost to the creditor nations. If large-scale debt relief is carried out correctly, the cost to taxpayers will be small—ridiculously small compared with the cost of America's purely domestic financial messes. It would be a pity if the United States and other industrial countries did not take advantage of the opportunity to do so much good for so little money.

ENDNOTES

1 The financial engineering required by debt reduction is complicated by the fact that a significant part of Third World debt is owed to mutilateral institutions like the World Bank rather than to private banks. This makes the direct costs to banks of debt reduction higher, since part of the gains from a lower debt burden accrue to these publicly owned institutions. These gains, however, indirectly benefit the same taxpayers who must compensate the banks, so that the true cost of debt reduction remains very low.

SECTION X

Eastern Europe/U.S.S.R.

In the late 1980s and early 1990 we have witnessed unprecedented changes in the global world order. The decline of communism and the movements to embrace markets in Eastern Europe and the former Soviet Union have created a complex web of opportunities and adjustment dilemmas. The consensus among reformers is that macroeconomic stability, price liberalization, production sector reforms, and financial-sector reforms are key elements of a successful reform program. The order of implementing these reforms is the subject of intense debate, as are the distributional consequences of the altered economic systems. In the articles in this section, the prospects and difficulties of these transformations are discussed by William Nordhaus and in a survey of issues written by economists at the International Monetary Fund.

READING 20

Macroeconomic Developments and Systemic Reforms in Eastern Europe and the U.S.S.R.

International Money Fund

In most of Eastern Europe, and to a lesser extent in the U.S.S.R., a broad consensus has recently emerged on the need to move toward market-based economies.[1] While the extent of reform has varied considerably across countries, there has been a general trend during the past year to accelerate the process of systemic change. After two decades of partial reforms, Hungary and Poland have taken significant steps to speed up the transformation of their economic systems and Yugoslavia has intensified reform efforts. The Czech and Slovak Federal Republic (Czechoslovakia), Bulgaria, and Romania have begun to implement comprehensive programs designed to achieve a rapid transition from a highly centralized system to a market economy. Market-oriented reforms are, however, considerably less advanced in the U.S.S.R. The "Guidelines for the Stabilization of the Economy and the Transition to a Market Economy" (Presidential Guidelines) that were announced by the President of the U.S.S.R. and approved by the Supreme Soviet in October 1990 recommend a relatively gradual transition, and to date there has been little progress with the implementation of systemic reforms.

In the majority of countries, severe economic dislocations have emerged as the traditional system of central planning has largely collapsed and market-based coordination mechanisms are only beginning to develop. Moreover, the adjustment of relative prices to conditions prevailing in world markets generally requires far-reaching restructuring of enterprises and industries. While this restructuring eventually will result in a more efficient allocation of resources, it is likely to entail substantial losses in output and employment in the short run.

Most countries have begun the transition to a market economy in a relatively unfavorable macroeconomic and external environment. The economic policies pursued in the recent past have left many countries in Eastern Europe and the U.S.S.R. with a legacy of large domestic and external imbalances, including substantial amounts of excess liquidity. At the same time, regional trade has begun to decline, reflecting the impact of economic dislocations in most countries in the region, notably the U.S.S.R. and the dissolution of trade arrangements among the members of the Council for Mutual Economic Assistance (CMEA), which entails considerable terms of trade losses for the Eastern European countries. These initial conditions complicate the process of transition and require tight financial policies to avoid a rapid acceleration of inflation and unsustainable external deficits. The next section of this chapter reviews macroeconomic policies and developments in Eastern Europe and the U.S.S.R., the following sections examine recent progress with systemic reforms in the domestic economy and in the external sector, and the final section provides a summary and conclusions.

MACROECONOMIC CONDITIONS: RECENT DEVELOPMENTS AND PROSPECTS

Stance of Policies

Faced with a sharp acceleration of inflation during 1989, Poland and Yugoslavia adopted comprehensive stabilization programs that combined tight fiscal and monetary policies with fixed exchange rates and controlled wages as nominal anchors.[2] Both programs were initially successful in bringing down inflation, but in mid-1990 slippages occurred as wages and credit to the non-government sector increased considerably faster than planned.[3] In Hungary, the emergence of large domestic and external imbalances prompted a substantial tightening of financial policies in 1990. Czechoslovakia continued to pursue cautious fiscal and monetary policies, and began the transition to a market economy in a relatively stable macroeconomic environment without a large monetary overhang. By contrast, in Bulgaria and Romania financial policies were not sufficiently tight to reduce existing imbalances and excess liquidity remained substantial. Macroeconomic imbalances remained particularly severe in the U.S.S.R., despite a reduction of the fiscal deficit from 11 percent of GDP in 1988 to 8-1/4 percent in 1990. The rapid expansion of credit to the enterprise sector added to the existing monetary overhang, which is now estimated at about one third of the stock of financial assets.[4]

In most countries in the region, it is recognized that macroeconomic policies need to be tightened further in 1991 to contain the impact on inflation and the external balance of recent price and external sector liberalizations, including in particular changes in CMEA trade arrangements, which imply large terms of trade changes in favor of raw materials (including energy) and against manufactures.[5] Following sweeping price liberalizations, Bulgaria, Czechoslovakia, and Romania earlier this year adopted tight financial policies and wage controls to prevent an inflationary wage-price spiral. Hungary has maintained a tight policy stance, and recently Poland has again tightened policies to bring down inflation. However, in Yugoslavia and particularly in the U.S.S.R., stabilization efforts remain seriously hampered by differences between federal and republican authorities and by the lack of progress with structural reforms in the enterprise and banking sectors.

In most countries, the recent tightening of financial policies has been accompanied by a growing reliance on market-based instruments of monetary control, such as changes in the cost and availability of central bank refinancing.[6] In addition, there have been far-reaching structural changes in government finances, such as sharp cuts in consumer and producer subsidies,[7] a significant reduction of the financing of investment outlays through the budget, rising budgetary expenditures for social security, and a rationalization of tax systems, including substantial reductions in the taxation of enterprise profits.[8] These changes are generally reflected in substantial declines of government expenditures and revenues as a percentage of GDP, in the U.S.S.R., however, the share of government expenditure in GDP remained largely unchanged, while the share of subsidies actually increased through 1990.

Output and Employment

Following virtual stagnation in 1989, output in Eastern Europe and the U.S.S.R. declined by nearly 4 percent last year (Table 6). The decline affected all countries in the region and reflected a combination of domestic and external factors, including the dislocations resulting from the disintegration of the existing economic system, the restructuring necessitated by substantial changes in relative prices and greater exposure to foreign competition; the short-run effects of tight financial policies; falling exports to other CMEA countries; disruptions in oil supplies from the U.S.S.R.; and the economic impact of the events in the Middle East.

Output losses in 1990 were particularly severe in Bulgaria, Poland, Romania, and Yugoslavia. In Poland and Yugoslavia, output contracted sharply in early 1990 and recovered only moderately when financial policies were relaxed later in the year. In Bulgaria and Romania, the disruptions of trade with Iraq and the CMEA countries, particularly the U.S.S.R, exacerbated severe domestic dislocations. By contrast, in Hungary strong growth of convertible currency exports partly offset the contraction of ruble exports and domestic demand, while in Czechoslovakia domestic demand helped to contain the decline in output in the face of adverse external developments. Based on official estimates, output losses in 1990 were relatively moderate in the U.S.S.R., although a rapid expansion of nominal incomes was accompanied by persistent shortages. In all countries, output losses were concentrated in the state sector; activity in the private sector, which is not adequately reflected in official output

Table 6. Eastern Europe and the U.S.S.R.: Macroeconomic Indicators, 1988–96
(Annual percentage change, unless stated otherwise)

	1988	1989	1990	1991	1992	1993–96
Eastern Europe[1] and U.S.S.R.						
Real GDP	4.3	1.9	−3.8	−4.1	−2.1	1.2
Consumer prices	11.1	30.9	34.1	45.6	18.2	. . .
Fiscal balance[2]	−8.0	−6.7	−6.5	−4.2	. . .	. . .
Eastern Europe[1]						
Real GDP	1.2	−0.9	−8.6	−1.5	2.8	4.4
Consumer prices	44.3	139.0	149.7	78.0	13.3	. . .
Fiscal balance[2]	−0.2	−0.1	−1.8	−0.6	. . .	. . .
Current account balance[3, 4]	6.7	3.0	−1.3	−10.0	−11.2	. . .
Of which: Convertible currency	2.7	0.7	−2.8	. . .	. . .	. . .
Debt service ratio[4, 5]	19.2	18.5	14.9	18.5	16.8	. . .
Of which: Convertible currency	34.7	29.2	18.1	. . .	. . .	. . .
External debt[3, 4, 6]	97.9	98.4	105.0	110.2	118.3	. . .

[1] Eastern Europe is defined to include Bulgaria, Czechoslovakia, Hungary, Poland, Romania, and Yugoslavia.
[2] In percent of nominal GDP.
[3] In billions of U.S. dollars.
[4] Includes nonconvertible currency data that are converted into U.S. dollars at national transferable ruble (TR)/U.S. dollar rates. These data are significantly influenced by distortions in intra-CMEA trade prices and by differences between the national TR/U.S. dollar cross rates and the official TR/U.S. dollar exchange rate of the International Bank for Economic Cooperation (IBEC). From 1991 onward, all data are in convertible currencies.
[5] Debt service paid in percent of exports of goods and services.
[6] Excluding liabilities to the Fund.

statistics, expanded rapidly, notably in Hungary, Poland, and Yugoslavia, but it is estimated that this had little impact on the overall level of activity, given the small size of the sector.

In most Eastern European countries, output is expected to continue to decline in 1991, albeit at a slower rate than last year. This decline would reflect the further dissolution of traditional trade patterns among the CMEA countries, sharp increases in the cost of imports, accelerating industrial restructuring, and further tightening of financial policies. From 1992 onward, output is projected to recover gradually as the private sector expands and efficiency begins to improve. Of course, this projection hinges critically on the assumption that the necessary systemic reforms will be implemented without delays and that tight macroeconomic policies will succeed in controlling inflation and containing external imbalances. In this regard, the prospects are considerably less favorable in the U.S.S.R. than in Eastern European countries. In the absence of a marked reorientation of economic policies, output in the U.S.S.R. is likely to continue to decline.

In all Eastern European countries and in the U.S.S.R., unemployment has begun to rise. Nonetheless, the decline in employment has tended to lag behind the fall in output, and unemployment rates are generally still considerably lower than in Western Europe. In Poland, unemployment rose from a negligible level in late 1989 to 6 percent of the labor force in late 1990. At the same time, the unemployment rate in Yugoslavia, which was already high, rose further to over 12 percent. While unemployment also has increased in Hungary, Romania, and the U.S.S.R., unemployment rates in these countries have remained in the range of 1 to 2 percent in 1990. Unemployment is projected to increase further this year as the process of enterprise restructuring accelerates; particularly large increases are expected in Bulgaria, Czechoslovakia, and Romania where the process of structural transformation has started only recently. Over the medium term, as the Eastern European economies begin to recover, unemployment rates are expected to decline gradually in all countries, except the U.S.S.R.

Prices, Wages, and Exchange Rates

The weighted average annual rate of inflation in Eastern Europe rose in 1990 but is expected to decline this year reflecting the impact of recent stabilization programs in Poland and Yugoslavia.[9] In both countries inflation fell rapidly during the first half of 1990—in Poland from a monthly rate of nearly 80 percent in January to 3-1/2 percent in June, and in Yugoslavia from 64 percent in December 1989 to zero in April 1990. Inflation picked up later in the year following a relaxation of financial policies and sharp price increases for oil imports, but the recent acceleration has been relatively moderate, and it is expected that both countries will be able to avoid a return to very high inflation. While in Czechoslovakia the impact of the recent price liberalization on the overall price level appears to have been relatively moderate, price liberalizations in Bulgaria and Romania have resulted in sharp increases in the price level owing to a large monetary overhang. However, financial policies have been tightened substantially in these countries, and it is not expected that the initial price adjustments will lead to a permanent increase in the rate of inflation. In the U.S.S.R., the consumer price index is likely to rise substantially this year as a result of recent adjustments in administered prices. Moreover, as price controls remain pervasive and shortages persist, registered price increases substantially understate the severity of domestic imbalances.

Wage restraint plays a key role in current stabilization efforts in the Eastern European countries. All countries have adopted some form of incomes policy, either by directly limiting or by taxing excessive wage increases. As a result, measured real wages stagnated or declined in 1990 in all countries, with the exception of Romania and the U.S.S.R., where nominal wages rose considerably faster than the official retail price index.[10] In Poland and Yugoslavia, a sharp compression of real wages in early 1990 was later partially offset by substantial wage increases.

Table 7. Eastern Europe: Shares of Exports to CMEA Countries and to the U.S.S.R. in 1989[1]
(In percent of total exports)

	Share of Exports to CMEA Countries	Share of Exports to the U.S.S.R.
Bulgaria	83.0	65.8
Czechoslovakia	53.7	30.5
Hungary	41.0	25.1
Poland	34.3	20.5
Romania[2]	35.8	21.4
Yugoslavia	34.3	20.9
U.S.S.R.	55.2	. . .

Source: National authorities and staff estimates.
[1] The shares in this table are based on national currency data on exports to CMEA countries and to the convertible currency area. Estimates of CMEA exports are strongly influenced by distortions in intra-CMEA foreign trade prices and exchange rates. See also footnote 4 to Table 6.
[2] Based on data for 1985.

Since late 1989, all Eastern European countries and the U.S.S.R. have substantially depreciated their nominal exchange rates, in most cases to boost competitiveness and support external sector liberalization. However, in several countries, notably in Poland, Yugoslavia, and Hungary, price increases subsequently outpaced the magnitude of the nominal devaluations and real effective exchange rates appreciated significantly. Nonetheless, with wage increases lagging price increases, it appears that in most cases, the impact on competitiveness was considerably less severe than indicated by the real exchange rate indices, which are based on consumer prices.

Trade and Current Account Balances

In 1990, the external payments positions of the Eastern European countries and the U.S.S.R. were strongly affected by the decline in intra-regional trade volumes, the expansion of trade with the convertible currency area, and by oil price developments. The disruptions in intra-regional trade were caused mostly by the virtual collapse of trade with East Germany and by the economic dislocations in the U.S.S.R. A 6 percent decline in Soviet oil output resulted in a fall in oil exports that triggered a matching fall in the volume of Eastern European exports to the U.S.S.R. In a number of

Table 8. Soviet Petroleum Exports to Eastern Europe in 1989–91[1]

	1989	1990[2]	1991[3]
	(In millions of barrels)		
Volume	483	343	258
	(In billions of U.S. dollars)		
Value[4]	4.2	2.9	4.9
Value[5]	8.3	7.5	4.9

Source: Soviet authorities and staff estimates.
[1] Oil and oil products.
[2] Estimate.
[3] Projection.
[4] At CMEA prices converted into U.S. dollars at the unweighted average of national TR/U.S. dollar cross-exchange rates, with the exception of exports to Yugoslavia, which are based on world market prices.
[5] At world market prices.

countries, export volumes to former CMEA members may have declined by 20 to 30 percent last year. The impact of these disruptions on total trade and economic activity is related to the degree of dependence of each country on the markets in

Chart 19. Eastern Europe: Current Account Balances[1]
(In billions of U.S. dollars)

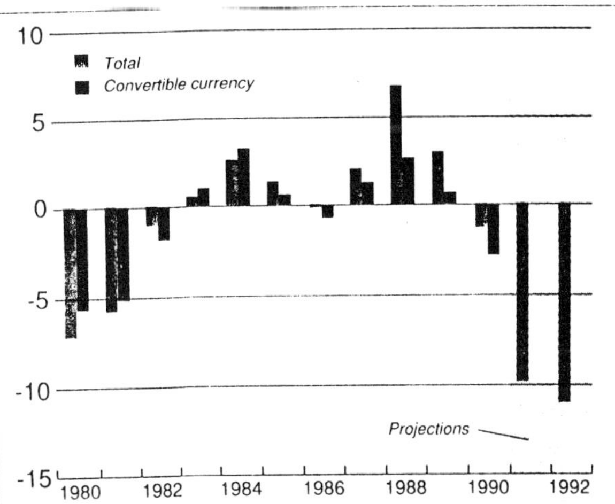

[1]Excluding the U.S.S.R. Total current account data include nonconvertible currency transactions converted into dollars at national TR/U.S. dollar cross-exchange rates. See Footnote 4 to Table 4.

CMEA countries, particularly the U.S.S.R (Table 7). Extensive trade liberalization pursued by several countries also unsettled the established channels of foreign trade and contributed to a reorientation of trade toward the convertible currency area. As a result, trade with the convertible currency area expanded rapidly.

Despite the sharp rise in oil prices in the second half of the year, the value of total Soviet exports was broadly unchanged in 1990, owing partly to a decline in the volume of oil exports and the considerable lag in the adjustment of intra-CMEA oil prices to world market levels (Table 8). The shortfall of oil supply from the U.S.S.R. forced the Eastern European countries to buy oil on the world market at much higher prices, adding significantly to their import bill in convertible currencies.

The shift in the aggregate current account position of the Eastern European countries in 1990 reflected primarily dramatic changes in the balances in convertible currencies (Chart 19).[11] The combined current account position in convertible currencies in Czechoslovakia, Romania, and Yugoslavia deteriorated sharply in 1990 largely because of a very large increase in imports. By contrast, the combined current account position in convertible currencies of Hungary and Poland improved, in large part because of a favorable export performance. The impact of regional trade disruptions on current account positions in nonconvertible currencies was small because the fall in the value of Eastern European imports was matched by a corresponding decline in export. The current account position of the U.S.S.R. deteriorated substantially in 1990, both in convertible and in nonconvertible currencies.

Predicting developments in trade and payments for 1991-92 is unusually difficult owing to considerable uncertainty about the impact of prospective changes in the regional trade and payments arrangements and of continued economic dislocations. The transition to world market prices with settlement in hard currencies in 1991 will generate a large deterioration in the terms of trade of the Eastern European countries, as their trade with the U.S.S.R. is dominated by imports of energy and raw materials whose relative prices in terms of manufactures were previously well below world market levels. The impact of this deterioration on aggregate trade balances is projected to be mitigated

Chart 20. Eastern Europe: Debt and Debt Service Ratios[1]

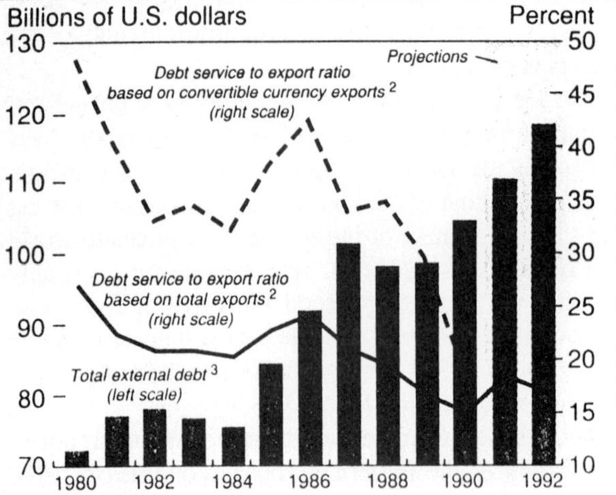

[1]Excluding the U.S.S.R.
[2]Based on debt service actually paid.
[3]Excludes liabilities to the Fund.

by a likely decline in the region's demand for imported oil. Intra-regional trade is projected to contract further this year as the transition to world market prices is likely to amplify the impact of economic dislocations throughout the region; in some cases the trade volumes are expected to decline by as much as 50 percent in 1991.

According to staff projections, the aggregate current account deficit of the Eastern European countries will reach about $10 billion in 1991 and $11 billion in 1992, reflecting the widening of external deficits with the traditional convertible currency area, and deteriorating trade balances vis-à-vis the U.S.S.R. The current account deficit of the U.S.S.R. with countries outside the CMEA grouping is unlikely to decline significantly in 1991. The overall current account deficit, however, could be considerably reduced in 1991 to the extent that the U.S.S.R. is able to run a trade surplus with the CMEA countries. This will depend on the financing available to these countries and on the disposition of their accumulated transferable ruble claims on the U.S.S.R.

External Financing and Debt

The marked widening of current account deficits in Eastern Europe in 1990 required substantial amounts of additional financing to support the stabilization and reform programs adopted by individual countries. The Fund has played an active role in designing the adjustment programs and has collaborated with the European Community in coordinating financial and technical assistance. During 1990, the Fund approved arrangements for Hungary, Poland, and Yugoslavia with total commitments amounting to $1 3/4 billion. In 1991, over $5 billion financing under the stand-by and extended financing facilities have already been approved for Bulgaria, Czechoslovakia, Hungary, Poland, and Romania, with additional access of up to $2 billion for higher cost of oil imports under the compensatory and contingency financing facility. In addition, up to $1.5 billion in possible contingency financing will be available to offset the impact of unexpected external shocks in these countries. By early 1991, large amounts of external financing had also been committed by the group of 24 (OECD area countries) to Eastern Europe. By contrast, there were virtually no new syndicated credit commitments from commercial banks; only the U.S.S.R. receive $3 billion worth of commitments in 1990 that were guaranteed by the governments of the creditor banks. Czechoslovakia, Hungary, and the U.S.S.R. borrowed $1 1/2 billion in the bond markets.

The total external debt of Eastern Europe amounted to $105 billion at the end of 1990, an increase of almost 7 percent over the previous year (Table 6). The largest increase was accounted for by Poland which continued to incur payments arrears. During 1991-92, the debt of Eastern Europe is projected to increase to $118 billion, reflecting in part large borrowings by Czechoslovakia and Romania. The debt-service ratio is projected to increase from 15 percent in 1990 to 18 1/2 percent in 1991 (Chart 20), but is expected to fall over the medium term as a result of the anticipated debt restructurings in some countries and improved export performance.[12]

SYSTEMIC REFORMS IN DOMESTIC ECONOMY

Key Issues

The recent move toward systemic reforms aiming at a complete transformation of the economic system into a market economy marks a significant departure from previous partial reform efforts in countries such as Hungary and Poland, which sought to combine administrative coordination and market mechanisms. These earlier reforms greatly reduced the role of direct central planning, but left intact elaborate mechanisms of indirect administration influence over resource allocation, production and distribution, and generally failed to impose financial discipline on enterprises. As a result, there were only marginal improvements in efficiency while financial control became increasingly difficult.

Current reform efforts throughout Eastern Europe, suggest that there is a broad consensus on the main elements of the domestic reforms that are required to establish a market economy. These include the development of a competitive private enterprise sector and price liberalization; the creation of efficient financial institutions and the liberalization of financial markets; the deregulation of labor markets, and the establishment of a social safety net. Views differ on the appropriate timing of specific measures in key areas such as price liberalization, the transformation of the state enterprise sector and in the liberalization of the external sector, but there is a growing recognition that a relatively rapid and broad-based approach to systemic reforms is required. Although the gradual introduction of financial discipline and market-determined prices may limit the cost of adjustment in the short run, it is likely to involve considerably higher cost in the longer run as the persistence of rigidities and price distortions would prevent significant efficiency gains, while the lack of financial discipline would jeopardize macroeconomic stability. Moreover, given the linkages between the distortions in different areas, rapid progress in one particular area is unlikely to yield significant results, and may even be harmful, if it is not accompanied by reforms in other areas.

Reform of Enterprise Sector

While earlier reform efforts in Hungary and Poland entailed a gradual liberalization of the regulations governing private economic activity, private enterprises remained constrained by numerous formal and informal restrictions, including limits on the size, discriminatory taxation, and limited access to credit and inputs. During the past three years, however, efforts to remove restrictions affecting private business activity on the part of residents and nonresidents have been intensified throughout Eastern Europe. Poland, Hungary and, more recently, Bulgaria, Czechoslovakia, Romania, and Yugoslavia have eliminated legal restrictions on the establishment of private enterprises and have passed legislation placing private and state enterprises on an equal footing. Despite the recent changes in the legal framework, however, informal restrictions, such as limited access to financial resources and inputs, are only gradually disappearing. In the U.S.S.R., most economic activity outside the state sector has been in the form of cooperatives, which have been subject to periodic waves of harassment.

In most countries, the removal of restrictions on the private sector has stimulated the creation of small firms that had been all but absent in the formerly centrally planned economies in which highly concentrated industrial sectors predominated. While this trend is important for the development of an efficient and competitive market economy, it is unlikely to have a significant impact on the structure of the enterprise sector in the short and medium run given the dominant role of the state enterprises, which in most countries still account for over 90 percent of industrial output.[13] Transformation of the state enterprise sector has thus become a major focus of systemic reforms in all countries. As previous attempts to enhance efficiency without changing the basic ownership structure have proven unsuccessful, it has become widely accepted that fundamental changes in ownership rights are required.

Czechoslovakia, Hungary, Poland, and Romania, and to some extent, Yugoslavia have recently prepared or enacted legislation that establishes a framework for privatization.[14] This framework generally provides for a variety of privatization techniques, depending on the size of the enterprises involved. Small enterprises, mainly in the services sector (retail, catering, and other services), are to be sold through direct tender or public auction. Privatization of these enterprises has begun and is expected to be completed within two years in Czechoslovakia, Hungary, and Poland. Bulgaria has recently established a framework for the privatization of small enterprises.

By contrast, the privatization of large state enterprises is expected to be considerably more difficult. A key issue in the current debate about privatization is whether enterprises should be restructured and rationalized before ownership changes. While restructuring would facilitate proper valuation of the enterprises[15]—a difficult task under current circumstances—it would also substantially delay the process, given the large scale of the envisaged privatizations.[16] It is estimated that in Poland, for example, approximately 8,000 state enterprises will change ownership whereas in the United Kingdom fewer than 20 public enterprises were privatized between 1979 and 1989. Current privatization plans in Czechoslovakia, Hungary, Poland, and Romania emphasize a relatively rapid process and do not require a major restructuring of the companies involved. In most cases, enterprises are expected to transform into joint stock companies prior to privatization; large conglomerates will be split up into separate entities. Hungary and Poland began to break up large state enterprises several years ago, and Czechoslovakia has recently adopted a similar approach.

Another important issue in the debate on privatization is whether shares in enterprises should be sold or distributed to the population. While the distribution of shares is generally considered more equitable and is believed to strengthen public support for privatization,[17] asset sales can be used to absorb excess liquidity, which, in some countries, notably the U.S.S.R., Bulgaria and Romania, is estimated to be substantial.[18] Current privatization plans in Hungary, Poland, Czechoslovakia, Romania, and Yugoslavia focus on sales, but except in Hungary and Yugoslavia, they also envisage some form of distribution of shares to the population. In Czechoslovakia and Romania, a certain fraction of the equity of most enterprises will be distributed, with the remainder available for sale to other parties.[29] The government agency overseeing the privatization program is generally expected to start the privatization process, but in Czechoslovakia, Hungary, Poland, and Yugoslavia privatization can also be initiated by a state enterprise. Hungary's privatization laws also permit privatization through corporate takeover initiated by an interested buyer. In Hungary and Poland, the privatization of large state enterprises has already begun.

Even though the privatization programs involve expeditious procedures, it is expected that the privatization of the bulk of the large state enterprises will take several years.[20] In the short run, commercialization of the enterprises that remain in the state sector is therefore an important task in all Eastern European countries and in the U.S.S.R. Operating state enterprises on a commercial basis requires the introduction of financial discipline and autonomy in decision making. Most countries have begun to tighten enterprises' budget constraints by limiting budgetary support and bank credit, and by placing restrictions on inter-enterprise credit. At the same time, enterprise autonomy has increased as central planning has been abandoned. In the U.S.S.R., however, lack of financial discipline in the state enterprises remains a matter of serious concern, while state orders and central allocation of certain inputs continue to play an important role.

The commercialization of state enterprises will require restructuring or liquidation of those firms that are no longer viable. Most countries have taken steps to facilitate this process. Hungary, Poland, and Yugoslavia have strengthened bankruptcy procedures and have begun to expedite the process of liquidation and restructuring.[21] Bulgaria, Czechoslovakia, and Romania are expected to introduce or revise bankruptcy legislation this year.

Price Liberalization

The transition to a market economy cannot succeed without a general decontrol of prices and the removal of the comprehensive systems of direct and indirect taxes and subsidies that distort relative prices in the formerly centrally planned economies. It has been argued that owing to the lack of competition, full price liberalization at an early stage of the transition process would lead to excessive price increases.[22] However, the experience with gradual price liberalization in Hungary and Poland during the 1980s has shown that a step-by-step approach does not necessarily avoid inflation. Tight financial policies which are the key to controlling inflation, are difficult to implement without significant cuts in subsidies and hence far-reaching price liberalization. Moreover, a competitive and efficient enterprise sector, which is essential for the proper functioning of the price mechanism, is unlikely to develop as long as severe price rigidities and distortions persist.

Most countries in Eastern Europe have recognized the importance of rapid price liberalization and have recently made considerable progress in this area. In Poland, the share of sales at market determined prices in the total value of sales was raised from 50 percent in 1989 to 90 percent in early 1990. Hungary has achieved a similar degree of price liberalization although as a result of a more gradual process. Czechoslovakia freed most prices in early 1991, thereby increasing the share of sales at free prices in the value of sales to 85 percent. More recently, Bulgaria and Romania have introduced comprehensive price liberalizations.[23] In most countries only the prices of a few basic food staples, of some key inputs, and of public utilities remain controlled.[24] In the U.S.S.R., however, government intervention in the process of price determination remains pervasive even after the partial price reform in April 1991. Enterprises have only very limited influence on prices through negotiated contract prices for certain commodities, and the Presidential Guidelines of October 1990 recommend a relatively gradual approach to price liberalization.

Financial Sector Reform

Competitive financial institutions that ensure the efficient allocation of savings are essential for the functioning of a market economy. Yet earlier reform efforts in Poland and Hungary paid relatively little attention to the financial sector, which, as in other Eastern European countries, continued to play a passive role by accommodating the financing needs of the state enterprises and the government. Since the late 1980s, however, financial sector reforms have begun to assume a more prominent role in Eastern Europe and the U.S.S.R.[25]

In recent years, all countries in the region have introduced a two-tier banking system by reorganizing the commercial functions of their central banks into separate entities as a first step toward the creation of a competitive commercial banking sector. They have also removed most restrictions limiting the regional proliferation of branch networks, the range of activities that individual banks can perform, and the enterprises' choice of bank services. However, in most countries, competition among banks is hampered by a continuing high degree of specialization along regional or industry lines, and by the effective segmentation of household and enterprise related banking business. Moreover, newly established private banks, as for example the cooperative banks in the U.S.S.R., frequently play a minor role, and licensing of foreign banks has until recently remained restricted in most countries.[26]

While still lacking a fully fledged competitive banking system, most countries have taken steps to liberalize interest rates. In Poland, banks are now largely free to determine deposit and lending rates, and Yugoslavia has introduced market-determined rates. Bulgaria and Romania liberalized interest rates earlier this year. In Hungary, many interest rates have been free for some time and the remaining ceilings on deposit rates are expected to be removed this year. Interest rates in Czechoslovakia have also been liberalized but the government has been monitoring developments to protect depositors and borrowers in view of a highly monopolistic commercial banking system that was established only recently. A number of countries, notably Hungary and Poland, have also taken steps to reduce interest subsidies for special activities.

The lack of financial discipline in the state enterprises has left banks in all Eastern European countries and the U.S.S.R. with a legacy of large portfolios of non-performing assets, which is a major impediment to the development of efficient financial institutions.[27] Yugoslavia has begun to institute a program of bank liquidation and rehabilitation and is simultaneously beginning the restructuring of enterprises to avoid renewed accumulation of bad loans. Following an evaluation of banks' balance sheets, Hungary has begun to prepare a program that addresses deficiencies in the financial sector;

Czechoslovakia and Poland have begun to evaluate banks' balance sheets with a view to injecting, if necessary, new capital. Several countries have started to introduce or strengthen prudential regulations and banking supervision to prevent banks from extending new credit to avoid losses on nonperforming loans.

In most Eastern European countries and in the U.S.S.R., the range of financial instruments has essentially remained confined to bank deposits and loans as a result of restrictions previously placed on other types of instruments. Only Yugoslavia and Hungary have developed rudimentary markets for a limited range of short- and long-term securities. More recently, however, several other counties have begun to broaden the range of financial instruments. The government of Poland began to issue treasury bills in late 1989; Bulgaria issued treasury bonds in late 1990; and there is a small but growing market for securities in the U.S.S.R. Czechoslovakia has recently legalized the issuance and trading of bonds. As the privatization of state enterprises proceeds, securities markets are expected to play an increasingly important role.

Labor Market Deregulation and Social Safety Nets

A well-functioning labor market requires the freedom for employers and employees to make employment decisions within a clearly defined legal framework but without government interference. However, the move in past years toward greater enterprise autonomy in several Eastern European countries and the U.S.S.R. generally did not significantly reduce restrictions regarding hiring and firing.[28] In addition, inadequate housing and retraining facilities have severely hampered labor mobility. As a result of these distortions and the existence of soft budget constraints, labor hoarding has been widespread in all countries.

The recent tightening of enterprises' budget constraints in countries such as Poland, Hungary, and Czechoslovakia has required greater freedom for enterprises to dismiss employees. Unemployment in these and in other countries has begun to rise and is expected to increase substantially as the restructuring of the enterprise sector advances. All countries in Eastern Europe and the U.S.S.R. have recently begun to develop the essential elements of a social safety net, including basic systems of unemployment benefits. In most countries, these schemes are currently financed by budgetary transfers, which can give rise to a serious fiscal burden. However, Hungary has introduced an insurance scheme based in part on contributions by employers and employees, and Bulgaria has increased social security contributions by employers to an extra-budgetary fund. Poland has established a fund for unemployment benefits and retraining, which is financed by employers' contributions and budgetary transfers.

Most countries have abandoned detailed intervention in the process of wage determination and have accepted the principle of wage bargaining. However, there is a broad consensus that an incomes policy is essential to avoid an inflationary wage-price spiral at the initial stage of the transition process when macroeconomic imbalances still prevail and prices are being liberalized. Poland, Hungary, Czechoslovakia, and, more recently, Romania have adopted tax-based incomes policies and imposed a punitive tax on excessive wage increases, while Bulgaria plans to place direct limits on enterprises' wage bills.

SYSTEMIC REFORMS IN EXTERNAL SECTOR

Key Issues

The anticipated benefits of broader participation in the world economy have prompted the Eastern European countries to make external sector liberalization one of the key elements of their transformation to market-based economies.[29] External sector liberalization involves the phasing out of quantitative restrictions and the reduction of implicit or explicit taxes and subsidies on international transactions. This requires steps toward currency convertibility, that is, the removal of restrictions on the use of domestic currency for international transactions, and trade liberalization, that is, the reduction or elimination of direct barriers to international trade.

In several Eastern European countries, notably Yugoslavia, Hungary, and Poland, current efforts to liberalize the external sector were preceded by some

20 years of gradual economic reforms in which the transformation of the external trade and payments regime was generally more advanced than reforms in other areas of the economy. The reforms involved a gradual dismantling of the state monopoly of foreign trade, the unification of exchange rates, and the introduction of linkages between domestic and foreign prices of traded goods. In the late 1980s, several countries established foreign exchange retention schemes, which allowed exporters to keep a certain percentage of their foreign currency earnings, and introduced foreign exchange auctions. In addition, licensing requirements for certain classes of imported and exported goods were effectively removed.[30] However, because these measures were not accompanied by far-reaching domestic reforms, the countries could not fully benefit from the degree of external liberalization that was achieved.

While the current move toward currency convertibility and trade liberalization in the Eastern European countries is part of a comprehensive reform effort comprising all sectors of the economy, many of the reforms in the domestic economy that are necessary to realize the full benefits of external sector liberalization, notably those enhancing the responsiveness of domestic enterprises to market signals, are typically only beginning to take place. Nonetheless, all countries have begun to introduce external sector liberalization at an early stage of the reform process in order to reap the anticipated benefits of "importing" competition and a more rational structure of relative prices. Following the experience of the industrial countries, external sector liberalization has begun with the current account while restrictions on capital account transactions remain generally in place.[31] In the U.S.S.R., however, there has been only limited progress with the liberalization of the domestic economy and external sector liberalization is proceeding relatively slowly.[32]

Convertibility

By early 1991, all Eastern European countries with the exception of the U.S.S.R. had established the essential elements of currency convertibility. There are, however, significant differences in the practical implementation of external sector reforms, which are largely related to the specific economic situation and, in particular, the availability of foreign exchange. The differences include the degree of the unification of exchange rates, the restrictions on convertibility for the non-enterprise sector, the determination of exchange rates, and the scope of restrictions on profit remittances and capital account transactions.

Most countries have established a unified official exchange rate for commercial transactions, although some temporary restrictions remain in place.[33] In Hungary, Poland, and Yugoslavia, official exchange rates for trade with the convertible currency area were already largely unified in the 1980s, and various exchange subsidies, the level of which was dependent on the user of foreign exchange, were gradually eliminated.[34] In Bulgaria and Czechoslovakia, all exchange rates for commercial transactions were unified between December 1990 and February 1991. The U.S.S.R. maintains a fixed commercial rate that applies to a specified range of transactions and an auction-determined market rate. Romania still retains a dual exchange rate system in which an official rate, set by the central bank, applies to purchases of foreign exchange for imports of a limited number of goods (for example, energy) and for certain central government transactions.

There are considerable differences across countries in the way exchange rates are determined. Poland and Yugoslavia have pegged their exchange rates to a single foreign currency, while Czechoslovakia and Hungary have tied their currencies to a basket.[35] In Bulgaria and Romania, the (free) exchange rate will be determined by market forces. In early 1991, Bulgaria introduced a decentralized framework of foreign exchange allocation based on the interbank market where commercial banks are permitted to buy and sell foreign currencies at free market rates.[36] In Romania, a temporary system of foreign exchange retention accounts, which can be used freely for current account transactions and for sale in the interbank market, has been introduced in early 1991 and functions in parallel with an interbank foreign exchange market.[37] In the U.S.S.R., the existing auction system is likely to be broadened; in the interim the retention quotas for exporters will be raised.[38]

In the majority of countries convertibility is limited to the enterprise sector, and in most countries limits on travel allowances have been maintained. In

Poland, however, individuals may acquire foreign exchange in the parallel market at the going rate. In Czechoslovakia, Hungary, and Poland, residents are authorized to hold foreign currency accounts and to use them freely. In Yugoslavia, internal convertibility was achieved in January 1990, but various restrictions were reintroduced toward the end of the year. All countries allow foreign investment, but with the exception of Czechoslovakia and Hungary, they restrict the repatriation of profits. In Czechoslovakia, entities participating in foreign trade will be allowed both to receive and to extend trade-related credits; current laws allow for a liberal repatriation of capital and transfers of shares in the event of liquidation of the enterprise.

Trade Liberalization

All Eastern European countries have effectively eliminated the state monopoly of foreign trade and have drastically reduced import restrictions, although various degrees of tariff protection are still in place. In some countries, such as Hungary and Yugoslavia, up to 90 percent of imports are free from quantitative restrictions.[39] In Poland, most nontariff restrictions were removed in 1990, and in Bulgaria import licensing requirements were practically eliminated in February 1991. As a means of mitigating the impact of rapid liberalization on the domestic industry, tariff protection is still given to some categories of goods in Poland, and a temporary import tax was introduced in Bulgaria and Czechoslovakia.[40] In January 1991, Romania eliminated various discriminatory features in its tariff code, such as the dependence of tariff rates on the end-users, and cut the highest tariff rates. A new tariff structure will be introduced in mid-1991, with a limited number of tariff rates ranging from 10 to 30 percent, depending on the type of product and the stage of processing. In the U.S.S.R., according to the Presidential Guidelines, the external sector reform will emulate measures introduced in Hungary and Poland during the 1980s. The guidelines envisage a further reduction of state involvement in foreign trade and the introduction of a new tariff schedule.

Important measures were also introduced to liberalize exports. Export subsidies have been largely removed and export licensing has been significantly reduced in the majority of countries. In Poland, all export quotas except those imposed as a result of agreements with third countries were removed by October 1990. In Bulgaria and Czechoslovakia, export restrictions and licensing remain in place for foodstuffs and raw materials to prevent production disruptions during the adjustment process. However, the existing export premium scheme was abolished. Romania will maintain export licensing only with regard to products that are subject to domestic price controls or those that are imported at the official exchange rate.

Changes in Regional Payments Arrangements

External sector liberalization in Eastern Europe and the U.S.S.R. has been facilitated by recent changes in bilateral payments arrangements. In January 1990, at the meeting of the CMEA in Sofia, the Eastern European countries and the U.S.S.R. agreed that starting from January 1, 1991, their mutual trade will be based on convertible currencies and world market prices. Existing arrangements were to remain in force until the end of 1990.

Notwithstanding the expected cost resulting from the reorientation of trade and significant changes in the terms of trade,[41] the Eastern European countries view the switch to convertible currency and world market prices as important elements of their external sector liberalization. In order to limit immediate trade disruptions, all countries have been negotiating agreements aimed at maintaining some minimum trade levels with the U.S.S.R. and other regional partners.[42] Trade relating to these agreements is expected to be balanced on a bilateral basis, but like all other trade among the CMEA countries, is to be conducted at world market prices and settled in convertible currencies. In some cases particularly in trade with the U.S.S.R., the agreements would include lists of commodities and manufactured goods to be exchanged for the agreed quantities of energy imports, although the scope of such barter arrangements is uncertain. Some agreements are expected to permit the use of accumulated trade surpluses to pay for future imports. Hungary, for example, has agreed with the U.S.S.R. that its accumulated trade surpluses denominated in transferable rubles will be converted into dollars and repaid over time. The shift to convertible currency settlements and unrestricted trade arrangements among the CMEA countries is expected to be completed by the end of 1991.

SUMMARY AND OUTLOOK

Since 1989, the Eastern European countries have begun to implement comprehensive reform programs that aim at transforming the formerly centrally planned economies into more efficient market-based systems. All countries have introduced sweeping price liberalizations and have taken significant steps toward currency convertibility and trade liberalization. There has also been considerable progress in the implementation of the legal and institutional reforms that are necessary to transform the enterprise sector and to create efficient financial institutions. All countries have liberalized the framework for private sector activity and have begun to prepare, or have enacted, legislation for the privatization of state enterprises. In some countries, notably in Hungary and in Poland, privatization is already under way. Nonetheless, it is recognized that the development of a competitive enterprise sector and the creation of efficient financial institutions will take time.

There is a broad consensus that these systemic reforms are unlikely to succeed if the macroeconomic imbalances, which most countries had inherited as a result of the policies pursued in recent years, are allowed to persist. In addition, the dissolution of existing trade arrangements in the CMEA has resulted in a sharp contraction of intra-regional trade and significant terms of trade losses for the Eastern European countries. In response to these domestic and external conditions, all Eastern European countries have taken steps to tighten financial policies in order to contain inflation and limit external imbalances.

By contrast, the U.S.S.R. has to date made relatively little progress with macroeconomic stabilization and systemic reforms. The Presidential Guidelines approved by the Supreme Soviet in October 1990, while endorsing in principle the transition to a market economy, signal a relatively gradual approach to systemic reforms, particularly in the area of price liberalization.

The structural transformation of the Eastern European countries requires substantial external support in the form of technical assistance and financing. The Fund, in cooperation with other international institutions, has assumed a major role in providing technical assistance, in financing, and in helping mobilize additional financial resources. In addition, the World Bank, the European Community, and other members of the Group of 24, as well as the European Investment Bank and the European Bank for Reconstruction and Development, are committed to provide substantial support. However, while external support can greatly facilitate the reform process in the Eastern European countries, the key to a successful transition to a market economy remains a sustained effort of systemic reform and macroeconomic stabilization.

ENDNOTES

1 Eastern Europe is defined to include Bulgaria, Czechoslovakia, Hungary, Poland, Romania, and Yugoslavia.

2 After a large initial devaluation, the Polish zloty was pegged to the U.S. dollar, the Yugoslav dinar was pegged to the German mark. The incomes policy in Poland was based on high and progressive taxation of excessive increases in enterprises' wage bills, while in Yugoslavia nominal wages and the prices of key industrial goods, transportation, housing, and public utilities were frozen for six months.

3 In Yugoslavia, efforts to bring wages, credit, and the fiscal situation under control were complicated by deteriorating relations between the federal government and the republics.

4 See *The Economy of the USSR.*, a study undertaken in response to a request by a Houston Summit. "Summary and Recommendations," International Monetary Fund, International Bank of Reconstruction and Development, Organisation for Economic Cooperation and Development, and European Bank for Reconstruction and Development, December 1990.

5 Owing to shortfalls in oil shipments from the U.S.S.R., most Eastern European countries already werre forced to import significantly larger amounts of oil at world market prices in 1990.

6 These instruments are, however, only at an early stage of development, and most countries continue to use direct credit ceilings or moral suasion to keep monetary conditions appropriately tight.

7 In Poland, the ratio of subsidies to GDP was halved in 1990 and is expected to decline further this year. In Czechoslovakia, budgetary subsidies are to decline by 7 percentage points of GDP in 1991, after a decline by 4 perentage points in 1990. In Bulgaria, subsidies are targeted to decline by more than 10 percentage points of GDP this year.

8 Bulgaria, Czechoslovakia, Poland, and Romania are planning to complete over the next several years a far-reaching reorganization of their tax systems, including the introduciton of a general value added tax, a unified personal income tax, and a

reform of the enterprise profit tax. Hungary implemented a similar tax reform in 1988-89.

9 The increase in the average annual rate of inflation in 1990 reflected mainly price adjustments in Poland following the liberation of prices in January 1990.

10 It should be noted that in the presence of widespread price controls and shortages, developments in real wages do not adequately reflect changes in purchasing power. Moreover, measured real wages to not include income from secondary employment in the private sector which is increasing rapidly in most Eastern European countries.

11 Because of price and exchange rate distortions, the nonconvertible currency data included in the aggregate current account figures may not accurately reflect actual developments. See also footnote 4 to Table 6.

12 These projections do not include the impact of the recently agreed debt restructuring package for Poland.

13 Even in Hungary where restrictions on private sector activity were less severe than in most other Eastern European countries, state enterprises accounted for over 90 percent of industrial output in 1988. See Paul G. Hare, "Reform of Engerprise Regulation in Hungary—from 'Tutelage' to Market." *European Economy*, No. 43, March 1990, p. 40. In the services and agricultural sectors, however, private economic activity already played a significant role in several Eastern European countries prior the introduction of recent reforms. In Poland, for example, farming land was predominantly privately owned.

14 The legislation also defines the ownership rights of the different levels of government. In the past, the lack of clearly defined ownershiip rights in Poland and Hungary gave rise to spontaneous privatizations that were initiated by enterprise managers largely to their own benefit. Clarification of ownership rights is also a key issue in Yugoslavia where most enterprises are socially owned.

15 See, for example, David Newbery, "Tax Reform, Trade Liberalization, and Industrial Restructuring in Hungary." *European Economy*, No. 43, March 1990, pp. 67-106.

16 It has been argued that existing administrations and enterprise managers lack the expertise and probably also the incentives to carry out the required restructuring. See Olivier Blanchard and others. "Reform in Eastern Europe and the Soviet Union." unpublished, November 1990.

17 Distribution schemes combined with the establishment of intermediaries such as mutual funds or holding companies have been proposed to overcome monitoring problems. See, for example, Olivier Blanchard and others (1990); and Roman Frydman and Andrzej Rapaczynski. "Markets and Institutions in Large-Scale Privatizations." unpublished manuscript presented at the World Bank Conferenced on "Adjustment and Growth: Lessons for Eastern Europe" (Poland: October 1990).

18 However, the transfer of income-producing assets to the private sector results in a loss of revenue for the government which must be compensated by new taxes. For a discussion of this point, see Guillermo A. Calvo and Jacob A. Frenkel, "From Centrally Planned to Market Economies. The Road from CPE to PCPE." IMF Working Paper 91/17 (Washington: International Monetary Fund, 1991).

19 In Poland, Romania, and Yugoslavia a certain percentage of shares can be bought by employees at a discount. In Yugoslavia, part of wage increases have been paid in shares.

20 Hungary plans to privatize 35 to 40 percent of business assets by 1993.

21 Hungary and Poland introduced bankruptcy laws in the mid-1980s, but these laws were rarely invoked.

22 See, for example, the Presidential Guidelines adopted by the Supreme Soviet of the U.S.S.R. in October 1990.

23 In order to limit excessive price increases that might result from lack of competition, Bulgaria, Czechoslovakia, Poland, and Romania have introduced regulations that permit government intervention in cases of monopolistic price setting.

24 In Yugoslavia, most prices were liberalized in 1988, after a long period of "on-off" price controls.

25 Guillermo A. Calvo and Jacob A. Frenkel (1991) discuss the importance of an early development of domestic financial markets.

26 Bulgaria has recently licensed the first foreign bank, and Romania has allowed licensing; Poland has permitted the establishment of new banks with majority foreign participation. There are plans to facilitate foreign participation in Czechoslovakia. In Hungary, foreign banks or joint ventures have operated for several years providing banking services to enterprises, more recently licensing of foreign banks has been extended to retail banking business for the household sector.

27 See Lawrence Brainard, "Strategies for Economic Transformation in Eastern Europe. The role of financial market reform," in *Finance and the International Economy:* IV, ed. by Richard O'Brien and Sara Hewin (Oxford University Press: 1991).

28 In Hungary, enterprise managers had greater freedom in employment decisions but were constrained by relatively restrictive labor laws.

29 Developing countries that pursued external sector liberalization and outward-oriented development policies have enjoyed higher rates of economic growth and employment, lower incremental capital-output ratios, and better export performance, and have demonstrated better ability to adjust to external shocks. For a review of the findings on this point, see, for example, Sebastian Edwards, "Openness, Outward Orientation, Trade Liberalization and Economic Performance in Developing Countries." PPR Working Paper No. 191, International Economics Department, World Bank, Washington, D.C., June 1989.

30 For further discussion of external sector liberalization in Eastern Europe, see Thomas Wolf, "Market-Oriented Reform of Foreign Trade in Planned Economies," in *Market Forces in Planned Economies*, ed. by O. Bogomolov (London: Macmillan, 1990), pp. 199-216.

31 The order of current and capital acocunt liberalization is usually justified on the basis of differences in the adjustment speed in goods and asset markets. See, for example, Jacob Frenkel, "Remarks on the Southern Cone: Discussion." IMF *Staff Papers*, 30 (March 1983). pp. 164-73. Note, however, that since the early 1980s in the industrial countries capital account liberalization has outpaced the liberalization of current account transactions.

32 See *The Economy of the USSR.* (1990).

33 Restrictions apply largely to trade with other former CMEA

partners and the availability of foreign exchange to households, both of which are reviewed below.

34 The bulk of trade was transacted at official commercial rates, but the enterprises could also acquire foreign exchange at specially held auctions or via the foreign exchange retention accounts.

35 On December 18, 1989, Yugoslavia pegged the exchange rate of the new dinar to the deutsche mark at 7 dinars per DM, and Poland pegged the zloty to the U.S. dollar on January 1, 1990, at a rate of 9,500 zloty per U.S. dollar.

36 In effect, the existing informal market was allowed to function without restrictions, on the condition that all transactions are channeled through the banking system.

37 The retention quota amounts to over 50 percent of export earnings.

38 Most countries require enterprises either to surrender a certain percentage of foreign exchange or to repatriate foreign exchange receipts within one month of export delivery.

39 Hungary and Yugoslavia exemplify the rapid pace of recent import liberalization in Eastern Europe. the share of liberalized imports in Yugoslavia increased from 15 percent in 1986 to 90 percent in 1989. In Hungary, the import liberalizaion program has resulted in the freeing of 90 percent of imports over a three-year period.

40 The average import tax amounts to 15 percent in Bulgaria, and to 20 percent for consumer goods imports in Czechoslovakia.

41 The macroeconomic impact of these changes was discussed above.

42 So far, only a few countries have concluded preliminary agreements.

READING 21

Soviet Economic Reform: The Longest Road

William D. Nordhaus

The struggle of the command economies to rediscover the market brings to mind the Hungarian joke: "Question: what is communism? Answer: the longest road from capitalism to capitalism." Having spent up to seven decades systematically attempting to eradicate market forces, the Soviet Union and the other socialist countries of Eastern Europe have reversed field in an attempt to revive "the market." The effort reveals much about both systems.

My paper is divided into three general areas. I begin with an overview of the aggregate performance in the socialist countries, particularly the Soviet Union, and compare their performance with that of Western countries. Next I discuss the goals and roadblocks on the road to reform, reform plans for the Soviet Union, and the macroeconomic issues facing socialist countries. I conclude with an assessment of the prospects for reform in the Soviet Union.

BACKGROUND: STAGNATION AND DISILLUSIONMENT

After decades of rapid growth in output and living standards, the socialist countries began a marked slowdown in economic growth around 1970. Table 1 shows Angus Maddison's estimates of the growth in output and in output per capita in the United States and in the Soviet Union over this century. Soviet growth has been respectable, but was particularly so in the early stages. Table 2 presents estimates, using data prepared by the U.S. Central Intelligence Agency, on total factor productivity in the Soviet Union since 1961. The data suggest that output growth in the Soviet Union has derived primarily from forced-draft increases in inputs; total factor productivity has shown only modest growth or, in recent years, a decline.

Why did growth slow so dramatically? Analysts suggest numerous causes: a decrease in the growth of inputs (depletion of low-cost resources such as oil, aging of the capital stock, and deterioration of labor discipline); lowered technological change and efficiency (because of numerous planning errors and diversion of R&D activities to the military); exogenous economic shocks (poor weather and declining prices of exported raw materials); and greater complexity of economic activity (with more products and greater technical complexity).[1]

Numerous analysts, including some Soviet economists, suggest that despite efforts to correct misleading Soviet statistics, Western estimates have overstated Soviet economic growth. Many indications of poor and even deteriorating quality in Soviet industries (both in terms of the products themselves and in the quality of service) suggest that exaggerated claims of quality improvement bias Soviet price statistics downward and lead to overstated output and hence target attainment.[2]

The declining growth in Soviet output is reinforced by the low share of consumption in GNP and a rising defense and investment burden. The CIA estimates that defense and investment currently absorb around 40 percent of Soviet GNP, up from roughly 34 percent in 1960. By contrast, investment and defense absorb some 25 percent GNP in the United States. The low Soviet consumption share implies that the per capita GNP figures overstate the level of economic welfare of the population.

Table 1. Average Annual Growth of Output and Productivity, Soviet Union and United States, 1900–87, Various Periods
Percent

	Gross domestic product		GDP per capita	
Period	United States	Soviet Union	United States	Soviet Union
1900–13	4.0	3.5	1.9	1.5
1913–50	2.8	2.7	1.2	2.3
1950–73	3.7	5.0	1.4	3.6
1973–87	2.5	2.1	1.0	1.2
1900–87	3.2	3.3	1.8	2.3

Source: Authors' calculations based on Maddison (1989, pp. 113, 128).

Table 2. Average Annual Growth of Output, Inputs, and Productivity, Soviet Union, 1961–85, Various Periods
Percent

			Inputs	
Period	Gross national product	Total factor productivity	Capital	Labor
1961–70	5.0	0.6	8.1	1.8
1971–80	2.7	−1.3	7.5	1.5
1981–85	1.9	−1.0	6.2	0.7

Source: Kurtzweg (1987, pp. 126–55).

In this area, as in assessments of military power, much confusion has been generated by Western estimates that inflate the quality and quantity of Soviet production. According to CIA estimates, the per capita output of the Soviet Union is equal to that of Spain and well above that of Greece. Alternative estimates of per capita output, as calculated by different agencies and by using different measurement concepts, are shown in table 3. Even the relatively low estimates by the International Comparison Project (ICP) may give too optimistic an impression of living standards. It would be necessary to make further corrections—adjusting for the large share of output devoted to nonconsumption purposes in defense and investment, for the low quality and lack of availability of goods, and for the frightening deterioration of environmental quality and public health—to obtain an accurate assessment of living standards in socialist countries.

Yet another way to measure living standards—calculating incomes at black market exchange rates—gives a Soviet per capita income of roughly $225, surely a lower bound on real incomes. With an overvalued exchange rate and exchange controls, the *black market* rate reflects the incremental value of imported goods, services, or safe foreign assets to the desperate buyer; it will therefore place an extremely high value on foreign currency. In addition, this rate will tend to underestimate real incomes because of the omission of nontradable goods. Still, while understating per capita income, this figure shows dramatically the uncertainty about the level of Soviet real income and the extent to which common estimates may overstate real incomes in socialist countries.

Perhaps the most striking comparison is the performance of East and West Germany. At the end of World War II, the two Germanys had roughly equal levels of productivity and similar industrial structures.[3] After four decades of capitalism in the West and socialism in the East, productivity in East Germany had fallen to a level estimated between one-third and one-half of that in West Germany. Yet CIA estimates produce the absurd conclusion that the per capita GNP of East Germany is more than 80 percent that of West Germany as estimated by the ICP (see table 3).

Of course, individuals living in socialist countries are unlikely to be persuaded by even the finest Divisia indexes. The simple unavailability of many goods is sufficient to convince consumers of the relative attractiveness of the different systems.

Table 3. Alternative Estimates of Per Capita GNP, Various Countries, 1987
U.S. dollars

Country	Measured by purchasing-power parity: International Comparison Project	Measured by purchasing-power parity: Central Intelligence Agency	Measured by exchange rates: Official	Measured by exchange rates: Market
United States	18,550	n.a.[a]	. . .[b]	18,530
West Germany	13,680	n.a.[a]	. . .[b]	14,400
United Kingdom	12,250	n.a.[a]	. . .[b]	10,420
Spain	8,520	n.a.[a]	. . .[b]	6,010
Greece	6,580	n.a.[a]	. . .[b]	4,020
Soviet Union[a]	6,930	8,380	4,800	225
Hungary	5,780	7,910	2,240	n.a.
Poland	4,540	6,930	1,930	n.a.
East Germany	9,660	11,300	n.a.	n.a.

Sources: Numbers in the first column are estimates of purchasing-power parity (PPP) levels of per capita GNP based upon the International Comparison Project (ICP) estimates. For countries other than the Soviet Union and East Germany, the source is World Bank (1989, table 30, p. 233). For the Soviet Union and East Germany, estimates are rough projections from Summers and Heston (1988). Data on 1985 PPP relatives are applied to 1987 U.S. per capita GNP. Numbers in the second column are from Central Intelligence Agency (1988). Numbers in the third column are from World Bank (1989, table 1, p. 165) except for the Soviet Union, which applies official exchange rate for commercial transactions to CIA estimates of ruble-value GNP. Numbers from the fourth column are from World Bank (1989, table 1), except for the Soviet Union, which applies current black market rate of 13.5 rubles to the dollar.

n.a. Not available.

a. CIA does not provide independent estimates for these countries.

b. These currencies are convertible at market rates and do not have separate official rates.

This point was forcefully put in the comment of the flamboyant president of the Russian republic, Boris Yeltsin, on his voyage to America:

> There were...shattering experiences of another sort—the supermarkets, for example. When I saw those shelves crammed with hundreds, thousands of cans, cartons and goods of every possible sort, for the first time I felt quite frankly sick with despair for the Soviet people. That such a potentially superrich country as our has been brought to a state of such poverty![4]

THE REFORM AGENDA IN SOCIALIST COUNTRIES

Virtually all reform movements in the Soviet Union and Eastern Europe have endorsed a market economy as the ultimate goal of economic reforms. The "Abalkin report," the most comprehensive published analysis of the plans of Soviet economic reformers, states:

> The main features of the model of a new economic system [are] ...the use of the market as the main form of coordinating the activities of the participants in production. We have become convinced on the basis of our own experience that there is no worthy alternative to the market mechanism as the method of coordinating the activities and interests of the economic subjects.[5]

Actual reform plans, however, reveal a less than whole-hearted adoption of a market economy. In already-reformed countries like Poland or Hungary, the vast bulk of economic activity is still produced in state-owned firms, and housing prices are closer to zero than to market levels. *Radical Reform* explicitly advocates continued primary state ownership of energy, defense, transportation, and communications, an unspoken presumption is that the state will continue to own and operate normal government services, education, and health, and may control housing prices for many years.[6] A rough guess is that these sectors would comprise only half of GNP in today's Soviet economy.

In addition, popular discussion in the Soviet Union reveals both egregious misconceptions and deep reservations about the consequences of living in a market economy. Hostility toward entrepreneurial activity is profound, and "speculation" is a four-letter word. In her insightful "Letter from Europe," Jane Kramer writes, "The mystique of the market has nothing to do with a marketplace. When Russians talk about the market, they are talking about everything from a new Communism to whatever government of the left or right they happen to admire."[7] Hearing an oxymoron like "free-market Communism" makes one suspect that the market under discussion is closer to the Hegel of political theorists than to the haggle of the Fulton Fish Market.

A final puzzle concerns the scant attention in the reform debates to the implications of a market economy for the distribution of income. Many Westerners are offended by the excesses of income, wealth, and power generated by market rewards. They wonder about a society in which newly minted lawyers get paid more than their professors, in which the rich paint their names on their personal airlines or trade ball players like baseball cards, and in which a financier pays a $600 million fine for the investment banker's equivalent of a speeding ticket and has plenty left over. It was just such excesses that led Arthur Okun to give, "Two cheers for the market, but not three."

The vanities of capitalism, however, are the price of a market economy—where wages and prices reflect how well products sell rather than how much some elite thinks they are really worth. Prices and incomes in the market are determined by dollar votes in the marketplace, not ballot votes in elections or bullet votes at the barricades. Have the socialist reformers absorbed the reality of the income distribution in markets in their doctrines?

Roadblocks on the Route to the Market

To reach the ultimate goal of a market economy, the socialist countries must overcome numerous obstacles that prevent the emergence of market forces. For the Soviet Union, the hurdles are daunting. It is as if, having spent seven decades pouring herbicide on every growing thing in the backyard, they suddenly decide to cultivate a garden. Among the chief difficulties that the Soviet Union faces are the following.

Price Reform and Free Market Pricing.

Prices of both inputs and outputs are often far from market-determined levels. Perhaps the most thorough study of relative prices in socialist and market economies was made in the international comparison study of incomes, which included Poland but not the Soviet Union. The study found coffee selling in Poland at 9.1 times the U.S. price, personal automobiles at 5.1 times the U.S. price. At the other extreme rent was 45 percent of U.S. rents for equivalent dwellings, and dentist services were 7 percent of U.S. levels.[8] Anecdotal reports today indicate that apartments in major cities rent for as little as 2 percent to 3 percent of income (perhaps $1 or $2 a month).

Sooner or later, if prices are to be market-determined, relative prices must be allowed to move to the appropriate levels. One of the important vehicles for introducing realistic prices is to open the economy to international trade. In addition, free markets would involve dramatic changes in the functioning of capital and labor markets; unprofitable firms must be forced to close or allowed to lay off workers or threaten unproductive workers with unemployment.[9]

One measure of the sparseness of markets in the Soviet economy is the number of prices. According to Nikolay P. Shmelev, there are, in the Soviet Union, 25 million distinct prices—upon reflection, an absurdly small number for a modern economy. For example, there are at any time in the United States some 25 million trucking tariffs, as well as some 50 million airline prices (some may wonder whether this is overdoing it a bit).[10] George Stigler and James Kindahl report that one can get price quotations on 135 million varieties of hot rolled carbon steel sheets.[11] A rough guess would be that the number of products on which one can get price quotations at any time in the United States must be in the tens of billions.

Although somewhat artificial, this price count reveals an important defect of a command economy: the price system does not operate in many sectors of the economy. Because most capital assets are owned by the state, markets for land, capital goods, and risk-bearing are virtually nonexistent. Socialist ideology has prevented the development of thick markets in financial capital or in housing. Households have as sparse a menu of financial assets as of foodstuffs. There is relatively little differentiation in labor remuneration for different labor skills. In short, Soviet prices are doing neither the gross tuning nor the fine tuning that they do in an advanced market economy.

Hard Budget Constraints.

Soviet enterprises operate with "soft budget constraints," a term signifying that operating losses lead to more bank credits rather than to bankruptcies. In planned economies that have turned to price instead of quantity rationing, such as Hungary, firms engage in endless haggling with the central authorities about taxes or credit conditions.[12] Of course, the United States is no stranger to the peril of soft budget constraints; its taxpayers will be paying hundreds of billions in extra taxes over the next few years because of the lack of budget discipline in the federal deposit insurance system.

Stabilization.

Some of the socialist economies have growing problems of large budget deficits and repressed inflation. Developing a full market economy will require achieving fiscal balance, a topic addressed in the next section. It is likely that stabilization will require budget reforms, such as the substitution of income-tested transfer payments for heavily subsidized food and housing prices. Imposing hard budget constraints on Soviet enterprises will also involve reforming the free granting of credits or subsidies to unprofitable enterprises.

Privatization of Individual Sectors.

In the United States and other market economies, output is primarily produced in private firms. Despite the alarums about the growth of the public sector in the United States, only 3 percent of U.S. GNP is produced in the federal sector and 10 percent in all levels of government and government enterprises. In socialist countries, the analogous figure is probably between 80 percent and 90 percent. Even today, after the market reforms introduced in Poland at the beginning of 1990, somewhere around 80 percent of Polish GNP is produced in government enterprises.[13] At some point, in a gradual or abrupt way, the actual decisions about buying, selling, pricing, producing, borrowing, and lending must be made on a decentralized basis by private agents.

Competition.

One underrated element in economic reform is introducing competition into markets. Centrally planned economies have pursued Engels' view that socialism is "one giant factory." Monopoly is pervasive. This industrial structure must be replaced with one with workable competition—say, three or more independent firms and exposure to international competition.

Institutions of the Market.

Above all, the Soviet economy lacks the institutions and infrastructure that are required to operate a market economy. These include accountants and accounting standards, lawyers and contract laws, market research and sales people, banking regulations and bankers, a list emphasizing that the written rules—the decrees that proliferate in socialist economies—may be much less important than the human capital embodied in experienced people who understand and operate the institutions of the market. Property rights must be completely redefined.

In addition, people will have to adopt the attitudes of the market. As Professor Yevgeniy Yasin puts it:

> The market is a social institution that requires certain rules of conduct from people. "Economic man"—with his inherent rational conduct, strongly motivated by considerations of personal profit, calculating, driven by the spirit of enterprise, ready to take risks and assume personal responsibility for his actions—should be given public recognition.
>
> The model that is currently prevalent in the Soviet Union is of "administrative man," to use H. Simon's term. He is typically used to submission and giving orders, to living in a structure of prevailing vertical links. In his subordinate role, he is likely to show pro forma obedience, turning to actions without rules. Lower strata of the hierarchy expect the upper strata to protect them in most relations with the outside world and recognize social paternalism as the norm.[14]

Table 4 provides a summary list of the obstacles on the road to a fully developed market economy. The list is long, and introducing any one measure will encounter formidable institutional and political obstacles. Moreover, a simple catalogue does not capture the interconnection of the different obstacles. For example, hard budget constraints are a prerequisite to allowing realistic cost calculations for free-market pricing, to bank reform, to reducing the government deficit, to reducing enterprise subsidies in the budget reform, to efficient private decision-

Table 4. Roadblocks to Economic Reform

1. **Price reform and free-market pricing**
   Eliminate central allocation and rationing
   Raise prices on necessities
   Free competitive sectors
   Privatize and regulate natural monopolies
2. **International**
   Remove quantitative restrictions and substitute tariffs
   Align different exchange rates
   Allow foreign investment
   Convertibility of currency
3. **Capital market changes**
   Free interest rates
   Commercial (retail) banking separated from central bank
   Control money supply
4. **Labor markets**
   Free firms to lay off workers
   Unemployment insurance and welfare reforms
   Housing reforms for mobility
5. **Hard budget constraints**
   Reform accounting
   Profit constraints
   Credit constraints
   End tax and regulatory haggling
6. **Stabilization**
   Reduce budget deficit
   Raise interest rates
   Anti-inflation policies (tax-based incomes policies, foreign competition)
7. **Budget reform**
   Remove redistributional pricing and substitute income-tested transfers
   Remove subsidies to failing firms
8. **Decentralize economic decisions**
   Allow private property
   Separate firms from government
   Privatize firms and production
9. **Competition**
   Break up monopolistic state firms
   Antitrust laws and regulation
   Entry of foreign firms
   Encourage small enterprises
10. **Institutions of the market**
    Contract and bankruptcy law
    Train managers
    Nurture homo economicus
    Change anti-market sentiments

making, and to nurturing homo economicus and the spirit of enterprise.

Sequencing the Transition: the Three Approaches

There is little disagreement among reformers about the need to move quickly to a market economy. The critical question is the sequencing and speed of the transition. Socialist economics have so many problems, and they are so interconnected, that reformers are unsure where to begin. Should they start with the budget, with privatization, with property reforms, with capital markets, with reducing subsidies, with freeing the ruble, or what? Should reform begin with budget reform so as to prevent a price-wage-price spiral when prices are decontrolled? Or should price inflation and wage controls be used to reduce real aggregate demand? Should there be a first step to get prices close to the market before letting prices go? Or is it hopeless to try to guess the "right" market price? Should prices be decontrolled now, so that incentives to production are enhanced? Or should the monopolies be broken up first to prevent the exercise of monopoly power? Should governments avoid political peril by postponing an increase in the prices of necessities (housing, food, and energy)? If so, will the resulting queues and inefficiencies restrict labor mobility, impede adjustments, and reduce incentives to work and bear risk? This list could be multiplied indefinitely.

The reform debate is currently divided into three camps: the radical (sometimes called the "big bang") approach, which would introduce the market reforms simultaneously; the step-by-step approach, which would phase in reforms gradually; and the conservative approach, which advocates moving cautiously if at all toward a market.

Big Bang Approach.

The approach currently being tested in Poland is the simultaneous introduction of numerous pro-market measures. The Polish authorities are removing barriers to entry and exit in most markets, decontrolling many prices, liberalizing foreign trade, reducing subsidies, and stabilizing the economy. The example most often pointed to as a historical precedent is the 1948 monetary reform in West Germany.[15] It should be emphasized, however, that virtually no privatization or demonopolization has yet occurred in Poland, and some observers believe that this may be responsible for part of the steep price increases in early 1990.

Staged Approach.

The approach currently favored by economic reformers in the Soviet Union is the step-by-step or gradual introduction of economic reforms. The Abalkin plan described in *Radical Reform* espouses this approach, which envisages three stages over six to ten years. The first stage is to create the legal framework (law on property, law on bankruptcy, and so forth) in which markets can grow. A second stage would take a number of substantive reforms (reduce the budget deficit, reform prices, close unprofitable enterprises, and reform credit). The third stage would allow a significant amount of market determination of prices and introduce foreign competition and partial ruble convertibility.

Conservative Approach.

In late 1989, different approaches to reform were debated in the U.S.S.R. Council of Ministers. The Abalkin plan was criticized, and a substitute introduced by Prime Minister Nikolay Ryzhkov was adopted. The conservative plan had three elements: stabilize the economy by balancing the state budget, retighten central controls in wage and price determination, and reallocate resources from defense and investment to consumer goods.[16] It is noteworthy that the most painful and politically sensitive step—price reform—has been repeatedly postponed during *perestroika*. The price of bread is scheduled to increase in July 1990, and some other goods may see price increases in January 1991, but a thorough price reform is still a distant goal.

In the spring of 1990, after Gorbachev was elevated to his position as president with strong executive powers, there was a great deal of speculation about whether he would use his powers to introduce a big bang, or at least to move quickly with the first phase of the step-by-step reform advocated by his close advisers. While it is difficult to read the tea leaves, it appears that the big bang approach has been rejected and that the first steps of reform will be introduced in the summer of 1990. It seems likely that the steps will take the form of continued property reforms and liberalization of the rules of enterprise.

The most treacherous steps involve "price reform," which is the euphemism for raising consumer prices. Given the periods of speculative hoarding, it would clearly be foolish to announce a major price reform far in advance. On the other hand, imposing reforms without popular support invites strikes, dissension, and loss of confidence in the government.

Reflections on the Three Strategies

In weighing the relative attractiveness of the three approaches, the experience of economic reforms in other countries can usefully be applied.[17] To begin with, it is clear that if by a big bang we mean moving immediately to a genuine market economy, this is simply impossible. As table 4 shows, the steps necessary to create a genuine market economy require a great deal of fundamental restructuring, some of which (such as development of capital markets, education, fostering the spirit of enterprise, and full privatization of state enterprises) will require years or decades to accomplish.

What is usually meant by a big bang is in fact a simultaneous partial liberalization (such as occurred in Poland). This would involve freeing prices in a substantial part of the economy (most of the tradable sector along with small enterprises) while opening the economy to foreign trade. Such an approach would seem feasible where a country is relatively small and open, where the public is hostile to a socialism imposed by a foreign power, and where there is some experience or at least memory of markets. These criteria would apply in most of the countries of Eastern Europe, particularly Poland,

East Germany, Hungary, and Czechoslovakia. Obviously, a big bang could be used for isolated sectors within a largely capitalist economy (as in lifting government regulation of the airlines in the United States or in privatizing nationalized enterprises in Japan and the United Kingdom).

But is the big bang appropriate for the Soviet Union? However appealing this approach is to frustrated reformers, I am skeptical about its acceptability or advisability for the Soviet Union as of mid-1990. The Soviet economy is large, closed, and extremely hierarchical. The obstacles to reform are higher and deeper in the Soviet Union than in other Eastern European countries. Unlike other socialist countries, the Soviet yen for the market is primarily confined to mathematical economists. While the system is barely creaking along today, it could be worse. The short-term gains from a big bang are limited, while the risks include the possibility of a complete breakdown of the economy, mass unemployment, political unrest, widespread economic distress, breakdowns in the distribution chain, hunger, or famine.

If the Soviet leaders choose instead a step-by-step approach, are there any lessons about the best sequence for reforms? With one exception, the sequence envisioned by the Abalkin plan discussed above seems on the whole a reasonable plan. The Abalkin plan begins by fostering the institutions of the market, then moves on to stabilize the economy and align relative prices, and finally to free markets. My only reservation about the plan is that it may place too little emphasis on macroeconomic stabilization efforts needed to reduce the queues and prevent serious macroeconomic imbalances. This important issue will be addressed in greater detail in the next section.

Although there are strong reasons for favoring the step-by-step approach as the only realistic path for the Soviet Union, one important danger must be acknowledged—that the transition will be phased in so slowly as effectively to stall reform. This is, indeed, a reasonable description of the progress of the Gorbachev reforms through May 1990; they have almost surely exacerbated the economic problems of the Soviet economy. It appears that the liberalization of the economy after 1985 allowed firms to raise wages above planned levels with the result that incomes outran production. As the shortages grew more severe, the government *recontrolled* prices and tightened central control; the extent of rationing is greater now than at any time since World War II.

A defender of the recontolled might cite Lenin's dictum that progress requires two steps forward and one step backward. Without great vigilance, this easily becomes two steps backward for every step forward—and thwarts reform altogether.

These reflections raise an intriguing possibility, a Murphy's Law of Reforms. This holds that reforming an internally consistent economic system makes things get worse before they get better. Any single reform (or perhaps any limited set of pro-market reforms) will aggravate the difficulties of a command economy. The reason is that socialist states have evolved a set of rules, incentives, and expectations designed to optimize economic performance within the confines of a command economy. Changing any rule, however sensible in the framework of a market economy, may lead to distortions that worsen performance in the partially reformed command economy.

In other words, within the framework of the command economy, planners, consumers, and enterprises adapt their behavior to optimize their objectives. For a given set of institutions, planners devise incentives that lead economic agents to perform relatively efficiently. If the planners are competent, they achieve a local optimum subject to the fundamental ideological and political constraints of socialism. Removing one or two of the constraints will defeat some of the rules that have produced the local socialist optimum.

A biological metaphor that captures the adaptive nature of economic systems comes to mind. No one doubts that a fish swims better than a dog. But dogs do swim in their own funny way. And replacing dog's legs with a fish tail, in a step-by-step reform of canine navigation, would quickly produce one sad pup.

ECONOMIC STABILIZATION

A central task of managing economic reform will be to maintain macroeconomic stability during the transition. On the whole, this is a new topic for socialist reformers. Until recently, socialist macroeconomics referred to economic planning and ensuring plan fulfillment. Unemployment was nonexistent in principle and, for the most part, in fact. Inflation of official prices was contained by leaving official prices fixed for long periods. When aggregate demand became excessive, these economies suffered "repressed inflation," a syndrome in which too-low prices result in high black market prices, long lines for goods, and forced saving. What Western economists call "macroeconomics," in the sense of the determinants of national income and output in the short run, is not yet a discipline among Soviet economists.

As socialist economies begin to liberalize their prices and allow enterprises to fire workers, the familiar symptoms of a market economy emerge. People lose their jobs, liberalized prices (in both the state and private sectors) begin to rise, and the populace complains about unemployment and inflation. At this point the Soviet Union will come up against the need for stabilization policy as the nation makes the transition to the market.[18]

The task of short-run macroeconomic policy is to ensure that the economy is in overall or aggregate balance. Using fiscal and monetary policies, policymakers aim for *internal balance*, which signifies that nominal aggregate demand is close to the potential output of the economy at the existing price level.[19] Internal balance involves both a *level* (or stock) and a *growth* (or flow) requirement. The level requirement is that desired spending in the economy (by households, enterprises, and the government) be close to the current-price value of output; the growth requirement is that total incomes and total spending grow at about the same rate as potential output. If desired spending in the economy greatly exceeds the current-price value of potential output, then the economy will tend toward repressed or open inflation.

By these criteria, the Soviet economy currently has many serious macroeconomic problems. To begin with, the government budget is seriously out of equilibrium, resulting in flow imbalance. The budget deficit has grown from 2 percent of GNP in the early 1980s to around 11 percent of GNP in 1989. There is also stock imbalance, with the government debt at around 44 percent of GNP and growing. In a market economy, such a large deficit and debt could be mopped up by borrowing; in the Soviet economy, however, the absence of marketable securities means that the deficit is effectively monetized. The large quasi-monetary imbalance is sometimes referred to as a "ruble overhang," which denotes a large accumulation of undesired holdings of money and other liquid assets by households and enterprises.

The easiest way to determine the size of the ruble overhang is to calculate the ratio of household liquid assets to household income. Based on fragmentary data, this ratio is estimated to have risen from around 0.6 in the 1970s (when there was little ruble overhang) to around 0.95 in 1989.[20] Applying the crude quantity theory suggests that prices would have to rise more than 50 percent to extinguish the overhang.[21] Unless neutralized, the ruble overhang will produce a sharp, one-time rise in prices when prices are decontrolled.

An understandable response to the peril of a large and growing ruble overhang—indeed a policy followed by the Soviet government since late 1989—is to clamp down tighter on prices. But that strategy works no better than tightening the lid on an overheated pot. It is not possible for centrally planned economies to avoid difficulties from excessive demand by controlling prices. In an economy with price controls—whether the Soviet Union in 1990 or the United States in 1944—the result of excess demand is shortages, long lines, and an increasingly inefficient distribution system. One result of the German decontrol of 1948 or of the Polish decontrol of 1990 is that goods magically appear in the shops. (The problem is that they are too expensive to buy.) The inefficiencies of repressed inflation are yet another reason why it is imperative for East European economies to get and retain control of their fiscal and monetary policies.

Figure 1 illustrates the impact of a growing ruble overhang. At an initial equilibrium, with aggregate demand of *AD* and aggregate supply of *AS*, prices are fixed below market-clearing levels. State firms are producing at point *a*, and the excess of desired spending over output is given by the segment *ac*. The actual outcome depends upon the rationing mechanism, but we can simplify by assuming that goods are rationed by queuing, that the length of the queue adjusts to balance supply and demand, and that the goods obtained by queuing are then resold at black market prices.[22] Under these assumptions, point *b* in figure 1 is the "true" price as measured either by the black market prices or by the shadow prices of output including costs of waiting, bribing, and using influence.

As the budget deficit increases the ruble

Figure 1. Impact of Ruble Overhang: Increase of Demand from Deficit

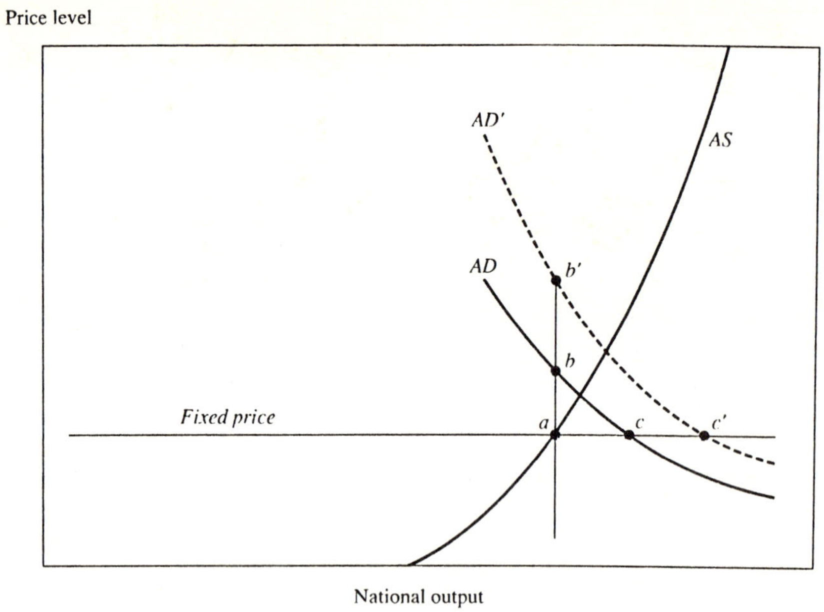

overhang, aggregate demand rises to *AD'*. Because prices are fixed, there is of course no official inflation. But the excess demand gets worse as the amount people wish to buy at the official price level increases while the supply is unchanged. The ex ante shortage—which is the difference between aggregate demand and supply at official prices—grows to *ac'*. The black market prices or shadow prices rise to *b'*.

What is the result? The shelves get barer and barer; lines get longer and longer; the stores have nothing to offer but rusty tins and rotten cauliflower; the street price of hard currency diverges even further from the official rate; the free prices in farmers' stalls rise sharply; consumers must spend more and more time foraging for goods; consumers buy goods they don't need as a desperate form of saving; people from high-shortage regions take long trips to the cities and other low-shortage regions, exacerbating regional tensions; those who have to sell goods at the high social shadow prices are vilified and accused of profiteering; economic planners are driven to ration basic goods - like soap, meat and sugar - in effect replacing he devalued ruble with a multitude of local and commodity-specific currencies in the form of rationing coupons. In essence, by an extension of Gesham's law, overvalued things (rubles) are driven out undervalued things (goods).

It is clear that, whatever the pace of reforms, the Soviet government must restore macroeconomic balance. One approach often discussed is to attack the problem by soaking up the ruble overhang. Some call for a "monetary reform," which in effect confiscates some of the ruble overhang by introducing a new currency at unfavorable rates to existing rubleholders. Another approach is to introduce a "parallel currency," perhaps one convertible into hard currencies. Yet a third approach, similar to that taken in Poland at the beginning of 1990, would be to let prices rise sharply so that the real value of the ruble holdings declines to the level desired by ruble owners.

In fact, these ideas will at best solve the stock, or level, problems and leave the flow, or growth, problem of a large budget deficit untouched. If the budget deficit continues at high levels, aggregate demand will grow rapidly, and the "inflationary gap" between desired spending at existing prices and real output will continue to widen, producing continued repressed or open inflation. A durable solution to the macroeconomic problem of excess demand will require a reduction in the budget deficit.

This point leads to an important linkage between macroeconomic and structural policies. Almost all observers of the Soviet economy believe that the structure of the budget is inefficient and undesirable. There are substantial subsidies to food and agriculture (amounting to 24 percent of the Soviet budget, or 12 percent of GNP) and to unprofitable enterprises (about 10 percent of the budget, or 5 percent of GNP). Defense probably absorbs 20 percent to 30 percent of the budget, although the exact size of the Soviet defense establishment at realistic prices is probably known by no one.[23] A promising approach to reform, therefore, is to restructure the budget to ensure macroeconomic stability, to align relative prices with social priorities, and to make room for growth in private consumption.

Some Soviet economists have recommended creating a two-level banking system to help limit money growth as a means of controlling inflation. Without doubt, creating a market-oriented banking system will be a vital part of a reformed Soviet economy. but it seems certain that there is today no way that monetary policy can operate to control spending independently of fiscal policy. There are virtually no retail banks, no credit market instruments, and no variable-price or variable-yield assets. The total value of equity-like "stocks" is around 0.02 percent of national income. Mortgages are unheard of. The chief household nonmonetary financial assets are savings accounts and lottery bonds, both of which are virtually perfect substitutes for money.

Because of the structure of financial markets, most of the government deficit is effectively monetized. Even with a broader menu of assets, it is difficult to identify components of spending that are interest sensitive. For example, without hard budget constraints, why would firms tighten their belts in response to interest or credit signals? For all these reasons, monetary policy is not an independent macroeconomic policy instrument at this time. In the near term, therefore, the task of controlling excessive aggregate demand will fall largely on fiscal policy.

In studying the performance of socialist economies, a Western macroeconomist cannot fail to notice the disastrous side effects of producers operating in a sellers' market. Until now, socialist enterprises have had no fear of depressions or idled capacity. The symptoms of high-pressure economies have been queues for any reasonably high-quality good, sellers' rationing, deterioration of product quality and variety, poor service, lack of labor discipline, and low rates of innovation.

The experience of Eastern Europe leads one to wonder whether Arthur Okun overestimated the advantages of a high-pressure economy in promoting many economic objectives when he wrote in 1973, "The greater diffusion of opportunity and of upward mobility in a full-utilization economy is a vital social benefit; and that benefit helps to explain why the pursuit of full employment is an integral part of a liberal's creed."[24]

The conventional worry about Okun's emphasis on a high-pressure economy has been the dangers of high inflation.[25] There may in addition be subtler macroeconomic costs involving lowered overall market discipline. The unhappy lesson of Eastern Europe is that super-full employment and chronic full utilization of capacity seem less effective than unemployment and excess capacity in promoting attention to quality and variety of product, product and process innovation, adjustments to structural change, and a general sense of market discipline among workers and managers.

In sum, there will be no substitute for governmental budget discipline—reducing the budget deficit and perhaps mopping up the ruble overhang—in reducing the pandemic and growing shortages and excess demand in the Soviet economy today. Although fiscal austerity may have unpopular elements, it can be sweetened if the fiscal reforms involve reducing defense spending and uneconomic subsidies. However, the primary attraction of a tight fiscal policy will be to restore value to the currency and to reduce inefficient nonmonetary rationing devices like queues, coupon rationing, and bribery.

OVERALL ASSESSMENT

At the end of the day, how likely are the Soviet reform efforts to succeed? Before voicing certain gloomy thoughts about the future economic reform, I must begin by applauding the immeasurable contribution that the Gorbachev *political* reforms have made to freedom in socialist countries and peace in the entire world. Even if he were to step down today, he would surely stand among the great leaders of the modern world.

On the *economic* front, however, the road has proven rockier. We should place little confidence in prognostications about the economics of Eastern Europe. Nonetheless, it is hard to have high hopes for a rapid turnaround in economic growth for the Soviet Union.

To begin with, economic reform has been long on rhetoric and short on substance. The small steps toward liberalization since 1985 have mainly increased income growth and have had little impact. Shortages have increased, rationing is widespread, and relative prices are probably more distorted than they were in 1985. No substantial successes have been achieved in removing the roadblocks to reform listed in table 4. Moreover, while the political changes won by Gorbachev have augmented his executive powers, Soviet reformers appear deeply divided on the sequence of reforms and no coherent reform plan has emerged. Both stabilization policy and price liberalization seem further away today than they have been since 1985.

In addition, while political sentiments are difficult to assess, the strong pro-market sentiments found in many Eastern European countries—particularly Poland and Hungary—have not become widespread in the Soviet Union. Recent polls put confidence in the Communist party and the KGB above that in the State Commission on Prices or the Ministry of Retail Trade. The growth of political democracy, with its traditional antipathy to taxes or increases in the prices of basic necessities, augurs poorly for reaching consensus in favor of a dramatic increase in consumer goods prices. Moreover, in the face of continued struggles among nationalities, political energies may be siphoned off into keeping Lithuania, Russia, and other republic in line instead of pushing through unpopular reforms. It may well be necessary to have a regime change and a repudiation of communist government in the Soviet Union before the transition to the market can be completed.

Most important, as the economic experience of both the advanced industrial countries and the third world amply demonstrate, successful reform programs leading to rapid economic growth are the exception rather than the rule. Latin America is littered with failed reform programs. Hungary, which has more than two decades of reform behind her, has yet to find a way out of the swamp of central planning. The socialist countries of Eastern Europe have undertaken numerous reforms over the past four decades, yet none has yet produced a vibrant and rapidly growing economy. Perhaps the Poles have discovered the magic potion in their 1990 experiment, but it surely is off to a rocky start. Even those successful reform efforts in East Asia have taken many years to bear fruit.

All this is not an argument for halting the process of economic reform. Fitful capitalism may be preferred to stagnant socialism, and the reform process must start somewhere. I end on an optimistic note by concluding that if the advocates of the market convince a skeptical public, overcome their conservative protagonists, design their reforms wisely, choose the correct sequence of measures, eliminate the budget deficit, have good luck with harvests, survive the political turmoil of a disintegrating empire, and persist for a decade—with all these, they have a ghost of a chance.

ENDNOTES

1 See Levine (1982)

2 The upward bias in the Soviet growth rate is described in Aganbegyan (1988, p. 2). By contrast, as Martin Baily and Robert Gordon showed recently in this journal, there may be significant quality understatement in U.S. national account statistics and a consequent understatement of real economic growth. See Baily and Gordon (1988).

3 For a discussion of income levels and performance in different parts of Germany, see Wallich (1955).

4 Yeltsin (1990, p. 255) contains a fascinating and almost believable autobiography.

5 *Radical Reform* (1989, pp. 2-4). The Abalkin report, *Radical Economic Reform: Top-Priority and Long-Term Measures* (hereafter called *Radical Reform*), was presented by Leonid Abalkin, Deputy Prime Minister, to the Organizing Committee of the All-Union Conference and Workshop on the Problems of Radical Economic Reform. This proposal was debated at a meeting of the Council of Ministers in November 1989 but was ultimately rejected in favor of a more conservative approach. Among the chief drafters of *Radical Reform* were Academician Stanislav Shatalin (Secretary of the Economics Division of the Soviet Academy of Sciences and recently appointed to Gorbachev's cabinet) and Professor Yevgeniy Yasin

(formerly of TSEMI and currently director of the U.S.S.R. Commission on Economic Reform).

6 *Radical Reform* (1989, p. 25).

7 Kramer (1990, p. 82).

8 Author's calculations based on Kravis, Heston, and Summers (1982, appendix table 6.3).

9 In principle, Soviet firms that lay off workers today have the obligation to find them jobs.

10 Shmelev (1988, p. 320). I am told that this figure comes from counting the number of distinct products for which prices are quoted. This example was developed in discussions with Alfred Kahn.

11 See Stigler and Kimdahl (1970, p. 5).

12 See Aven (1990).

13 *Economic Report of the President, February 1990*, table C-8. For socialist countries, private conversations. We might wonder whether the market-oriented Poles have inadvertently invented a form of market socialism quite unlike that envisioned by Oskar Lange and others.

14 See Yasin (1990, p. 16), with slight changes in translation.

15 As a matter of historical accuracy, however, it should be noted that there are two big differences between the German reforms of 1948 and the current situation in socialist countries. First, although Germany had been subjected to considerable central rationing and price controls, which began in 1935, many of the institutions of the market remained in place—banks, large private corporations, accounting systems, and, most important, human capital in the market skills and knowledge of the functioning of markets. Second, the movement to a full market was phased in over an extended period, with many prices controlled and the currency partially inconvertible until the 1950s. This episode is described in detail in Wallich (1955).

16 See the discussion in Ofer (1990, p. 3).

17 Particularly useful are the lessons from development economics. A thoughtful analysis is presented in Ranis (1990).

18 A discussion of the issues from a Soviet perspective is contained in Kagalovsky and Khandruyev (1990). The authors are directors of research at, respectively, the State Committee on Construction and the State Bank of the Soviet Union. Many of the macroeconomic issues are addressed in Ofer (1990).

19 Macroeconomic balance also entails external balance, in which the current account and capital flows are in balance. I concentrate on issues of internal balance as these seem more pressing for the Soviet Union in the near term.

20 See Ofer (1990, table 2, pp. 36-37).

21 The reasoning based on the quantity theory runs as follows. Assume that household liquid assets (which are primarily currency and savings accounts) are the only "outside money." That is, they are the only nominally denominated exogenous variable in the economy. Further suppose that the economy was in macroeconomic equilibrium with an asset-income ratio of 0.60 and that the asset-income ratio rose to 0.95 today. Then, if the only factor out of equilibrium were the ruble overhang, prices would have to rise by a factor of 0.95/0.60, or slightly over 50 percent, to reestablish the earlier desired asset-income ratio.

22 An illustration of such a mechanism is provided in the paper by David Lipton and Jeffrey Sachs in this issue. Note that the assumption concerning queuing will lead to a relatively benign outcome. If some of the scarce goods are siphoned off to the nomenclatura or to low-priority users, the shortages will be relatively worse.

23 Ofer (1990, table 1, p. 35); CIA (1988, p. 19).

24 Okun (1973, pp. 246).

25 See, for example, the discussion of Okun's position by William Fellner and Alan Greenspan that follows his article.

SECTION XI

Supplementary International Economic Data

SUPPLEMENTARY DATA 1

Uruguay Round: Structure and Summary of Status of Negotiations

International Monetary Fund

The Uruguay Round of multilateral trade negotiations was due to have been completed by the end of 1990. Meeting in Brussels in December 1990, however, ministers agreed that it was not possible to conclude the negotiations at that time; they were relaunched in late February 1991, with understandings having been reached that the main agricultural issues would be addressed specifically. The table below summarizes the main objectives of the negotiating groups in the Uruguay Round, and dictates the status of the negotiations at the time they were resumed, and the main issues that remain to be resolved.[1] The negotiations are conducted by the Trade Negotiations Committee (TNC), with its subsidiary bodies, the Group of Negotiations on Goods (GNG) and the Group of Negotiations on Services (GNS).

URUGUAY ROUND: STRUCTURE AND SUMMARY OF THE STATUS OF THE NEGOTIATIONS

Group	Main Goals	Main Remaining Issues[2]
1 Tariffs[3]	One-third trade-weighted tariff cut, reduction of peaks and escalation; increased tariff bindings.	Achieving targeted cuts. Tariff peaks in sensitive sectors and tariff escalation.
2. Nontariff measures (NTMs)[4]	(a) Significant reduction of NTMs by all participants.	(i) Ensure that tariff cuts are reinforced, not offset.
		(ii) Ensure against reversals.
	(b) Establish and harmonize rules of origin; assure they do not become trade barriers.	
	(c) Establish multilateral rules to minimize delays in preshipment inspection.	

URUGUAY ROUND: STRUCTURE AND SUMMARY OF THE STATUS OF THE NEGOTIATIONS *(continued)*

Group	Main Goals	Main Remaining Issues[2]
3. Natural resource-based products (RRBPs)[5]	Fullest liberalization.	(i) Tariff escalation. (ii) Product coverage: EC would include fishing resources; others see this covered by Law of the Sea.
4. Textiles and clothing	Phase out Multifibre Agreement (MFA) and integrate the sector into GATT.	(i) Length of phase out. (ii) Percentage of products to be covered in each stage of the phase out.
5. Agriculture	(a) Establish a market-oriented trading system.	(i) Extent of specific commitments on reduction of internal support, export subsidies and border protection; EC would "rebalance," by raising some bound tariffs. (ii) Food security (e.g., rice).
	(b) Establish rules to clarify and harmonize sanitary and phytosanitary measures.	(i) How to cover state, provincial, and local governments.
6. Tropical Products[6]	Fullest liberalization.	(i) Tariff escalation. (ii) Product coverage. (iii) Loss of regional preferences of some countries.
7. GATT articles		
(a) Bound tariff schedules, under Article II:1(b)	Also bind "other duties and charges."	
(b) Balance of payments provisions (Articles XII, XIV, XV and XVIII:B)		Industrial countries seek stronger disciplines; developing countries see no need for change.
(c) State-trading enterprises (Articles XVII)	Enhance transparency; improve notification and review procedures.	

URUGUAY ROUND: STRUCTURE AND SUMMARY OF THE STATUS OF THE NEGOTIATIONS *(continued)*

Group	Main Goals	Main Remaining Issues[2]
(d) Customs unions and free-trade areas (Article XXIV); GATT compliance by state, provincial, and local authorities (Article XXIV:12)	Enhance transparency and desciplines re formation and enlargement of regional arrangements; improve compliance of subgovernments.	(i) Ensure that regional groupings do not raise trade barriers. (ii) Ensure that members take all reasonable measures for GATT compliance by subgovernments.
(e) Waivers from GATT obligations (Article XXV:5)	Time limits and stricter surveillance	Time limits on existing GATT waivers, including a 1955 U.S. waiver on some agricultural import restrictions.
(f) Renegotiation of tariff bindings (Article XXVIII)	Broaden number of countries with negotiating rights when a tariff binding is broken.	
(g) Nonapplication of the GATT (Article XXXV)	Allow use of nonapplication provisions after start of bilateral tariff negotiations with a prospective member.	
(h) "Grandfather clause" (in Protocol of Provisional Application). under which inconsistent measures that predate GATT membership are maintained.	Phase out the clause under agreed time limits.	
8. MTN agreements and arrangements (Tokyo Round codes).		
(a) Antidumping	Strengthen rules on antidumping measures.	(i) Prevent harassment. (ii) Prevent circumvention of duties.
(b) Customs valuation	Make code universal; include measures on falsification of customs valuation and transitional period for implementation by developing countries.	

URUGUAY ROUND: STRUCTURE AND SUMMARY OF THE STATUS OF THE NEGOTIATIONS *(continued)*

Group	Main Goals	Main Remaining Issues[2]
(c) Government procurement	Make code universal; clarify procedures.	
(d) Import licensing procedures	Reduce discretion in the issuance of licenses.	Develop export licensing procedures after Round.
(e) Technical barriers to trade	Improve coverage and transparency of code.	Extent to which obligations apply to subgovernments.
9. Safeguards (Article XIX)	Improve rules for the use of temporary import restrictions.	Replace recourse to quantitative restrictions by price-based measures; reformulate conditions to bring grey-area measures under GATT; nondiscriminatory or selective measures.
10. Subsidies and countervailing measures	Restrain use of all subsidies and produce clear rules on countervailing	Should there be outright prohibition of subsidies; how defined?
11. Trade-related aspects of intellectual property rights, including trade in counterfeit goods (TRIPs)	Develop or adapt rules to protect intellectual property rights (IPRs): establish disciplines on trade in counterfeit goods.	(i) Whether enforcement of IPRs should be under GATT. (ii) Patent rights on technology transfers, e.g., for pharmaceuticals. (iii) Harmonization of patent laws, e.g., U.S. law based on "first to invent," others on "first to file."
12. Trade-related investment measures (TRIMS)[7]	Elaborate disciplines to avoid adverse trade effects..	(i) Should there be outright prohibitions; how defined? (ii) Whether disciplines should apply to directly imposed TRIMS, or also to indirect ones; such as incentive management, e.g., subsidies, taxes.

URUGUAY ROUND: STRUCTURE AND SUMMARY OF THE STATUS OF THE NEGOTIATIONS *(continued)*

Group	Main Goals	Main Remaining Issues[2]
13. Dispute settlement	Strengthen dispute settlement mechanism.	(i) Shorten delays in adoption and implementation of panel reports. (ii) Commitment not to resort to unilateral measures not consistent with GATT.
14. Functioning of the GATT System	Enhance GATT surveillance, improve overall effectiveness of GATT, and increase its contribution to coherence in economic policymaking.	(i) GATT management structure. (ii) Strengthened Secretariat. (iii) Declaration on policy coherence.
15. Group of Negotiations on Services	Bring about liberalization and establish multilateral rules and disciplines.	(i) Coverage: some participants seek to exclude sectors or limit access significantly (e.g., civil aviation, maritime, telecommunications, audio-visual). (ii) Unconditional MFN contingent on sufficiency of liberalization. (iii) Degree of up-front liberalization: those with open systems require substantial up-front commitments, others would freeze current access and negotiate liberalization after the Round. (iv) Formulate safeguard provisions, including on measures for balance of payments need. (v) Cross-retaliation in disputes—sector specific retaliation or across sectors and/or in goods.

ENDNOTES

1 The table updates the material provided in Supplementary Note 3 of the October 1990 *World Economic Outlook*, pp. 94–101.
2 In the absence of additional comments, each reference to an agreed text indicates that the main goals have been achieved.
3 With full reciprocity from its major trading partners, the United States would reduce tariffs to zero or very low rates on some 2,000 tariff lines in the areas of beer, certain electronic products, nonferrous metals, construction equipment, pharmaceutical and some chemicals, paper, wood products, fish, and steel. The approach touches sensitive sectors for some countries, e.g., fish for the EC and Nordic countries.
4 The measures include variable levies, quantitative restrictions (including voluntary export restraints (VERs), nonautomatic licensing and restraints under the MFA), price control measures, customs clearance procedures and health and sanitary regulations.
5 The negotiations cover fisheries, forestry, and nonferrous metals, as well as other products that participants agree to negotiate on a bilateral basis; thus, in the latter case, Australia has discussed with the EC a possible lowering of EC coal subsidies, with no reported outcome to date.
6 The product categories covered by the negotiations are tropical beverages (coffee, cocoa, and tea); tropical spices, flowers and plants; oilseeds, vegetable oils and oilcakes; tobacco, rice and roots; tropical fruits and nuts; tropical woods and rubber; and jute and hard fibre.
7 As identified by some countries, TRIMs include local content rules, domestic sales rules, export performance requirements and its variants, trade balancing rules, and exchange restrictions.

SUPPLEMENTARY DATA 2

Summary of U.S. International Transactions

U.S. Department of Commerce

Table A.--Summary of U.S. International Transactions
[Millions of dollars, seasonally adjusted]

Line	Lines in tables 1 and 10 in which transactions are included are indicated in ( )	1989	1990
1	Exports of goods, services, and income (1)	606,593	652,936
2	Merchandise, excluding military (2)	361,451	389,550
3	Services (3)	116,491	133,295
4	Income receipts on investments (11)	128,651	130,091
5	Imports of goods, services, and income (15)	-697,407	-722,730
6	Merchandise, excluding military (16)	-477,368	-497,665
7	Services (17)	-94,076	-106,919
8	Income payments on investments (25)	-125,963	-118,146
9	Unilateral transfers (29)	-15,491	-22,329
10	U.S. assets abroad, net (increase/capital outflow (-))(33)	-128,610	-57,706
11	U.S. official reserve assets, net (34)	-25,293	-2,158
12	U.S. Government assets, other than official reserve assets, net (39)	1,320	2,976
13	U.S. private assets, net (49)	-104,637	-58,524
14	Foreign assets in the United States, net (increase/capital inflow (+))(48)	216,549	86,303
15	Foreign official assets, net (49)	8,624	32,425
16	Other foreign assets, net (56)	207,925	53,879
17	Allocations of special drawing rights (62)	....	....
18	Statistical discrepancy (63)	18,366	63,526

SUPPLEMENTARY DATA 3

Balance of Payments Tables for the United States, Japan and Germany

International Monetary Fund

Table A4. United States: Balance of Payments, 1987–Third Quarter 1990
(In billions of U.S. dollars)

	1987	1988	1989	1989 I	1989 II	1989 III	1989 IV	1990 I	1990 II	1990 III
Current account	−162.2	−129.0	−110.0	−22.9	−27.6	−31.6	−28.0	−17.9	−21.0	−30.1
Net direct investments	15.9	42.2	40.5	14.3	6.9	1.8	17.5	−4.7	−0.1	−12.6
Abroad	−31.0	−16.2	−31.7	−7.0	−10.1	−10.6	−4.0	−10.2	−7.4	−20.2
In the United States	46.9	58.5	72.2	21.3	17.1	12.4	21.5	5.5	7.2	7.6
Financing need	**−146.4**	**−86.8**	**−69.5**	**−8.6**	**−20.6**	**−29.8**	**−10.5**	**−22.6**	**−21.1**	**−42.6**
Change in official reserves	9.1	−3.9	−25.3	−4.0	−12.1	−6.0	−3.2	−3.2	0.3	1.7
Acquisition of liabilities by foreign monetary authorities	47.7	40.2	8.5	8.0	−5.4	13.4	−7.4	−7.8	4.5	13.4
Residual financing need	**−89.5**	**−50.5**	**−86.3**	**−4.6**	**−38.1**	**−22.5**	**−21.1**	**−33.6**	**−16.4**	**−27.5**
Financing										
Portfolio investments[1]	**31.1**	**40.3**	**44.8**	**14.0**	**6.6**	**12.5**	**11.8**	**−6.7**	**−8.1**	**−2.7**
Public sector bonds	−2.3	27.2	40.9	10.6	5.1	14.5	10.7	1.0	1.4	−0.7
Assets	—	—	—	—	—	—	—	—	—	—
Liabilities	−2.3	27.2	40.9	10.6	5.1	14.5	10.7	1.0	1.4	−0.7
Other bonds	15.7	14.5	14.0	4.3	2.4	0.7	6.6	−4.5	−0.1	1.0
Assets	−7.4	−7.0	−5.3	−1.2	−1.7	−2.1	−0.3	−7.6	−5.6	−0.5
Liabilities	23.1	21.4	19.3	5.5	4.1	2.8	6.8	3.2	5.5	1.4
Corporate equities	17.7	−1.4	−10.1	−0.9	−0.9	−2.7	−5.5	−3.3	−9.4	−3.0
Assets	2.1	−0.9	−16.7	−0.9	−4.5	−7.5	−3.8	0.1	−5.7	−0.5
Liabilities	15.6	−0.5	6.6	−0.1	3.5	4.8	−1.7	−3.4	−3.7	−2.5
Deposit money banks[1]	**46.5**	**16.1**	**8.2**	**−5.8**	**−1.0**	**8.6**	**6.4**	**7.1**	**−3.4**	**23.3**
Long-term, net	0.6	10.6	0.2	−2.5	−0.9	−3.1	6.7	6.1	3.9	2.5
Short-term	45.9	5.5	8.0	−3.3	−0.1	11.7	−0.2	1.1	−7.3	20.8
Assets	−40.9	−57.3	−41.6	−15.4	24.4	−13.7	−36.9	41.1	−11.5	−6.2
Liabilities	86.7	62.8	49.6	12.1	−24.5	25.4	36.7	−40.0	4.2	26.9
Other	**5.3**	**2.5**	**10.8**	**8.0**	**3.6**	**−1.1**	**0.3**	**14.2**	**−2.0**	**1.9**
Errors and omissions	**6.7**	**−8.3**	**22.6**	**−11.5**	**29.0**	**2.5**	**2.6**	**19.0**	**29.8**	**4.9**

Source: International Monetary Fund, *Balance of Payments Statistics*.
[1] Excluding liabilities held by foreign monetary authorities.

Table A5. Japan: Balance of Payments, 1987–Third Quarter 1990
(In billions of U.S. dollars)

	1987	1988	1989	1989 I	1989 II	1989 III	1989 IV	1990 I	1990 II	1990 III
Current account	87.0	79.6	57.0	16.0	14.2	14.9	11.9	12.3	7.9	7.4
Net direct investments	-18.4	-34.7	-45.2	-9.0	-11.6	-10.7	-13.9	-13.3	-12.4	-10.5
Abroad	19.5	-34.2	-44.2	-8.9	-11.6	-10.5	-13.2	-13.9	-12.8	-10.9
In Japan	1.2	-0.5	-1.1	-0.2	—	-0.2	-0.7	0.6	0.4	0.5
Financing need	**68.7**	**44.9**	**11.8**	**7.0**	**2.6**	**4.2**	**-2.1**	**-0.9**	**-4.6**	**-3.1**
Change in official reserves	-37.9	-16.5	12.8	-2.1	9.6	3.7	1.6	10.4	-0.6	-2.2
Acquisition of liabilities by foreign monetary authorities	—	—	—	—	—	—	—	—	—	—
Residual financing need	**30.7**	**28.4**	**24.5**	**4.9**	**12.2**	**7.9**	**-0.5**	**9.4**	**-5.1**	**-5.3**
Financing										
Portfolio investments[1]	**-91.3**	**-52.8**	**-32.5**	**7.0**	**-7.9**	**-12.4**	**-19.2**	**-6.0**	**-10.7**	...
Public sector bonds	-62.3	-106.5	-95.1	-15.9	-26.7	-20.6	-31.9	5.5	-4.6	...
Assets	-71.2	-84.1	-95.4	-13.4	-26.0	-25.0	-30.9	-0.4	-10.4	...
Liabilities	8.9	-22.4	0.2	-2.5	-0.7	4.4	-1.0	5.9	5.8	...
Other bond	30.7	49.9	73.5	13.7	31.1	12.3	16.4	5.2	-4.8	...
Assets	—	—	—	—	—	—	—	—	—	...
Liabilities	30.7	49.9	73.5	13.7	31.1	12.3	16.4	5.2	-4.8	...
Corporate equities	-59.7	3.8	-10.9	9.1	-12.3	-4.1	-3.7	-16.7	-1.3	-2.9
Assets	-16.9	-3.0	-17.9	0.1	-6.1	-4.8	-7.1	-5.0	-2.2	0.5
Liabilities	-42.8	6.8	7.0	9.0	-6.2	0.8	3.4	-11.7	0.8	-3.4
Deposit money banks[1]	**62.1**	**38.4**	**3.7**	**-23.0**	**9.1**	**-4.9**	**22.4**	**-15.4**	**1.4**	...
Long-term, net	-9.7	-6.1	-4.9	-1.3	-0.6	-0.1	-2.9	-1.5	-2.1	...
Short-term	71.8	44.5	8.6	-21.7	9.7	-4.8	25.3	-13.9	3.4	3.0
Assets	-107.1	-147.5	-133.9	-66.6	23.0	-74.3	-15.9	-17.9	18.9	-34.7
Liabilities	178.9	191.9	142.5	45.0	-13.2	69.5	41.3	4.1	-15.4	37.8
Other	**2.2**	**-17.1**	**26.1**	**7.2**	**-4.2**	**20.8**	**2.3**	**16.3**	**14.5**	...
Errors and omissions	**-3.7**	**3.1**	**-21.8**	**3.9**	**-9.2**	**-11.5**	**-5.1**	**-4.4**	—	**-6.6**

Source: International Monetary Fund, *Balance of Payments Statistics*; and Bank of Japan, *Balance of Payments Monthly*.
[1]Excluding liabilities held by foreign monetary authorities.

Table A6. Germany: Balance of Payments, 1987–Third Quarter 1990

(In billions of U.S. dollars)

				1989				1990		
	1987	1988	1989	I	II	III	IV	I	II	III
Current account	46.1	50.5	55.4	16.7	14.0	11.1	13.6	17.0	10.8	8.2
Net direct investments	−7.3	−9.9	−7.7	−1.1	−1.9	−2.0	−2.6	−5.5	−2.0	−4.1
Abroad	−9.2	−11.2	−13.6	−2.7	−2.7	−3.0	−5.2	−5.6	−4.0	−4.3
In Germany	1.9	1.4	5.9	1.6	0.7	0.9	2.7	0.1	2.0	0.2
Financing need	**38.8**	**40.6**	**47.8**	**15.6**	**12.1**	**9.1**	**11.1**	**11.6**	**8.8**	**4.1**
Change in official reserves	−21.5	15.4	−2.8	1.4	−1.5	−0.8	−1.9	−1.4	−2.2	−0.6
Acquisition of liabilities by foreign monetary authorities	1.2	3.0	13.4	3.4	7.2	0.8	2.0	0.5	0.5	0.8
Residual financing need	**18.5**	**59.0**	**58.4**	**20.4**	**17.7**	**9.1**	**11.1**	**10.6**	**7.1**	**4.2**
Financing										
Portfolio investments[1]	**−2.5**	**−43.8**	**−4.4**	**−16.4**	**1.1**	**−1.3**	**12.2**	**−8.1**	**−6.1**	**−3.5**
Public sector bonds	11.7	2.6	8.9	−4.1	3.9	3.3	5.9	−6.5	1.7	2.0
Assets	—	—	—	—	—	—	—	—	—	—
Liabilities	11.7	2.6	8.9	−4.1	3.9	3.3	5.9	−6.5	1.7	2.0
Other bonds	−12.9	−39.0	−21.0	−10.6	−2.4	−6.7	−1.3	−6.3	−4.2	−2.5
Assets	−13.6	−31.2	−21.5	−9.5	−2.4	−7.5	−2.1	−5.6	−4.3	−3.9
Liabilities	0.7	−7.8	0.6	−1.1	—	0.9	0.8	−0.7	0.1	1.3
Corporate equities	−1.3	−7.3	7.6	−1.7	−0.4	2.1	7.6	4.7	−3.5	−2.9
Assets	−0.1	−10.3	−5.0	−3.0	−1.2	−1.0	0.2	0.3	−0.6	—
Liabilities	−1.2	3.0	12.6	1.3	0.8	3.1	7.4	4.3	−3.0	−2.9
Deposit money banks[1]	**−8.0**	**−2.8**	**−25.0**	**12.9**	**−7.7**	**−6.5**	**−23.8**	**7.9**	**−7.1**	**−3.0**
Long-term, net	−1.3	6.9	6.3	2.4	1.7	1.9	0.4	−4.9	−1.2	−5.2
Short-term	−6.7	−9.6	−31.3	10.6	−9.4	−8.4	−24.1	12.8	−5.9	2.2
Assets	−8.8	−15.8	−43.2	6.9	−15.1	−8.4	−26.7	8.1	−6.1	−5.9
Liabilities	2.1	6.2	12.0	3.6	5.7	—	2.6	4.7	−0.2	8.1
Other	**−7.1**	**−14.9**	**−32.1**	**−16.2**	**−9.7**	**−1.5**	**−4.7**	**−15.3**	**1.3**	**−1.9**
Errors and omissions	**−0.8**	**2.4**	**3.0**	**−0.8**	**−1.4**	**0.2**	**5.2**	**4.9**	**4.9**	**4.2**

Source: International Monetary Fund, *Balance of Payments Statistics*; Bundesbank, *Monthly Report*.
[1]Excluding liabilities held by foreign monetary authorities.

SUPPLEMENTARY DATA 4

Major Industrial Countries: Monthly Average Nominal and Real Effective Exchange Rates, January 1980 to Febuary 1991

International Monetary Fund

(Indices, 1980 = 100; Logarithmic scale)

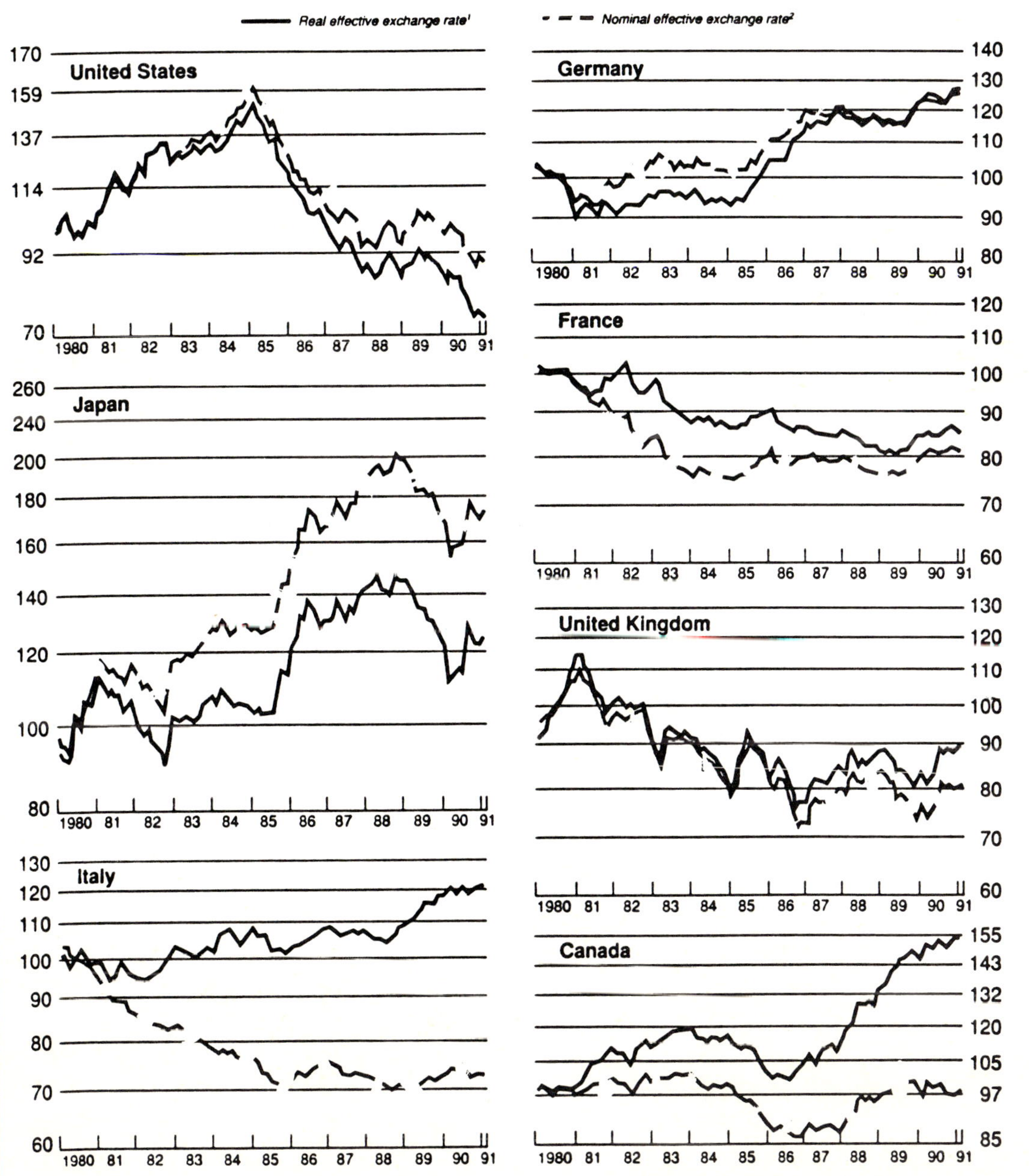

[1]Defined in terms of normalized unit labor costs in manufacturing and constructed using trade weights based on 1980 trade data (series ...reu in *IFS*).
[2]Constructed using same weights as real effective exchange rate indices (series ...neu in *IFS*).

SUPPLEMENTARY DATA 5

Developing Countries: External Debt and Debt Service, 1983–1992[1]

International Monetary Fund

(In percent of exports of goods and services, except where otherwise noted)

	1983	1984	1985	1986	1987	1988	1989	1990	1991	1992
External debt[2]										
Developing countries	**135.6**	**134.9**	**152.0**	**173.7**	**162.1**	**143.3**	**129.3**	**124.8**	**125.5**	**117.6**
(in billions of U.S. dollars)	889.0	930.0	1,004.5	1,096.3	1,216.0	1,223.7	1,234.1	1,306.4	1,362.2	1,388.3
By region										
Africa	166.5	168.8	189.5	244.8	252.9	250.8	244.9	231.6	232.1	221.1
Asia	95.3	90.8	104.3	106.5	91.7	78.3	68.8	68.7	68.1	65.4
Europe	149.2	143.4	164.6	179.6	183.0	156.3	156.1	168.3	162.4	155.7
Middle East	67.2	74.3	88.8	120.1	114.2	118.3	104.0	92.2	113.2	115.1
Western Hemisphere	290.5	274.0	293.5	348.6	344.2	297.6	268.6	254.9	248.9	216.5
By financial criteria										
Net creditor countries	32.4	30.8	34.4	41.4	40.3	38.0	30.7	26.4	37.7	42.6
Net debtor countries	173.2	168.0	185.7	207.8	193.1	168.2	153.3	149.5	146.1	134.5
Market borrowers	160.0	150.7	162.8	172.2	150.2	122.7	108.2	104.3	99.6	89.6
Diversified borrowers	155.6	158.3	177.8	210.6	211.0	199.3	185.0	190.7	193.3	175.9
Official borrowers	259.2	260.5	299.3	364.0	377.9	360.6	354.5	322.4	325.8	314.9
Countries with recent debt-servicing difficulties	240.3	234.0	254.7	306.1	302.2	272.0	253.0	250.8	251.7	224.2
Countries without debt-servicing difficulties	109.2	106.7	123.2	131.8	117.4	101.7	92.0	90.7	88.8	84.9
Debt service payments[3]										
Developing countries	**18.4**	**19.7**	**21.3**	**22.7**	**20.5**	**20.0**	**16.8**	**15.5**	**16.1**	**14.8**
(in billions of U.S. dollars)	120.6	135.8	140.9	143.3	153.9	171.1	160.7	161.8	175.0	175.1
By region										
Africa	22.7	26.3	28.1	28.7	25.1	31.4	27.5	26.0	28.9	24.5
Asia	12.2	12.8	15.3	15.2	14.8	11.1	10.5	9.0	8.1	8.2
Europe	20.3	20.2	24.5	27.3	23.7	24.1	22.2	20.5	24.1	21.4
Middle East	7.9	9.6	10.0	13.4	13.1	11.2	12.0	13.7	14.9	11.6
Western Hemisphere	42.5	42.0	41.2	44.9	40.2	47.3	33.2	29.3	32.8	31.4
By financial criteria										
Net creditor countries	4.4	5.1	4.7	5.9	5.6	4.2	4.3	3.3	3.7	3.9
Net debtor countries	23.5	24.3	26.1	27.0	24.3	23.8	19.9	18.5	19.0	17.3
Market borrowers	25.1	25.1	26.2	26.5	23.3	22.4	17.0	14.5	14.7	14.4
Diversified borrowers	19.7	21.7	25.3	26.8	26.0	28.9	26.7	25.8	25.5	22.3
Official borrowers	23.9	25.7	27.1	29.9	25.8	21.0	22.4	26.8	31.4	24.2
Countries with recent debt-servicing difficulties	31.8	33.1	33.1	35.6	31.3	35.6	27.1	26.8	30.8	26.3
Countries without debt-servicing difficulties	15.6	16.3	19.7	20.5	19.4	16.3	15.5	13.7	12.7	12.3

[1] Excludes liabilities and service payments to the Fund.
[2] Total debt at year-end as percentage of exports of goods and services in the year indicated.
[3] Debt service payments refer to actual payments of interest on total debt plus actual amortization payments on long-term debt. The projections incorporate the impact of exceptional financing items.